IN TWO VOLUMES

VOLUME II

M E D I C A L   C A R E E R S   P L A N N I N G

This book is dedicated to our three beloved children—
NASEEMA, RASHEEDA and SURRYA in the hope
they will make their own contribution toward
creating a happier world.

MEDICAL CAREERS PLANNING

A Comprehensive Guidance Manual on World-Wide Opportunities for Education, Training, Employment and Financial Assistance in All Fields of Medicine and Allied Health Professions

Attia Naseem, M.D. (Diplomate, American Board of Pathology), Assistant Director, Department of Pathology, Mount Vernon Hospital, New York 10550 (Affiliate New York University School of Medicine)

Kamil Mustafa, M.D., FFARCS (England) (Diplomate, American Board of Anesthesiology), Assistant Professor, Department of Anesthesiology, Albert Einstein College of Medicine at Lincoln Hospital, New York 10454

MEDICAL CAREERS PLANNING

A Comprehensive Guidance Manual on World-Wide Opportunities

for Education, Training, Employment and Financial Assistance in All

Fields of Medicine and Allied Health Professions

ATTIA NASEEM, M.D.

(Diplomate, American Board of Pathology)
Assistant Director, Department of Pathology,
Mount Vernon Hospital, New York 10550
(Affiliate New York University School of Medicine)

KAMIL MUSTAFA, M.D.

FFARCS (England) (Diplomate, American Board of Anesthesiology)
Assistant Professor, Department of Anesthesiology,
Albert Einstein College of Medicine, New York 10461

BUREAU OF HEALTH & HOSPITAL CAREERS COUNSELING

The authors have used their best efforts in collecting and preparing material for inclusion in this work, but do not assume and hereby disclaim all liabilities to any party for any loss or damage caused directly or indirectly by errors or omissions in the compilation of facts for this publication.

Library of Congress Number 73-86751
ISBN 0-917364-01-5
Copyright © 1975 Attia Naseem, M.D.

To obtain additional information or personal guidance on all matters pertaining to health careers planning, the reader is advised to write to:

> Bureau of Health & Hospital Careers Counseling
> P.O. Box 238
> Scarsdale, New York, 10583

"The purpose of human life is to serve and to show compassion and the will to help others."

—ALBERT SCHWEITZER
(1875–1965)

STATEMENT OF PURPOSE

The book is designed to offer a comprehensive and a unified source of information on professional career planning in all fields of medicine and allied health vocations. Because of the growing complexities of the role and functions of the multiple job categories in the modern health care industry, the need for such a guidance manual has become increasingly urgent. The primary aim of the publication is to provide an authentic and an easily accessible reference source to the following category of persons who are concerned intimately with the educational and training aspects of the health care delivery system in North America:

- Career guidance counselors
- Educators
- Students
- Guardians
- Physicians
- Placement advisors
- Health and hospital personnel employers
- Health Institutions administrators and departmental supervisors.

The preparation of this work has entailed a prolonged and an exhaustive research of the current informative literature produced by various professional organizations and central governing bodies concerned with each occupation category. It needs, however, to be stressed at the very outset, that some of the information material can become outdated in a relatively short span of time because of the constant changes being brought about in the modern health care practices as a result of the rapid pace of progress in bio-medical technology. In order to obviate the necessity of too frequent printing of new editions, a permanent advisory service has been established as an integral part of the publication project of this manual. The readers can thus always have a ready access to a source of information—accurate and updated—as well as to personal counseling, simply by addressing their inquiries to: Bureau of Health & Hospital Careers Counseling, P.O. Box 238, Scarsdale, New York 10583.

The Book is divided into two Volumes:

VOLUME I deals exclusively with the guidance material relevant to the needs of an aspiring physician. It is designed primarily to answer the fundamental question: "HOW DOES ONE PREPARE ONESELF TO BECOME A PHYSICIAN?" Commencing from the high school level, the reader is presented with all the factual information, in a chronological order, on the years of premedical and medical education that is requisite to his qualification as a licensed physician.

Relevant data is presented on some of the major medical institutions around the world, especially those which offer medical education opportunities to the foreign applicants, particularly from the U.S. The medical schools in North America are described in greater detail with particular reference to: Admission requirements, tuition fee schedules, financial aid and scholarship sources, approximate living expenses and all other matters of academic and scholastic interest to the intending student. Separate chapters are devoted to the undermentioned topics of vital interest both to the undergraduate students of medicine as well as the qualified physicians at all levels of professional standing:

- Medical education opportunities for U.S. citizens in countries abroad
- Postgraduate specialty training programs in hospitals in the U.S. and Canada
- Immigration procedures, and postgraduate training and employment opportunities for foreign physicians in North America
- Financing of premedical and medical education

At the end of the section and also as appendices of various chapters, comprehensive listing is provided on:

i. All hospital facilities in the U.S. with bed capacity over 100
ii. Employment agencies and placement bureaus for physicians in various geographical regions in the U.S. and Canada
iii. State licensing bodies and specialty boards in the U.S.
iv. Voluntary organizations of medical and paramedical interest, which constitute valuable source of information in several areas of health care industry
v. Major pharmaceutical manufacturing concerns in North America which offer job opportunities to qualified physicians in their research and development programs.

VOLUME II provides an authentic and a comprehensive source of information on all aspects of professional career planning in health care vocations allied to medicine. Approximately two hundred job categories are discussed in detail with special reference to the educational and training requirements, work descriptions, professional affiliations and promotion opportunities in each category. Brief notations are included on the workers desirable trait in terms of aptitude and temperament for individual career pursuits. The volume also includes a complete listing of the postal addresses of all professional organizations in the health care technology in North

America; the readers can thus avail themselves of current information source in specific areas of their vocational interest.

In conclusion, it is a pleasure to express our sincerest gratitude to Miss Milagros Parades, the Librarian-in-Chief at the Lincoln Hopital, Albert Einstein College of Medicine for her invaluable assistance and cooperation in procuring for us all the photographic material and the factual information data from various sources in this country and abroad; and also for obtaining the copyright permissions, where needed.

Attia Naseem, M.D.
Kamil Mustafa, M.D.
Greenwich, Connecticut

IN TWO VOLUMES
VOLUME II

———

Allied Health Care Professions

CONTENTS—VOLUME ONE

CONTENTS—VOLUME TWO

5. HOSPITAL AND HEALTH CARE ADMINISTRATION 730

INTRODUCTION

Young people who choose careers related to medicine or health care can be sure that their services will always be in demand, and that their work will be rewarding, meaningful and beneficial to society.

It is difficult to realize that only a hundred years ago the first school of nursing had not yet been established in the United States. Antiseptics, inoculation against disease, X-ray, and the electrocardiograph were still unknown. Physicians stood virtually alone in the battle against disease.

In 1970, according to the United States Department of Labor, 4,000,000 persons were engaged in medical or health-related work in this country, and only nine of every 100 of them were physicians. The remainder were employed in about 200 different kinds of jobs, all contributing to modern health care. Eighteen of these workers were medically-related technicians, such as laboratory personnel, radiologists, and biomedical engineers. Fifty of them were nurses. Seven were engaged in dentistry, six in the management of hospitals, and the rest in various other facets of health care, such as social work, mental health, and environmental science.

In combination, medicine and health care now rank as the third largest industry in the United States, surpassed only by agriculture and construction in the number of persons employed. The Department of Labor predicts that 6,000,000 persons will be employed in some phase of health care by 1980.

The phenomenal expansion of health care as an industry in recent years is due to several factors:

- Since the end of World War II, medicine and related science and technologies have advanced at a pace faster than ever before in human history. During this period, antibiotics came into general use; nuclear medicine was born; and the science of medical electronics blossomed into a full-fledged specialty of biomedical technologies. Progress in medical electronics led to the evolution of several monitoring devices for continuous observation and recording of the vital functions of critically ill patients. Automated machines were developed to take over temporarily the functions of the heart, lungs, or kidneys. Life-prolonging surgical procedures such as open heart surgery, blood vessel replacements and by-pass vascular operations designed to improve the impoverished circulation

In the middle of the last century, the British nurse Florence Nightingale reformed the practice of hospital nursing. She earned the gratitude of her country during the Crimean War, when she headed a band of nurses at the battlefront. Until then, soldiers often lost their lives or limbs due to infection in wounds. By insisting on strict adherence to principles of asepsis and antisepsis, she saved many lives. In this painting, she is depicted supervising care of patients in Florence Nightingale Home, which was founded in her honor at St. Thomas's Hospital, London, in 1860.

Painting by Robert Thom, courtesy of Pake, Davis and Company

to various parts of the body became commonplace. Complete organ transplant emerged from the realms of science-fiction fantasies into real-life surgical procedures of routine nature at the specialized centers.

- During these same years, the population of the United States increased at both ends of the life span. Since early childhood and old age are the periods in life when people are most susceptible to disease, increased facilities for health care became necessary. Although the national birth rate now seems to be leveling off, the proportion of older persons in the population continues to grow.

- In general, Americans have enjoyed increasing affluence in recent years, and they are also increasingly well informed about good health practices and the benefits of prompt medical care. Quite naturally, as medical and surgical science gained in ability to prevent or cure various conditions, the demand for access to health and medical services grew.
- Finally, a large proportion of American workers now have some kind of private prepaid health insurance as one of the "fringe benefits" of their employment. Similar protection is provided for indigent and elderly citizens through Medicaid and Medicare. While rising costs of hospitalization and modern care have made these coverages less than full protection, the fact that a "third party" —government or a private insurance company—will pay at least part of the bills induces patients to seek medical attention more readily than they would have done in years past. As some form of national health insurance becomes a reality in the near future, there will be even more demand for medical and health services.

The combination of intensified public demand and the proliferation of new medical, surgical, and health care techniques has resulted in unprecedented need for additional man- and woman-power to accomplish delivery of essential services. Specialists in many fields—not necessarily physicians—are required to operate sophisticated new machines, perform necessary laboratory tests, provide physical and occupational therapy, care for patients, keep medical records, and administer hospitals, clinics, public health services, and voluntary health agencies.

The Scope of Health-Related Occupations

Altogether, there are now about 200 job classifications in the health industry. Many of them have been created in recent years; others will be added as further techniques and equipment develop.

About 85 per cent of these jobs are at the aide, assistant, or technician level, and require one or two years of education beyond high school graduation. This training is usually offered by junior colleges, community colleges, vocational or technical schools, hospitals, or health departments. There are likely to be such facilities close to a student's home, and both tuition and living expenses are frequently less than attendance at a major college.

Some job classifications require only high school graduation for entrance, with necessary special training being given on the job.

Other classifications, at professional levels, do require four or more years of training at colleges, universities, or specialized schools.

Whatever your personal talents and interests, there is a place for you somewhere in the health care industry.

Do you have a liking for science, and the ability to keep a cool head in time of

At the University of California at Davis, a Technologist receives a specimen of a patient's blood for analysis.

crisis? Perhaps you should train as a paramedic, or an ambulance emergency technician.

Are you good at mathematics, and possessed of an analytic mind? Your place might be as a computer operator in health data.

If you have a bent for mechanics or electronics, you may be just the person needed to monitor or repair the intricate devices now widely used in intensive care units.

If you enjoyed laboratory science in high school, your help is certain to be needed as a technician in any one of a variety of disciplines.

Is art your hobby? You might look toward a career as an art therapist, medical illustrator, or photographer.

Careers are also available in music therapy, occupational therapy, and physical therapy.

If you have good typing skills, dictaphone experience, and a command of spelling, you might train as a medical records transcriber.

Perhaps food preparation is your forte. There is always need for dietitians and nutritionists.

If you like to work directly with people, nursing may be the career for you; or you may wish to go into social rehabilitation service, or work in mental health.

There is no doubt that the need for additional health care personnel will continue. Reliable estimates indicate that before the year 1980 it will be necessary to secure:

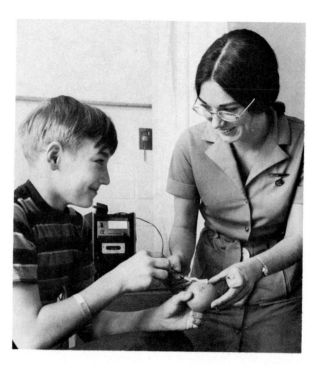

A Registered Nurse shows a young diabetic patient how to inject his daily dosage of insulin.

    30,000 more dental auxiliaries;
    25,000 to 30,000 more medical laboratory personnel;
    20,000 more environmental health personnel;
    10,000 more medical record personnel;
    10,000 more dietetic and nutritional personnel;
     6,000 more workers in physical therapy;
     3,000 to 4,000 more occupational therapy personnel.

Among the professions requiring a bachelor's degree, 93,000 more personnel will be needed in 1980 than were available in 1970.

Advantages in Selection of a Health Care Career

The health services offer young persons great flexibility.

Since there is a growing demand for health care personnel everywhere, there is practically no geographic limitation on the area in which you can live and work. You need not even confine your ambition to the United States.

There are many overseas opportunities for American health workers. The Public Health Service, the Agency for International Development, and the World Health Organization are only a few of the organizations that send health personnel abroad, sometimes in teams, to help other nations eradicate disease, set up clinics, and train workers from the indigenous populations of the developing countries.

On the other hand, if you are not obsessed by wanderlust, and wish to settle down

Good health is a matter of world-wide concern, and countries cooperate through international agencies to improve conditions in under-developed areas. Here, an American public health worker assigned to such an agency administers BCG inoculation to children in Africa.

and raise a family, there are many full-time health occupations that are performed in normal business hours, and need not disrupt your personal life. There are also many part-time jobs that will allow you to accommodate your work to your family's demands upon you.

Because of the recent abolition of compulsory military service, it is no longer necessary for young men to plan their lives around a period of years in uniform. However, the armed services remain a possible source of basic training in many health occupations that can be applied later to a career in civilian life. Both the military and the United States Public Health Service offer careers as commissioned officers for health professionals. About five per cent of all the men in uniform, both commissioned and enlisted, rate as medical personnel.

Veterans who have received medical training in the military can capitalize on their skills through MEDHIC (Military Experience Directed into Health Careers), sponsored jointly by the Department of Defense and the Department of Health, Education and Welfare.

Because all health care occupations are associated with the professionalism of medicine, they carry an aura of prestige. In terms of monetary reward, they pay as well as, or better than, the jobs requiring equal education and training in other sectors of the economy. At higher levels, workers are allied with professional associations, which tend to set standards both for working conditions and quality of workmanship. At lower levels, many workers are members of trade unions, which protect their interests.

At all levels, health care workers justifiably feel a sense of satisfaction with the value of their contribution to an improved quality of life.

1

MAJOR TYPES OF HEALTH SERVICE
ORGANIZATIONS AND FACILITIES

There is a wide variety of organizational and institutional structures in which the career health worker may be employed. Sometimes he (or she) has a chance to choose the situation of his (or her) preference.

Hospitals

Community hospitals are located close to the people they serve. Most persons have visited one at some time. They are general hospitals, which treat patients of all ages, with all kinds of illnesses, on an acute, short-term basis. Their patients stay an average of one week.

Chronic disease hospitals treat patients who need long-term care for mental or physical illness.

Some hospitals specialize in certain groups of patients, such as children, old people, patients with eye or ear problems, patients with orthopedic handicaps, or those who suffer from malignant diseases.

Hospitals may be supported by local, state, or Federal taxes: they may be privately owned by a group of physicians; they may be church-supported; or they may be maintained by charitable gifts and endowments.

They range in size from a few beds to institutions with 1,000 and more beds.

The largest hospitals often evolve into medical centers, comprising several specialized hospitals and a general hospital. They are usually associated with a university or medical college, and combine the training of physicians and nurses with research projects as well as providing direct patient care.

What you see when you walk into one of these institutions is only the surface of its activity. The calm efficiency you observe would not be possible without well-planned housekeeping. The pills in the vial on a patient's table were prepared in the hospital pharmacy. The patient probably has had X-rays taken, and specimens of blood and urine analyzed in the hospital laboratories for diagnostic purposes. If he underwent surgery, he was visited by the anesthesiologist, who cooperated with the surgeon to determine the specific agent or anesthetic technique most suitable for

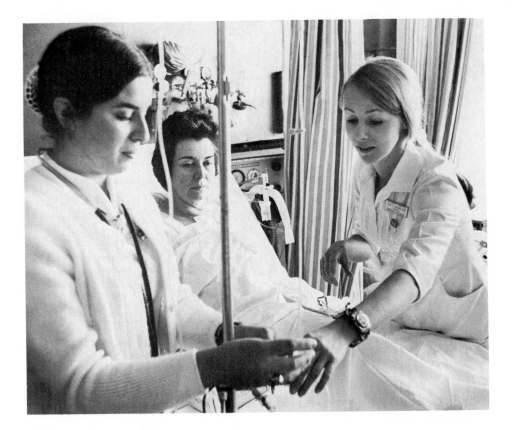

At New York University Medical Center, a Registered Nurse assists a Physician to adjust the intravenous drip which is being given to a patient suffering from cardiovascular disease.

his needs. As he recovers from surgery, he may spend a day or so in an oxygen tent, under supervision of the Department of Respiratory Therapy. He may be on a special diet. In a few days, his physician may prescribe physical therapy as a means of speeding his recovery.

Meanwhile, his medical chart is being maintained, and will finally be tabulated and stored in the Records Department. The Admitting Office has taken steps to advance his insurance claims. The Administrative and Business Offices have performed all the multiple functions vital to the smooth and coordinated working of the hospital staff in the interest of care and safety of the patient.

In addition to all these activities and many more that are carried out for the patient in hospital, the institution probably conducts an outpatient clinic for people in the neighborhood, and an emergency room. It is probably involved in community health education, and preventive medical services, as well as social counseling and home care to assist patients after they leave the hospital.

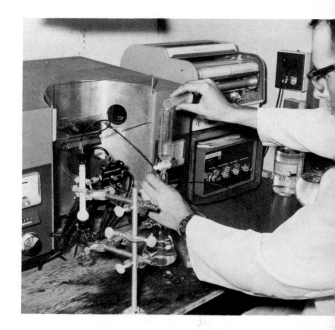

The quality of our environment is important to health. At the Rome Pollution Laboratory a Technologist in the New York State Department of Environmental Conservation tests fish taken from the State's waters, to detect and measure the amount of mercury they contain. He is using a "cold vapor phase technique," pouring acid through a funnel into the flask containing samples of fish. As mercury vapor forms it will be measured in ratio to the fish sample by the atomic absorption spectrophotometer at the right of the Technologist.

Public Health Departments

Public health departments are tax-supported, and exist on the local, state and Federal levels. Since their work is interrelated to a great extent, they usually maintain a constant liaison with each other.

For example, local health departments keep track of all births and deaths in their respective areas. They maintain accurate and current records of age, sex and race of the deceased persons, together with the specific cause of death as far as could be ascertained from clinical and laboratory reports. These facts are communicated to the regional state health departments for forwarding to the United States Public Health Service for the final compilation of a comprehensive unified statistical report. Such information is absolutely vital for the development of future health programs on a national scale.

On the other hand, local health departments depend on state and Federal departments for services they cannot supply themselves. For instance, a community might turn to its state for assistance in stopping upstream pollution of a river that furnishes its drinking water. Local health departments expect the larger units to inform them when an epidemic of influenza can be expected, or an epidemic of measles or encephalitis has broken out in a nearby area. When the local department receives such information, it warns the public through newspapers, radio, and television. It takes steps to assure adequate supply of appropriate vaccines or gamma globulin, and urges susceptible persons to get suitable protection.

The local health department is responsible for guarding the purity of the water, air, and food in its community, and for regulating the disposal of sewage and waste products. It is obligated to control mosquitoes, vermin, rats, and other disease-

An Environmental Technician assists in taking samples of municipal water supplies.

carrying creatures, and educating the public in disease control. It provides inoculations against communicable diseases, and traces epidemics to their source in order to control them when they occur. It inspects restaurants and food markets for cleanliness, and requires health examinations of workers who handle food. It also inspects apartments and public buildings on receiving complaints of unsafe, unsanitary, or unhealthy conditions.

It provides and maintains maternal and child welfare clinics, and services for the mentally ill and the mentally retarded.

Large cities usually have their own public health laboratories, in which samples of water, soil, air, and food can be tested for contamination, traces of radiation, poison, or harmful bacteria. Some of these laboratories also conduct research programs.

Smaller communities may have to rely on the state health department laboratories for the above services.

In general, state health department services supplement those of local communities, and function in situations that go beyond local boundaries, or beyond the financial capability of local units. For example, most large, long-term-care institutions for the mentally ill or mentally retarded are state-supported and administered.

The United States Public Health Service functions on a national, and sometimes international, plane. It conducts and promotes research into the causes, treatment, and prevention of physical and mental diseases; disseminates health information to the public; supervises the manufacture and sale of drugs and other biologic products; and grants assistance to individual states in maintaining adequate public health services, including grants for the training of personnel.

It also institutes and administers nationwide programs for control of specific infections, such as tuberculosis and venereal disease.

Because travelers can now reach the United States from any part of the world in less time than it takes the symptoms of many dread diseases to become evident, the United States Government conducts health examinations of all immigrants, passengers, and crews who come into this country from infected regions. At times, it takes the initiative in helping to eradicate such scourges as bubonic plague, smallpox, tuberculosis or malaria in other countries. It may send teams of health workers abroad for this purpose. It also cooperates with international organizations in global health projects.

Certain other agencies in the United States Department of Health, Education and Welfare affect our national health, as does the Food and Drug Administration, which enforces the pure food, drug, and cosmetic laws, and laws requiring proper labeling of poisons. It inspects factories and processing plants which produce food and drug products.

The Maternal and Child Health Service conducts continuing studies, many of which affect future national health programs. It furnishes consultation to states, and administers grants-in-aid for maternal and child welfare and for physically handicapped children.

From even this brief recounting, it is evident that public health agencies at all levels require an enormous diversity of personnel. In addition to physicians, nurses, dentists, administrative and clerical personnel, they need veterinarians, sanitary engineers, sanitarians, statisticians, computer operators, educators, nutritionists, information specialists, social workers, economists, sociologists, just about every kind of laboratory technician, environmental scientists, and dozens of other types of personnel.

School Health Departments

School nurses have played a role in the American educational system for several generations. However, the modern concept of school health programs is much broader than periodic checking of sight and hearing, alertness to symptoms of infectious disease, and emergency care of illness or accident cases.

Regularly scheduled, physician-conducted school health examinations have become routine in most school systems. These examinations are designed to assure proper and timely inoculation as well as detection of early signs and symptoms of any serious disability or illness.

Modern programs, often directed by a school health specialist, are concerned with the total environment in which the students live and learn. Their goals include provision of safe, healthful conditions in all parts of the school buildings, gymnasiums, lunchrooms, playgrounds, and athletic fields. They extend into achievement of the best possible home and community conditions. Accident prevention and public health education are considered equally as important as dealing with health emergencies. Good nutrition, dental health and hygiene, comprehensive health education, and mental health all come within the scope of present programs, as does provision for exceptional children, whether handicapped or gifted.

Close cooperation is established and maintained between the school and the community at large, particularly in relation to parents' organizations and other health agencies.

Although the school nurse is still the most visible symbol of school health programs, educational systems also require school physicians, dentists and dental hygienists, dietitians and nutritionists, psychologists, mental health counselors, and social workers.

Occupational Health Services

In every business and industry, physical surroundings affect the health and productivity of workers; and absenteeism due to illness or accidents is unprofitable, as are inefficiency and errors. For these reasons, as well as genuine concern for their employees, many commercial organizations have established in-house health units, to protect and maintain the health of workers.

Such units may consist only of a nurse in attendance and a physician on call; or they may be completely staffed on a full-time basis, according to the needs of the particular industry.

In the nature of their business, some companies may have more likelihood of health problems developing than others. Hazard to an office worker may be limited to eye strain from working in bad light, but danger of lung damage may threaten a worker who handles asbestos insulation material, or the possibility of excessive radiation may be inherent in working with radioactive substances. However, regardless of the size of the industrial complex or of its occupational health staff, it must concern itself with safety on-the-job as well as with other health problems.

Company staffs may also cooperate with community agencies to improve health and safety conditions off-the-job.

In terms of worker efficiency, poor mental health—whether due to problems on-the-job or in personal life—may be as detrimental as physical injury. Consequently, many occupational health programs include facilities for counseling.

Beyond a nurse and physician, occupational health staffs may include a safety engineer, industrial hygienist, radiologic health specialist, sanitary engineer, sanitarian, dentist, dietitian and nutritionist, public health educator, and specialists in mental health and rehabilitation.

Mental Health Occupations

The term "mental illness" is defined as describing psychiatric disorders or diseases that appear as personality problems and behavioral difficulties. Usually it is re-

A Physical Therapist conducts an exercise class to keep psychiatric patients in good physical condition.

served for disabilities severe enough to need specialized professional treatment.

Mental illness has long been one of our most serious problems, and strenuous efforts are being made toward its prevention. To this end, public health departments take more and more responsibility for promoting mental health. Public health nurses, school health personnel, industrial health personnel, and social workers are often able to detect early symptoms, and refer patients to proper counseling or care before illness becomes severe. And, of course, schools as well as health agencies both voluntary and public, are engaged in educating the general population on the importance of mental health.

Nevertheless, many persons do require long-term treatment and care. If hospitalization is necessary, these patients may be admitted to mental hospitals, or be treated in community mental health centers or psychiatric wards of general hospitals.

In terms of staff, these institutions need all the basic services of other hospitals, plus psychiatrists, psychologists, psychiatric nurses and aides, social workers, and specialized therapists.

Advances in drug therapy and other improvements in treatment make the outlook for mental patients more hopeful than in the past. A relatively new development is the emphasis placed on enabling patients to return to useful lives in their communities. Halfway houses, through which patients can be re-introduced to community life gradually, and specialized rehabilitation techniques are means to this end.

Occupations in Treating the Mentally Retarded

Mental retardation is due to organic causes, and not to mental illness. Abnormalities occurring before birth, accidents before or during birth; or infectious diseases, accidental poisoning, brain injury, or inadequate nutrition in early childhood are its prime causes. Symptoms usually appear while the child is very young.

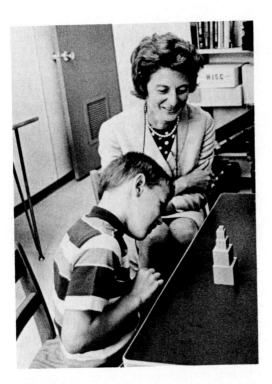

Training mentally retarded children and adults to function in society is a modern aspect of health care, and evaluation of patients' abilities is a first step in which psychologists as well as medical personnel participate.

Until very recent years, it was believed that such children were incapable of learning or ever becoming self-sufficient and useful members of society.

Thanks to intensive research, a few of the many causes of retardation have now been identified, and medical scientists are working to find means of controlling and treating them. Prevention is possible in some cases, and many children brought to early treatment can be helped.

Given rehabilitation therapy and specialized treatment and training, many more children can be taught to care for themselves, and to earn their own living.

Since retarded persons are susceptible to the same general health problems as other people, they need all of the usual health services, plus the services of physicians in many medical specialties—in fields of neonatology, pediatrics, psychiatry, neurology, and physical medicine and rehabilitation.

The institutions and agencies that serve them also need nurses, psychologists, occupational therapists, physical therapists, speech pathologists, recreational therapists, vocational therapists, and medical social workers.

Rehabilitation Services

The purpose of rehabilitation is to help people who are disabled by injury or illness to recover function and resume their lives as normally as possible.

As a specialty, rehabilitation received its greatest impetus during and immediately

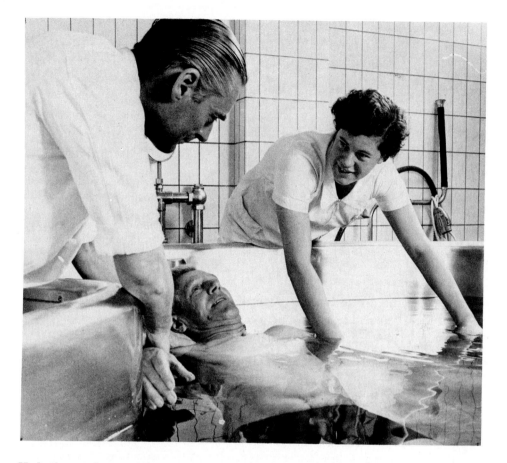

Hydrotherapy is one of the techniques by which Physical Therapists treat patients whose muscles have been weakened by accidents, strokes, or disease. Because water is buoyant, patients can move their arms and legs more easily than when they must combat gravity.

following World War II, when, as a direct result of efforts with paraplegics, amputees, and other seriously injured military men, the same techniques were transferred to care of civilians.

Victims of paralytic poliomyelitis and cerebral palsy, older persons who had experienced "strokes," and patients who had survived crippling industrial or traffic accidents were those first benefited by the establishment of specialized rehabilitation centers.

A wide variety of services is needed in these institutions. Medical care is a necessity, and so is counseling to enable the patient to face and adjust to his problem.

Members of rehabilitation services include physical therapists, nurses, orthotists and prosthetists, rehabilitation counselors, occupational therapists, speech pathologists, audiologists, corrective therapists, experts in homemaking rehabilitation, manual arts therapists, vocational counselors, music therapists, recreational therapists, educational therapists, psychologists, plus all the administrative and manage-

Voluntary health agencies fulfill many community health needs, as in this class for prospective parents conducted by the Memphis, Tennessee, chapter of the American Red Cross.

ment personnel needed to run the center. Even when the patient has regained all possible physical function, he may need retraining for a new type of employment in which his handicap will not be a hindrance, and the services of an employment specialist to help him get a job.

Voluntary Health Agencies

The first voluntary health agency in the United States was the American Red Cross, which was founded by Clara Barton in 1881. It was followed by the National Tuberculosis Association—now the American Lung Association—and the American Cancer Society. Today we have a multitude of voluntary health agencies, each devoted to a special interest or disease entity, and supported by public memberships and contributions. They are involved in almost every kind of health service, and employ a wide variety of professional and technical personnel to carry on their work.

One of their major functions is to inform the public about the particular health problem with which they are concerned, and tell people what they can do about it individually or as part of a general effort. They make critically needed health services available when they cannot be provided otherwise.

They take leadership in developing professional understanding of their health fields, and provide grants for research. They are especially active in promoting career opportunities in their fields, and making scholarships available to promising young people.

The range of workers they employ is as diverse as the fields they represent. Occupations that would constitute a basic staff would include administrative specialists, public health educators, information specialists, health statisticians, medical specialists, nurses, social workers, home economists, and sociologists.

There are many opportunities for careers in medical research and related fields. Research scientists find employment in universities, medical centers, public health departments, industries that manufacture pharmaceuticals, and in the Federal Government's National Institutes of Health.

Careers in Research

If a single word could characterize the twentieth century, it might well be "research." And the research that benefits medicine and health care is not always intended for that purpose. Medical and surgical science and health care have profited by fall-out from research in chemistry, physics, biology, engineering, automation, mathematics, electronics, atomic energy, space, sociology, economics, administration, and the technologies of mass communication.

Although medical science has utilized discoveries made in all these disciplines, there is definite need for research directed to its specific problems. The first part of this kind of research may take place in Federal laboratories and those of state health departments, pharmaceutical manufacturers, or universities. University laboratories are in a fortunate position in being able to draw upon the resources of faculty talent in the physical, biologic, and social sciences, as well as those in departments directly related to health and medicine. Some university projects in basic research are sponsored by the universities themselves, or by grants from voluntary health agencies. Many are funded by the United States Public Health Service, through the National Institutes of Health.

Other Federal agencies that contribute to health research are the Atomic Energy Commission, the National Science Foundation, the National Aeronautics and Space

Administration, the Environmental Health Administration, the Defense Department, the Food and Drug Administration, and the Veterans' Administration.

Altogether, Federal agencies supply about two-thirds of the funding for medical and health research in this country.

The second part of research in medicine and health care takes place in hospitals, clinics, and the private practice of selected physicians. This is known as "clinical research," and is a vital prerequisite for general adoption of any agent or procedure by physicians. Universities that have medical schools and teaching hospitals are major participants in this kind of research.

2

CHOOSING A HEALTH CAREER

The choice of a career is one of the most important decisions a young person must make. It determines the direction his life will take, and the circumstances and people with whom he will spend it.

Success and future happiness depend heavily on realistic analysis of his own talents and capabilities and the things he likes and doesn't like; and an honest appraisal of whether his personal characteristics and qualifications truly fit what seems to be the "dream job." An honest appraisal of whether it is possible to reach the desired goal in terms of opportunity and cost is equally essential.

Obviously, the first thing to do is to gather all the information you can about careers in the health field, and select those that interest you most. The job descriptions in this book will assist you in doing that.

Since everyone's evaluation of himself is influenced by what he'd *like* to think himself to be, it is wise to consult someone who knows about the kind of job you are seeking, and who can give you an objective view of its suitability for you. Your school counselor, and the appropriate counselor at your local office of the state employment service, are good persons with whom to start. In addition to helping you with your choice, they probably can tell you where and how to get further help and information.

When you have narrowed your job choices in this way, it will be up to you to use your own initiative in further exploration of those that seem most promising. It is probable that you will still have many questions:

- Where can you get the required training?
- What will it cost?
- Where can you find out about available scholarships?
- Is there any other form of student assistance available?
- What is the employment outlook for the jobs you like in your own town, in the state, or in the nation as a whole?
- Where can you see people actually at work in these jobs, to learn what they do?

The first step in finding answers to these questions is to scout your school library and your community library for any career information they may have. If you don't know how to go about looking for such material, ask the librarian to help you.

A student at Oxford College of Emory University works in the microbiology research laboratory with Dr. Margaret Drummond, Associate Professor.

Another very good method of getting information is to write to various sources for their publications on the subject: career information literature produced by the Federal Government, by national professional organizations, by other interested national organizations, colleges, state education departments and community career guidance centers. To assist you in making these inquiries, an "Information Guide" of sources classified according to health-occupation areas of work is provided as an Appendix in this book.

A further step is to get in touch with people in your own town who are either working in such jobs, or who are very well-informed about them. In addition to your school counselor and local public employment officer counselor, you might contact your local health department, local community health council, city or county medical and hospital associations and their women's auxiliaries, local professional societies and voluntary agencies, hospitals and clinics, or any local employment counseling agency approved by the American Board of Counseling Services, such as those sponsored by B'nai Brith or the Urban League.

In many localities, health career committees exist, and they cooperate with the high school health career clubs that have become a popular student activity in many schools. These local committees often take part in school assemblies, or career days, and put on programs or exhibits of their own at county fairs, or organize tours of hospitals or public health facilities, or visits to nearby professional schools. If these activities exist in your community, you will find them profitable.

Sometimes these clubs also carry on work-experience programs, for which you can volunteer, and thus get to see the workings of a hospital, public health agency, or voluntary agency from the inside. In some cases, you may find that there are part-time or summer vacation jobs for which you might qualify. There may also be summer trainee programs, which offer promising students on-the-job experience in health occupations. These opportunities are often sponsored by an organization, and are most likely to be found in the scientific or technological fields.

Educational Requirements

As you study the Job Descriptions which make up much of this volume, you will notice that there is a wide range in the education or training required for the various occupations. However, it can safely be said that the more nearly professional a job is, the greater are the number of years that are to be spent in education and training.

At the University of Wisconsin Center for Health Sciences, a student examines cells, in preparation for a career as a Medical Technologist.

For example, high school graduation is all that is needed for a laboratory helper, who simply washes up glasses and does other odd jobs as he is required to do under direct supervision.

High schools and vocational schools offer the training needed in office skills, or in manual arts. Also, some high schools and vocational schools give specialized training for nurse aides, practical nurses, dental assistants, and institutional food workers.

Hospital orderlies and opticians are among another group of careers for which training is given on-the-job, although the period of training in the hospital may extend over several years.

By far the largest proportion of job classifications requires two to three years of training beyond high school graduation. Many hospitals have nursing schools that offer two-year associate nursing and three-year diploma programs in registered nursing. Other occupations that require less than a college degree include various laboratory technicians, electronics technician, and medical assistant in a doctor's office.

A bachelor's degree earned in four years of college is the basic requirement for the baccalaureate nursing program, and for physical therapists, and sanitarians. The jobs of child-health associate and medical-record administrator require an additional year of internship.

Other professional occupations, such as pharmacist, speech pathologist, or occupational therapist, require a five-year combination of college and professional training before beginning the career.

Medicine, dentistry, and some other health careers require even longer periods of education and training.

Cost of Education and Training

How much it will cost to train for any health career depends on the kind of school, the area of the country where it is located, the availability of loans and scholarships, financial support by the government, changes in tuition charges, and many other variables.

It can be said that the most economical way to get professional training is to live at home and be able to attend a local institution. Then your main expenses will be tuition, books, and laboratory fees. If you go to a college supported by your city or state, tuition is likely to be much less than in a privately supported college. (This difference is also true of publicly supported junior colleges or other institutions offering less than four-year programs.)

If you are going away from home, your own state university will be less expensive in tuition than a state university in another state, or a private college. Another point to consider is that if you go far from home, travel becomes an important item in expense.

Write for catalogs of all the schools you consider attending, and as you study

A pharmacy student at the University of Wisconsin Center for Health Sciences prepares an injection under a laminar flow hood.

them be certain to find out the costs of tuition, dormitory or other living arrangements, what the college advises that you allow for books, laboratory and other fees, and for general expenses.

By this means you will be able to estimate the total cost at each school, and compare one with another.

If the career you are considering entails graduate school, or other training beyond the bachelor's degree, you will want to evaluate the cost in a similar manner, in order to have a general idea of what it will take in both time and money to realize your ambition.

The next order of business is to make an inventory of your own resources, so that you know how much of the cost you can meet by yourself. In many colleges, three out of four students pay some of their expenses by working part-time, or summers, or both. If you intend to do this, and have good assurance that you can get such employment and carry it along with your school work, it should be considered as part of your personal resources.

When you have done all this, you will be able to determine how much more money you will need and must secure through full or partial scholarship, grants-in-aid loans, or other means.

Financial Aid

Because of the great demand for additional personnel in health careers and occupations, many kinds of financial aid have become available. These include full or

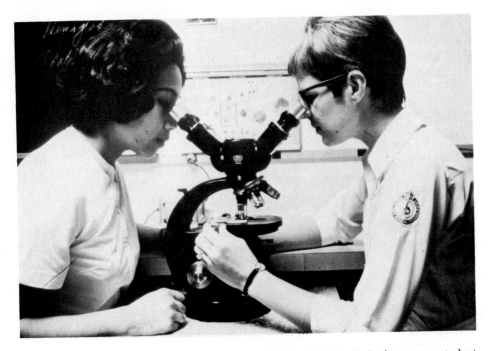

Using a double-headed microscope, a Registered Medical Technologist instructs a student concerning the cells on the slide they are observing.
Photo courtesy of the National Committee for Careers in the Medical Laboratory

partial scholarships, grants-in-aid loans, part-time work programs, and combinations of these. It is possible for a student to finance the entire cost of his education by these means.

The sources for such aid are numerous, and it would be impossible to list all of them, particularly since there are additions and changes from year to year. In order for your information to be up-to-date, you need to contact the source organization for the financial aid for the category or career of your choice.

When you have decided on your career, and estimated the amount of help you need, your first port of call should be your high school guidance counselor. Other promising sources of specific information are the financial officer or admissions counselor of the college of your choice, and state or local health career programs. (A listing of state and local health career programs, with their addresses, is given in the appendix of this book.)

In addition, at the end of each job description in this book, you will find the names of the professional societies associated with it. The addresses of these societies will be found under the heading "Information Guide" in the appendix.

At the close of this chapter, you will find a bibliography of source books on financial aid that are probably in your school or public library.

Scholarships and Grants

Some scholarships are earmarked for students who want to go into health careers. Others, not so earmarked, are awarded to students on the basis of ability and need.

Almost all private colleges offer partial and full scholarships to outstanding students depending on the extent of their need. Student's need, academic record, and test scores, are all taken into consideration.

You should request scholarship information from the schools to which you wish to apply for entrance. The application forms you will receive usually entitle the student to consideration for all types of financial aid. Both the student and his parents should make it a point to fill out these forms (and any others you receive in response to inquiry) as completely and promptly as possible.

The Federal Government and many states award merit scholarships to promising students on the basis of examinations taken during the last year of high school. In addition, the Federal Government has grants for children of deceased or disabled veterans, and young people who previously received social security benefits. The GI Bill of Rights offers educational assistance to veterans who were honorably discharged from the Armed Forces after January 31, 1955.

Private, Federal, and state medical and allied health associations and societies offer full and partial scholarships and grants for individuals who wish to pursue professional training in certain specified fields.

Other possible sources of scholarship funds include hospitals and their auxiliaries, private industry, labor unions, local religious organizations, civic and special-interest groups.

Educational Loans

High school graduates who have been accepted for enrollment, or college students enrolled in full- or half-time degree programs, and who need financial aid for educational expenses, are eligible for National Defense Education Act (NDEA) loans. An undergraduate may borrow up to $1,000.00 annually, and need not pay either interest or principal until nine months after he ends his studies. Then a three per cent interest rate is applied to the unpaid balance of the loan until it is fully repaid.

Many states underwrite higher education loans for students who are state residents and enrolled in full- or half-time degree programs. The money is borrowed by the student from a bank or other participating state-lending institution. Repayment does not begin until nine months after the student ends his study, and payments can be spread over as much as ten years. Interest rates vary, but interest, too, does not begin until nine months after the student has left school.

Part-Time Employment

Students who need a job to help pay for college expenses are eligible for employment under federally-supported work-study programs that permit students to work on campus or in nonprofit organizations up to 15 hours a week during the school term, and up to 40 hours a week during vacations.

Most schools and colleges have placement services, to help students find part-time jobs in the community. The schools themselves frequently need capable employees either full- or part-time.

Most colleges have tuition remission plans for full-time employees, so that they can take a limited number of courses free of charge, usually in evening classes.

Aid for Graduate Training

The trend toward support of financial aid for graduate training is very favorable.

The Health Training Improvement Act of 1970 (P.L. 91–519) allows 21 categories of health professions of less than baccalaureate level to receive financial aid for advanced training. These include, among others, medical and X-ray technologists, dietitians, and technicians and technologists at all levels.

The Comprehensive Health Manpower Training Act of 1971 (P.L. 92–157) and the Nurse Training Act of 1971 (P.L. 92–158) expanded the Federal program so that a broader spectrum of students attending professional schools could receive low-cost loans. The categories now include students of medicine, osteopathy, dentistry, nursing, pharmacy, optometry, podiatry, and veterinary medicine.

Loans for graduate study are also available under the National Defense Education Act (NDEA).

Grants for graduate study are available in a number of specialties, such as public health, mental health, rehabilitation and nursing education. Many of the grants (frequently termed "fellowships") are financed by the Federal Government. Some are offered directly by universities; and others are provided by foundations, voluntary health agencies, industries, and some state governments.

The Forgiveness Clause

Recent legislation allows students who have borrowed from the Federal Government under the above laws to be "forgiven" part of their debt on agreement that they work in areas where their specialty is badly needed for a specific period of time. This is one way in which health-care services are made available to the places where they are needed the most.

General Federal Support

The number of Federal programs that support health manpower training is increasing constantly, including training on-the-job; continuing education at all levels; training that leads to a diploma, an associate, a baccalaureate, or advanced degrees.

The Federal Government also makes grants to states, local communities, schools, public and private agencies, or directly to individuals to fulfill the expanding demands for health manpower.

REFERENCES

A Chance to Go to College. New York: College Entrance Examination Board, 1971, 248 pp.

"A Letter to Parents: Financial Aid for College, 1970–71." Margolius, Sidney. New York: College Entrance Examination Board, 1970, 10 pp.

Complete Planning for College. Sulkin, Sidney. New York, Harper & Row, Publishers, 1968, 324 pp.

Counselor's Manual for: How About College Financing? American Personnel and Guidance Association, American School Counselor Association, 1607 New Hampshire Avenue, N.W., Washington, D.C. 20009. 1968. Fiengold, S. Norman, (Ed.).

Financial Aid for Higher Education. U.S. Office of Education, Washington, D.C.: Government Printing Office, 1968, 110 pp.

"Need a Lift? Educational Opportunities." American Legion Education and Scholarship Program. Indianapolis: Revised annually.

How to Earn Money in College. Cambridge, Mass.: Harvard Student Agencies, Inc., 1968, 238 pp.

The Presentation of Job Descriptions

Opportunity in many health-related careers is not confined to a single type of health service or setting. For example, nurses are needed in schools, industries, public-health departments, rehabilitation centers, volunteer agencies, social service work, and physicians' offices as well as in hospitals. Laboratory technicians are in demand for research and public-health laboratories and those of pharmaceutical manufacturers, as well as for hospitals. Dietitians are employed by schools, industries, employee cafeterias, and in the laboratories of food processors, as well as by hospitals.

However, the criteria established in the operation of hospitals are basically the same for each profession as those of other potential employers: hospitals employ a greater diversity of health care workers than any other single type of organization or institution: and the structure of hospitals provides an orderly means of presenting job categories.

Therefore in detailing career opportunities, greatest stress is placed on conditions and requirements as they exist in hospitals, with additions and exceptions noted in later chapters dealing with employment opportunities in other sectors of society.

SUGGESTED ORGANIZATION CHART FOR A TYPICAL LARGE GENERAL HOSPITAL BY DEPARTMENTS

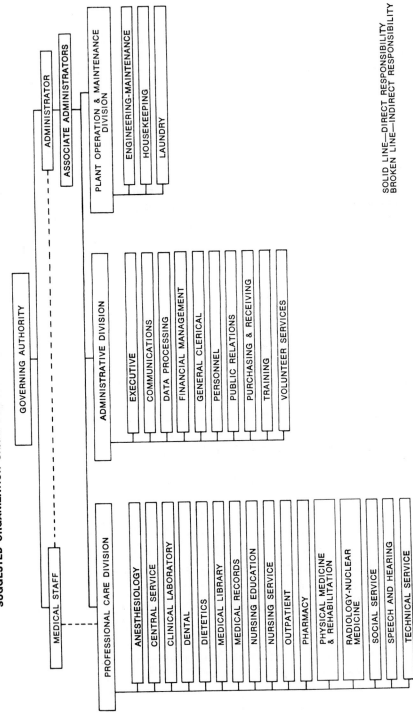

GOVERNING AUTHORITY

MEDICAL STAFF

ADMINISTRATOR

ASSOCIATE ADMINISTRATORS

PROFESSIONAL CARE DIVISION

- ANESTHESIOLOGY
- CENTRAL SERVICE
- CLINICAL LABORATORY
- DENTAL
- DIETETICS
- MEDICAL LIBRARY
- MEDICAL RECORDS
- NURSING EDUCATION
- NURSING SERVICE
- OUTPATIENT
- PHARMACY
- PHYSICAL MEDICINE & REHABILITATION
- RADIOLOGY-NUCLEAR MEDICINE
- SOCIAL SERVICE
- SPEECH AND HEARING
- TECHNICAL SERVICE

ADMINISTRATIVE DIVISION

- EXECUTIVE
- COMMUNICATIONS
- DATA PROCESSING
- FINANCIAL MANAGEMENT
- GENERAL CLERICAL
- PERSONNEL
- PUBLIC RELATIONS
- PURCHASING & RECEIVING
- TRAINING
- VOLUNTEER SERVICES

PLANT OPERATION & MAINTENANCE DIVISION

- ENGINEERING-MAINTENANCE
- HOUSEKEEPING
- LAUNDRY

SOLID LINE—DIRECT RESPONSIBILITY
BROKEN LINE—INDIRECT RESPONSIBILITY

NOTE: This chart is for illustrative purposes only and should not be considered a recommended pattern of organization.

The Manpower Administration of the United States Department of Labor, in cooperation with the American Hospital Association, has made a nationwide survey of hospital organization as it is most often practiced, and the job classifications found in each department. In general, the departments of hospitals fall into one of three divisions: professional care, administration, and operation and maintenance. The overall pattern of organization appears in the following chart.

Classifications are presented by departments, with the highest–rated job first, followed by others in declining order. Where several jobs are at the same level, the descriptions will follow the departmental organization chart so far as possible, working from left to right, and following each related staff of workers down, then moving to the next column to the right.

If a job appears on the organization chart of a department but is not described in full detail, it can be assumed that qualifications for it are high school graduation or less, possibly plus a short-course or on-the-job training.

For the convenience of employment counselors and career guides, each job description is followed by a notation as to its classification and number in the *Dictionary of Occupational Titles* (2 volumes, 3rd edition; Washington, D.C.: United States Department of Labor, Manpower Administration, 1965). These will be found on the left margin: Superintendent, Hospital: (DOT) 187.118–062.

Classification numbers are given for all jobs that show on charts, including the laborer jobs that are not described in detail.

It should be remarked that health-care occupations comprise so dynamic a field that new job classifications and specialties develop continually. Consequently, not every most-recent or near-future career possibility may be classified yet, or have been assigned a suffix. In these cases, judgment will need to be made from similar existing classifications.

Because the same job is not always called by the same name everywhere, each description is headed by the title most commonly used, with alternate titles listed beneath it.

3

BASIC SCIENCE AND PROFESSIONAL CARE

Basic science underlies all health care and offers many challenging career opportunities. In the hospital it is best represented by the Clinical Laboratory, and the Research Laboratory, if the hospital is part of a large medical center.

A generation ago, any knowledgeable person would have stated confidently that there were only three basic sciences: biology, chemistry, and physics. Today, mathematics must be added, and is as indispensable as the others in prevention and treatment of disease.

A Clinical Laboratory is a prime necessity for any hospital. It is headed by a Clinical Pathologist, who—with his assistants—performs tests that give physicians the information they need to guide them in diagnosis and treatment. Having these services conveniently on the premises is a great advantage in modern hospital care. Many physicians have small laboratories within their offices, staffed by a Medical Assistant who can do routine tests. For more complicated tests, they call on one of the independent laboratories that do clinical work, or utilize the facilities of the hospital.

A Research Laboratory is concerned with solving unanswered basic questions about causes of disease and disability, and developing new ways to predict, prevent, or treat the ills that plague mankind. They are frequently associated with universities, medical schools, private foundations, some industries, and Federal and state agencies.

Clinical and Research Laboratories frequently complement each other. Physicians engaged in clinical practice often are also involved in research in their specialty, and their experience with patients—supported by the work of the clinical laboratory—contributes to ultimate results.

Broad-scale cooperation is essential in some of the most challenging research efforts. For example, working together in molecular biology and in brain research are the physician and surgeon, the anatomist and physiologist, the biophysicist and biochemist, the biomathematician, and the medical engineer.

Drawing upon the knowledge and skill of these and other specialists, research activities seek to discover substances in the body cells that cause cancer or aging; in blood, that cause kidney transplants to fail; in the interaction of complex acids and proteins in cells that may permit control of human heredity. As surgeons and immunologists push forward their studies of how failing human organs can be "traded in" for new ones, others who are equally dedicated strive to arrest aging, the process of deterioration that begins at birth.

The principal Federal agency that supports health-related research—and concomitant education of professionals in the health field—is the National Institutes of Health of the United States Department of Health, Education and Welfare. Support for special types of research and education of young scientists is also provided by the National Science Foundation, the Atomic Energy Commission, the National Aeronautics and Space Administration, the Veterans' Administration, the Department of Agriculture, and some other agencies.

Clinical Laboratory

The Clinical Laboratory performs tests in six fields of basic science—bacteriology, biochemistry, cytology, hematology, histopathology, and serology—to assist the medical staff of the hospital in making or confirming diagnoses. In addition to making specialized tests, clinical laboratories in general hospitals are responsible for making all routine tests, such as urinalyses, blood cell and hemoglobin count for all patients on admission; and gross and microscopic examination of all tissues re-

The Clinical Laboratory in a hospital devotes its efforts to solving immediate problems of diagnosis and treatment of patients. A Clinical Pathologist, who is a physician, heads the Laboratory, and supervises the Technologists, Technicians, Assistants, and other workers. He confers with the staff, instructs and assists them in difficult procedures, and makes judgments when the results of tests are unusual.

Photo courtesy National Committee for Careers in the Medical Laboratory

moved at surgery. They also determine causes of communicable diseases, and—upon request—render bacteriological service as a control and continual check on all apparatus used for sterilization.

Laboratory Units

In larger hospitals, the clinical laboratories are divided into a number of specialized units.

Bacteriology: Micro-organisms found in body fluids, exudates, skin scrapings, or autopsy or surgical specimens are cultivated, classified, and identified, in order to provide data on the cause, cure, and prevention of disease. Research is undertaken to develop new or improved methods for discovering and identifying pathogenic organisms. Investigation is made of the biology, distribution, and mode of transmission of bacteria, and the nature and efficiency of chemotherapeutic treatment.

Biochemistry: Chemical tests of body fluids and exudates are performed, to provide information for diagnosis and treatment of disease. Investigation is made of the chemical processes in functioning and malfunctioning of the human body. The effects of chemical compounds upon physiological and biochemical functions of the body are studied, to provide information on the most effective methods of treating pathological conditions.

Cytology: Human cells are examined, to detect evidence of cancer in its early stages, and to determine other diseased conditions. Research is carried on to develop new cytological methods, and new strains, to produce greater clarity during examination of cell structures.

Hematology: Blood specimens are tested, and the results interpreted, to provide a basis for treatment of diseases. The unit engages in research related to hematologic methods and diagnosis.

The blood bank, if a hospital has one, is usually part of the hematology unit. The bank provides for storage and preservation of blood and its various constituents. Blood may be procured either directly from donors, or from other blood banks. When it is obtained from donors, this unit extracts blood and makes the necessary laboratory tests for the purpose of determining its suitability for transfusion.

Histopathology: Tissue is prepared and examined, to provide data on cause and progress of disease. Microscopic examinations of tissue pathology are made. Research is carried on to develop new histopathologic methods, and new strains that will produce greater clarity during examination of special tissue structures or chemical components. Personnel of this unit perform autopsies, and interpret gross and microscopic autopsy findings in conferences with the medical staff and technologists, toward improving future diagnosis and treatment of patients.

Serology: This unit prepares the serums used to treat and diagnose infectious diseases and immunize against these diseases, and to identify diseases based on characteristic reactions of various serums. It investigates the safety of new commercial antibiotic products, and the accuracy of therapeutic claims. It directs immunology tests and injections, and investigates problems of allergy. It conducts tests to determine therapeutic and toxic dosages, and the most effective methods of administering serums, vaccines, antibiotics, antitoxins, antigens, and related drugs.

The Clinical Laboratory may be responsible for a number of other functions, such as basal metabolism tests, activities of the clinical photographic laboratory, medical illustration unit, and the morgue. Care and treatment of the animals used in research may devolve upon it. Teaching programs for student nurses, interns, residents, and medical technologists and other laboratory personnel may also be a function of the laboratory.

Authority in the Laboratory

The hospital Pathologist is also the head of the Clinical Laboratory. He has the responsibility for the organization and operation of all pathological services and the supervision of all personnel assigned to the laboratory. He is a physician who has a specialty in pathology. Since his job combines administrative and professional functions, he reports to both the Assistant Administrator and the Chief of Medical Staff.

Interrelations

Laboratory services must be coordinated with all other diagnostic functions of the hospital. This requires consultation with members of the medical staff, administrators, and department heads. A system is necessary whereby all routine laboratory tests can be performed within a specified period of time after a patient is admitted. Thus, the laboratory must be operative—at least on an emergency basis—24 hours a day.

Close cooperation is essential between the laboratory and the Outpatient Department. Personnel in the laboratory have occasional contact with patients, and with medical, admitting, and nursing staff, and with other employees. The Pathologist may lecture to student bodies, professional societies, and medical organizations. There is cooperation with other department heads, private physicians, and personnel in other laboratories, and related activities in radiology and technical services.

Standards

All regularly employed laboratory technologists and technicians should be on the registry sponsored by the American Society of Clinical Pathologists. They must have complete instruction in a school for technologists or technicians approved by the Council on Medical Education and Hospitals of the American Medical Association. Many hospitals, particularly those connected with schools of medicine or osteopathy, offer courses in medical technology. These schools must also meet the standards formulated by the Council on Medical Education and Hospitals of the American Medical Association.

Physical Facilities and Staffing

The physical facilities of the clinical laboratory will depend upon its workload. In a small hospital, where only a minimum of routine work is performed, a minimum of space and equipment is required. In a large hospital, space may be divided into a number of specialized units, including an office for the Pathologist, and a central workroom for procedures utilized by all units. If a large amount of outpatient work is performed, the hospital may maintain a small branch laboratory in the Outpatient Department or Clinic.

The director of the laboratory is a doctor of medicine or osteopathy, with qualifications in pathology acceptable to the Council on Education and Hospitals of the American Medical Association, or the Committee on Hospitals of the Bureau of Professional Education of the American Osteopathic Association. If a hospital is unable to secure the full-time services of a qualified person in this capacity, arrangements should be made to share services with another institution in the area. It is imperative that a duly qualified Pathologist be responsible for the issues and post mortem examinations and for the interpretation of tests and examinations.

Depending upon the hospital, requirements for a Clinical Laboratory Director can be met by: (1) a full-time Clinical Pathologist; (2) a part-time Clinical Pathologist shared with a nearby institution; (3) a Consulting Pathologist to whom materials can be sent for diagnosis, and who will come to the hospital periodically to supervise services and meet with the medical staff; or (4) a member of the medical staff who has had training in clinical pathology and will supervise the laboratory in situations where the workload is insufficient to warrant the full-time services of a specialist. In the last case, tissue examinations requiring specialized equipment and skill can be sent to the nearest clinical laboratory that is headed by a qualified pathologist.

CLINICAL LABORATORIES DEPARTMENT

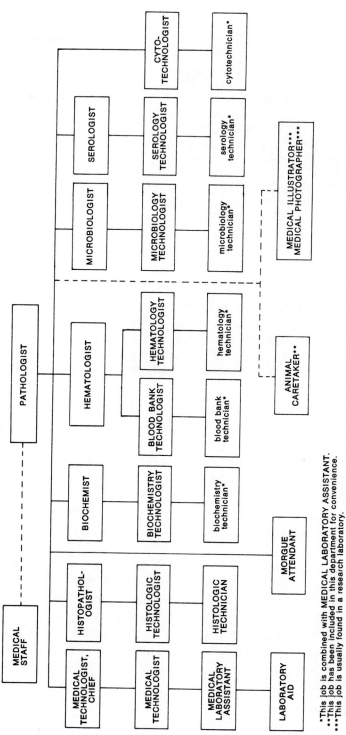

*This job is combined with MEDICAL LABORATORY ASSISTANT.
**This job has been included in this department for convenience.
***This job is usually found in a research laboratory.

NOTE: This chart is for illustrative purposes only and should not be considered a recommended pattern of organization.

A Chief Medical Technologist calls the attention of the Pathologist to an unusual formation of tissue cells.

MEDICAL TECHNOLOGIST, CHIEF
Laboratory Supervisor

The Chief Medical Technologist, who has a broad background of college science and clinical laboratory experience, holds a key to quality performance in the laboratory. In addition to her skills as a technologist, she is a supervisor, teacher, and research assistant. She is the "right-hand person" of the Pathologist. (The majority of medical technologists today are women, although men are beginning to enter the field.)

In a small hospital laboratory, one Chief Medical Technologist will supervise the work of other personnel in all 6 branches of clinical pathology. In large hospitals, there may be a Chief Microbiology Technologist, a Chief Biochemistry Technologist, a Chief Cytotechnologist, a Chief Hematology Technologist, an Histologic Technologist, a Chief Serology Technologist, and a Chief Blood Bank Technologist.

Whether the Chief Laboratory Technologist supervises the work of the entire laboratory or of only one unit within it, she is directly responsible to the Pathologist, and next in authority. Her opportunities are as unlimited as the horizons of research and preventive medicine, and as valuable as any work related to health care.

JOB DUTIES

She supervises, coordinates, and participates in activities of workers performing various chemical, microscopic, and bacteriologic tests of body fluids, exudates, skin scrapings, or autopsy or surgical specimens to obtain data for diagnosis and treatment of disease.

She consults with the Pathologist to plan priorities of work to be completed each day, and supervises workers in her assigned section or area of specialization in the laboratory. She checks the validity and accuracy of test results obtained by laboratory personnel on a sample basis by performing the same test and comparing the results. She keeps records pertaining to tests performed, and charts the results to insure that variation in test results and standards are within acceptable quality control ranges. She may keep time records, and make ratings and recommendations for promotions. She gives instructions to new workers regarding procedures and techniques of performing tests. She may direct the training and instruction of students in medical terminology. She may interview and hire new laboratory workers.

She performs experimental testing procedures and reports to the Pathologist, suggesting changes to increase validity and reliability of tests. She demonstrates newly approved methods to personnel, and implements standard procedures. She studies current medical literature, to obtain information on new test methods and procedures.

She may assist the Pathologist during autopsies. She may schedule appointments, and may be responsible for ordering replacements to maintain stock of equipment and supplies.

She should obviously be capable of performing all the duties of the Medical Technologists working under her.

EDUCATION, TRAINING, AND EXPERIENCE

Three years of college is required, with courses in biology, chemistry, and mathematics, plus one year of training in a school of medical technology approved by the American Society of Clinical Pathologists.

The applicant must be registered as a Medical Technologist by the Registry Board of the American Society of Clinical Pathologists.

Some states require a license issued by the State Board of Health as a prerequisite to practice.

Usually requires from two to five years' experience in a clinical laboratory.

JOB RELATIONSHIPS

Workers supervised: Medical Technologists, Medical Laboratory Assistants, and Laboratory Aides.
Supervised by: Pathologist.
Promotion from: Medical Technologist.
Promotion to: No formal line of promotion.

PROFESSIONAL AFFILIATIONS

American Society of Medical Technologists
Suite 25, Hermann Professional Building
Houston, Texas 77025

Medical Technologist, Chief (DOT) 078.168-010

MEDICAL TECHNOLOGISTS

Medical technology is one of the newest and fastest growing professions associated with modern advances in medical science. It is a field in which women have predominated until the present, although men are beginning to come into it. It is estimated that 80,000 to 90,000 professional Medical Technologists will be needed by 1980. Graduates usually find employment opportunities in every part of the country, and salaries compare favorably with those of teachers and other professional workers of whom equivalent education is required.

Not all of the work that the technologist performs in the laboratory is dramatic, but all of it is vital. In blood transfusions, where—in addition to testing for blood groups A, B, and the Rh factors—final crossmatch verification can involve anywhere from six to twenty highly sensitive and specific determinations, the knowledge and skill of the Medical Technologist are crucial. Tests performed by Medical Technologists are indispensable to physicians in establishing diagnosis and determining treatment of individual patients.

In large hospitals, and those engaged in research, Medical Technologists may be specialists, working in only one field of clinical pathology, such as microbiology, biochemistry, cytology, hematology, histology, serology, or handling of the blood bank. In smaller hospitals, a technologist may work in all these fields. In all accu-

A Medical Technologist carefully measures a laboratory solution, following standardized procedures.

racy, the one who works in all fields is properly called a "Medical Technologist," and the others should be known by the specific fields in which they work, as "Biochemistry Technologist," for example.

The Medical Technologist, by whatever title, performs various chemical, microscopic, and bacteriologic tests to obtain data for use in diagnosis and treatment of disease.

She receives written requisitions sent by physicians to the Clinical Laboratory and assigned to her by the Chief Medical Technologist or the Pathologist who heads the laboratory. These may be requests for routine or special laboratory tests. She sets up and adjusts laboratory equipment and apparatus, such as chemical glassware, balance, microscope, slides, and reagents.

She obtains laboratory specimens, such as urine, blood, and sputum, from wards or directly from the patients, using established laboratory techniques. She adds reagents or indicator solutions, and subjects specimens for processing to such operations as heating, agitating, filtering, or titrating, according to established procedures. She prepares slides for microscopic analysis as necessary. She observes reactions, changes of color, or formation of precipitates, studies slides using microscope, or subjects treated specimens to automatic analyzing equipment to make qualitative and quantitative analyses. She posts all test findings to laboratory slips for study by the Pathologist or other laboratory supervisors. She also posts results of laboratory analyses to record cards, and files reports. She indicates the amount to be charged to the patient's account, identifies and labels all specimens to be retained, and files them for further reference or research.

EDUCATION, TRAINING, AND EXPERIENCE

Education for medical technology requires at least three years of a baccalaureate degree program in an accredited college or university, including 16 semester hours each of approved courses in chemistry, biological science, and mathematics. This is followed by a 12-month hospital laboratory educational program in medical technology accredited by the Council on Medical Education of the American Medical Association and approved by the American Society of Clinical Pathologists. The AMA accreditation is recognized by the United States Office of Education and the National Commission on Accrediting.[1]

More than 775 AMA-approved hospital programs are now affiliated with colleges or universities that count the clinical experience as the senior year, and award a bac-

[1] An alternative program allows the applicant who has completed four years of college and holds a bachelor's degree to substitute five years of laboratory experience for the hospital laboratory program.

calaureate degree upon its completion. Little or no tuition is charged for the hospital laboratory programs, and many schools offer scholarships and/or stipends averaging about $100 a month. A number have student loan funds.

Following this training, students are eligible to take the national examination of the Board of Registry of the American Society of Clinical Pathologists, giving them certification and the professional title, MT(ASP). Professional Medical Technologists must be so registered, and some states require a license issued by the State Board of Health as a prerequisite to practice.

JOB RELATIONSHIPS

Workers supervised: Medical Laboratory Assistant; may supervise Laboratory Aide.
Supervised by: Medical Technologist, Chief or Pathologist.
Promotion from: No formal line of promotion.
Promotion to: Medical Technologist, Chief.

PROFESSIONAL AFFILIATIONS

American Society of Medical Technologists
Suite 25, Hermann Professional Building
Houston, Texas 77025

Medical Technologist (DOT) 078.281-018

MEDICAL LABORATORY TECHNICIAN

The Medical Laboratory Technician is the newest member of the laboratory team. In recent years, demands on Medical Technologists to do more and more supervisory work and to undertake on-the-job teaching and instruction have made it impossible for them to perform all of the actual testing. The Medical Technician, who fills the gap between the Technologist and the Medical Laboratory Assistant, is qualified to do routine work without close supervision, and special testing with supervision. She does not have the supervisory and educational responsibilities of the professional Medical Technologist.

The position of Technician provides a new intermediate level on the career ladder, and offers an excellent point of entry to a profession in which age and experience become increasing assets, and workers are assured of steady employment. It is the kind of work in which a woman can take time out for marriage and family, and return with little difficulty, or work on a part-time basis during child-rearing years. For persons seeking advancement in a lifetime career, it offers opportunity to work in one's chosen field while continuing education.

Proficiency examinations for laboratory personnel have been developed by the Educational Testing Service for the National Committee for Careers in the Medical Laboratory, under a Labor Department contract. These measure an individual's competence, so that he or she may be considered for placement at an appropriate

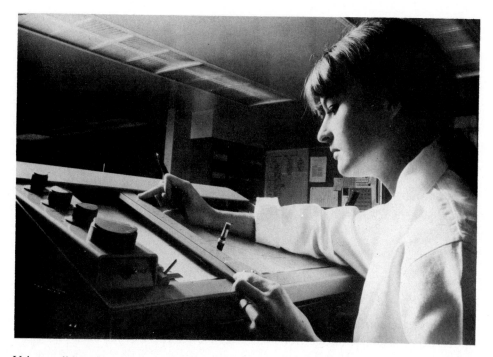

Using a slide rule, a Medical Laboratory Technician calculates the results of a test she has just completed.

Photo courtesy of the National Committee for Careers in the Medical Laboratory

job level, irrespective of degrees or credentials earned. The examinations were designed especially for military corpsmen and those who have primarily learned and progressed on the job. Equivalency examinations are available to give academic credit for acquired knowledge.

Medical Laboratory Technicians, as well as Technologists, are employed in clinical and bio-analytical laboratories of clinics, hospitals, physicians' offices, medical, dental, and veterinary colleges, pharmaceutical companies, state and municipal public health departments, insurance companies, public and private research institutions, medical departments of industrial firms, and Federal government agencies. There are no geographic limitations on employment.

JOB DUTIES

The Medical Laboratory Technician performs various chemical, microscopic, and bacteriologic tests to obtain data for use by physicians in diagnosis and treatment of disease. She does routine testing with relatively little supervision, and specialized procedures under supervision of a Medical Technologist.

She receives written requisitions, as provided by physicians, on assignments made by the Pathologist or Medical Technologist. She sets up and adjusts laboratory equipment and apparatus, such as chemical glassware, balance, microscope, slides, and reagents.

She obtains laboratory specimens, such as urine, blood samples, and sputum, from wards or directly from patients, using established laboratory techniques, adds reagents or indicator solutions, and subjects specimens for processing to operations such as heating, agitating, filtering or titrating according to established procedures. She prepares slides for microscopic analysis as necessary. She observes reactions, changes of color, or formation of precipitates. She studies slides, using microscope, or subjects specimens to automatic analyzing equipment to make qualitative and quantitative analyses. She posts all test findings to laboratory slips for approval by the supervising Medical Technologist. She identifies and labels all specimens to be retained and files them for further reference and research.

EDUCATION, TRAINING, AND EXPERIENCE

Preparation for medical laboratory technician requires a high school education followed by an associate degree from an accredited junior or community college and by clinical experience in an approved laboratory. Students with this experience may receive certification of MLT(ASCP) by the Registry of Medical Technologists.

They may also receive certification by the American Medical Technologists registry. This registry gives certification as a Medical Laboratory Technician to the high school graduate who has completed a two-year work-school experience in programs approved by the Accrediting Bureau of Medical Laboratory Schools. It will also give certification as Medical Laboratory Technician to students who have completed a 50-week Armed Forces course in medical laboratory techniques together with approved laboratory experience. All applicants for American Medical Technologists Registry must pass a registry examination.

JOB RELATIONSHIPS

Workers supervised: None.
Supervised by: Medical Technologist.
Promotion from: Medical Laboratory Assistant.
Promotion to: No formal line of promotion.

PROFESSIONAL AFFILIATIONS

American Medical Technologists
710 Higgins Road
Park Ridge, Illinois 60068

American Society of Clinical Pathologists
2100 West Harrison Street
Chicago, Illinois 60612

American Society of Medical Technologists
Suite 1600
Hermann Professional Building
Houston, Texas 77025

National Committee for Careers in the Medical Laboratory
9650 Rockville Pike
Rockville, Maryland 20014

Medical Laboratory Technician: (DOT) 078.281-026

MEDICAL LABORATORY ASSISTANT
Assistant Laboratory Technician
Certified Laboratory Assistant
Biochemistry Technician
Blood Bank Technician
Cytotechnician
Hematology Technician
Laboratory Assistant
Microbiology Technician
Serology Technician

Medical Laboratory Assistants are the foot soldiers in the clinical laboratory's battle against disease. They are the people who perform the routine chores, and their work is extremely valuable in the total operation of the laboratory.

In a small hospital, the Medical Laboratory Assistant might have to be proficient at tasks in all the scientific branches of testing. In large institutions, she is likely to concentrate on only one of the basic sciences, and is identified with it, as a Hematology Technician, or a Serology Technician.

JOB DUTIES

The Medical Laboratory Assistant conducts routine tests in clinical laboratories for use in treatment and diagnosis of disease, and performs related duties.

She performs tests in various areas, such as serology, hematology, chemistry, microbiology, histology, and cytology, using standard techniques and equipment. She may make qualitative determination of sugar in urine, by adding prescribed reagents to specimens and noting change of color or appearance of precipitate. She makes blood cell counts by adding reagents to sample and then checking against standard color scales or color comparisons in a colorimeter; or separates plasma from whole blood, using a centrifuge. She stores and labels plasma. She may tend automatic equipment, such as diluting-titrating machine, blood cell counter, and spectrophotometer to prepare specimens and perform analytical tests.

She prepares sterile media such as agar in plates, jars, or test tubes, for use in growing bacterial cultures. She incubates cultures for specific times at prescribed temperatures. She may make preliminary identification of common types of bacterial cultures for confirmation by her supervisor. She prepares solutions, reagents, and stains, following standard laboratory formulas and procedures. She maintains laboratory stock of chemicals and glassware. She may collect specimens from patients. She keeps detailed records of all tests performed and reports laboratory findings to all persons authorized to receive such information.

EDUCATION, TRAINING, AND EXPERIENCE

Preparation for Medical Laboratory Assistant requires graduation from high school, plus a 12-month training program in a certified laboratory-assistant school approved by the American Medical Association. Many hospital laboratory schools are accredited to provide this training, and their graduates are eligible to take the American Society of Clinical Pathologists' Board of Registry examination, whereby they are certified, and may place the letters CLA(ASCP) after their names.

Medical Laboratory Assistants may also receive limited certification as Laboratory Technicians (CT Limited Certification) from American Medical Technologists. The applicant must be a graduate of an accredited high school or equivalent, and have completed not less than 24 months of on-the-job training in an approved laboratory. He must also pass a certification examination.

Veterans who are high school graduates and have completed the basic military medical laboratory course plus one year of acceptable experience may also qualify under the American Medical Technologists certification program.

JOB RELATIONSHIPS

Workers supervised: None.
Supervised by: Medical Technologist.
Promotion from: No formal line of promotion.
Promotion to: No formal line of promotion.

PROFESSIONAL AFFILIATIONS

Board of Certified Laboratory Assistants
9500 South California Avenue
Evergreen Park, Illinois 60642

Medical Laboratory Assistant: (DOT) 078.381-000

LABORATORY AIDE
Clean-up Man
Equipment Washer
Laboratory Attendant
Tester Helper
Utility Man, Laboratory

JOB DUTIES

The Laboratory Aide cleans laboratory equipment, such as glassware, metal instruments, sinks, tables, and test panels. He uses solvents, brushes, and rags. He assists the Medical Technologist by performing routine duties in the Clinical Laboratory.

He mixes water and detergents or acids in containers to prepare cleaning solutions according to specifications. He washes used glassware and instruments in a container by rinsing them in water, and drying, using cloth, hot air drier, or acetone bath. He examines cleaned equipment to detect breakage and discards damaged or broken equipment. He carries cleaned items to the appropriate section of clinical laboratory for storage. He may sterilize instruments and glassware, using autoclave.

He pours, measures, and mixes liquid, powder, and crystalline chemicals to prepare simple stains, solutions, and culture media, following established formulas and using uninvolved chemical and bacteriological procedures. He may label tubes and bottles, and fill them with specified solutions.

As assigned, and under close supervision, he may perform such simple laboratory tests as qualitative determinations of sugar and albumen in urine. He adds specific reagents to urine samples, and notes change in color or appearance of precipitate.

He collects patients' specimens from wards and returns them to laboratory for analysis. He assembles equipment used in collecting communicable disease specimens. He distributes supplies and laboratory specimens to the designated area. He keeps records of specimens held in the laboratory. He maintains an inventory of supplies. He repairs laboratory apparatus, using hand tools. He scrubs walls, floors, shelves, tables, sinks, using cleaning solutions and brush. He may tend the still that provides the laboratory with distilled water.

In smaller hospitals, the Laboratory Aide may also assume the post of Animal Caretaker.

EDUCATION, TRAINING, AND EXPERIENCE

High school education is required, preferably including chemistry and bacteriology. Experience is not essential, although the worker usually requires approximately two months' training in a clinical laboratory to be capable of normal productivity.

JOB RELATIONSHIPS

Workers supervised: None.
Supervised by: Medical Technologist, or may be supervised by Medical Technologist, Chief.
Promotion from: No formal line of promotion. This is an entry job.
Promotion to: No formal line of promotion.

PROFESSIONAL AFFILIATIONS

None.

Cleaner, Laboratory Equipment: (DOT) 381.887-018

MORGUE ATTENDANT

The Morgue Attendant makes a valuable contribution to the work of the Clinical Laboratory. He is directly responsible to the Pathologist who heads the laboratory and who handles autopsies upon which confirmation of diagnoses is based. From autopsies, too, information is gathered in regard to the nature and progress of disease, often in direct relation to specific research projects. The Morgue Attendant expedites this essential work. While he seldom receives public recognition, his work is indispensable.

The location in which he works is as professional as any other part of the hospital or laboratory. Some walls of the room are lined with metal lockers, and look much like the wall of storage lockers in an airport or bus terminal. However, these lockers are six feet deep, and each contains a removable tray upon which a body rests. The lockers are refrigerated, and bodies remain only temporarily. An operating table occupies the center of the room, and storage cabinets containing surgical instruments, linens, and other equipment are nearby.

The Morgue Attendant is more than a janitor. Frequently, he performs simple autopsy procedures that save the Pathologist's time before and after autopsy, and he assists during the examination. He renders valuable assistance in the preparation of various organs for detailed microscopic examination.

JOB DUTIES

The Morgue Attendant maintains the hospital morgue room and equipment in clean and orderly condition.

He receives bodies of deceased persons in the morgue and assists the porters in placing them in compartment trays, taking care to verify identification of body by armband, compartment label, and record-of-death form accompanying the body.

When an autopsy is to be performed, he transfers the body from the compartment tray of the morgue refrigerator to the autopsy table, using a wheeled stretcher. He lifts the body manually, or uses a portable hoist to lift it from the stretcher to the table. He lays out cutting and surgical instruments, glass specimen jars, and test tubes in readiness. He writes information such as name of deceased person and date of autopsy on specimen labels and also in the autopsy logbook for identification and record purposes.

During the autopsy, he hands the Pathologist surgical instruments such as knives, saws, scalpels, forceps, and also linens, as needed or directed, so that the Pathologist need not divert his attention from the field of study. He flushes blood and other fluids from the body, using water and suction evacuation hoses. Occasionally he performs minor prosecting duties, such as opening the skull, using an electric band-saw. As organs are removed, he weighs them and posts the weights for the Pathologist's use in making diagnostic reports. He places organs and specimens in pre-labeled specimen containers. He may photograph the specimens. He locates and ties off major arteries and stumps of organs, and closes the incision in the body cavities to prepare the body for the undertaker. This may require filling the cranium with plaster. He then preserves the body in the refrigerated area until it is removed by the undertaker. The Morgue Attendant is responsible for release of the body only to an authorized person.

He cleans the surgical instruments, equipment, and morgue area, using water, sterilizing equipment and solutions, and cleaning equipment. He selects powders and liquids and mixes in prescribed solutions to replenish supply of preserving solutions. He gathers soiled linens for laundering, and replaces with fresh supply. He requisitions supplies from the storeroom to maintain stock in the morgue.

EDUCATION, TRAINING, AND EXPERIENCE

High school graduation is usually required, but this job usually requires no previous experience. Some employers may require some morgue room experience.

Three months' on-the-job training is required.

JOB RELATIONSHIPS

Workers supervised: None.
Supervised by: Pathologist.
Promotion from: No formal line of promotion. This may be an entry job.
Promotion to: No formal line of promotion.

PROFESSIONAL AFFILIATIONS

None.

Morgue Man: (DOT) 335.887.010

HISTOPATHOLOGIST

Histopathology is the branch of science that deals with the composition, structure, and function of body tissues, particularly as they are affected by disease. It is basic to any understanding of the causes and cure of cancer, and therefore is very important in cancer research.

In the clinical laboratory, the histopathologist is most concerned with isolating and identifying malignant cells in the tumors or other suspected tissues of patients whose physicians think they may have cancer. By microscopic examination of tiny, gossamer-thin slices of tissue, called sections, taken from the affected area of a patient, the histopathologist can tell not only whether the cells are malignant, but what kind of malignancy is present. This knowledge helps the physician decide whether radiological, surgical, or a combination of treatments is necessary. When the tissue is taken from a living person, this procedure is called a biopsy.

Naturally, the patient is most pleased when the histopathologist finds that the tissue taken for biopsy is benign, or not cancerous.

Surgeons make use of histopathology during actual operations. After incision has been made, and the tumor or other suspected tissue is exposed, the surgeon quickly excises samples and sends them to the laboratory, where the specimens are frozen, sectioned, stained, and examined while the patient is still on the operating table. From the results, the surgeon knows how extensively he must operate.

Histopathologic techniques are also employed at the time of autopsy, when it may be important to determine whether cancer was present, and may have been the cause of death. This kind of examination is important in adding to the scientific body of knowledge about the progression of various forms of cancer. If the deceased person has been receiving treatment, post mortem examination of tissues indicates how effective the treatment proved to be. A significant proportion of clinical research consists of projects in which a physician, or team of physicians and laboratory personnel, keeps records and reports on the effectiveness of certain kinds of treatment, or accuracy of a certain kind of diagnostic method, in a series of patients having similar conditions.

JOB DUTIES

The Histopathologist works directly under the Pathologist who heads the clinical laboratory. He directs and supervises preparation of tissue specimens and examines specimens to provide data on body functions or cause and progress of disease.

He trains and supervises laboratory personnel in fixing, embedding, cutting, staining, and mounting tissue sections, or prepares tissue material from surgical and diagnostic cases or from autopsies. He examines tissue section structures. He assists personnel with the more difficult tissue sections, and directs uses of special stains and methods for isolation, identification, and study of functions, morphology, and pathology of obscure cells, tissues, and connecting fibers. He writes diagnostic reports of microscopic examinations for approval by the pathologist.

He may lecture to students of medicine, medical technology, or nursing, or to the interns and residents in training in hospital.

He may conduct autopsies to select tissue specimens for study. He may engage in research to develop new histopathologic methods and new stains to bring out special tissue structure of chemical components.

He may study formation of organs and related functions to obtain data on body function.

EDUCATION, TRAINING, AND EXPERIENCE

A master's degree or doctorate in histopathology is usually required, plus three years of experience in histopathology in an approved medical laboratory.

JOB RELATIONSHIPS

Workers supervised: Histologic Technologist and Histologic Technician.
Supervised by: Pathologist.
Promotion from: No formal line of promotion.
Promotion to: No formal line of promotion. May be promoted to Pathologist in charge of clinical laboratory, if histology training includes M.D. degree and experience in other branches of pathology.

PROFESSIONAL AFFILIATIONS

American Medical Association
535 Dearborn Street
Chicago, Illinois 60610

American Society of Clinical Pathologists
445 North Lake Shore Drive
Chicago, Illinois 60611

American Society of Medical Technologists
Suite 25, Hermann Professional Building
Houston, Texas 77025

Histopathologist: (DOT) 041.181-010

HISTOLOGIC TECHNOLOGIST
Histopathology Technologist
Medical Technologist, Histology
Tissue Technologist

The Histologic Technologist works directly under the Histopathologist. She cuts, stains, mounts, and studies specimens of human tissues to provide data on structural changes in the tissues and organs under study at the cellular level.

At times she must work under the pressure of knowing that the work she is doing will affect surgery in progress, and though the team in the operating room is awaiting the results of her investigation, she cannot sacrifice accuracy for speed. Much of the time, she knows that the physician who has prescribed the examination of a patient's tissue specimen will be influenced in his diagnosis and treatment by the outcome of her work.

A Histologic Technologist dips very thin sections of body tissue into special dyes to make cells stand out clearly during microscopic examination to detect possible malignancy.

Photo courtesy of the National Committee for Careers in the Medical Laboratory

JOB DUTIES

The Histologic Technologist trims tissue, fixes it in formaldehyde or other fixing solution to preserve it, and dehydrates it by immersion in acetone or alcohol baths. She places specimens in paraffin or imbeds them in colloidin until they are ready for processing.

She prepares specimens for immediate study by freezing them with carbon dioxide. She inserts prepared tissue in microtome and stains it to define essential feature, then mounts the tissue sections on microscopic slide and inserts the slide into the microscope.

She examines slides for indications of malignancy or disease and reads instructions on work slips to determine the initial approach to pathological search. She examines nucleus to detect characteristics, such as variation in thickness of nuclear membrane, overall shape of membrane, and disproportionate size of nucleus; and she examines chromatin in cell by checking color against chart, and appraising concentration of granules. She compares findings with graphic illustrations, or makes determinations based on experience, to detect signs of malignancy or disease. She examines cytoplasm and nucleus to detect deviations from the norm in color, thickness, clumping, concentration of bodies, and shape, as further indication of the nature and extent of malignancy or disease. She prepares reports, itemizing abnormalities, for study by the Histopathologist or Pathologist.

She stains and covers Papanicolaou smear slides, and examines the prepared slides through the microscope to determine whether they meet established standards. She takes the slides to the Pathologist for diagnosis.

She stains specimens of fat globules, bone, and bone marrow, using specified reagents, and prepares slides for study by the Histopathologist or Pathologist. She may examine the slides for abnormalities.

The Histologic Technologist prepares and maintains paraffin, reagents, and other solutions and stains according to standard formulas.

She keeps detailed records of tests performed in the laboratory. She may assist the Histopathologist or pathologist in autopsies.

The duties of this job may be combined with those of the Histologic Technician.

EDUCATION, TRAINING, AND EXPERIENCE

The Histologic Technologist must have three years of college, with courses in biology, chemistry, and mathematics, plus one year of training in a school of medical technology approved by the American Society of Clinical Pathologists.

She must be registered as a Medical Technologist by the Registry Board of the American Society of Clinical Pathologists.

Some states require a license issued by the State Board of Health.

JOB RELATIONSHIPS

Workers supervised: Sometimes may supervise the Histologic Technician.
Supervised by: Histopathologist or Medical Technologist, Chief.
Promotion from: No formal line of promotion.
Promotion to: No formal line of promotion.

PROFESSIONAL AFFILIATIONS

American Society of Medical Technologists
Suite 25, Hermann Professional Building
Houston, Texas 77025

Histologic Technologist: (DOT) 078.381

HISTOLOGIC TECHNICIAN
Medical Laboratory Assistant
Medical Technician
Tissue Technician

The Histologic Technician does the day-to-day routine work of preparing tissue specimens for examination by the Pathologist, the Histopathologist, the Histologic Technologist, or herself. In small laboratory units, the positions of Histologic Technologist and Histologic Technician are often combined. In others, the Medical Technician does the work of the Histologic Technician.

The Technician receives specimens of tissue from surgical or diagnostic patients and from autopsy, sorts them in accordance with the priority and difficulty of the work, and identifies specimens by number.

She trims the specimens into blocks and fixes the tissues in formalin or other fixing solution for a prescribed length of time to kill any organisms present and preserve cellular composition. She dehydrates tissue sections by immersion in acetone or alcohol baths, and clears the sections (that is, renders the tissue transparent) by use of special liquid reagents. The tissues are then impregnated with paraffin in vacuum. The technician may use an autotechnicon for these procedures.

She prepares specimens by frozen section method, by placing tissues on the freezing stage of a special microtome, and freezing with carbon dioxide gas. She prepares microsections of ophthalmological and bony specimens by colloidin embedding.

She cuts thin slices of specimens, using various types of microtome knives, and stains sections for diagnosis. She assists the Pathologist or Histologic Technologist to select proper stains in accordance with the type of embedding material used and steps involved, in order to bring out certain tissue elements as needed for diagnosis. She mounts and labels the stained and finished slides.

She examines sample of stained slides with microscope to be sure that materials are properly prepared, and determines when prescribed techniques and apparatus should be modified to meet special conditions and expedite diagnosis.

She prepares solutions and reagents in accordance with standard procedures. She sharpens and hones microtome knives, and maintains laboratory equipment. She records the number of blocks handled and number of slides prepared. She files tissue blocks, checking to insure that each is appropriately labeled. She keeps file of current data concerning histopathological methods and procedures. She takes periodic inventory of supplies and equipment used in the unit, and prepares requisition forms to replenish depleted supplies.

EDUCATION, TRAINING, AND EXPERIENCE

High school graduation with courses in biology, chemistry, and mathematics plus a year of supervised training in a clinical laboratory in histologic techniques are required, plus certification as a Histologic Technician by the Board of Registry of Medical Technologists of the American Society of Clinical Pathologists.

JOB RELATIONSHIPS

Workers supervised: None.
Supervised by: Histologic Technologist or Histopathologist.
Promotion from: No formal line of promotion.
Promotion to: No formal line of promotion.

PROFESSIONAL AFFILIATIONS

Registry of Histologic Technicians
P.O. Box 2544
Muncie, Indiana 47302

Histotechnician: (DOT) 078.381-018

BIOCHEMIST
Chemist, Biological

Biochemistry, which in the context of the hospital laboratory is synonymous with clinical chemistry, is concerned with the functioning of cells down to their most fundamental aspects—the chemical processes that go into the cell's nutrition, growth, and reproduction. It reveals how these processes are disturbed by illness, and how these disturbances may be corrected.

It is an applied, practical science, but its scope is as broad as the individual biochemist's interests and opportunity for research. Therefore, it is not surprising to hear of basic research by a clinical chemist on an enzyme system, or the mechanism of blood-clotting, while he is serving as head of a chemistry service in a hospital. This science is oriented toward both immediate and ultimate relief of human disease.

The Biochemist is interested in five areas within the scope of his profession: service, teaching, research, quality control, and administration.

As a service, clinical chemistry uses a variety of analytical tests to aid the physician in his diagnosis and prevention of disease, and to assist him in determining and monitoring the course of treatment for his patients. Both routine and special tests are made on blood and other body fluids. Some of the special tests are performed frequently, and may require extra skill and a separate area in the laboratory. Among these are tests for hormones (endocrinology), and of poisons (toxicology). Other specializations are often made into individual laboratory units for blood gases, pulmonary function, kidney function, chromatography, metabolic screening, and pediatric microchemistry.

The chemist has an amazing array of mechanical, automated, and electronic instruments at his command. It is commonplace for a machine to sample blood automatically from a tray and to analyze it for ten or more constituents. The results are then fed into a computer which records the data for patients' charts. Automatic analyzers are used wherever possible for tests ordered in large numbers. Tests performed singly, or in small numbers, may be run manually, using such instruments as the atomic absorption spectrophotometer, amino acid analyzer, blood gas apparatus, or osmometer.

However, manual analysis remains essential. New tests, or modifications of old ones, appear frequently, and the biochemist must evaluate them; and, if they are useful, make them part of his service even before convenient machines are available. This evaluation is called "development," and is a primary duty of the clinical chemist.

Imitation of natural substances by synthesis of their chemical elements is one of the biochemist's important contributions to medical science. Here, Dr. J. Edwin Seegmiller, Professor of medicine at the University of California, San Diego School of Medicine explains the process used in his laboratory for analysis of purine, a synthetic compound that duplicates the basic uric acids.

The Biochemist continually engages in teaching the personnel in his laboratory, and he may be on the faculty of a medical school or university. He may lecture to interns, and participate in seminars, scientific meetings, and workshops.

In addition to conducting research activities in line with the demands of his hospital and his own interests, as mentioned earlier, the Biochemist has a duty to report his findings in professional journals, so that his discoveries can be shared by other professionals. Or he may present the results of his work in scientific meetings. Frequently, he is called upon to participate in research projects involving a team drawn from several medically related disciplines.

As director of the chemistry unit of the hospital's clinical laboratory, the Biochemist is responsible for the quality of the results reported. It is up to him to devise and employ methods to check on the reliability and accuracy of tests as they are performed. He is also responsible for the personnel in his unit, and for the smooth, efficient operation of all its elements.

Because his work is so broad in scope, a full listing of his job duties in a large instiution would be difficult to envision. A basic description follows.

JOB DUTIES

The Biochemist directs and supervises chemical tests of body fluids and exudates of hospital patients to provide information for diagnosis and treatment of illness.

He trains and supervises biochemistry technologists and biochemistry technicians in collecting specimens from hospital patients and in conducting tests to identify chemical composition of body fluids. He assists technologists with more difficult analyses, interprets results, and performs unusual or complicated tests. He submits diagnostic reports for approval by the Pathologist. He studies, refines, and modifies established techniques to produce more accurate qualitative and quantitative analyses, and improves methods for identifying changes of a chemical nature caused by disease.

He devises methods for testing toxic or therapeutic effect of new and experimental drugs, toxins, or poisons on humans, and on microorganisms or parasites. He determines which elements of a mixture are responsible for toxic effects. He conducts tests to identify chemical processes involved in functioning of living tissues and organs, and studies metabolism, utilization, and oxidation of foodstuffs in the body, using experimental animals as needed. He isolates, identifies, synthesizes, and studies characteristics of natural organic products, such as enzymes, hormones, and vitamins. He investigates chemical aspects of allergies, allergens, antigens and antibodies and serums, and studies related problems of immunology and serology.

He may conduct biochemical research in highly specialized areas, such as metabolism of steroid hormones, or origins of cancer.

He may lecture to lay and professional students.

He prepares the budget for laboratory supplies and equipment for the biochemistry unit. He writes reports, recording numbers of tests performed, kinds of tests, amount of supplies used, and progress made on research projects. He may interview and hire new laboratory workers and conduct on-the-job training.

The duties of the Biochemist and Biochemistry Technologist may be combined.

EDUCATION, TRAINING, AND EXPERIENCE

A Clinical Chemist must earn an academic degree at the bachelor's level, preferably in a university accredited by the American Chemical Society. His course should have included 32 semester hours (or equivalent) in chemistry. Hours obtained in medical technology are valuable, but cannot substitute for hours in chemistry. If possible he should gain a minor in mathematics, and his chemistry courses should represent a balance of inorganic, analytic, biochemical, organic, and physical chemistry.

A master's degree is desirable, and although the basic 32 semester hours of chemistry is still the requirement, the aspiring biochemist should obtain some practical experience in clinical chemistry, and complete a research thesis related to clinical chemistry.

A candidate for the doctorate should acquire a minimum of 48 semester hours of chemistry, including clinical chemistry, and should complete an original research thesis appropriate to clinical chemistry.

Since only a few universities offer graduate and postgraduate training in clinical chemistry, graduate education is usually confined to biochemistry, physiological chemistry, or analytical chemistry. Practical experience in clinical chemistry is then gained on the job.

The minimum requirement for entrance into this position is a bachelor's degree in chemistry and biochemistry, plus at least three years of experience in biochemistry in a medical laboratory.

JOB RELATIONSHIPS

Workers supervised: Biochemistry Technologist.
Supervised by: Pathologist.
Promotion from: No formal line of promotion.
Promotion to: No formal line of promotion, except through increased administrative and supervisory duties.

PROFESSIONAL AFFILIATIONS

American Society of Biological Chemists, Inc.
9650 Rockville Pike
Bethesda, Maryland 20014

Biochemist: (DOT) 041.081-030

BIOCHEMISTRY TECHNOLOGIST
Medical Technologist, Biochemistry

The post of Biochemistry Technologist ranks below that of the Biochemist, and above that of the Biochemistry Technician. In small laboratories and hospitals, her functions may be absorbed by the Biochemist, or she may work under the Biochemist and absorb the functions of the Biochemistry Technician. However the clinical chemistry unit is organized, she is the Biochemist's second pair of hands. The actual testing and record-keeping that she does serves to release him for the broader aspects of the unit's work in teaching, research, and efforts to improve the methods and techniques in the laboratory.

JOB DUTIES

The Biochemistry Technologist performs chemical tests on body fluids and exudates from hospital patients, to provide information for diagnosing and combating disease.

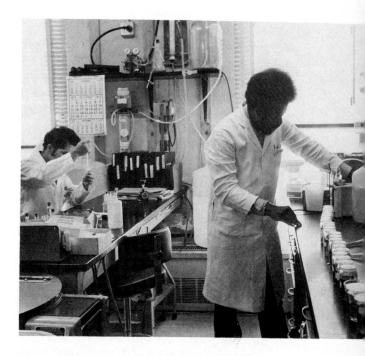

In the Clinical Laboratory, Biochemical Technologists and Technicians conduct tests of various kinds of specimens taken from patients. The results they obtain, using standard procedures, assist physicians in making accurate diagnoses.

She receives patient specimens such as urine, blood, spinal fluid, and gastric juices, or collects specimens directly from patients. She centrifuges the fluids, to separate cells and sediment from serum or supernatant fluids. She adds specific quantities of reagents or solutions to the specimens, and heats, filters, shakes, or otherwise subjects them to prescribed procedures. She notes the appearance, change of color, or resulting precipitate, or examines results by means of photometer, spectograph, colorimeter, and microscope to identify chemical composition and concentrations, and to observe processes of change. She titrates specimen samples against standard reagents to make quantitative determinations. She calculates and tabulates results, and makes reports of her observations.

She performs other qualitative and quantitative tests using titration apparatus, centrifuge, incinerator-furnace, filters, shakers, pH meter, and microgasometer. She records readings of machine registers on work sheets and logs. She examines graph tracings made by machine analyzers to locate or plot test values. She calculates test findings, using mathematical formulas, conversion tables, and slide rule. She posts test findings to laboratory slips, logbooks, and quality-control records.

She performs a number of specific tests. She tests urine for determination of sugar and albumin content, alkalinity, and presence of acetone bodies, blood, bile derivatives, Bence-Jones protein, sulfonamides, uric acids, and various drugs and poisons. She adds specific reagents, which act as indicators, to urine samples, and notes change of color or appearance of precipitates. She makes quantitative determinations by comparing resultant colors against standards, or by making simple calculations based on quantity of reagent or sample used to obtain specific color. She may detect the presence of blood by means of a spectroscope. She centrifuges urine and examines resultant sediments under a microscope to detect the presence of various types of cell bodies. She determines the specific gravity of urine, using a urinometer, and notes general color, odor, and turbidity of sample. She tests blood to determine urea nitrogen, carbon dioxide, sulfonamides, calcium, iron, chlorides, creatinine, uric acid, phosphorous content, and glucose tolerance. She tests gastric content for free and total acidity and occult blood; spinal fluid for chlorides, globulin, and total proteins; and feces for bile, occult blood, and urobilinogen. She tests for the presence of vitamins and hormones, using established procedures, or by observing their effect on test animals under experimental conditions. She may test purity, alkalinity, and total solid contents of water, milk, and food products.

EDUCATION, TRAINING, AND EXPERIENCE

The Biochemistry Technologist must have three years of college with courses in biology, chemistry, and mathematics, plus one year of training in a school of medical technology approved by the American Society of Clinical Pathologists.

She must be registered as a Medical Technologist by the Registry Board of the American Society of Clinical Pathologists.

Some states require a license issued by the State Board of Health in order to practice.

Workers will usually receive three to six months' on-the-job training by the Biochemist to become familiar with procedures and practices of hospital.

JOB RELATIONSHIPS

Workers supervised: Medical Laboratory Assistant specializing in biochemistry, may be designated Biochemistry Technician.
Supervised by: Biochemist, or Medical Technologist, Chief.
Promotion from: No formal line of promotion.
Promotion to: No formal line of promotion.

PROFESSIONAL AFFILIATIONS

American Society of Medical Technologists
Suite 25, Hermann Professional Building
Houston, Texas 77025

Biochemistry Technologist: (DOT) 078.281-010

BIOCHEMISTRY TECHNICIAN
Medical Laboratory Technician

The Biochemistry Technician may work directly under the Biochemist in a small laboratory. In larger laboratories, she may be supervised by a Biochemistry Technologist.

Her role, like that of the Medical Laboratory Technician, is to relieve the Biochemist or Biochemistry Technologist of much of the routine work in the laboratory, so that the energies of her superiors can be directed toward activities that require more extensive specialized training. She is capable of doing routine work without close supervision, and some specialized work with supervision.

The general classification of this job is that of Medical Laboratory Technician, and represents a new development in the organization of laboratories, with relatively low entrance requirements and broad prospects for employment.

JOB DUTIES

The Biochemistry Technician performs a number of specific chemical tests on body fluids and exudates from hospital patients, to provide information for diagnosis and treatment of disease conditions. Her work is assigned by the Biochemist or Technologist.

She receives patient specimens, such as urine, blood, spinal fluid, and gastric juices, or collects specimens directly from patients. She centrifuges the fluids, to separate cells and sediment from serum or supernatant fluids. She adds prescribed amounts of specified reagents or solutions, and subjects the specimens to prescribed procedures, such as heating, filtration, shaking, or titration. She notes the appearance, changes of color, or resulting precipitates, and posts her findings on laboratory slips for inspection by the Biochemist.

She performs a number of specific tests: She tests urine for determination of sugar and albumin content, alkalinity, and presence of acetone bodies, blood, bile derivatives, Bence-Jones protein, sulfonamides, uric acids, and various drugs and poisons. She determines the specific gravity of urine, using a urinometer, and notes general color, odor, and turbidity of the sample.

She tests blood to determine urea nitrogen, carbon dioxide, sulfonamides, calcium, iron, chlorides, creatinine, uric acid, phosphorous content, and glucose tolerance.

She tests gastric content for free and total acidity and occult blood; spinal fluid for chlorides, globulin, and total proteins; and feces for bile, occult blood, and urobilinogen. She tests for the presence of vitamins or hormones, using established procedures.

She may test for purity, alkalinity, and total solid content of water, milk, or food products.

She keeps records of the tests that she has made, and labels and files any specimens that are to be retained for future reference or research.

EDUCATION, TRAINING, AND EXPERIENCE

Preparation requires a high school diploma followed by an associate two-year degree from an accredited junior or community college, and by clinical experience in an approved laboratory. Students with this experience may receive certification by the Registry of Medical Technologists of the American Society of Clinical Pathologists, with the designation MLT (ASCP).

They may also be certified by the American Medical Technologists registry, which gives certification to high school graduates who complete a two-year work-school course in programs approved by the Accrediting Bureau of Medical Laboratory Schools. Veterans who have completed a 50-week Armed Forces course in medical laboratory techniques and have approved laboratory experience can also be certified by American Medical Technologists. All applicants for registry by this organization must pass an examination.

JOB RELATIONSHIPS

Workers supervised: None.
Supervised by: Biochemist or Biochemistry Technologist.
Promotion from: Medical Laboratory Assistant.
Promotion to: No formal line of promotion.

PROFESSIONAL AFFILIATIONS

American Society of Medical Technologists
Suite 1600
Hermann Professional Building
Houston, Texas 77023

Medical Laboratory Technician: (DOT) 078.281-026

HEMATOLOGIST

The Hematologist specializes in the blood and blood-forming organs, and the diseases associated with blood disorders, such as anemia, sickle cell anemia, and leukemia.

Science has long known that people have varying blood types, of which O (Universal) is most common, followed by A and B and combinations of these plus M, N, and P. In the mid-twentieth century, numerous "blood factors" were discovered, of which Rh-negative and Rh-positive are the best-known. Certain blood types are allergic to each other, and so cross-matching of blood types between patient and donor is vitally important in transfusions, and in successful plastic surgery and organ transplants. Special precautions must be taken when an Rh-negative mother bears the children of an Rh-positive father.

The work of the Hematologist is complex, and essential in almost every medical and surgical procedure. Blood samples are taken from every patient on admission to hospital, and analyzed in the laboratory, as a guide for the physician in making his diagnosis and selecting treatment.

JOB DUTIES

The Hematologist directs and supervises analysis and testing of blood specimens, interprets test results to provide a basis for treatment of disease, and directs the operation of the hospital blood bank.

He trains and supervises Hematology Technologists and Technicians in performance of blood tests and microscopic analysis of blood smears, or makes tests and prepares materials for microscopic study. He instructs workers by practical demonstration, to correct faulty techniques or introduce new procedures and equipment. He assists workers with more difficult tests and analyses of unusual test results, and performs specialized or highly complex tests. He may rerun tests to determine accuracy of results. He reviews and interprets test results, examines blood film slides and cultures under the microscope, and writes diagnostic reports for approval by the Pathologist.

He supervises the Blood Bank Technologists and Blood Bank Technicians in collecting, processing, and dispensing blood and blood plasma. He participates in educational conferences to exchange information pertinent to latest trends in the field of hematology. He may lecture to students of medicine, medical technology, or nursing arts, or to interns. He may engage in research related to hematological methods and diagnosis.

In some hospital laboratories, this job may be performed by a doctor of medicine or osteopathy, particularly a pathologist, who has specialized in hematology. In small institutions, this job may include the duties of Hematology Technologist and Blood Bank Technologist.

EDUCATION, TRAINING, AND EXPERIENCE

The Hematologist may be a doctor of medicine. The minimum requirements are a master's degree or doctorate in hematology and three years of experience in hematology in a medical laboratory.

JOB RELATIONSHIPS

Workers supervised: Blood Bank Technologist; Hematology Technologist.
Supervised by: Pathologist.
Promotion from: No formal line of promotion.
Promotion to: No formal line of promotion. May be promoted to Pathologist in charge of clinical laboratory, if holding an M.D. degree.

PROFESSIONAL AFFILIATIONS

American Medical Association
535 Dearborn Street
Chicago, Illinois 60610

American Society of Clinical Pathologists
445 North Lake Shore Drive
Chicago, Illinois 60611

American Society of Medical Technologists
Suite 25, Hermann Professional Building
Houston, Texas 77025

American Osteopathic Association
212 East Ohio Street
Chicago, Illinois 60611

American Osteopathic College of Pathologists
3921 Beecher Road
Flint, Michigan 48504

Hematologist: (DOT) 078.231 T

HEMATOLOGY TECHNOLOGIST
Medical Technologist, Hematology

The Hematology Technologist works under the direction of the Hematologist, and in turn supervises the Hematology Technicians or the Medical Laboratory Assistants who are assigned to the hematology unit. She is responsible for day-to-day routine blood tests, and performs some special tests under supervision. She studies the morphology of constituents of blood, to obtain data for use in diagnosis and treatment of disease.

JOB DUTIES

The Hematology Technologist receives blood specimens sent to the laboratory or she draws blood from the patient's finger or ear lobe, or by venipuncture, observing strict principles of asepsis and antisepsis, to prevent infection of the patient and contamination of specimens. She centrifuges blood specimens in test tubes and capillary tubes to separate cells and sediment from the blood serum. She measures blood quantitatively by pipettes, making necessary dilutions in accordance with standard procedures.

She performs such tests as red and white blood cell counts, platelet counts, differential white blood cell counts, reticulocyte counts, sickle cell counts, hemoglobin estimations, fragility tests, and determinations of color index, sedimentation rate, coagulation time, bleeding time, clot reaction time, volume index, and mean corpuscular volume, using specialized laboratory equipment such as photometer, sedimentation rate stand, and fibrometer. She records direct scale readings or converts readings to per cent and grams, using converting tables. She consults with the Hematologist or Pathologist regarding difficult analyses or abnormal findings.

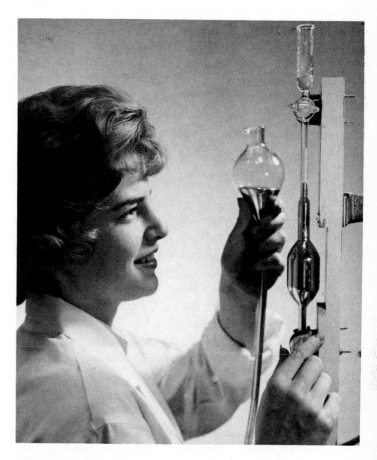

At St. Francis Hospital in Wichita, Kansas, a Hematology Technologist performs a blood-gas analysis.
Photo courtesy of the National Committee for Careers in the Medical Laboratory

She transfers blood from pipettes to counting chambers in making cell counts, and counts the number of cells within ruled squares of the chamber as reviewed through a microscope. She calculates the number of cells per cubic centimeter of blood sample. She stains blood sample cells for clearer definition, and to distinguish between various types of cells.

She adds prescribed reagents to blood samples and compares the resultant color with standard color scales, such as those representing blood containing various amounts of hemoglobin or she makes color comparisons in a colorimeter or photometer, and converts scale readings into per cent and grams.

She groups or types blood by mixing red cells of the person to be typed with typing serums, and notes whether clumping of cells occurs. She cross-matches donors' and patients' blood to determine compatibility.

She studies morphology of red blood cells in terms of proportion of cells in various stages of development and other characteristics of red corpuscles that may be related to disease processes. She studies slides made from bone marrow specimens, since bone marrow is the site of blood cell manufacture.

She may calculate prothrombin time (time used in the second stage of blood coagulation) by drawing blood samples into an anticoagulant solution of specific strength, and measuring—with a stopwatch—the appearance of a coagulum upon addition of thromboplastin. She may prepare and examine thick and thin blood film slides for malaria or other parasites such as filaria and trypanosomes.

She may prepare solutions and reagents used in conducting blood tests. She records all results of tests conducted in the laboratory log.

This job is often combined with that of the Hematologist or the Blood Bank Technologist.

EDUCATION, TRAINING, AND EXPERIENCE

A Hematology Technologist must be registered with the designation H(ASCP) by the American Society of Clinical Pathologists. Preparation requires four years of college with a Bachelor of Science degree including courses in biology, chemistry, and mathematics, plus two years of training in a school of medical technology approved by the American Society of Clinical Pathologists, and a registry examination.

Persons who hold a Medical Technologist certification may qualify for certification as a Hematology Technologist through one year of experience in hematology in an acceptable laboratory, plus the examination.

Some states require a license issued by the State Board of Health in order to practice.

JOB RELATIONSHIPS

Workers supervised: Medical Laboratory Assistant specializing in hematology, who may be designated as Hematology Technician.
Supervised by: Hematologist or Medical Technologist, Chief.
Promotion from: No formal line of promotion.
Promotion to: No formal line of promotion.

PROFESSIONAL AFFILIATIONS

American Society of Medical Technologists
Suite 25, Hermann Professional Building
Houston, Texas 77025

American Society of Clinical Pathologists
445 North Lake Shore Drive
Chicago, Illinois 60611

Hematology Technologist: (DOT) 078.281

HEMATOLOGY TECHNICIAN
Medical Laboratory Assistant

The Hematology Technician performs procedures more complex than those assigned to a general Medical Laboratory Assistant, and she concentrates on work

A Hematology Technician prepares a microscope slide with a sample of blood taken from a patient suspected of having sickle cell anemia. She will treat the slide with a special reagent, so that when it is examined microscopically the crescent-shaped cells become clearly visible.

related to blood and the diseases that affect it. Under supervision of the Hematologist or the Hematology Technologist, she conducts the routine blood tests that must be performed for every patient on admission to hospital. Her work contributes to the information upon which physicians base their diagnoses and treatments.

JOB DUTIES

The Hematology Technician makes blood cell counts by adding reagents to blood samples and comparing the samples with standard color scales, or makes color comparisons by means of a colorimeter. She separates plasma from whole blood, using a centrifuge. She stores and labels plasma.

She may operate automatic equipment, such as the diluting-titrating machine, blood cell counter, and spectrophotometer.

She groups or types blood by mixing red cells of the patient to be tested with typing serums, and notes whether clumping of cells occurs. She cross-matches donors' and patients' blood to determine compatibility. She may be called upon to determine the coagulation time in certain blood samples.

She frequently performs such tests as red and white blood cell counts, platelet counts, differential white blood cell counts, reticulocyte counts, sickle cell counts, and hemoglobin estimations. She uses various laboratory equipment in making tests, including the centrifuge, to separate cells and sediment from blood serum; the sedimentation stand, in calculating sedimentation rates; and microscopes, to make cell counts, and examine bone marrow. She needs mathematical skill, to translate readings from various devices into percentages or grams, using prescribed formulas or mathematical conversion tables.

The Hematology Technician records the results of every test she performs onto laboratory slips, for checking by the Hematology Technologist or the Hematologist. She calls the attention of her superiors to any unusual findings she may make during routine tests. She may prepare solutions and reagents used in testing, following standardized specifications and procedures.

She cleans and sterilizes laboratory equipment, glassware, and instruments, and maintains the laboratory stock of chemicals and glassware.

EDUCATION, TRAINING, AND EXPERIENCE

This job falls into the category of Medical Laboratory Technician, a new classification between Technologist and Assistant. The present criteria for certification by the Board of Registry of the American Society of Clinical Pathologists (ASCP) are an associate degree (two years) from a junior or community college, in a program combining general education, laboratory sciences (including clinical laboratory) and related subjects, as approved by the American Medical Association Council on Medical Education in collaboration with the ASCP Board of Schools. Students with this background are eligible for the registry examination, and certification of MLT(ASCP).

Certification may also be obtained through the American Medical Technologists Registry. This registry gives certification to high school graduates who have completed a two-year work-study program approved by the Accrediting Bureau of Medical Laboratory Schools. In this program, credit is given for previous certification as Certified Laboratory Assistant. Certification is also granted to students who have completed a 50-week Armed Forces course in medical laboratory techniques, together with approved laboratory experience.

Examination for registry is required in all programs of certification.

JOB RELATIONSHIPS

Workers supervised: None.
Supervised by: Hematology Technologist or Hematologist.
Promotion from: No formal line of promotion.
Promotion to: No formal line of promotion.

PROFESSIONAL AFFILIATIONS

American Medical Technologists
710 Higgins Road
Park Ridge, Illinois 60068

American Society of Clinical Pathologists
2100 West Harrison Street
Chicago, Illinois 60612

American Society of Medical Technologists
Suite 1600
Hermann Professional Building
Houston, Texas 77025

National Committee for Careers in the Medical Laboratory
9650 Rockville Pike
Rockville, Maryland 20014

Board of Certified Laboratory Assistants
9500 South California Avenue
Evergreen Park, Illinois 60642

Medical Laboratory Technician: (DOT) 078.281-026

BLOOD BANK TECHNOLOGIST
Medical Technologist, Blood Bank

The Blood Bank Technologist finds many opportunities for her skills. Not only hospitals, but clinics and special blood bank centers need her services.

Until World War II, the uses of blood transfusion were severely limited, because patients frequently are allergic to blood types other than their own, and because storage and preservation of whole blood was extremely difficult.

It had been discovered that when the whole blood of eight or more adults was mixed together, regardless of types, and the blood corpuscles suspended by centrifuge or sedimentation, the resulting fluid—or plasma—could be treated to prevent clotting, and used as a blood replenisher for almost anyone. But this did not solve the problems of storage and preservation.

Then, in 1940, a young black American surgeon who was a Fellow at the Columbia University Medical School found a way to dry plasma and preserve it.

The Royal College of Surgeons in London heard of Dr. Charles S. Drew's discovery, and, expecting a Nazi *blitzkrieg,* called upon Dr. Drew to supply large quantities of dried plasma. Almost none existed at that time, and quantities could not be produced quickly enough to send to Britain, but Dr. Drew founded a "Blood for Britain" campaign in the United States, collecting and shipping plasma.

Fortunately, the expected "blitz" did not develop, and by the time the United States entered the War, Dr. Drew, as head of the American Red Cross Blood Bank and assistant director of blood procurement for the National Research Council, had solved the problem of drying plasma in quantities, and there was a supply of dried plasma on hand, ready for use by American forces. It is credited with saving innumerable lives.

Gradually, hospitals set up their own blood banks, and eventually private blood banks augmented their resources and those of the pioneering Red Cross. Today,

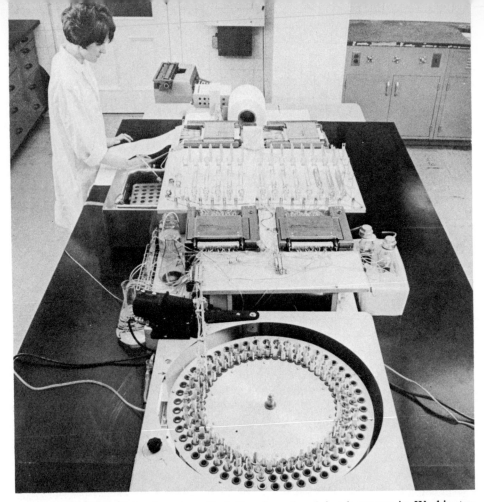

This autoanalyzer at the American Red Cross's national headquarters in Washington, D.C. checks blood samples for rare combinations of blood factors. It makes 14 different tests on 120 blood samples in one hour. The Red Cross rare blood file now has computerized availability of donors of rare blood factors, so that such blood can be made available anywhere in the United States in an emergency.

plasma is not the only agent supplied by blood banks. They also collect and store individual types of blood, to be in readiness for situations that require them.

Usually, when either blood plasma or whole blood is needed, the patient is in grave condition. The Blood Bank Technologist has the satisfaction of knowing that her work will give life to some patient.

JOB DUTIES

The Blood Bank Technologist collects, tests, and stores blood, administers transfusions, and maintains records of blood donations or transfusions. He (or she) supervises or performs the following procedures of a blood bank:

She schedules donors' appointments to maintain adequate supply of various types of blood. When the donor arrives, she confers with him to obtain medical history data that is needed as safeguard against collecting diseased or otherwise unusable blood. She takes the donor's temperature, blood pressure, and pulse, following specified procedures, and records this data. She then cleans the area of the puncture site with disinfectants, and distends a vein, using a rubber tourniquet. She inserts the needle on a disposable siphon tube into the donor's medical-cubital vein, following strict procedures of asepsis and antisepsis to avoid infection of the patient or contamination of the blood being obtained. She inverts the bottle and opens the clamp on the tube to allow the siphoning process to begin. She shakes the bottle to be sure that the blood mixes with the anticoagulant agent already in the bottle, or she shakes the substance with an electric-powered device. Throughout the procedure, she observes the donor, to be alert to any signs of adverse reaction. If complications arise, she calls the physician or nurse who is on duty. When she has filled the blood bottle and test tubes used for performance of blood tests, she withdraws the needle and observes the donor throughout his immediate convalescence, to verify his strength and color. She posts data to record the donation of blood into the log.

The Blood Bank Technologist groups or types blood by mixing red cells of persons to be typed with typing serums, noting whether clumping of cells occurs. She prepares and examines microscopic test slides to determine the blood group of donor or patient, using a pipette and microscope. She verifies the blood group of patient or donor by back-typing the blood samples, using the microscope. She cross-matches the blood samples, to determine compatibility. She identifies antibodies in either the donor's or patient's blood that could react ?dversely during transfusion and cause harm to the person receiving the transfusion. She performs tests for syphilis and allied venereal diseases. She records all test results in the laboratory logbook, files the transfusion slips, and enters the data regarding the performance of the transfusion into the log.

The Blood Bank Technologist processes blood plasma for future use in blood transfusion, by separating plasma from the red blood cells with a centrifuge machine and separating devices.

She prepares solutions and reagents in accordance with standard formulas. She maintains written records of tests performed and keeps the inventory of the blood bank. She inspects stored blood to detect signs of spoilage, and removes spoiled blood for discard.

In the event that an adverse transfusion reaction occurs, she retests samples of both donor and patient blood to aid the Pathologist in determining the possible cause of the reaction.

EDUCATION, TRAINING, AND EXPERIENCE

The Blood Bank Technologist must first be a registered Medical Technologist, as certified by the American Society of Clinical Pathologists. This requires three years of college, with stress on courses in biology, chemistry, and mathematics, and one year of work-study in a school approved by the ASCP. Following this, one year of specialized training in a blood bank school approved by the American Association of Blood Banks is required before the student is eligible for examination and registration as MT(ASCP)BB.

Some states require a license issued by the State Board of Health before a Blood Bank Technologist is allowed to practice.

JOB RELATIONSHIPS

Workers supervised: Medical Laboratory Assistant specializing in hematology, who may be designated as Blood Bank Technician.
Supervised by: Hematologist, or Medical Technologist, Chief.
Promotion from: No formal line of promotion.
Promotion to: No formal line of promotion.

PROFESSIONAL AFFILIATIONS

American Society of Medical Technologists
Suite 25, Hermann Professional Building
Houston, Texas 77025

American Association of Blood Banks
30 North Michigan Avenue
Chicago, Illinois 60602

Blood Bank Technologist: (DOT) 078.281

BLOOD BANK TECHNICIAN
Medical Laboratory Assistant, Blood Bank

The Blood Bank Technician relieves the Blood Bank Technologist of much of the routine work in the blood bank, releasing her to concentrate on the more difficult or special procedures, and on responsibility for record-keeping and other administrative tasks.

In present practice, the Blood Bank Technician is something more than a Medical Laboratory Assistant, although she may incorporate the duties of an Assistant into her daily schedule. Since she works only in the blood bank, she becomes proficient in her tasks, and capable of doing an increasing number of procedures with a minimum of supervision, and some more difficult tests with supervision.

JOB DUTIES

The Blood Bank Technician may schedule appointments with donors, and confer with them to obtain medical history data, to be sure no diseased or otherwise unusable blood is collected. She may take the donor's temperature, blood pressure, and pulse, and record this data. She may be responsible for setting out the equipment necessary to collect the blood, and for seeing that the proper reagents are in readiness, and labels provided for the blood collected.

The Technician groups or types blood by mixing red cells with typing serum, noting whether clumping occurs. She prepares and examines test slides to determine the blood group, using a pipette and microscope, and she verifies by back-typing. She identifies antibodies in the blood that could cause adverse reaction in the patient receiving it.

The Technician processes blood plasma for future use in patients, by separating the fluid from the red cells, using a centrifuge and separating devices.

When a transfusion is to be performed, she may be called upon to cross-match the patient's blood sample with that of a suitable donor. In emergency or accident cases, she may have to do this very quickly, but with no loss of accuracy.

The Technician is responsible for proper labeling, filing, and storage of all blood and blood samples that she handles, and for precise record-keeping on laboratory slips and in the laboratory logbook.

She probably will be responsible for preparing solutions and reagents, following closely specified instructions; and for cleaning and sterilizing all laboratory equipment, glassware and instruments, and for maintaining the laboratory stock of chemicals and glassware.

EDUCATION, TRAINING, AND EXPERIENCE

This job falls into the category of Medical Laboratory Technician, a new classification between Technologist and Assistant. The present criterion for certification by the Board of Registry of the American Society of Clinical Pathologists (ASCP) is an associate degree (two years) from a junior or community college, in a program combining general education, laboratory sciences (including clinical laboratory) and related subjects, as approved by the American Medical Association Council on Medical Education in collaboration with the ASCP Board of Schools. Students with this background are eligible for the registry examination, and certification of MLT(ASCP).

Certification may also be obtained through the American Medical Technologists Registry. This registry gives certification to high school graduates who have completed a two-year work-study program approved by the Accrediting Bureau of Medical Laboratory Schools. In this program, credit is given for previous certification as Certified Laboratory Assistant. Certification is also granted to students who have completed a 50-week Armed Forces course in medical laboratory techniques, together with approved laboratory experience.

Examination for registry is required in all programs of certification.

JOB RELATIONSHIPS

Workers supervised: None.
Supervised by: Blood Bank Technologist or Hematologist.
Promotion from: No formal line of promotion.
Promotion to: No formal line of promotion.

PROFESSIONAL AFFILIATIONS

American Medical Technologists
710 Higgins Road
Park Ridge, Illinois 60068

American Society of Clinical Pathologists
2100 West Harrison Street
Chicago, Illinois 60612

American Society of Medical Technologists
Suite 1600
Hermann Professional Building
Houston, Texas 77025

National Committee for Careers in the Medical Laboratory
9650 Rockville Pike
Rockville, Maryland 20014

Board of Certified Laboratory Assistants
9500 South California Avenue
Evergreen Park, Illinois 60642

American Association of Blood Banks
30 North Michigan Avenue
Chicago, Illinois 60602

Medical Laboratory Technician: (DOT) 078.281-026

MICROBIOLOGIST
Medical Bacteriologist

Although microbiology is one of the newer branches of science, in recent decades it has affected man's life from the core of the earth to the far reaches of space.

Microbiologists have discovered vaccines for the prevention of diseases, such as smallpox and poliomyelitis, and new drugs, such as penicillin, for the treatment of disease. They have discovered vitamins and other basic food materials. What we know about the chemistry of cells is due to work by microbiologists, as well as what we know about the function of certain cell parts in heredity. Biologists are considering microorganisms as possible sources of food for space travelers, and geologists use microorganisms in their search for oil.

In the clinical laboratory, the Microbiologist fulfills many functions. From specimens taken from patients, he isolates and identifies the virus or bacteria causing each patient's illness. He may assist the physician in determining whether a par-

The electronic microscope permits magnifications so enormous that Microbiologists and the technical personnel who assist them can peer into a wonder-world of organisms too tiny to be detected by conventional light microscopy.

ticular antibiotic or other agent will be effective against a given microorganism by cultivating the organism in culture mediums, and injecting it into small animals, in whom the proposed treatment can be tried.

His work is of great importance when epidemics occur and it is necessary to trace the infection to its source.

Opportunities for microbiologists are extremely broad. They are in demand by public health laboratories, and in agriculture, industry, space science, and studies of marine life. Students who are interested in microbiology as a career should begin their preparation in high school, taking as many science courses there as possible, so that they will have the best groundwork for intensive college study.

JOB DUTIES

The Microbiologist directs and supervises the cultivation, classification, and identification of microorganisms found in patient body fluids, exudates, skin scrapings, or in autopsy and surgical specimens, to provide data on cause, cure, and prevention of disease.

He trains and supervises Microbiology Technologists and Technicians in collecting swabs and smears from patients, and preparing bacterial growth under a microscope. He assists them with more difficult cultures and analyses, and studies and identifies less common bacteria, Rickettsiae, fungi, protozoa, and viruses. He posts all test findings, and writes diagnostic reports for approval by the Pathologist.

He performs research to develop new or improved bacteriological methods for discovering and identifying pathogenic organisms.

He correlates laboratory findings with clinical data supplied by hospitals and medical practitioners regarding human illnesses.

He may supervise the inoculation of small animals as a means of determining the infectious nature, virulence, and course of a disease. He may investigate the biology, distribution, and mode of transmission of bacteria, and the nature and efficiency of chemotherapeutic treatment.

He may lecture to students of medicine, medical technology, or nursing, or to interns.

He maintains production records, including data pertinent to total number of cultures, and interpretation of specific cultures.

The job of Microbiologist is often combined with that of Serologist, and may also include the duties of Microbiology Technologist.

EDUCATION, TRAINING, AND EXPERIENCE

A bachelor's degree in bacteriology or microbiology is essential. A master's degree or doctor's degree is desirable, and frequently required.

Some employers may require certification by the American Board of Microbiology of the American Academy of Microbiology (at the doctorate degree level), or the National Registry of Microbiologists of the American Board of Microbiology (at the bachelor's degree level).

At least three years of experience in microbiology in a medical laboratory is usually required.

JOB RELATIONSHIPS

Workers supervised: Microbiology Technologists.
Supervised by: Pathologist.
Promotion from: No formal line of promotion.
Promotion to: No formal line of promotion. Promotion is through additional administrative and supervisory duties.

PROFESSIONAL AFFILIATIONS

American Academy of Microbiology
P.O. Box 897
Vero Beach, Florida 32960

American Society for Microbiology
115 Huron View Boulevard
Ann Arbor, Michigan 48103

Microbiologist: (DOT) 041.081-094

MICROBIOLOGY TECHNOLOGIST
Bacteriology Technologist
Medical Technologist, Microbiology

In her work, the Microbiology Technologist studies various microorganisms: algae, bacteria, fungi, protozoa, Rickettsiae, viruses, and yeasts. By no means all of such organisms are harmful. In fact, many are helpful. Yet epidemics of diseases caused by microorganisms have decimated populations in the course of history.

In the clinical laboratory, the Microbiology Technologist is concerned with isolating and identifying those microorganisms that do cause disease, and finding means to combat them. It is difficult to realize that practically all the vaccines we know—against typhoid fever, yellow fever, whooping cough, influenza, and poliomyelitis—are products of microbiologic research within this century; and so are all of the antibiotics upon which we rely. Clinical laboratories, as well as research laboratories, were involved in their development, and will be involved in man's future conquests over disease.

JOB DUTIES

The Microbiology Technologist cultivates, isolates, and assists in identifying bacteria and other microorganisms present in body fluids, exudates, skin scraping, or

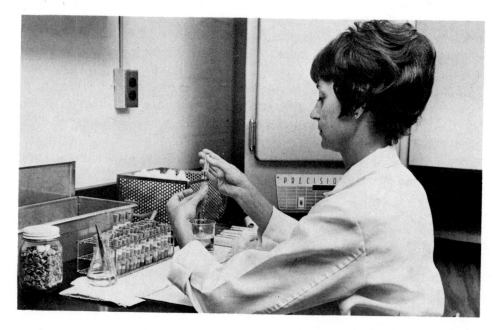

A Microbiology Technologist injects microorganisms into suitable culture medium for incubation under controlled conditions, to encourage growth of colonies and permit later microscopic identification.

autopsy and surgical specimens, and performs various bacteriological, mycological, virological, and parasitological tests to provide data on cause and progress of disease.

She receives specimens of human or animal body materials, such as feces, pus, sputum, serous fluids, and urine, from patients or from autopsies.

She injects and incubates cultures for prescribed lengths of time under aseptic conditions in suitable media such as meat extracts, sugars, and body products and discharges. She makes periodic observations of material derived from cultures, and identifies the type of bacterial colony found by determination of cultural requirements and biochemical reactions in chemically defined media.

She places specimens from culture on microscopic slides with plantinum wire sterilized over gas burner. She stains specimen under examination to define essential features more clearly, using one or a combination of standard stains, and dries with blotting paper. She mounts the slides on microscope; studies, identifies, and counts bacteria or other microorganisms present; and writes reports of findings. She discusses findings, and consults with the Microbiologist or Pathologist when results are conflicting or do not fall into recognized patterns. She may examine growth to identify pathogens. She performs macroscopic and microscopic agglutination and precipitation tests to detect presence of pathological bacteria in human hosts through identification of specific antibodies that are found. She may cultivate and identify fungi, Rickettsiae, protozoa, and viruses.

She prepares culture media according to established formulas, titrating them to determine degree of acidity. She sterilizes media under standard conditions, and stores all media in refrigerators. She prepares bacteriophage (agents which destroy microorganisms), by filtering feces or pus through special filters. She tests potency of phage by adding various dilutions to test tubes containing growth of organisma, and noting reactions. She sterilizes equipment and apparatus.

In inoculating animals, she injects material derived from patients either directly or after cultivation, into mice, rats, guinea pigs, or rabbits. She observes disease produced in these animals and determines the nature, pathogenicity, and virulence of the bacteria or other agents.

The job duties of Microbiology Technologist may be combined with those of the Microbiology Technician, or with those of the Microbiologist.

EDUCATION, TRAINING, AND EXPERIENCE

Certification as a Microbiology Technologist, with the designation M(ASCP), requires a Bachelor of Science degree in bacteriology plus one year of experience in microbiology in a laboratory approved by the American Society of Clinical Pathologists, and a registry examination.

Some states require a license issued by the State Board of Health in order to practice.

JOB RELATIONSHIPS

Workers supervised: Medical Laboratory Assistant, specializing in microbiology, may be designated Microbiology Technician.
Supervised by: Microbiologist or Medical Technologist, Chief.
Promotion from: No formal line of promotion.
Promotion to: No formal line of promotion.

PROFESSIONAL AFFILIATIONS

American Society of Medical Technologists
Suite 25, Hermann Professional Building
Houston, Texas 77025

Microbiology Technologist: (DOT) 078.281-022

MICROBIOLOGY TECHNICIAN
Medical Laboratory Assistant

The Microbiology Technician may be a Medical Laboratory Assistant who has been assigned to the microbiology unit. However, in many clinical laboratories today, the Technician is better qualified, and fills a role between that of the Technologist and the Assistant. She is able to carry on routine tests with very little supervision, and some more difficult procedures with supervision. As she takes increasing responsibility, the Technologist's time is released to concentrate on the more involved procedures, and to relieve the Microbiologist of some of the administrative load. This becomes increasingly necessary when the Microbiologist also fulfills a teaching function, or is engaged in original research.

JOB DUTIES

The Microbiology Technician prepares sterile media, such as agar, meat extracts, or body products, and titrates them to determine acidity. She stores all media in plates, jars, or test tubes, under refrigeration.

When specimens for culturing are assigned to her, she injects the required specimen material into the proper culture for a prescribed length of time, under prescribed temperature, according to standard procedures.

She places specimens from the culture on microscopic slides, using a platinum wire sterilized over the gas burner. She stains the specimen to be examined, using one or a combination of stains according to standard procedure, in order to be able to define the essential features more clearly. She mounts the slides on the microscope, and views them, to identify and count bacteria or other organisms that are present, and writes a report of her findings for review by the Technologist. If anything unusual occurs, or if she has any uncertainty about her findings, she consults the Technologist.

In addition to culture media, the Technician prepares solutions, reagents, and stains following standard laboratory procedures. She cleans and sterilizes laboratory equipment, glassware, and instruments. She maintains the laboratory stock of chemicals for her unit. She keeps detailed records of all tests performed, and reports her findings to the Technologist.

EDUCATION, TRAINING, AND EXPERIENCE

This job falls into the category of Medical Laboratory Technician, a new classification between Technologist and Assistant. The present criterion for certification by the Board of Registry of the American Society of Clinical Pathologists (ASCP) is an associate degree (two years) from a junior or community college, in a program combining general education, laboratory sciences (including clinical laboratory) and related subjects, as approved by the American Medical Association Council on Medical Education in collaboration with the ASCP Board of Schools. Students with this background are eligible for the registry examination, and certification of MLT(ASCP).

Certification may also be obtained through the American Medical Technologists Registry. This registry gives certification to high school graduates who have completed a two-year work-study program approved by the Accrediting Bureau of Medical Laboratory Schools. In this program, credit is given for previous certification as Certified Laboratory Assistant. Certification is also granted to students who have completed a 50-week Armed Forces course in medical laboratory techniques, together with approved laboratory experience.

Examination for registry is required in all programs of certification.

JOB RELATIONSHIPS

Workers supervised: None.
Supervised by: Microbiology Technologist.
Promotion from: No formal line of promotion.
Promotion to: No formal line of promotion.

PROFESSIONAL AFFILIATIONS

American Medical Technologists
710 Higgins Road
Park Ridge, Illinois 60068

American Society of Clinical Pathologists
2100 West Harrison Street
Chicago, Illinois 60612

American Society of Medical Technologists
Suite 1600
Hermann Professional Building
Houston, Texas 77025

National Committee for Careers in the Medical Laboratory
9650 Rockville Pike
Rockville, Maryland 20014

Board of Certified Laboratory Assistants
9500 South California Avenue
Evergreen Park, Illinois 60642

Medical Laboratory Technician: (DOT) 078.281-026

SEROLOGIST

Serology is the branch of science that deals with the disease-fighting properties of the blood; and, conversely, with the discovery, production, and utilization of agents that will stimulate the growth of antibodies in the blood, and confer immunity to a disease before an individual is exposed to it.

It was Edward Jenner, a British physician, who first noticed that milkmaids who were exposed to cowpox did not contract smallpox during epidemics. He reasoned —correctly—that their blood had developed antibodies from the mild cowpox infection, and that these were effective protection against the more virulent smallpox. From this reasoning, he developed the first smallpox vaccine.

Today we have vaccines against several diseases, based on the same principle. We also have serums other than vaccines, and antitoxins, antibiotics, antigens, and other drugs that combat diseases by utilizing the natural mechanisms of the blood.

In the clinical laboratory, the Serologist is not so much concerned with the development or manufacture of such agents, as he is with determining the effectiveness, safety, and best methods of administration of those that exist. In some instances, he may use them to help identify an infection.

JOB DUTIES

The Serologist directs and supervises the preparation of serums used in treatment and diagnosis of infectious diseases, and immunizations against these diseases. He performs or directs laboratory tests to identify diseases, based on characteristic reactions of various serums.

The Serologist trains and supervises the Serology Technologists and Serology Technicians in collecting specimens from hospital patients; making serums by inoculating laboratory animals, and conducting serological laboratory tests to diagnose infectious diseases. He observes workers during performance of tasks to determine that established procedures are utilized. He conducts or assists with more difficult tests, and devises improved methods for preparing serums, diagnostic antigens and antibodies. He writes diagnostic reports for approval by the Pathologist.

He investigates the safety of new commercial antibiotic products, and the accuracy of their therapeutic claims.

He directs immunology tests and injections, investigates problems of allergy, and conducts tests to determine therapeutic and toxic dosages, and most effective methods of administering serums, vaccines, antibiotics, antitoxins, antigens, and related drugs, using laboratory animals as controls.

He may lecture interns or students of medicine, medical technology, or nursing. He participates in educational conferences to exchange information pertinent to trends in bacteriology, serology, and immunology.

This job is frequently combined with that of Microbiologist. The job duties of Serology Technologist may be included with those of the Serologist.

EDUCATION, TRAINING, AND EXPERIENCE

Bachelor's degree in bacteriology or serology is essential. A master's degree or doctor's degree is desirable, and frequently required.

At least three years of experience in serology in a medical laboratory is usually required.

JOB RELATIONSHIPS

Workers supervised: Serology Technologists.
Supervised by: Pathologist.
Promotion from: No formal line of promotion.
Promotion to: No formal line of promotion. Promotion may be through increased administrative and supervisory duties.

PROFESSIONAL AFFILIATIONS

American Society for Microbiology
115 Huron View Boulevard
Ann Arbor, Michigan 48103

Serologist: (DOT) 041.081

SEROLOGY TECHNOLOGIST
Medical Technologist, Serology

In smaller laboratories, the duties of the Serology Technologist may be combined with those of the Serologist, or those of the Microbiology Technologist, or of the Blood Bank Technologist.

In large institutions, where the Serologist has educational and supervisory duties, the Serology Technologist becomes responsible for much of the day-to-day testing, and immediate supervision of Technicians and Assistants.

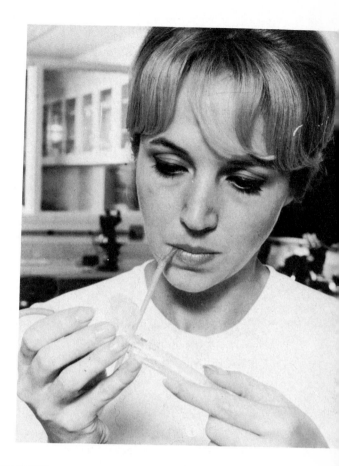

The Serology Technologist performs tests on body fluids of patients to assist physicians in diagnosing specific diseases. She also makes serums and vaccines for inoculation and treatment of patients.

Photo courtesy of the National Committee for Careers in the Medical Laboratory

JOB DUTIES

The Serology Technologist performs routine serological tests on body fluids and materials such as blood, exudates, scrapings, and spinal fluids, to ascertain pathogenic qualities of specimens and test them for specific diseases.

She makes antibacterial and antitoxic serums and vaccines. She mixes or dilutes manufactured serums according to standard formulas, for use in tests and for inoculation and treatment of patients, to create resistance to specific infections, or to destroy microorganisms that enter the body. She makes diagnostic and treatment serums by periodically injecting antigens (dead bacteria or certain proteins that when injected into the body incite tissues to produce disease-fighting antibodies) into laboratory animals. She draws blood from the animals, removes the antiserum (serum that contains specific antibodies) from the blood, and uses the antiserum for tests or for injection into patients. She preserves serum in the laboratory refrigerator.

The Serology Technologist receives specimens of blood for testing from the wards, or collects them directly from patients. She centrifuges them, to separate cells from serum. For the purpose of serological diagnosis of certain diseases, like syphilis, typhoid, Brucellosis or infectious mononucleosis, she mixes the serum drawn from patient with known bacterial specimens or anti-sera. She observes reactions, macroscopically or microscopically, to detect characteristic clumping or agglutination in the test solution.

She performs tests for syphilis, using one of the established laboratory methods, such as Wassermann, Kahn, Kline, Kolmer, or Eagle. She performs biological diagnostic tests, such as Widal tests for typhoid fever, heterophile antibody tests for infectious mononucleosis, and tests for typing pneumococci and streptococci.

She performs other agglutination tests, complement fixation test, or capsular swelling tests, using the centrifuge, incubators, test tubes, microscopes, and balances.

In all testing, she follows strict principles of asepsis and antisepsis in use of glassware and serum, and in preparation and titration of reagents. She records all results in the laboratory test logbook. She consults with the Serologist when test findings are abnormal, or when difficulties are encountered in testing.

The Serology Technologist performs immunology tests and injections, such as pollen sensitization tests, by direct injection of antigens into the patient. She observes and records reactions to injections.

She may conduct tests to determine the susceptibility of microorganisms to sulfa drugs, penicillin, and other antibiotics, and to chemical and physical agents. She may conduct pregnancy tests. She may also test, collect, process, and dispense blood and plasma from the hospital blood bank.

EDUCATION, TRAINING, AND EXPERIENCE

The Serology Technologist must have three years of college with courses in biology, chemistry, and mathematics, plus one year of training in a school of medical technology approved by the American Society of Clinical Pathologists. She must be a registered Medical Technologist by the Registry Board of the American Society of Clinical Pathologists.

Some states require a license issued by the state's Board of Health in order to practice.

JOB RELATIONSHIPS

Workers supervised: Medical Laboratory Assistant specializing in serology, who may be designated Serology Technician.
Supervised by: Serologist or Medical Technologist, Chief.
Promotion from: No formal line of promotion.
Promotion to: No formal line of promotion.

PROFESSIONAL AFFILIATIONS

American Society of Medical Technologists
Suite 25, Hermann Professional Building
Houston, Texas 77025

Medical Technologist: (DOT) 078.281-018

SEROLOGY TECHNICIAN

The Serology Technician performs procedures more complex than the routine duties assigned to Laboratory Assistants, and requires only limited supervision, but she does not undertake the supervisory and educational responsibilities of the Technologist.

JOB DUTIES

The Serology Technician performs routine serological tests on body fluids and materials, such as blood, exudates, scrapings, and spinal fluids, to ascertain pathogenic qualities of specimens and test them for specific diseases.

She makes antibacterial and antitoxin serums and vaccines, to be used for diagnosis or treatment, by injecting antigens (dead bacteria or certain proteins that incite issues to produce disease-fighting antibodies) into laboratory animals. She draws blood from the animal, removes the antiserum (which contains the antibodies) from the blood, and uses it for tests or for injection into patients. She preserves serum by refrigeration.

She mixes or dilutes manufactured serums according to standard formulas, for use in tests and for inoculation and treatment of patients, in order to increase their resistance to a specific infection, or destroy microorganisms that have invaded the body.

She performs agglutination tests, complement fixation tests, and capsular swelling tests, making observations macroscopically and microscopically, using the centrifuge, incubators, test tubes, microscopes, and other laboratory equipment.

She performs tests for syphilis, using one of the established laboratory methods. She also performs skin tests, such as those for typhoid fever, and tests to detect pollen sensitization and other allergies, as well as tests for typing various bacteria. She may conduct pregnancy tests, and tests to determine the effectiveness of given antibiotics against specific microorganisms. In some clinical laboratories, she may have the responsibilities of the Blood Bank Technician.

In all testing, she follows strict principles of asepsis and antisepsis in her handling of serums, specimens, glassware, and laboratory instruments. She cleans and sterilizes equipment used in the laboratory.

She records the results of all tests she has made, for the approval of the Technologist or Serologist.

EDUCATION, TRAINING, AND EXPERIENCE

This job falls into the category of Medical Laboratory Technician, a new classification between Technologist and Assistant. The present criterion for certification by the Board of Registry of the American Society of Clinical Pathologists (ASCP) is an associate degree (two years) from a junior or community college, in a program combining general education, laboratory sciences (including clinical laboratory) and related subjects, as approved by the American Medical Association Council on Medical Education in collaboration with the ASCP Board of Schools. Students with this background are eligible for the registry examination, and certification of MLT(ASCP).

Certification may also be obtained through the American Medical Technologists Registry. This registry gives certification to high school graduates who have completed a two-year work-study program approved by the Accrediting Bureau of Medical Laboratory Schools. In this program, credit is given for previous certification as Certified Laboratory Assistant. Certification is also granted to students who have completed a 50-week Armed Forces course in medical laboratory techniques, together with approved laboratory experience.

Examination for registry is required in all programs of certification.

JOB RELATIONSHIPS

Workers supervised: None.
Supervised by: Serology Technologist.
Promotion from: No formal line of promotion.
Promotion to: No formal line of promotion.

PROFESSIONAL AFFILIATIONS

American Medical Technologists
710 Higgins Road
Park Ridge, Illinois 60068

American Society of Clinical Pathologists
2100 West Harrison Street
Chicago, Illinois 60612

American Society of Medical Technologists
Suite 1600
Hermann Professional Building
Houston, Texas 77025

National Committee for Careers in the Medical Laboratory
9650 Rockville Pike
Rockville, Maryland 20014

Board of Certified Laboratory Assistants
9500 South California Avenue
Evergreen Park, Illinois 60642

American Association of Blood Banks
30 North Michigan Avenue
Chicago, Illinois 60602

Medical Laboratory Technician: (DOT) 078.281-026

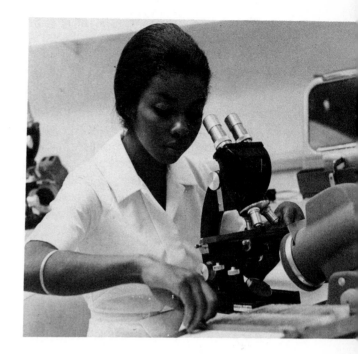

A Cytotechnologist reviews a series of microscope slides on which are tissues taken at biopsy from women who underwent surgery for breast cancer. Data from the slides will be used by a team of physicians in a scientific report on their study of this malignancy.

Photo courtesy of the National Committee for Careers in the Medical Laboratory

CYTOTECHNOLOGIST
Medical Technologist, Cytology

Cytology is the science of cells, and particularly of cell structure and growth. The secret of life itself is locked in the mysteries of the cell.

Understanding of cells is relevant to almost every aspect of health and disease, but perhaps nowhere more critically than in relation to cancer, which is characterized by unruly, unnatural, abnormal, and unnecessary growth of cells. The disease reveals itself in disordered cell growth long before it becomes evident in any other way. Progress in ability to make early diagnosis of cancer is due largely to progress in the science of cytology.

The study of cells in the clinical laboratory takes place under the supervision of the Pathologist, with Cytotechnologists and Cytotechnicians searching through high-powered microscopes to trace clues to the disease in the delicate patterns of cytoplasm and nucleus, and observe the shapes of cells. When tissue or smears are stained, and magnified a thousand times, abnormalities in color, size, and shape of cells signal the early presence of cancer.

A factor contributing to the difficulty of this work is the wide variation in normal cells in different organs of the human body. The Cytotechnologist and Cytotechnician must be thoroughly versed in all the variations among normal cells before they can expect to recognize the abnormal ones.

JOB DUTIES

The Cytotechnologist may sometimes collect specimens directly from patients, but usually they are sent to the clinical laboratory in the form of tissue or fluid, by physicians or surgeons who are diagnosing or treating patients.

Because a characteristic of cancer is that the diseased tissue discards cells from deep layers up to the surface, where they are washed away by body fluids, such fluids are often the most accessible specimens.

In preparing a fluid specimen, the Cytotechnologist centrifuges it, to separate cells from the supernatant, and places a bit of the resultant material on a glass microscope slide, using a pipette, spatula, or swab. She then draws a blank slide across it, to spread it evenly. She immerses the slide in a fixative solution to preserve the specimen, and then into a series of stains, to dehydrate, clear, and color the slides in such a way that specific parts of the cell are more visible under microscopic study.

She mounts the slide on a microscope, and examines the cells to detect evidence of cancer or other pathological conditions.

When she has completed her study, she classifies the slides according to standard classifications ranging from normal to cancerous cells, with strict adherence to her training and experience of typical and atypical cell structures. She records the classification on each slide, and presents those with unusual cell structures to the Pathologist for further examination and decision as to whether further biopsy or study is necessary.

She compiles listings of patients from whom the Pathologist has requested followup specimens, with his notations as to the specific periods of time within which they should be analyzed. When the followup specimens are received, she studies them in similar fashion, and reports whether cell abnormalities are the same, have been eliminated, or intensified.

She maintains records of all work performed in the unit, and catalogs and files all slides to be used as part of patients' medical records.

She may take periodic inventory of supplies and equipment. She may prepare chemical reagents and stains used in performing tests.

EDUCATION, TRAINING, AND EXPERIENCE

Two years of college are required, and must include 12 semester hours in science, at least eight of which must be in biological sciences. In addition, the Cytotechnologist must have completed 12 months in a school of cytology approved by the American Medical Association, the last six months of which can be in an acceptable cytology laboratory. The applicant then is eligible for examination by the Board of Registry of Medical Technologists of the American Society of Clinical Pathologists, and receives the certification CT (ASCP).

Some states require a license issued by the State Board of Health as a condition to practice.

JOB RELATIONSHIPS

Workers supervised: Medical Laboratory Assistant specializing in cytology, may be designated Cytotechnician.
Supervised by: Pathologist or Medical Technologist, Chief.
Promotion from: No formal line of promotion.
Promotion to: No formal line of promotion.

PROFESSIONAL AFFILIATIONS

American Society of Medical Technologists
Suite 25, Hermann Professional Building
Houston, Texas 77025

Cytotechnologist: (DOT) 078.281-014

CYTOTECHNICIAN
Medical Laboratory Assistant

The Cytotechnician relieves the Cytotechnologist of routine inspection of body materials and fluids in which cancerous or other pathological cells may be suspected. She is able to do these tests with a minimum of supervision, and some more difficult tests with supervision.

In many clinical laboratories, a considerable part of her work may be investigation of cervical and vaginal smears submitted by physicians in the intensive effort to detect cancer of these organs in its earliest stages. The Cytotechnician has the satisfaction of knowing that she is playing a vital role in a worldwide campaign to eliminate these forms of cancer, which have been among the most deadly for women in past generations. Today, as the result of "Paps"* smears and similar diagnostic measures, these forms of cancer claim far fewer fatalities.

JOB DUTIES

The Cytotechnician is assigned certain specimens of body tissues, fluids, or other specimen materials for analysis.

If the specimen is in the form of tissue, she may freeze it, and slice it into very thin sections for mounting on the microscope. If it is fluid, it may have to be centrifuged, to separate cells and sediment. In either instance, she places the prepared specimen on a microscope slide, drawing a clean slide across it to smooth it out if it is fluid. The slide is then immersed in a fixative solution, and subsequent staining

---

* Abbreviation of Papaniculaou, for George Papaniculaou, a Greek-born physician, citizen of the United States, and discoverer of the technique.

solutions, to preserve the specimen and to make the characteristics of the cells easier to see.

She mounts the slide on a microscope and examines the cells, to discover whether there is an evidence of abnormality.

In all of these procedures, she follows standard techniques meticulously, and observes all rules of asepsis and antisepsis, in order to prevent any possibility of contamination.

She records her findings on laboratory slips for the approval of the Technologist, and carefully classifies each slide in accordance with her findings and standard methods of classification. If anything unusual occurs during her investigation of any slide, she consults the Cytotechnologist for assistance.

She may take periodic inventory of supplies and equipment in the cytology unit, and enter requisitions for replacements. She may have responsibility for preparation of chemical reagents and stains used in the performance of tests. She may also be responsible for sterilization of glassware and other equipment used in the laboratory.

EDUCATION, TRAINING, AND EXPERIENCE

This job falls into the category of Medical Laboratory Technician, a new classification between Technologist and Assistant. The present criteria for certification by the Board of Registry of the American Society of Clinical Pathologists (ASCP) are an associate degree (two years) from a junior or community college, in a program combining general education, laboratory sciences (including clinical laboratory) and related subjects, as approved by the American Medical Association Council on Medical Education in collaboration with the ASCP Board of Schools. Students with this background are eligible for the registry examination, and certification of MLT(ASCP).

Certification may also be obtained through the American Medical Technologists Registry. This registry gives certification to high school graduates who have completed a two-year work-study experience program approved by the Accrediting Bureau of Medical Laboratory Schools. In this program, credit is given for previous certification as Certified Laboratory Assistant. Certification is also granted to students who have completed a 50-week Armed Forces course in medical laboratory techniques, together with approved laboratory experience.

Examination for registry is required in all programs of certification.

JOB RELATIONSHIPS

Workers supervised: None.
Supervised by: Microbiology Technologist.
Promotion from: No formal line of promotion.
Promotion to: No formal line of promotion.

PROFESSIONAL AFFILIATIONS

American Medical Technologists
710 Higgins Road
Park Ridge, Illinois 60088

American Society of Clinical Pathologists
2100 West Harrison Street
Chicago, Illinois 60612

American Society of Medical Technologists
Suite 1600
Hermann Professional Building
Houston, Texas 77025

National Committee for Careers in the Medical Laboratory
9650 Rockville Pike
Rockville, Maryland 20014

Board of Certified Laboratory Assistants
9500 South California Avenue
Evergreen Park, Illinois 60642

Medical Laboratory Technician: (DOT) 078.281-026

ANIMAL CARETAKER

In a clinical laboratory, most of the animals needed for biological testing and re-search are small creatures, ranging from chicks, mice, hamsters, guinea pigs, rabbits, to cats and dogs. Sometimes monkeys are used. Neither the range of animals, nor their use, is likely to be as extensive as in a research laboratory.

Nevertheless, animals are essential for the purposes of testing the efficiency of drugs, chemical agents, and medical and surgical procedures before they are tried in humans; for the training of surgeons; and for use in numerous diagnostic pro-cedures.

Animals in clinical and research laboratories are always treated with compassion, and spared unnecessary pain through anesthesia when a procedure is difficult. They are well-fed, well-cared-for, and frequently become pets—not only of the laboratory personnel, but often of other members of the hospital staff. It is not unusual for a staff member to adopt an animal after it has served a laboratory purpose, and take it home. It is also not unusual for hospital and research laboratories to serve as outposts of the local Society for the Prevention of Cruelty to Animals, providing a shelter for strays, and offering unneeded animals for adoption.

Some animals, such as chicks, mice, hamsters, guinea pigs and rabbits are "farmed" by persons or companies outside the laboratory—that is, raised for the express purpose of sale to laboratories. In some instances, this is necessary, in order to obtain certain kinds or strains of animals.

A sick animal could not be of any value in clinical testing, and so it is in the interest of the laboratory to keep animals in excellent health. It should also be added that because discoveries made to benefit humans are beneficial to animals, too, the laboratories often aid the advancement of veterinary medicine.

Cleanliness of the animals, and preservation of a sterile atmosphere in the laboratory are essential to the validity of any scientific tests that are to be made.

Responsibility for all these matters falls upon the Animal Caretaker. While it may not be necessary for him to have achieved a high level of formal education, he must be dependable, and a person of intelligence and compassion.

JOB DUTIES

The Animal Caretaker prepares the animals' food, by weighing, grinding, chopping, measuring, and mixing specified amounts of ingredients according to the directions he is given. He feeds and waters the animals as indicated by schedules and diet lists. He records the amount consumed by each animal, and removes any unfinished food and disposes of it.

He cleans and sterilizes the cages, pens, and surrounding areas, such as walls, windows, and floors, using steam and germicidal solutions. He places portable cages, water bottles, feed troughs, and similar items in the sterilizer. He repairs cages and equipment, using hand tools. He sprays insecticides, and spreads powder in animal quarters to exterminate vermin.

On instruction to do so, he may puncture the ear lobes of designated animals, and draw blood samples for experiments to be made by physicians, using scalpel, gauze, and alcohol. He positions a laboratory test tube or glass slide under the incision and catches drops of blood sample. He labels the test tube or slide, and carries the sample to technicians for analysis.

He observes animals, and records their general behavior and specific reactions to experimental treatment. He visually inspects animals for observable symptoms of contagious disease. He prepares animals for surgery by bathing, shaving hair from the body areas, and administering anesthetic. He transports animals in and out of surgery, by carrying, or using special fixtures.

The Animal Caretaker controls temperature and humidity in the rooms, to maintain a prescribed environment. He may have responsibility for ordering feed and supplies. He may remove dead animals for cremation.

He makes full reports, including any unusual behavior of animals, to his superiors. He is ultimately responsible to the Pathologist, but may take direction from a Veterinarian, or from physicians and technologists who are conducting specific experiments.

EDUCATION, TRAINING, AND EXPERIENCE

High school graduation, with courses in chemistry and biology, is preferred. Some employers accept applicants with the ability to understand oral and written instructions. Some employers require the worker to be certified by the Animal Care Panel of the United States Department of Health, Education, and Welfare.

Previous experience is not usually required.

Usually one to three months' on-the-job training is required to attain adequate job proficiency. This will depend upon the size and complexity of the animal section of the clinical laboratory.

JOB RELATIONSHIPS

Workers supervised: None.
Supervised by: Animal Quarters Supervisor or Veterinarian.
Promotion from: No formal line of promotion. This is an entry job.
Promotion to: No formal line of promotion.

PROFESSIONAL AFFILIATIONS

American Association for Laboratory Animal Science
P.O. Box 10
Joliet, Illinois 60434

Animal Caretaker (DOT) 356.874-014

MEDICAL ILLUSTRATOR
Artist, Medical

Although some kind of illustration has accompanied medical texts and materials since the beginning of time, the upsurge of research, discoveries, and the proliferation of scientific journals in recent years has put the skills of the professional Medical Illustrator at a premium.

It is no longer enough that the artist have a command of his artistic materials and techniques. It is now necessary that he (or she, since there are about as many women as men in the field) have a strong foundation of medical knowledge as well. Of the fewer than 300 professional Medical Illustrators in the United States today, most handle an ever-changing variety of assignments, although a few specialize in only one field, such as ophthalmology or neurosurgery. Quite a number of artists free lance.

Medical Illustrators are more commonly employed by research institutions than clinical laboratories, and often are members of a research team. They must be able not only to render a true anatomical likeness, but also to create simple explanatory diagrams to show complex ideas, or to script a program of visuals for a television presentation, or sculpture body parts for use in demonstration of organ functions.

The Medical Illustrator must have imagination, versatility, and technical capability in a number of art skills.

There are relatively few schools of medical illustration that are accredited by the Association of Medical Illustrators, and classes are usually limited to a half dozen students each year, so competition for entrance is keen. However, ultimate rewards in employment are great.

JOB DUTIES

The Medical Illustrator makes drawings, diagrams, and three–dimensional models to illustrate medical and surgical findings and procedures, for use in exhibits, publications, and research and teaching activities.

He confers with the supervisor of each project to ascertain the purpose of the desired illustrative material, and to obtain guidelines for the project. He studies any sketches provided, and researches data in medical and scientific publications to become acquainted with the subject matter.

He makes sketches of surgical procedures, anatomical specimens, microscopic structures of plants and animal tissue, and other medical conditions. He prepares rough sketches, preliminary drawings, and finished illustrations to scale, using crayon, pen, ink, water colors, and mixed media. He plots and matches reference points on drawings and transparent overlays to provide for printing multicolored designs. He lays out, cuts, and affixes adhesive color, type, and pattern screens to the drawing, or completes details of the drawing in freehand. He submits drawings as part of medical case history, to be used in postoperative consultations, research and teaching activities, and as illustrations for textbooks, monographs, and scientific papers.

He constructs, or directs construction of, models for scientific exhibits or teaching purposes. He makes plaster and wax castings to show anatomy, physiology, and articulation of various parts of the body. He offers advice on construction of glass-blown models and those made from other synthetic materials. He meets with faculty members, research fellows, and authorized affiliated agencies to determine their needs regarding exhibits or illustrations.

He assists in styling and overall design of medical books, monographs, and scientific papers in order to coordinate text with the illustrative material. He advises on presentation of such material for publication and exhibits.

He letters and lays out charts, tables, graphs, diagrammatical representations, and other mechanical plans to accompany research publications. He designs and prepares commercial art products, such as leaflets, bulletins, posters, and announcements. He may design titles for motion pictures and television media. He designs and directs production of audio and audiovisual presentations and aids, as well as exhibits for research, educational, and public relations purposes, and for use in conferences and seminars. He may design backgrounds and related artwork.

He maintains files of visual and audiovisual records of research data, making them available to medical men, researchers, and faculty. He collects descriptions of unusual medical occurrences from scientific literature which may be needed for illustrations.

EDUCATION, TRAINING, AND EXPERIENCE

Completion of a minimum two years of college, including courses in biology, zoology, and comparative anatomy, plus twenty months of special training in a recognized school of medical illustration is required.

Some employers require certification by the Association of Medical Illustrators.

JOB RELATIONSHIPS

Workers supervised: None.
Supervised by: Pathologist or Associate Administrator.
Promotion from: No formal line of promotion.
Promotion to: No formal line of promotion. Promotion may be through increased supervisory or administrative duties.

PROFESSIONAL AFFILIATIONS

Association of Medical Illustrators
738 Keystone Avenue
River Forest, Illinois 60305

Medical Illustrator: (DOT) 141.081

MEDICAL PHOTOGRAPHER

Medical photography, which is a significant aspect of biological photography, is a method of scientific recording. It is valued for its clarity and accuracy rather than art—although some biological photography does attain that status in the course of revealing the awesome intricacies of nature that the human eye could never see.

The field has become far too complex for anything but the most professional training to develop a competent Medical Photographer. Today he has at his command ultraviolet and infrared rediation for illumination; high-speed cinematography, to slow down events that happen too fast to see; slow-motion and stop—motion, to condense processes such as the growth of a colony of bacteria that might take several days; X-ray photography, to penetrate surfaces; and electronic microphotography to make visible incredibly small microorganisms. The Medical Photographer may also be called upon to direct closed-circuit television systems, such as those used to transmit details of a surgical procedure from the operating room to a medical classroom or seminar.

The Medical Photographer must have a thorough knowledge of photographic optics, light theory, and the characteristics of photosensitive materials, as well as adequate knowledge of the subject matter he is recording. He must become a multimedia communications expert, and at the same time be cognizant of the scientific milieu in which he is working, so that his activities do not disturb the essential scientific processes.

He has become a valuable and highly skilled member of the scientific team, helping the research scientist in his work, and the practicing physician in delivery of improved health care. His work also enriches the training of students.

JOB DUTIES

The Medical Photographer receives requests from faculty of the medical staff for photographic recordings of patients, anatomical structures, pathological specimens, surgical techniques, diagnostic and therapeutic methods, and other procedures to be produced in monochrome or full color, using still and motion picture cameras.

He positions the patient or specimen to be photographed, determining place, background, and most suitable illustrative technique. He arranges illumination and optical equipment, and sets up cameras at best distances and angles. He selects the proper type of film and lens and filter arrangement. He adjusts the lens and camera shutter for proper focus and time exposure, and exposes the film.

He makes photographic records of microscopic structures of plant and animal tissues, or studies of various diseases. He provides photographic followup records to illustrate a series of the same or similar medical cases, such as preoperative and postoperative photographs, to illustrate effects of treatment.

He makes copies of charts, electrocardiograms, roentgenograms, and other original material. He consults with the individuals who made the requests, to determine the effectiveness of the completed project.

He engages in developmental and investigative activities in the field of medical photography, and presentation of scientific data, including such problems as time-lapse and ultraspeed photography; use of infrared or ultraviolet light sources to produce visible records of normally invisible phenomena; and development of new equipment or adaptation of existing equipment to produce more accurate pictorial records.

He develops film in accordance with established photographic procedures, and makes contact and projection prints and transparencies, including lantern slides and photomontages. He retouches negatives, and spots and mounts prints for exhibits. He mixes and tests standard processing formulas and alters formulas to obtain special effects.

He cuts and edits motion pictures, suggesting titles, trailers, and other continuity material. He plans illustrations and scripts for visual education aids in cooperation with teachers, physicians, and other scientists. He plans layout of exhibits.

He trains assistants in photographic techniques and procedures. He establishes work schedules and assigns tasks. He suggests method of performance and reviews completed assignments.

He requisitions material to maintain stock at adequate operating levels. He maintains files and indices. He repairs equipment not requiring factory adjustment. He may occasionally run motion picture and slide projectors.

EDUCATION, TRAINING, AND EXPERIENCE

High school graduation is required. College-level courses in physics, chemistry, anatomy, physiology and other biological fields are desirable.

Courses in mathematics and statistics are desirable.

Training in all basic techniques and procedures used in commercial photography, and special training in medical and related photographic fields, are required.

A number of colleges now offer courses leading to science degrees in biological photography.

JOB RELATIONSHIPS

Workers supervised: May supervise staff of other Medical Photographers and clerks.
Supervised by: Pathologist or Associate Administrator.
Promotion from: No formal line of promotion.
Promotion to: No formal line of promotion. Promotion may be on basis of increased administrative and supervisory duties.

PROFESSIONAL AFFILIATIONS

Association of Medical Illustrators
738 Keystone Avenue
River Forest, Illinois 60305

Biographical Photographic Association, Inc.
P.O. Box 12866
Philadelphia, Pennsylvania 19108

Biological Photographic Association
Stanley J. McComb, Executive Secretary
P.O. Box 1057
Rochester, Minnesota 55901

Biological Photographer: (DOT) 143.382-010

Research Laboratories

The basic research that underlies advances in medicine and health care takes place in a variety of contexts. They include (i) universities and medical schools that frequently are associated with hospitals, and in which projects are usually headed by physicians; (ii) Federal institutions, such as the National Institutes of Health, the Food and Drug Administration, and the Veterans Administration, in which projects are often physician-directed; and (iii) industries, primarily those concerned with manufacture of pharmaceuticals or food, in which project directors frequently are specialists in one of the basic sciences, rather than medical doctors. To a lesser extent, research may be conducted in private commercial laboratories, or those supported by foundations or voluntary organizations.

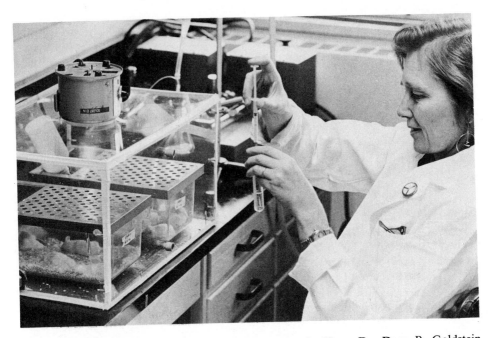

Small animals are frequently used in medical research. Here, Dr. Dora B. Goldstein, Senior Scientist and Lecturer, Department of Pharmacology, Stanford University School of Medicine, conducts a study of alcoholism, utilizing mice.

The history of medical discoveries is replete with illustrations of valuable knowledge gained by accident while the scientist was looking for something else. Alertness to the potential of everything that may be revealed is the hallmark of the research scientist. Consequently, earmarking funds for research solely for a narrow medical problem or single-disease entity may work to a disadvantage.

Methods of funding directly influence the course of research, and two-thirds of the funding for medical research is provided by Federal allocations. In the past, these were distributed as grants, very often to physicians in universities and medical centers who combined the clinical approach with basic research.

In recent years, allocations of government funds have been cut back drastically, with the lion's share earmarked for research into cancer, heart disease, and sickle cell anemia: and, instead of grants, funds are distributed by contract in many instances. If this trend continues, it may lead to less research in medical centers, and a larger proportion in industrial laboratories and independent research organizations, which are better attuned to the contract method of funding.

Whatever the outcome, industrial laboratories and independent research organizations will be prime employers of a wide range of scientists, not necessarily physicians. Young people who obtain a master's degree or a Doctor of Philosophy degree in any of the basic sciences can look hopefully to them for positions of importance, possibly at higher levels than they might attain in laboratories related to medical centers. Their requirements are high, but the opportunities they offer are great.

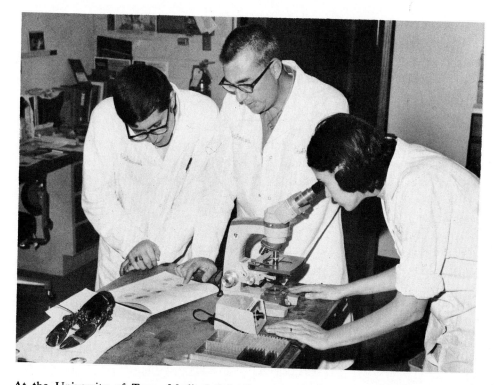

At the University of Texas Medical School at San Antonio, Dr. Frederick Rommel, Assistant Professor of Pediatrics and Microbiology (center) and two Research Assistants examine the blood hemolymph of a lobster microscopically.

Photo by Thurman Hood, Jr., The University of Texas Medical School at San Antonio

If your interest is primarily in basic sciences related to medicine, the best places to train are the specific basic sciences departments in medical schools; those in anatomy, biochemistry, bioengineering, biophysics, cell biology, genetics, microbiology, pathology, pharmacology and physiology are the most common. Your letter of inquiry about programs and courses in the schools you might like to attend should be directed to the department in which you would like to specialize. Be sure to include state university medical schools in the list to which you write. They are less likely to suffer faculty cutbacks than private schools, if Federal funds are reduced.

Graduate and post-doctoral classes in these basic science departments are always small, which is a great advantage to students. However, their entrance requirements are high, and competition for admission is keen. It is well to investigate their possibilities while you still have time to complete necessary undergraduate courses.

The structure and organization of any research laboratory depend on its specific purpose. In a pharmaceutical laboratory, for example, there is usually a director of research, possibly a biochemist, who has the most authority of anyone in the company. He may or may not also be a physician. If not, there probably is a medical director on the staff.

Below the top echelon, there are usually many jobs for which a master's degree or doctorate in science is required, and which are highly specialized.

There are job opportunities for technologists and technicians in all the areas of basic science delineated under the heading of clinical laboratories. For these, the job duties and educational or training requirements are the same as in clinical laboratories. Not all of them may be found in any one laboratory, of course. The type of work the laboratory is doing determines what jobs exist.

In laboratories other than those related to pharmaceuticals, still other job categories will be found. A food manufacturer, for example, would employ nutritionists, and other technical workers to evaluate preservatives and additives, and to maintain quality control. A textile manufacturer may maintain laboratory personnel to develop flame-proofing procedures for children's wear, or test the allergenic properties of various dyes.

The following pages present job categories that are more likely to be found in research than in clinical laboratories.

BIOMEDICAL ENGINEER
Bioengineer
Medical Engineer
Medical Electronics Engineer
Bioinstrumentation Engineer
Medical Instrumentation Engineer

The Biomedical Engineer (increasingly called the Bioengineer) applies theory from the physical sciences—chemistry, physics, and geology—and technology from science and industry to the solution of problems in medicine and the life sciences: physiology, biochemistry, biophysics, cytology, and neurophysiology. He has become an important partner with the physician and surgeon in every aspect of health care and preventive medicine. His contributions have revolutionized scientific and medical research, and are responsible for many of the recent dramatic advances in prevention and treatment of disease, and repair of damage done by injury or disease. Many current efforts fall into one of four areas:

- The development of new instruments for use in medical and surgical care, or in research.
- The invention and perfecting of devices to repair or replace parts of the human body that do not function properly.
- The adaptation of computer technology to serve a wide range of specialized requirements in the health services and in research.
- The application of engineering theory and methods to medical and biological research—for example, in studies of the structure of the living organism, and of the mechanisms by which the human body maintains itself in good health.

Basic research is vital to development of new techniques in health care, and many present studies are only possible because biomedical engineers have designed or adapted sophisticated modern devices and instruments for scientific purposes. Here, Dr. James H. Dewson III monitors a monkey's performance by means of closed circuit television and a computer. Dr. Dewson has taught monkeys to distinguish between two-element sequences of sound and noise, and has developed a method for measuring their normal memory capacity. The work is part of a study at Stanford University Medical Center aimed at finding a treatment to restore loss of speech in stroke victims.

Biomedical Engineers sometimes describe themselves as "creative borrowers," because they draw on the resources of both basic and applied sciences, and combine or adapt them for new and surprising purposes. For instance, techniques in monitoring the vital signs of astronauts during space flight are now put to work for round the clock surveillance of patients in intensive care units. As another example, plastics and techniques of plastic fabrication designed for manufacturers of women's hosiery are now used to make artificial pieces of arteries which the body does not reject when they are spliced into a diseased section of the circulatory system.

The diversity of fields from which they take inspiration is evident from only a partial list: analytical and physical chemistry, thermodynamics, transport phenomena, fluid mechanics, reaction kinetics, properties of materials, data acquisition, signal processing, microwaves, transduction, gas dynamics, optics, automation, servomechanisms, metal machining, and construction.

JOB DUTIES

Because the work of the Biomedical Engineer is so highly creative, there is probably no field in which specific job duties are so difficult to define. What the Biomedical Engineer does depends entirely upon the project with which he is involved. Even then, not even he may be able to predict the procedures he will have to go through to reach his desired goal. Examples of the kinds of work that he does will supply the best illustrations.

Instruments: A small sampling of the many instruments devised by biomedical engineers might include: (1) a tiny microphone that can be slipped through a vein into the heart to diagnose specific heart "murmurs," so that a surgeon can know what to expect when he operates; (2) completely automatic methods that improve speed and accuracy in chemical and visual analysis of biological specimens for diagnosis: (3) use of a laser beam as a surface and near-surgical tool, particularly in such delicate operations as that for detached retina of the eye.

The variety of new instruments may be illustrated by two that allow physicians to gain information from the interior of the body without exploratory surgery. The first is a method of "seeing" and measuring organs of the body, abnormal growths, or unborn babies. It is an adaptation of sonar, the ultrasound technique used by oceanographers to locate and plot the position of objects under water. It can be used much more freely than X-ray, because it causes no undesirable side effects.

The second is a tiny radio transistor, which, when the patient swallows it, reports fluctuations in body temperatures, pressures, pH, and other chemical indications of internal bleeding, ovulatory activity, and digestive activity.

Replacement and Repair Devices: Among the most exciting scientific stories of recent years have been those reporting development and successful use of devices to replace or repair organs of the body. Among them are: (1) an electronic obstacle–detector that helps blind persons avoid bumping into things or falling from curbs; (2) a lifelike artificial forearm powered electronically, and activated by the patient's own neural commands, which allows him to make a fist, lift weights, and write; (3) the heart-lung machine which takes over the work of those organs and permits open-heart surgery; (4) the battery-operated, portable defibrillator with built-in cardioscope, which employs electric shock to restore or regulate heartbeat during surgical emergencies, or such field emergencies as heart failure, drowning, or asphyxiation; (5) the battery-operated miniature pacemaker, which, implanted in the chest with electrodes contacting the heart, is prolonging life in good health for thousands of selected heart patients; (6) the artificial kidney, or dialysis machine, which prolongs the lives and functional activity of patients otherwise doomed to early death.

Computing Machines and Electronic Data Processing: Computers and other electronic business machines are widely used in handling administrative procedures in hospitals, public health departments, and other areas of health care. They are valuable in keeping health records, and in storage and retrieval of health statistics.

The direct use of computers and data processing in patient care is a relatively new development. Among applications already in use are (1) monitoring of vital signs in patients under intensive care; (2) swift analysis of hundreds of comparable case histories, to enable a physician to reach diagnosis of difficult or rare problems; (3) analysis of accumulated research material; (4) communication between computers at long distances, enabling a clinician in one area to forward data for diagnosis to a faraway medical center if necessary, for comparison with a stored volume of data and immediate consultation with specialists.

Research: Apart from the research that leads to tangible devices, Biomedical Engineers contribute ideas in almost every aspect of health-related sciences: (1) they are involved in simulation of complex biological systems to increase understanding of life processes; (2) they evaluate the quantitative effects of tranquilizer drugs on muscle fibers; (3) they are studying the molecular and crystal structure of the cell, and its genetic significance; (4) they are investigating the commnications network of the nervous system, studying how the brain achieves learning, memory, and thought, and how it operates in sleep.

EDUCATION, TRAINING, AND EXPERIENCE

Graduation from high school, with courses in mathematics, chemistry, physics, and biology plus four years of college, with a bachelor's degree in engineering are required. Courses in biology, physiology, biochemistry and other biophysical sciences are desirable. Supplementary on-the-job training and extensive outside reading and study are recommended. Specialized graduate courses are in process of development at some universities.

JOB RELATIONSHIPS

Workers supervised: Biomedical Engineering Technicians, Data Processors, persons engaged in construction of devices.
Supervised by: Research Director or Administrator.
Promotion from: No formal line of promotion.
Promotion to: No formal line of promotion.

PROFESSIONAL AFFILIATIONS

Alliance for Engineering in Medicine and Biology
3900 Wisconsin Avenue, N.W.
Washington, D.C. 20016

American Institute of Biological Sciences
3900 Wisconsin Avenue, N.W.
Washington, D.C. 20016

Association for the Advancement of Medical Instrumentation
9650 Rockville Pike
Bethesda, Maryland 20014

Bioinstrumentation Advisory Council of the American Institute of
Biological Sciences
3900 Wisconsin Avenue, N.W.
Washington, D.C. 20016

Biomedical Engineer: (DOT) (DOT number pending for this category)

BIOMEDICAL ENGINEERING TECHNICIAN
Biotechnician

The work of the Biomedical Engineering Technician is not confined to research. In fact, his work in manufacture and servicing of prostheses and other aids for handicapped persons has become so important that it is treated as a separate entity elsewhere in this book.

Similarly, his (or her) function in operation of heart-lung machines and kidney dialysis equipment is described in greater detail under individual headings.

JOB DUTIES

The job duties assumed by Biomedical Engineering Technicians are so diverse that they can best be described in terms of areas of work.

The Biomedical Engineering Technician may sometimes work at assembling, adapting, or maintaining new kinds of devices and instruments. He may work in a biomedical engineering shop, or in a research laboratory. He may work in plastics, metals, glass, or other materials. Watchmakers, for example, sometimes adapt their skills to making miniaturized devices. Glassblowers and plastics workers may direct their effort toward manufacture of artificial organs. Electronics technicians are involved in almost every phase of biomedical engineering. Technicians also program information gained by use of these devices into computers for analysis, storage, or communication to other computers.

EDUCATION, TRAINING, AND EXPERIENCE

No firmly established requirements exist, although training programs are being developed. Excellence in a specific skill is essential, coupled with on-the-job training.

JOB RELATIONSHIPS

Workers supervised: None.
Supervised by: Research Director, Biomedical Engineer, or Department Head.
Promotion from: No formal line of promotion.
Promotion to: No formal line of promotion.

PROFESSIONAL AFFILIATIONS

Alliance for Engineering in Medicine and Biology
3900 Wisconsin Avenue, N.W.
Washington, D.C. 20016

Electronic Engineer: (DOT) 003.081-034

Digital Computer Programmer: (DOT) 020.188-026

Programmer, Technical: (DOT) 020.188-030

4

PROFESSIONAL HOSPITAL SERVICES

Many hospital services directly related to professional care of patients are staffed by non-physicians. Other services, headed by physicians, employ assistants, technicians, technologists, and specialists in fields other than medicine.

Of all professional care services, the nursing service is the largest. However, many other job classifications bring workers into contact with patients, and offer rewarding careers in the field of direct patient care in a hospital setting.

Professional care departments include:

- Anesthesiology Department
- Central Service
- Dental Department
- Dietetic Department
- Medical Library
- Medical Records Department
- Nursing Education Department
- Nursing Service
- Outpatient Department
- Pharmacy
- Physical Medicine and Rehabilitation
- Radiology-Nuclear Medicine Department
- Social Service Department
- Speech and Hearing Therapy Department
- Technical Services

Job classifications in these services demand a wide variety of talents.

Requirements for education, training, and experience are equally varied. Some positions require little more than ability to speak, read, write, and follow instructions. Others require specialized training, a year or two of college, a baccalaureate degree, or advanced degrees with experience in approved training situations. In general, it can be said that the more professional the position, the more education and experience it requires.

Fortunately, scholarships and student loans are available for most of the higher job classifications.

Some positions that require only a high school diploma or less, with brief on-the-job training, are shown on the organization charts of the departments, but are not presented in full detail. Some others, in which there is no marked difference in requirements from those demanded in any business, also appear on the charts but are not fully described.

Anesthesiology Department

The Anesthesiology Department provides for the administration of anesthetics for all surgical, obstetric, and related medical procedures in the hospital.

> Anesthesiology is a practice of medicine dealing with but not limited to (1) the management of procedures for rendering a patient insensible to pain and emotional stress during surgical, obstetrical and certain medical procedures; (2) the support of life functions under the stress of anesthetic and surgical manipulations; (3) the clinical management of the patient unconscious from whatever cause; (4) the management of problems in pain relief; (5) the management of problems in cardiac and respiratory resuscitation; (6) the application of specific methods of inhalation therapy; (7) the clinical management of various fluid, electrolyte and metabolic disturbances. (*Standards for Patient Care in Anesthesiology*. Amended by ASA House of Delegates, October 11, 1973.)

Legally, the attending physician or surgeon is ultimately responsible for the total welfare of the patient. This responsibility could be interpreted to include the choice of agent and technique of administration of anesthetics. However, in the modern practice of medicine, the Anesthesiologist who is also a physician exercises his own judgment in these matters in consultation with the surgical and medical colleagues involved in the care of the patient.

The head of the Anesthesiology Department is always a physician. In smaller hospitals, a single Anesthesiologist may serve several institutions, or a member of the hospital medical staff who has special training in anesthesiology is named as Associate Administrator in charge of this department. Nurse Anesthetists assist the department head, and the Chief Nurse Anesthetist may assume some administrative duties.

In preparation of anesthesia, the Anesthesiologist or Nurse Anesthetist, studies the results of the physician's physical examination, including his clinical notes, and may visit the patient. Decision as to the type of anesthetic to use and the method of administration is based on this information. The Anesthetist observes the patient's condition before, during, and after administration of the anesthetic, and until all its effects have passed. He records the kind and amount of anesthetic administered, and any preoperative or postoperative medication that was given. He establishes and carries out safeguards in all procedures.

Personnel in the Anesthesiology Department must work closely with surgical, obstetric, X-ray, respiratory therapy, emergency room, pediatrics, and psychiatric services, and in recovery room and intensive care areas. The department head attends regular medical staff meetings, participates in discussions, and presents records of the department as a contribution to clinical research.

Minimum standards for safety and efficiency of anesthesiology services in hospitals have been set by the American College of Surgeons, the American Osteopathic Association, and the American College of Anesthesiologists.

NURSE ANESTHETIST, CHIEF

Advances in anesthesiology have produced a considerable number of agents and techniques of administration, from which the Anesthesiologist or Chief Nurse Anesthetist must select the one agent and method of administration most suitable for each individual patient. Many procedures are extremely sophisticated, and these are further refined by premedications that permit optimum result with minimum use of the prime anesthetic agent. Patient-monitoring during anesthesia is a very meticulous aspect of administration.

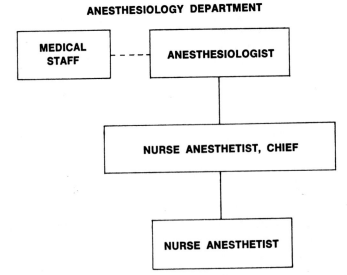

ANESTHESIOLOGY DEPARTMENT

NOTE: This chart is for illustrative purposes only and should not be considered a recommended pattern of organization.

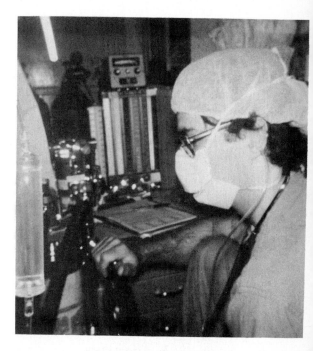

In management of individual patients, the Anesthesiologist or Nurse Anesthetist chooses the most suitable technique. Whatever method is selected, the Anesthetist monitors the patient's vital signs continuously during the progress of surgery, keeping the physician informed of his condition, and adjusting the flow of the anesthetic agent as necessary. Postoperatively, the Anesthetist supervises the patient until all effects of the anesthetic have passed. Here an Anesthesiologist administers an intravenous–drip anesthetic to a patient undergoing total dental extraction.

The Chief Nurse Anesthetist must have the background in education and training necessary to make such vital judgments, and the executive capability to direct and supervise the Nurse Anesthetists who may be doing the actual administration.

JOB DUTIES

She schedules assignment of cases to Nurse Anesthetists. She supervises the planning, securing, and arranging of necessary equipment, and directs the activities of the Nurse Anesthetist in the operating room. She performs anesthetist duties where the nature of the surgery or the patient's condition is such that serious problems might arise during surgery.

She assists the Anesthesiologist in planning courses of instruction for student nurses, and participates in the instruction. She directs students in practical application of the principles of anesthesiology, plans demonstrations of methods and techniques, and supervises their work experience. She may instruct medical interns and residents in methods and techniques of anesthesiology.

She participates in medical staff conferences concerning surgery and recovery procedures and training as related to anesthesia.

She analyzes data and prepares reports concerning specific anesthesia, drugs, techniques, and reactions of patients to them, as a basis for further medical research. She may participate in a research project in anesthesiology, including development of new techniques of administration of anesthesia, and observe and record patients' reactions.

EDUCATION, TRAINING, AND EXPERIENCE

The Chief Nurse Anesthetist should have graduated from both an accredited School of Nursing and an accredited School of Nurse Anesthesiology. The latter course is usually of 18- to 24-months' duration. She must be a Registered Nurse as well as a Registered Nurse Anesthetist in the state where she is performing this work.

She should also have from two to five years' experience as a Nurse Anesthetist, part of which was spent as an Instructor, before appointment as Chief.

If her appointment entails transfer to a strange hospital, a short period for orientation should be allowed, to learn the procedures of the specified hospital.

JOB RELATIONSHIPS

Workers supervised: Nurse Anesthetist; trainees and aides.
Supervised by: Anesthesiologist or Associate Administrator.
Promotion from: Nurse Anesthetist.
Promotion to: None.

PROFESSIONAL AFFILIATIONS

American Association of Nurse Anesthetists
Suite 310, Prudential Plaza
Chicago, Illinois 60601

Nurse Anesthetist, Chief: (DOT) 075.128-010

NURSE ANESTHETIST
Staff Anesthetist

The Nurse Anesthetist administers intravenous, inhalation, spinal, and other anesthetics to render patients insensible to pain during surgical procedures, childbirth, or other medical or dental procedures.

JOB DUTIES

She reviews her assignment of cases for each day, and the type of anesthesia prescribed for each one. She studies the physical findings of preoperative examination, to determine the probable effects of the anesthesia on the patient. She administers the preoperative medication prescribed by the physician, if this has not already been given.

She takes the necessary supplies and equipment to the operating room, and assembles such equipment as syringes and tubing, and the machine by which gas is administered, cheking it to insure that it is functioning properly. She prepares prescribed solutions for intravenous injections. She ascertains that blood of the proper type is available for emergency use.

After checking correct identification, she positions the patient on the operating table in accordance with established procedure for the type of operation to be performed. She takes the patient's blood pressure, respiration and pulse. If the patient is conscious, she explains the surgical procedure, to secure the patient's cooperation and confidence.

If the anesthetic is to be administered by inhalation, she fits the mask to the patient's face and starts the gas flow. She maintains the patient in the surgical anesthetic state, adjusting oxygen and gas flow, and keeping air tubes in position as necessary.

If the anesthetic is to be administered intravenously, she takes the necessary precautions to ensure that there is no leakage of the anesthetic agent in the perivenous tissue. Since most of these drugs are highly irritant, leakage may result in serious sloughing of the tissues.

In obstetric cases, she administers an analgesic agent to minimize pain, and anesthetic prior to delivery and for operative obstetric situations.

In every type of anesthetic used, she periodically takes the patient's blood pressure, respiration, and pulse, and watches for significant physical changes, such as change in skin color, or dilation of pupils. She keeps the surgeon informed of the patient's condition. If respiratory emergencies occur, she takes immediate remedial action.

She records the condition of the patient prior to, during, and following administration of the anesthetic, and the type of anesthetic used, on the patient's clinical chart.

She assists in moving the patient from the operating room to the recovery room or floor, and periodically checks the condition of the patient, and takes remedial measures to counteract any unfavorable postanesthesia effects. If unfavorable symptoms develop, she notifies the physician. When the effects of anesthesia on the patient have completely worn off, she submits her postoperative report.

She disassembles the equipment used, and cleans the work area, or directs others in doing so. She removes the supplies and accessories to the supply room, and cleans and sterilizes instruments, in accordance with established procedures.

She requisitions any necessary repairs or adjustments of equipment. Periodically, she inventories supplies, and orders replacements to maintain adequate stock of anesthetics, supplies, and accessories.

EDUCATION, TRAINING, AND EXPERIENCE

The Nurse Anesthetist must be a graduate of an accredited school of nursing, and should also have a graduate degree from an accredited school of nurse anesthetists. The training of a Nurse Anesthetist usually extends for a period of 18 to 24 months. She must be certified as a Registered Nurse, and as a Registered Nurse Anesthetist in the state where she is working. Whether she needs previous experience depends upon the hospital.

A short break-in period to learn procedures of the hospital is desirable.

JOB RELATIONSHIPS

Workers supervised: None.
Supervised by: Nurse Anesthetist, Chief or Anesthesiologist.
Promotion from: Nurse, Staff after formal training.
Promotion to: Nurse Anesthetist, Chief. Advancement may also be made through addition of supervisory, administrative, or teaching duties.

PROFESSIONAL AFFILIATIONS

American Association of Nurse Anesthetists
Suite 3010, Prudential Plaza
Chicago, Illinois 60601

Nurse Anesthetist: (DOT) 075.378-010

Central Service

In a hospital, medical and surgical supplies and equipment must be in readiness at all times. This in essence is the responsibility of the Central Service Department. It requisitions, stores, issues, assembles, and sterilizes all the equipment and materials used for care of patients. This amounts to a stock of hundreds of items, some of which are issued routinely, and others needed only occasionally. Routine items are often distributed on a regularly scheduled daily delivery, and only emergency requisitions are issued at other times of the day.

Records must be kept, so that articles that are consumed are charged against individual patient treatment, and are replaced.

A special sterilizing room is maintained in the department, since all equipment and supplies for bedside treatment, and those for the obstetrical and surgical departments, must be sterile. Sterile and nonsterile distilled water, and other irrigating solutions may also be prepared in Central Service.

Central Service also maintains and distributes such portable equipment as resuscitators, oxygen equipment, wheelchairs, orthopedic appliances, and surgical and emergency medical equipment. The Department provides instruction on use of such apparatus and equipment.

There is a growing trend toward consolidating Central Service to include a central cleanup area for processing all soiled supplies.

Central Service should be located near the Nursing Service, to which it is often attached, and to the Pharmacy and the Laundry.

The Director of Central Service is often a Registered Nurse, although there is a trend toward employing a manager without nursing training, but with a professional nurse as a member of his advisory committee. Other staff members are likely to include one or more registered or practical nurses, along with assistants, technicians, aides, orderlies, and messengers, who are trained on the job. Student nurses may be assigned to the service as part of their training, and volunteers may also be used.

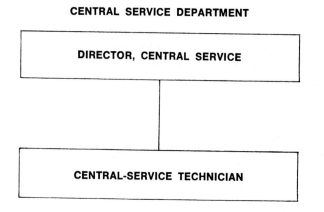

CENTRAL SERVICE DEPARTMENT

NOTE: This chart is for illustrative purposes only and should not be considered a recommended pattern of organization.

DIRECTOR, CENTRAL SERVICE

The Director of Central Service supervises and coordinates the activities of personnel in the department, in furnishing sterile and nonsterile supplies, equipment, and services for the care and treatment of patients.

JOB DUTIES

The Director establishes methods and work performance standards for preparing and handling sterile items. She shows personnel procedures such as proper use of sterilizing equipment, how to set up treatment trays, and otherwise maintain the equipment of the department. She insures that aseptic techniques are employed in preparing and handling supplies and equipment. She prepares instruments for repair, and maintains a regular schedule for checkup of electrical equipment by the maintenance department.

She insures that work and storage areas are clean and orderly. She takes microbiologic samples of air, surfaces, and equipment and sends them to the laboratory for sterility checks.

She supervises personnel engaged in decontaminating, assembling, packaging, and sterilizing linens, dressings, gloves, treatment trays, instruments, and related items: the preparation of standard irrigating solutions; the rotation of stock; and requisitioning, issuing, and controlling supplies and equipment. She maintains adequate stock on hand by visual inspection, and by consulting inventory records.

She recommends changes in budget and inventory level to meet current demands. She prepares and submits requisitions for additions and replacements, and stores received stock in appropriate areas of the supply room.

On presentation of proper authority, she dispenses stock for delivery to various hospital departments, and inspects returned equipment, to insure that all parts have been returned. She keeps inventory of items issued, and maintains a schedule of charges to be billed to the using department or patient.

She prepares reports on activities of the department, and keeps records on assigned personnel. She may interview applicants, and conduct in-service training for department personnel.

In hospitals having a school of nursing, she trains students in principles and procedures of sterilization, and aseptic techniques, and use and care of sterilizing equipment.

EDUCATION, TRAINING, AND EXPERIENCE

Graduation from an approved school of nursing and current licensure by State Board of Nursing is preferred. Some employers will accept workers with knowledge of nursing theory and practice but who are not professional nurses.

Sufficient experience is needed to understand and carry out hospital rules and regulations concerning sterilization and aseptic techniques. Operating room experience and some supervisory experience are also desirable.

JOB RELATIONSHIPS

Workers supervised: Central-Service Technicians and other personnel assigned to the department.
Supervised by: Assistant Administrator or Assistant Director, Nursing Service.
Promotion from: No formal line of promotion. May be promoted from a nursing position or a Central-Service Technician.
Promotion to: No formal line of promotion. May be promoted to a responsible position on another department, such as Purchasing, or Receiving.

PROFESSIONAL AFFILIATIONS

American Nurses' Association
10 Columbus Circle
New York, New York 10010

National League for Nursing
10 Columbus Circle
New York, New York 10019

American Society for Hospital Central Service Personnel
840 Lake Shore Drive North
Chicago, Illinois 60611

State and local nursing associations.

Supervisor, Central Supply: (DOT) 179.168

CENTRAL-SERVICE TECHNICIAN
Medical-Supply Clerk
Sterilizer
Supply-Room Helper

The Central-Service Technician cleans, sterilizes, and assembles equipment, supplies, and instruments according to prescribed procedures and techniques, performing all or any combinations of tasks necessary in the department.

JOB DUTIES

She decontaminates surgical instruments, containers, rubber gloves, syringes, and equipment such as aspirators, courpettes, and oxygen suppliers, using detergents and disinfecting solutions. She sterilizes instruments, equipment, surgical linens, and supplies such as surgical packs, treatment trays, using steam or gas sterilizer; or disinfects with antiseptic solutions. She places articles in sterilizer and processes according to the manufacturer's instructions. She operates semiautomatic to automatic sterilizing equipment. She may prepare standard irrigating solutions by prescribed formulas.

She prepares packs of supplies and instruments, dressing and treatment trays, needles, syringes, and gloves, according to designated procedures, and wraps, labels, and seals them. She prepares list of contents, and affixes list to each package or group of packages. She prepares control system to show supplies processed.

She may gather used supplies from hospital departments and return them after sterilization. She may fill requisitions, record charges, and inventory supplies.

EDUCATION, TRAINING, AND EXPERIENCE

High school graduation is preferred. Some employers prefer training as a Licensed Practical Nurse.

Some hospitals offer a formal program for Central-Service Technicians.

Previous experience is not required.

Up to six months' on-the-job training is needed to become familiar with the items handled in the department.

JOB RELATIONSHIPS

Workers supervised: None.
Supervised by: Director, Central Service.
Promotion from: No formal line of promotion. This may be an entry job.
Promotion to: No formal line of promotion. May be promoted to Chief Central-Supply Technician.

PROFESSIONAL AFFILIATIONS

None.

Central-Supply Worker: (DOT) 223.887-010

Dental Department

The Dental Department is a complete, self-contained unit, designed to furnish consultation, clinical services, dental research facilities, educational services on behalf of the hospital, and also may offer dental internships and residencies when appropriate.

Dental Department personnel establish and maintain relationships with appropriate clinical and administrative services of the hospital, participate in regular hospital staff conferences, and in work of the various committees of the hospital.

Standards for the Dental Department are set by the *Guidelines for Hospital Dental Services,* as formulated by the Council on Hospital Dental Services of the American Dental Association and the Council on Professional Practice of the American Hospital Association.

The Department must be under the direction of a dentist who is a graduate of a school approved by the Council on Central Education of the American Dental Association, and he must be licensed in the state in which the hospital is located.

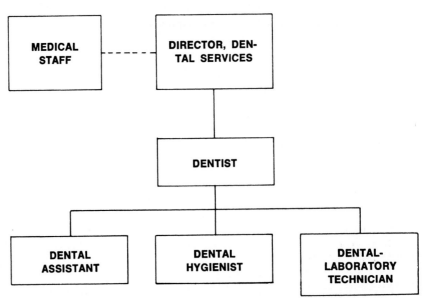

DENTAL DEPARTMENT

NOTE: This chart is for illustrative purposes only and should not be considered a recommended pattern of organization.

In addition to the Director, the staff includes qualified dentists, dental hygienists, dental technicians, dental assistants, and other personnel needed to meet the requirements of the program.

DIRECTOR, DENTAL SERVICES

The Director of Dental Services in a hospital administers the Dental Department and supervises all phases of its activities.

With members of other departments in the hospital, he participates in planning joint administrative and technical programs, and research programs, and recommends methods and procedures to coordinate dental services with medical, surgical, nursing, and other related services. He investigates and studies trends and developments in dental practices and techniques that may be applicable to his own Department of Dental Services.

JOB DUTIES

The Director assigns and supervises the activities of the department's personnel, requisitions supplies and equipment, prepares budget, and prepares narrative- and statistical-reports of activities and expenditures.

He recommends and approves personnel changes, such as hiring, transferring, and promoting staff members. Usually he interviews and hires professional staff members himself.

He resolves problems requiring administrative authority or professional knowledge, and outlines policy procedures and methods for resolving lesser problems.

He instructs students and interns in the theory and practice of dentistry, conducts diagnostic and clinical seminars, and lectures.

He may serve as dental consultant in cooperative health planning, and may address public health, medical, educational, or other scientific meetings and conferences. He may also have a dental specialty.

EDUCATION, TRAINING, AND EXPERIENCE

The Director must have a doctorate from an approved dental school. If he is practicing in a specialty field, he may be required to pass a specialty board examination, which usually requires two or three years' graduate education and approximately the same amount of specialized experience.

He must have a license to practice in state where employed, and one or more years in a supervisory or administrative capacity.

JOB RELATIONSHIPS

Workers supervised: All personnel assigned to Dental Department (professional, technical, clerical, and paramedical).
Supervised by: Associate Administrator for administrative purposes and Chief of Medical Staff for professional practice.
Promotion from: Dentist.
Promotion to: No formal line of promotion.

PROFESSIONAL AFFILIATIONS

American Association of Dental Schools
211 East Chicago Avenue
Chicago, Illinois 60611

American Dental Association
211 East Chicago Avenue
Chicago, Illinois 60611

National Dental Association
P.O. Box 197
Charlottesville, Virginia 22902

State and local dental associations.

Dentist: (DOT) 072.108-010

DENTIST

Most dentists are in private practice, working from their own offices, and providing a wide range of general care. However, a good many have taken additional professional training, and have entered a specialty field. The eight recognized dental specialties are:

- Endodontics (root treatment).
- Oral pathology (diseases of the mouth).
- Oral surgery (surgery of the mouth).
- Orthodontics (teeth straightening).
- Pedodontics (children's dentistry).
- Periodontics (treatment of the tissues or gums supporting the teeth and the underlying bone).
- Prosthodontics (making of artificial teeth or dentures).
- Public Health dentistry (prevention and control of dental diseases, and promotion of dental health through community efforts and education).

Dentistry is a highly respected profession, and offers many career opportunities. A dentist, if he chooses to take a salaried position, can find ready openings in industry, the Armed Forces, the Veterans' Administration, in public health, or dental research, as well as in hospitals. He will also find teaching opportunities in dental schools.

Up to now, only about two per cent of dentists have been women, but the field is open to them.

JOB DUTIES

In the hospital situation, the Dentist provides care for both inpatients and out-patients. He diagnoses and treats diseases, injuries, and malformations of teeth and gums.

He makes visual examination of the patient's teeth and gum structure, using X-rays, mouth mirror, explorers, instruments, and other diagnostic tools. He enters his findings on a dental chart and in the patient's medical record. He decides upon the most feasible plan of treatment, and carries it to conclusion.

He locates and repairs cavities in teeth. He extracts impacted, infected, or other-wise diseased or troublesome teeth, or performs root canal work. He makes impressions and models of jaws, in preparation of dentures. He fits orthodontic appliances for straightening and rearranging irregular teeth, and treating malocclusion of the jaws. He treats diseases of gums, teeth, and mouth with appropriate drugs, or by surgery.

He advises patients about dental health practices.

He consults with heads of other patient care services in planning dental treatments to be used for their patients.

He may perform dental procedures at chairside in an office, or at bedside with a portable dental unit. He may perform oral surgery at chairside, bedside, or in the hospital operating room.

The Dentist may have a specialty.

He has the assistance of a Dental Hygienist, Dental Assistant, or Dental Laboratory Technician in doing dental work.

EDUCATION, TRAINING, AND EXPERIENCE

A doctor's degree from an approved dental school is required, plus licensing in the state in which the Dentist is practicing or is on hospital staff.

If the Dentist is practicing in a specialty field, he may be required to pass a specialty board examination, which usually requires two or three years of graduate education and about the same amount of specialized experience as prerequisite for eligibility.

JOB RELATIONSHIPS

Workers supervised: Dental Assistants; Dental Hygienist; Dental-Laboratory Technician; clerical assistants.

Supervised by: Director, Dental Services.
Promotion from: No formal line of promotion.
Promotion to: No formal line of promotion. May be promoted to Director, Dental
Services.

PROFESSIONAL AFFILIATIONS

American Association of Dental Schools
211 East Chicago Avenue
Chicago, Illinois 60611

American Dental Association
211 East Chicago Avenue
Chicago, Illinois 60611

National Dental Association
P.O. Box 197
Charlottesville, Virginia 22902

State and local dental associations.

Dentist: (DOT) 072.108-010

Oral Pathologist: 072.081-010

Oral Surgeon: 072.101-010

Orthodontist: 072.018-014

Pedodontist: 072.108-018

Periodontist: 072.018-022

Prosthodontist: 072.018-026

Public Health Dentist: 072.018-030

DENTAL ASSISTANT
Dental Technician

The Dental Assistant has a pleasant, interesting, and rewarding job. She is the person who meets patients and makes them comfortable, as she prepares them for examination, treatment, or surgery.

The work that she does in assisting the Dentist is meticulous, and satisfying in the sense of work well done. The Assistant is also usually the office manager, handling appointments, business transactions, records, and other important matters.

The young woman who has taken the routine business courses in high school has an advantage. Beyond high school, she then requires only one or two years of training in a dental college, or in a junior or community college that has an approved program. Once she is qualified, her services will be in demand almost anywhere that she chooses to live. It is estimated that by 1980, more than 220,000 dental assistants will be needed, which is double the present number. She will find opportunities in private dentists' offices, and in public health work, as well as in hospital Dental Departments.

JOB DUTIES

The Assistant arranges dental instruments, materials, and medications or whatever is required for the patient's examination or treatment on the chairside tray, in the order that they will be used according to the scheduled procedure.

She prepares the patient by settling him in the chair and draping him with a sterile sheet or other covering.

During examination or treatment, the Assistant works with the Dentist at chairside, passing instruments to him, and keeping the patient's oral operating areas clear by use of suction devices, water sprays, cotton rolls, and holders, and by retraction of the cheek and tongue. She prepares restorative materials and dental cements, to have in readiness. She sterilizes instruments in the autoclave, or by chemical disinfectants.

If state dental laws allow it, she may take and develop X-ray films, and mount them.

She assists the Dental-Laboratory Technician in construction of models of teeth and mouth, and construction of dentures and other dental prostheses. She pours, trims, mounts, and polishes models of plastic or plaster made from impressions taken by the Dentist.

The Dental Assistant performs clerical and stenographic duties, arranges appointments, keeps records and accounts, receives cash, or sends charges to the hospital Financial Manager for billing to the patients' accounts. She records treatments, and keeps inventory of materials used and orders supplies when needed.

She may perform routine maintenance, such as lubricating equipment, sharpening dental hand instruments, replacing expendable parts, and cleaning equipment and treatment area.

She may determine the pulse, respiration, facial coloration, and pupillary reflexes of patients under anesthetic.

EDUCATION, TRAINING, AND EXPERIENCE

High school graduation, with business courses, biology, and chemistry are required. The aspiring Dental Assistant must then earn a certificate of completion of a dental-assistant course in a vocational school for one year, or a two-year junior college program. She should have one year of experience in a dentist's office.

These requirements having been completed, it should take about three months of on-the-job training to become familiar with the hospital routine.

JOB RELATIONSHIPS

Workers supervised: None.
Supervised by: Dentist or Dental-Laboratory Technician.
Promotion from: This may be an entry job.
Promotion to: May be promoted to Dental Hygienist or Dental-Laboratory Technician, after completion of additional formal education.

PROFESSIONAL AFFILIATIONS

American Dental Assistants Association
211 East Chicago Avenue
Chicago, Illinois 60611

Dental Assistant: (DOT) 079.378-010

DENTAL HYGIENIST
Hygienist
Oral Hygienist
Prophylactician

The Dental Hygienist is a practicing member of the dental health team, dedicated to helping individuals maintain oral health and prevent dental diseases and disorders. She is qualified by education and license to provide patient treatment prescribed by the Dentist, for the purpose of cleaning and protecting teeth.

Most Dental Hygienists are employed in private dental offices, but an increasing number are going into organized community health programs, school health programs, and hospital dental clinics.

The need for Dental Hygienists is steadily increasing, not only in this country, but in many other nations.

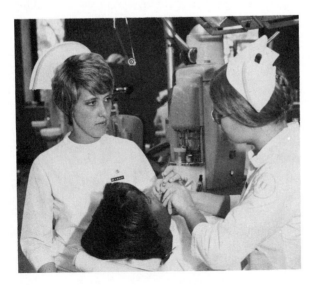

An instructor in dental hygiene at Loyola University Medical Center, Maywood, Illinois, demonstrates techniques to a student in the Dental School's baccalaureate program.

JOB DUTIES

Under supervision of the Dentist, the Dental Hygienist removes stains and deposits from the teeth by cleaning, scaling, and polishing. She applies agents that make teeth more resistant to decay, and prepares clinical and laboratory tests for interpretation by the Dentist. She takes, develops, and mounts X-rays.

In removing calcareous deposits from the teeth and under the gums, she uses small hand instruments and mirror, rotating brushes, rubber cups, and cleaning compound. She inserts a fine finishing strip between teeth to remove stains from parts of the teeth that are inaccessible by other methods. She applies medicants to gums and between teeth with cotton swabs.

She records her evaluation of the patient's mouth condition and extent of prophylaxis on the patient's dental chart, to provide the Dentist with information for more complete diagnosis and subsequent plan of treatment.

She cleans, sharpens, and sterilizes instruments, using autoclaves or disinfectant solutions; and mixes cleaning compounds and antiseptic solutions.

She advises and instructs patients on proper dental care and proper diet for good dental health. She may plan and deliver lectures to community organizations and other groups, or children, using posters, slides, models, motion pictures, and other visual aids.

She may provide bedside prophylaxis, using portable dental unit, and instruct nurses relative to patients' good dental care.

She may provide chairside assistance to the Dentist, by laying out instruments, mixing restorative materials, and aspirating the patient's mouth. She may schedule appointments, and perform miscellaneous clerical duties.

EDUCATION, TRAINING, AND EXPERIENCE

Graduation from an accredited dental hygiene school, with license to practice in the state in which the hospital is located are required. There are two types of training available: a four-year college program, leading to a Bachelor of Science degree; and the more widely offered two-year program, leading to dental hygiene certification. Scholarships are available, and inquiry should be made to the American Dental Hygienist Association. There are no specific requirements for length of experience or training after licensing.

JOB RELATIONSHIPS

Workers supervised: None.
Supervised by: Dentist.
Promotion from: No formal line of promotion. May be promoted from Dental Assistant after additional formal training.
Promotion to: No formal line of promotion. Some hospitals employ a Dental Hygienist in a supervisory position, in which case promotion is through addition of administrative or supervisory duties.

PROFESSIONAL AFFILIATIONS

American Dental Hygienist Association
211 East Chicago Avenue
Chicago, Illinois 60611

Dental Hygienist: (DOT) 078.368-014

DENTAL LABORATORY TECHNICIAN

The Dental Laboratory Technician makes and repairs such dental restorations as dentures, crowns, bridges, and inlays. He works under the direction, or according to the prescription, of the Dentist. His work is extremely painstaking, and when well done is often as delicate as the most dainty sculpture.

He is a specialist in his own right, and his skill in the use of many instruments and techniques contributes significantly to the science of dentistry.

JOB DUTIES

When fabricating complete or partial dentures from the mouth impression, the Technician builds a wax bite rim and arranges selected artificial teeth in the wax, in proper relation to each other. He mounts the wax denture in articulate, and makes final adjustments by melting and working wax with hand instruments, and grinding high points of teeth with the lathe. He encases the wax denture in plaster, plastic, or other special material, melts out the wax, and injects a plastic compound into the cavity. After this has cured, he removes the denture from the plaster casing and finishes it by polishing and buffing to a natural luster. (Detailed methods and techniques of laboratories and technicians may vary.)

For bridges and partial dentures, the Technician works from plaster models and the Dentists' prescriptions. In these models, he must consider the stress placed upon them by the other teeth. He measures the supporting teeth with a dental surveyor, and determines the correct position of the clasp ends to insure proper fit and adequate retention.

Broken bridges, dentures, and other restorations are repaired by cutting away brokens parts with a knife, and grinding rough edges to a level. Missing portions of the prosthesis are constructed in the same manner as new dentures.

Metal crowns and inlays are cast in a centrifugal casting machine; gold is melted in a crucible with a gas blowtorch or other heating device, and driven into the mold by centrifugal force. Porcelain crowns may be mixed and shaped by hand and glazed in an oven. Wire bridge attachments are shaped by hand and soldered, using a blowtorch or Bunsen burner. All crown and bridge components are tested for occlusal harmony on the articulator, and assembled with the aid of solder and gas torch to form the fixed bridge.

Appliances for straightening teeth are constructed and repaired.

At specified points in the process, the denture may be returned to the Dentist for fitting, so that the final product will be comfortable and pleasing.

Some Dental-Laboratory Technicians are "generalists," who do all types of work necessary. Others specialize, doing only one or two procedures, such as a Dental Ceramist; Contour Wire Specialist, Crown and Bridge; Orthodontic Technician; or Bite-Block Man.

The laboratory in which the Technician works may be in a hospital, but more probably is a commercial, privately owned business, unless the hospital is related to a dental school and students are being trained in these skills.

EDUCATION, TRAINING, AND EXPERIENCE

The American Dental Association and the National Association of Certified Dental Laboratories have together developed training requirements leading to certification as Dental-Laboratory Technician either as generalist or specialist within a particular area. Usually one to two years' classroom training, plus three or four years of experience in a dental laboratory are needed before taking the exam for certification.

No other experience is required if worker has certification.

JOB RELATIONSHIPS

Workers supervised: Dental-Laboratory Assistant working toward certification.
Supervised by: Dentist or Chief Dental-Laboratory Technician.
Promotion from: No formal lines of promotion.
Promotion to: No formal lines of promotion.

PROFESSIONAL AFFILIATIONS

National Association of Certified Dental Laboratories, Inc.
1330 Massachusetts Avenue, NW.
Washington, D.C. 20005

American Dental Association
211 East Chicago Avenue
Chicago, Illinois 60611

There may be a union affiliation or local or state organization.

Dental-Laboratory Technician: (DOT) 712.381-014

Dietetic Department

The Dietetic Department of the hospital is responsible for preparation and serving of all meals. This includes general menus served to the majority of patients, food served to hospital personnel in the cafeteria, and special diets prescribed by physicians. Since adequate nutrition is a basic essential to good health, the role of the Dietetic Department is very important to patient care.

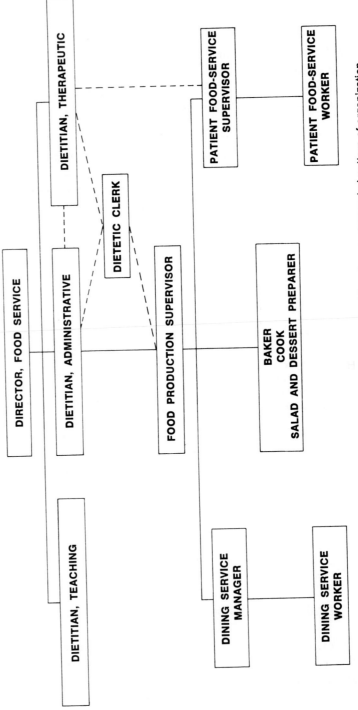

DIETETIC DEPARTMENT

NOTE: This chart is for illustrative purposes only and should not be considered a recommended pattern of organization.

The hospital Dietitian is trained to provide nutrition care to individuals and groups, and to apply the principles of management to planning and directing food service programs.

The Dietetic Department is organized as follows:

Within the framework of the hospital, dietitians also serve as advisors to clinic patients in the Outpatient Department, and may even give demonstrations of food preparation to groups of patients.

Frequently, dietitians are called upon to work as members of research teams, with physicians and other scientists. Dietitians who do this kind of work may also have faculty status if the hospital is associated with a school of medicine or nursing.

In addition to hospitals, dietitians find ready employment in industries, food processing companies, public health organizations, and schools. Discussion of some of these opportunities will be found in later presentation of Nutritionists and their work.

CHIEF DIETITIAN
Director, Food Service
Director, Dietetics

The Chief Dietitian, or Director of Food Service, has the overall responsibility for planning, directing, and coordinating the activities of the Dietetic Department to provide meals for both patients and hospital employees.

He establishes departmental regulations and procedures, and develops standards for organization and supervision of the service. He operates within the policies of the hospital administration, and, in coordination with the Administrative Dietitian, is responsible for hiring and training of personnel. He interviews and makes final selection of applicants, reviews work schedules for personnel, and rates job performance. He selects personnel for transfer, promotion, and special training, to insure the most effective use of individual skills of employees.

JOB DUTIES

The Chief Dietitian determines the quality and quantity of food required, plans menus, and controls food costs. She (or he) reviews regular diet menus as to cost and suitability to type of hospital, and standardized recipes for menu requirements. She makes frequent inspections of all work, storage, and serving areas to determine that regulations and directions governing dietetic activities are being followed. She recommends and institutes changes in techniques or procedures for more efficient operation.

She develops and implements policies and procedures governing handling and storage of supplies and equipment. She is also responsible for the proper sanitation of the premises and the maintenance of records and reports. She prepares job

A Dietetic Intern at the University of Wisconsin Center for Health Services talks to a young hospital patient about choosing nutritional foods.

descriptions, organization charts, manuals, and guidebooks for employees, covering all phases of departmental operation. She makes final determination of kinds and amounts of supplies and equipment needed.

She reviews records and reports covering kind and number of regular and therapeutic diets prepared, nutritional and caloric analysis of meals, costs of raw food and labor, computation of daily ration cost, inventory of equipment and supplies. She develops and directs the cost control system, and prepares and submits the department budget.

She confers with other department heads regarding technical and administrative aspects of the dietetic service. She establishes effective relationships with the medical staff, nurses, and other patient-care personnel. She attends hospital staff conferences in regard to new developments and trends.

She delegates authority to her supervisory staff for task details, to facilitate smooth flow of materials and services.

She attends professional meetings and conferences, to keep informed of current practices and trends in the fields of dietetics and nutrition. She may prepare articles for publication in professional journals, and lecture on various aspects of dietetic operations. She may discuss dietetic problems with patients or their families, and explain diet therapy for a specific case.

In smaller hospitals, the duties of Dietitian, Administrative Dietitian, and Therapeutic Dietitian may be combined.

A bachelor's or advanced degree from an accredited institution is required, with major in foods, nutrition, or food-service administration.

The Administrative Dietitian may have completed an internship in hospital offering dietetic internship approved by The American Dietetic Association or have met necessary experience requirements.

Varied experience in dietetics and administration is required.

JOB RELATIONSHIPS

Workers supervised: All employees assigned to the department.
Supervised by: Administrator or an Associate Administrator.
Promotion from: Dietitian, Administrative; Dietitian, Teaching; or Dietitian, Therapeutic.
Promotion to: No formal line of promotion. May be promoted to an Associate Administrator.

PROFESSIONAL AFFILIATIONS

American Society for Hospital Food Service Administrators
840 North Lake Shore Drive
Chicago, Illinois 60611

The American Dietetic Association
620 North Michigan Avenue
Chicago, Illinois 60611

Dietitian, Chief: (DOT) 077.118-010

DIETITIAN, TEACHING
Assistant Director, Dietetic Education

The Teaching Dietitian is responsible for the dietetic educational programs for nurses, medical and dental interns, dietetic interns, and other hospital personnel who need this instruction.

JOB DUTIES

The Teaching Dietitian plans schedules of instruction and on-the-job training. She may conduct classes in such subjects as nutrition, diet therapy, sanitation, infant nutrition, marketing, menu planning, food procurement, food cost control, and supervisory techniques. She arranges for additional lectures by the medical staff, teachers of dietetic subjects in colleges and universities, and members of professional associations. She supervises other dietitians in any training or teaching functions they may perform in connection with the program.

She may recommend and supervise procedures in orientation and on-the-job training of food-preparation and food-service workers; and institute orientation programs to acquaint employees with work assignments, schedules, and required performance standards.

She selects the textbooks and reference materials for the subjects to be presented in the classroom, and she prepares the course outlines. She prepares manuals and guidebooks for use in on-the-job training, and visual aids to supplement textbook information.

She requests literature on trends and practices in fields of dietetics and nutrition from accredited colleges, universities, and professional associations.

The Teaching Dietitian participates in meetings of professional associations.

In smaller hospitals, the duties of this job may be combined with those of Administrative Dietitian, Therapeutic Dietitian, or Food Service Director.

EDUCATION, TRAINING, AND EXPERIENCE

Both bachelor's and master's degrees from accredited institutions are required, with majors in foods, nutrition, or food service management. Completion of courses in methods and principles of teaching is also required.

The Teaching Dietitian may have completed an internship in a hospital that offers dietetic internship approved by the American Dietetic Association, or equivalent approved experience. At least one year of experience as an instructor in one or more phases of dietetics in a college or institution is preferred.

JOB RELATIONSHIPS

Workers supervised: All trainees and dietetic personnel who take part in training activities.
Supervised by: Director, Food Service.
Promotion from: No formal line of promotion. May be promoted from staff level position.
Promotion to: No formal line of promotion. May be promoted to Director, Food Service.

PROFESSIONAL AFFILIATIONS

The American Dietetic Association
620 North Michigan Avenue
Chicago, Illinois 60611

Dietitian, Teaching: (DOT) 077.128-014

DIETITIAN, ADMINISTRATIVE
Assistant Director, Food Service
Food Production Manager

The Administrative Dietitian works directly under the Chief Dietitian, and implements the policies and procedures that she sets. She directs and supervises the hospital personnel involved in planning, preparing, and serving the food to patients, staff, and visitors.

JOB DUTIES

The Administrative Dietitian plans basic menus, considering such factors as variety, season of the year, availability, known food preferences of the group to be served, nutritional and caloric content, and food costs. She estimates the number of people to be served, and computes quantity of food to be prepared, to insure that individual portions will be in conformity with dietetic standards. She prepares daily menus and portion specifications for the guidance of staff personnel, and inspects prepared food to insure adherence to specifications, observing the food's appearance, quantity, and temperature, and samples it for taste.

She develops and implements work standards, sanitation procedures, and personal hygiene requirements consistent with institutional rules, local, state and Federal regulations, and foodhandling principles. She inspects food preparation and serving areas, equipment, and storage facilities, observes the appearance and personal habits of the staff to detect deviations or violations of current health regulations, and orders corrective measures as necessary.

She prepares daily work schedules and assigns duties and responsibilities, through supervisors, to the staff. She employs the dietetic personnel; directs orientation and training; and initiates, recommends, and approves personnel transfers, promotions, and dismissals, according to procedures established by the hospital administration.

She is responsible for records and reports concerning technical and administrative operations, such as number of meals served, menus, analyses of diets, food costs, supplies issued, repairs to equipment, maintenance service and costs, and personnel data. She maintains a continuous inventory of supplies.

She may make suggestions as to revisions or adaptations of procedures for more efficient performance in the department, and for the training of employees.

She reviews technical publications, studies journals, and confers with food industry representatives concerning new developments in food packing and processing, new and modified equipment, and new nutritional concepts. She selects those with merit for possible incorporation into the hospital program.

Depending on the size and organization of the Dietetic Department, she may directly supervise food preparation personnel, and oversee the cooking, serving, and cleaning tasks. She may also supervise all dietetic personnel not specifically assigned to patient food-service or modified diet preparation. She may direct the employee food-service activity.

In smaller hospitals, the duties of the Director of Food Service or of Therapeutic Dietitian may be combined with this job.

EDUCATION, TRAINING, AND EXPERIENCE

A bachelor's or advanced degree from an accredited college or university is required, with major in foods, nutrition, or food-service administration.

The Administrative Dietitian may have completed a dietetic internship approved by The American Dietetic Association or have met necessary experience requirements.

Varied experience in dietetics and administration is required.

JOB RELATIONSHIPS

Workers supervised: All employees of food production unit.
Supervised by: Director, Food Service.
Promotion from: No formal line of promotion. May be promoted from staff level position.
Promotion to: Director, Food Service.

PROFESSIONAL AFFILIATIONS

American Society for Hospital Food Service Administrators
840 North Lake Shore Drive
Chicago, Illinois 60611

The American Dietetic Association
620 North Michigan Avenue
Chicago, Illinois 60611

Dietitian, Administrative: (DOT) 077.168-018

DIETITIAN, THERAPEUTIC
Assistant Director, Therapeutic Dietetics

The Therapeutic Dietitian specializes in the planning and preparation of diets for patients who have particular health care problems, such as diabetes, or high blood pressure; and for patients with temporary problems, such as immediate postoperative conditions.

The Therapeutic Dietitian has more contact with patients and their families than do other members of the dietetic staff, because she frequently must confer with them and their families to explain the necessary regimen, and be sure that they are capable of carrying it on after the patient is discharged. Frequently she has continuing contact with the patient, following his progress after he has gone home, and possibly seeing him on an outpatient basis. Often, once the patient is at home, he is tempted to eat what the family eats, and he needs supportive counseling to stay on his diet.

The Therapeutic Dietitian may also give part of her time to the Outpatient Clinic (or an additional Therapeutic Dietitian may be employed for this post), to instruct patients and groups of patients, on the elements of good nutrition. She may hold cooking demonstrations, to teach methods of food preparation, and may develop diet plans adapted to the ethnic or national diet preferences of the outpatients who come to the clinic.

The Therapeutic Dietitian is held in high regard by physicians. She must consult with them closely, and also with nurses, in setting up a meal plan for a patient that will meet all the conditions the doctor has prescribed and also meet the psychological needs of the patient. Many physicians know little about the fine points of nutrition, and must rely on the dietitian's expertise to fulfill their patients' needs.

JOB DUTIES

The Therapeutic Dietitian plans and directs preparation of modified diets prescribed by the medical staff for patients with therapeutic diet needs.

She receives medical orders for modified diets, and may interview patients to learn their food habits and preferences, so that she can plan their diets to fulfill medical requirements and still prove appetizing to the patient. She may be called upon to advise patients and their families on the types and quantities of food to be prepared for the patient at home, and instruct them in any necessary special techniques of preparation. She may initiate referral of specific patients to a community agency for followup, subject to the physician's approval.

In the hospital kitchen, she must instruct personnel as to the type and quantity of food to be prepared, and techniques to be used. She may inspect the meal assembly, to see that trays conform to the prescribed diets, and meet standards and directions as to quality, quantity, temperature, and appearance.

She is responsible for records and reports concerning technical and administrative operations, such as number of meals served, menus, analyses of modified diets, and food costs.

In smaller hospitals, the duties of this job may be combined with those of the Administrative Dietitian, or the Director of Food Service.

EDUCATION, TRAINING, AND EXPERIENCE

A bachelor's or advanced degree from an accredited institution is required, with a major in foods and nutrition.

The Therapeutic Dietitian may have completed an internship in a hospital that offers a dietetic internship approved by the American Dietetic Association, or have had equivalent approved experience.

JOB RELATIONSHIPS

Workers supervised: All employees of therapeutic or modified diet unit.
Supervised by: Director, Food Service.
Promotion from: No formal line of promotion. May be promoted from a staff level position.
Promotion to: No formal line of promotion. May be promoted to Director, Food Service.

PROFESSIONAL AFFILIATIONS

The American Dietetic Association
620 North Michigan Avenue
Chicago, Illinois 60611

Dietitian, Therapeutic: (DOT) 077.128-018

DIETETIC CLERK
Storeroom Clerk

The Dietetic Clerk performs a variety of clerical duties for the Dietetic Department. Although requirements in terms of education are low, he must be responsible for many details that facilitate the operation of the department.

JOB DUTIES

The Dietetic Clerk compiles dietetic information for use by kitchen personnel in preparation of food. He examines diet orders received and tallies portions and kinds of foods for each type of diet (regular or modified). He marks amount of tally on master menu, to inform kitchen personnel of food requirements. He processes new diets and changes as required. He may enter diet changes in patient's medical records.

He keeps records of, and prepares reports on, perpetual inventory, food purchases, total meals served, food costs, and equipment purchases. He may also be required to maintain files on the department personnel with regard to their respective duties and responsibilities.

He keeps the kitchen supply room in orderly condition. He may inventory supplies and equipment, and type requisitions to replenish supplies. He verifies invoices of goods received and reports discrepancies to his supervisor.

EDUCATION, TRAINING, AND EXPERIENCE

A high school diploma is required, and courses in bookkeeping and typing are desirable.

Usually, one year of experience in clerical work is required, though some employers may accept a substitute of one year of business school education in lieu of experience.

On-the-job training of about one month's duration is provided.

JOB RELATIONSHIPS

Workers supervised: None.
Supervised by: Dietitian, Administrative or Dietitian, Therapeutic.
Promotion from: No formal line of promotion. This may be an entry job.
Promotion to: No formal line of promotion.

PROFESSIONAL AFFILIATIONS

None.

Diet Clerk: (DOT) 079.588-010

FOOD PRODUCTION SUPERVISOR
Chef
Chief Cook
First Cook
Head Cook

The Food Production Supervisor oversees and coordinates the activities of kitchen workers in preparation and cooking of food for the hospital patients, staff, and visitors.

JOB DUTIES

He plans, or participates in planning, menus and utilization of foodstuffs and leftovers, taking into consideration the number and types of meals to be served and marketing conditions. He estimates goods consumption and requirements, to determine type and quantity of meats, vegetables, and other food to be prepared. He supervises cooking personnel, and coordinates their assignments to insure economical and timely food preparation. He reviews menus, and determines food quantities, labor, and overhead costs in cooperation with the Administrative Dietitian. He observes methods of food preparation, cooking, and sizes of portions, to insure food is prepared and served in the prescribed manner. He tests cooked foods by tasting and smelling. He may develop and standardize recipes.

He may inspect trays for attractiveness, palatability, and temperature of food.

He inspects purchased foods for standards of quality.

He may train new food service employees. He keeps records of work assignments and hours worked by personnel under his supervision.

EDUCATION, TRAINING, AND EXPERIENCE

A high school diploma is required. It is desirable that the applicants have completed a special one-year course including such subjects as sanitation, hygiene, quantity food preparation, supervisory techniques, estimating requirements, purchasing food, and managing kitchen and storeroom.

JOB RELATIONSHIPS

Workers supervised: Employees concerned with preparation of food.
Supervised by: Dietitian, Administrative or Dietitian, Therapeutic.
Promotion from: Cook or Baker.
Promotion to: No formal line of promotion.

PROFESSIONAL AFFILIATIONS

None.

Executive Chef: (DOT) 313.168

Kitchen Supervisor: (DOT) 310.138

COOK

The Cook prepares, seasons, and cooks food for hospital patients, employees, staff and visitors.

JOB DUTIES

The Cook reviews menus and work orders to determine type and quantities of meats, vegetables, soups, salads, and desserts to be prepared. He plans cooking schedule so that foods will be ready at specified times. He confers with the Food Production Supervisor or Dietitian regarding modified diet preparation and use of leftovers. He procures foodstuffs from refrigerator, freezer, or other storage areas, or requests other workers to perform this task. He cuts and trims meat and fowl.

He prepares or supervises the washing, trimming, cooking, and seasoning of food items. He measures and mixes ingredients according to recipes, using a variety of kitchen utensils and equipment, such as blenders, mixers, grinders, slicers, and tenderizers. He makes sauces, soups, stews, casseroles, and desserts. He bakes, broils, roasts, and steams meats, fish, vegetables and other foods. He observes and tastes food being cooked, and adds ingredients to season or improve texture. He tastes food being cooked, and adds ingredients to season or improve palatibility. He He adjusts heat controls and timers on stoves, ovens, steam kettles, and grills. He also prepares cold meats, sandwiches, griddle cakes, cooked cereals, and beverages.

He carves portions of meat, fish, and fowl for individual servings, and prepares or directs distribution of food to serving units. He apportions servings in accordance with orders for patients.

He inspects food and meats in storage, and directs sanitary maintenance of storage rooms and units, stoves, work tables, and equipment, using his knowledge to spot indications of the presence of vermin, insects, mold, and the appearance of deterioration of foodstuffs. He suggests menu or recipe changes so that food will be used before spoilage.

He may estimate food needs and requisition supplies.

He may be designated according to the food items he cooks, as Meat Cook, Pastry Cook, or Modified Diet Cook. He may also have an assistant or helper.

EDUCATION, TRAINING, AND EXPERIENCE

The Cook must be a high school graduate, although graduation from a formal technical school specializing in hotel or institutional cooking may be substituted if the worker has the required experience.

The experience required is one to four years in hospital, institutional, or restaurant cooking.

JOB RELATIONSHIPS

Workers supervised: Workers assigned to cooking duties.
Supervised by: Food Production Supervisor.
Promotion from: Patient Food-Service Worker.
Promotion to: Food Production Supervisor.

PROFESSIONAL AFFILIATIONS

None.

Cook: (DOT) 313.381-018

Baker: (DOT) 313.781-010

Pantryman: (DOT) 317.884-014

Kitchen Helper: (DOT) 318.887-010

The Dietetic Department of the hospital prepares food for the employees' cafeteria as well as for service to patients. *Photo courtesy of New York State Health Department*

DINING SERVICE MANAGER
Cafeteria Food-Service Supervisor
Counter Service Manager
Manager, Cafeteria

The Dining Service Manager supervises and coordinates the activities of dietetic personnel who serve meals in a cafeteria, dining room, or coffee shop.

JOB DUTIES

He assigns tasks to employees, and arranges work schedules. He sees that service is prompt and courteous, and makes adjustments following complaints.

He directs the setup of tables in the dining room, and the preparation and serving of food for regular and special luncheons and dinners. He inspects the cafeteria, dining room, coffee shop, and equipment for cleanliness.

He interviews and recommends employment of new workers, assigns them to various duties, and instructs them in work procedures. He maintains a record of meals served. He keeps cost records, and makes periodic reports of operating expenses. He orders food, supplies, and equipment, and assists in menu planning.

EDUCATION, TRAINING, AND EXPERIENCE

The Dining Service Manager should have graduated from high school, and some college education is desirable. Courses in foods and nutrition, and personnel management or supervisory training are also desirable.

Six months to one year of supervisory experience in a hospital department of dietetics, as manager of a cafeteria, or in the dining room of a hotel or restaurant is usually required. On-the-job training varies from one to three months, to learn policies and procedures of the hospital.

JOB RELATIONSHIPS

Workers supervised: All workers engaged in serving meals in the cafeteria, dining room, or coffee shop.
Supervised by: Food Production Supervisor or Dietitian, Administrative.
Promotion from: Qualified worker in the department.
Promotion to: No formal line of promotion.

PROFESSIONAL AFFILIATIONS

None.

Food-Service Supervisor: (DOT) 319.138-010

Dining Service Worker: (DOT) 311.—T

PATIENT FOOD-SERVICE SUPERVISOR
Kitchen Steward
Patient Tray-Line Supervisor
Sanitation Supervisor

The Patient Food-Service Supervisor trains and supervises the personnel who serve trays to patients. She maintains the cleanliness of food service areas and equipment, and otherwise assists the Therapeutic Dietitian, as directed.

JOB DUTIES

She instructs workers in methods of performing their duties, and assigns and coordinates the work of employees, to promote efficiency.

She observes filled trays, to assure that foods are properly apportioned, and attractively garnished, and arranged on trays properly. She directs workers in loading trays on carts or in automatic conveyor units, for dispatch to nursing stations, and in serving food trays to patients.

She interviews and recommends employment of new workers. She may visit patients, to learn of food preferences. She calculates routine modified diets.

EDUCATION, TRAINING, AND EXPERIENCE

High school graduation is preferred. Some college education is desirable. Courses in foods, nutrition, and personnel management, or supervisory training are desirable.

The Patient Food-Service Supervisor inspects trays that are to be served to patients in their rooms, and checks the temperature of the food.
Photo courtesy New York Health Department

The worker should have six months to one year of supervisory experience in a hospital food preparation unit.

One to three months' on-the-job training is provided to learn policies and procedures of the establishment.

JOB RELATIONSHIPS

Workers supervised: Patient Food-Service Workers.
Supervised by: Food Production Supervisor or Therapeutic Dietitian.
Promotion from: Patient Food-Service Worker.
Promotion to: No formal line of promotion.

PROFESSIONAL AFFILIATIONS

None.

Food-Service Supervisor: (DOT) 319.138-010

Medical Library

Medical libraries are of vital importance in quality medical care, because they are sources of information for every physician who is confronted by a difficult case. There he can discover the experience of other physicians all over the world who have encountered similar cases, along with descriptions of the most efficient techniques for establishing diagnosis, and the latest methods of treatment.

Medical libraries are maintained by all medical, dental, nursing, pharmacy, and veterinary schools; by pharmaceutical houses; research centers; public health laboratories; medical societies; and hospitals. The largest is the National Library of Medicine, which is associated with the office of the Surgeon General, in Washington, D.C., and which contains 125,000,000 volumes. The smallest may be 5,000 volumes or less, but the majority of medical libraries contain 20,000 to 75,000 volumes.

However, the number of books in a medical library is only the beginning of its measure. An up-to-date library also contains vast resources in medical and scientific journals and periodicals from every part of the world, monographs, rare books and manuscripts, and an assortment of audiovisual aids. Journals and periodicals in particular are of tremendous value to the clinician in securing the most contemporary information.

A hospital library is likely to include a separate category of books for use by patients, including current titles of general interest. Patients may never see the inside of the actual library, but make their selections from book carts that make the rounds of their rooms.

In a small library, the Medical Librarian may work virtually alone, ordering, receiving, classifying, indexing, storing, and dispensing its contents.

In large libraries, an extensive Medical Library Department is required, to augment basic services with such responsibilities as preparing bibliographies, abstracts, reviews, and excerpts of medical literature; translating foreign articles and journals; microfilming technical journals and manuscripts; using data processing equipment to index, organize, catalog, and classify the wide variety of information that must be stored; binding and repairing books; maintaining and circulating tapes, records, films, slides, and audiovisual equipment.

The library provides reading rooms, a lending service, and possibly a service by mail; and an interlibrary loan service for staff members, residents, interns, nurses, technicians, and students. If it is a large library, it may be open to the public, or have a subscription membership program that extends its services to science writers, other professionals such as lawyers, teachers, or architects, and industries, organizations, or research groups that are in need of medical information.

The Medical Library Department in a large hospital is directed by a Medical Librarian, who reports directly to the hospital administration. The hospital probably will also have a Library Committee, composed of members of the medical staff and interested members of its Board of Trustees or other governing body. In a small hospital, the Medical Record Librarian may also have responsibility for the library.

Standards for medical libraries are set by the Joint Commission on Accreditation of Hospitals of the American Hospital Association.

Large medical libraries may be divided into units, and Librarians may be assigned to concentrate on ordering, cataloging, reference and bibliography, historical and rare book collections, administration, machine data processing, or other specific activities.

Translators, abstractors, indexers, and audiovisual experts who are not neces-

MEDICAL LIBRARY DEPARTMENT

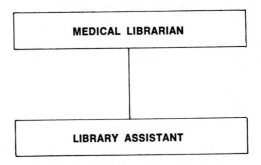

NOTE: This chart is for illustrative purposes only and should not be considered a recommended pattern of organization.

sarily librarians, but who specialize in medicine and science, may also be members of the library staff. If the library's storage and retrieval system is computerized, there will be personnel skilled in these processes. There may be microfilm experts. No generalizations can be made as to the job classification requirements of these workers.

MEDICAL LIBRARIAN

Career opportunities for medical librarians are practically unlimited, and advancement can be as rapid as the abilities of the worker justify.

Due to the rapid expansion of the medical field, and increase in number of new medical schools, there is a shortage of trained medical librarians, not only in the United States but in other countries. Salaries compare favorably with those of other professions, from the entry level to top positions.

The Medical Librarian is the specialist who bridges the gap between the scientist or student and the information he seeks. The places in which she works are more than ordinarily pleasant, and the clientele she serves more than ordinarily interesting.

In academic libraries the librarian may be accorded faculty status and privileges, and may have teaching responsibilities, particularly in regard to the use of the library and its resources and services.

JOB DUTIES

The Medical Librarian administers and maintains a hospital or other medical library, containing books, reports, journals, and bibliographic tools for use of physicians, staff, students, and other concerned persons.

She selects or assists in selecting books for purchase, and subscribes to pertinent periodicals. She assists physicians in searching the required references in the literature, compiles accession lists, and annotates or abstracts materials. She arranges special collections of books, periodicals, manufacturers' catalogs and specifications, film strips, motion pictures, microcards, and journal reprints.

She classifies, catalogs, and indexes textbooks, journals, and monographs. She establishes and maintains a card file. She examines all new books and classifies them. She assigns classification numbers to all printed materials, so that they can be found easily. She prints numerals and letters on books and other printed materials in accordance with the accepted system, and arranges them in order on the shelves.

She issues books and other materials to readers on request, checks out materials, and keeps pertinent records.

She assists readers in finding materials, by demonstrating the use of the catalog, and suggesting specific sources of information.

She contacts borrowers to retrieve overdue books, so that they will be available to others who may need them.

She contacts other libraries to find materials that are needed and are not available in the hospital's medical library.

She assists members of the staff and students by answering requests for information, and by preparing bibliographies, translations, abstracts, and reviews that are needed for lectures, articles for medical journals, theses, and classroom projects. She assists, and acts as consultant to, instructors, student nurses, and others who use the library facilities in conjunction with courses. She instructs new students on how to use the library, its rules, contents, and in particular the use of the catalog and other reference materials.

She examines pertinent books, and writes and posts reviews of them.

She may be a member of a hospital committee to determine library needs and policies for smooth operation.

If the library includes a section of general books and periodicals for loan to patients, she assumes responsibility for this as well, and may occasionally make patient rounds, to discover what materials will be of greatest interest to patients.

EDUCATION, TRAINING, AND EXPERIENCE

The Medical Librarian must have graduated from a college or university with a Bachelor of Arts, Bachelor of Science, or Bachelor of Science in Library Science degree, and completed graduate work in library science leading to a Master of Library Science degree. Majors may be in biological sciences, behavioral sciences, the humanities, or physical sciences.

Because many professional periodicals that are of value come from other than English-speaking countries, it is an advantage for the Medical Librarian to have as much fluency as possible in foreign languages, particularly French and German.

The Medical Library Association grants certificates for (1) completion of five years of professional experience; or (2) completion of an approved course of instruction plus six months' supervised experience in a medical library in addition to an advanced degree in library science; or (3) completion of examination given at the discretion of the Subcommittee on Certification.

Federal grants and loans are available to assist the student working toward a library degree, and many state and local organizations and library schools offer programs of assistance. Full or part-time scholarships are offered by the Medical Library Association and the Special Libraries Association. There are also ample opportunities for students to work in medical libraries while they are in school.

JOB RELATIONSHIPS

Workers supervised: Library Assistant and clerical workers.
Supervised by: Associate Administrator.
Promotion from: No formal line of promotion. Employees are usually recruited from outside.
Promotion to: No formal line of promotion.

PROFESSIONAL AFFILIATIONS

Medical Library Association, Inc.
919 North Michigan Avenue
Chicago, Illinois 60611

American Library Association
50 East Huron Street
Chicago, Illinois 60611

Librarian, Reference Library: (DOT) 100.168-030

LIBRARY ASSISTANT

The scope of this job classification is such that some employers require graduation from a college or university with a Bachelor of Arts, Bachelor of Science, or Bachelor of Science in Library Science degree, while others require only high school graduation and on-the-job training for six months to a year. Whatever the requirements, the Library Assistant's job is only an entry to a career as Medical Librarian, toward which generous scholarships are available, as are opportunities for students to do part-time work in the library while they are in school.

The responsibilities of the Library Assistant are largely routine, and are performed under the supervision and at the direction of the Medical Librarian. Nevertheless, the position offers very pleasant working conditions and personal associations, and is an excellent training ground for later, more professional, status.

JOB DUTIES

The Library Assistant compiles records; sorts and shelves books, reports, and journals; issues and receives medical library materials such as books, films, and recordings.

She issues books on loan to the hospital staff and students. She records the identifying data (by hand or by photographic equipment) of the loaned books and notes the dates that they are due. She inspects returned books for damage, verifies due dates, and computes and receives overdue fines. She reviews records to compile list of overdue books, and issues overdue notices to the borrowers.

She sorts books, publications, and other items according to classification code, and returns them to shelves, files, or other designated storage area. She files cards in catalog drawers.

She locates books and publications for patrons.

She issues borrower's identification card according to established procedures.

She repairs books, using mending tape, paste, and brush.

She answers inquiries of a routine nature on the telephone or in person, and refers requests for professional or technical assistance to the Medical Librarian. She may be required to type various types of material on special library cards and also be delegated the responsibility of preparing duty schedule for other personnel.

EDUCATION, TRAINING, AND EXPERIENCE

All employers prefer one to two years of library experience as a prerequisite to hiring. Beyond that, requirements vary from a high school diploma to graduation from college or university with a Bachelor of Arts, Bachelor of Science, or Bachelor of Science in Library Science degree.

JOB RELATIONSHIPS

Workers supervised: None.
Supervised by: Medical Librarian.
Promotion from: No formal line of promotion. This may be an entry job.
Promotion to: With additional academic training and considerable experience may be promoted to Medical Librarian.

PROFESSIONAL AFFILIATIONS

Medical Library Association, Inc.
919 North Michigan Avenue
Chicago, Illinois 60611

American Library Association
50 East Huron Street
Chicago, Illinois 60611

Library Assistant: (DOT) 249.368-050

Medical Record Library personnel are responsible for gathering together all reports pertinent to the treatment of every patient from each member of the medical staff who took part in the patient's care. These are coordinated and placed on permanent file in the Library.

Photo courtesy of the American Medical Record Association

Medical Records

The Medical Records Department provides a central file for the complete written case histories of all patients seen at the hospital's clinics or admitted to the hospital.

The importance of detail and accuracy in these records is readily apparent in terms of their use: Reference to them facilitates diagnosis and treatment of patients in any future illness. They are valuable in evaluating methods of treatment; in instruction of medical, nursing, and related personnel; and in planning community health programs, hospital and health care administration; and as elements in research on specific conditions. They are also considered valid as evidence in legal actions and insurance claims.

Each patient's record includes identification data, chief complaint on presentation, past medical history, review of medical records forwarded from another hospital if the patient was transferred, his family medical history, history of the present illness, results of physical examination on admission, and provisional diagnosis. These are followed by reports of consultations; clinical laboratory, pathology, X-ray, and any other test reports. The medical and/or surgical treatment of the case is delineated, complete with all physicians' orders, nurses' graphic charts, medication administered, periodic checks of vital signs, results of routine periodic laboratory tests, and progress notes. All significant items from the patient's continuous chart are entered. The final diagnosis and condition of the patient at time of discharge, as well as any followup notes, are reported. If the patient did not survive, report at autopsy is included, if one was performed.

As soon as the department receives medical records, a quantitative analysis is made, and if anything seems to be missing, a responsible physician or department head is asked to complete them. A review is also made of clinical records accompanying a patient in transfer from another hospital; if there are omissions, the department initiates action to obtain the missing data.

Because records must be easily understandable in any hospital, and interchangeable in filing systems, terminology for diseases and operations is standardized, as is the system of indexing. The patients' index is basic, in which records are filed alphabetically by patients' names. However, each patient also has an index number, which is cross-indexed in a variety of other categories, so that at any time the hospital can lay hand on a complete file of patients who had any single disease, any type of operation, or were attended by any one physician or surgeon.

The Medical Records Department makes a daily census report of patients, as well as monthly and annual statistical reports of services to patients, which assist the staff in evaluating and improving the professional work of the hospital.

The department may make group studies of diseases, and collect scientific data from literature for use by the medical staff. And, since medical records are often called for in certain legal actions, especially those in which defense of a physician's or the hospital's conduct of a case is relevant, the Medical Records Librarian may occasionally have to present this evidence in court.

The department maintains close relationships with the medical staff and that of the Nursing Services Department; and it works closely with related health groups, particularly local public health units, to which it provides statistical information, records, and reports.

Standards for medical records departments are set by the Commission on Accreditation of Hospitals of the American Hospital Association, or the Committee on Hospitals of the Bureau of Professional Education of the American Osteopathic Association. Among their rules are the requirements that, except in emergencies, complete to-date information on a patient must be recorded before surgery is undertaken; and that no medical record is complete until signed by the attending physician.

Authority and responsibility for proper functioning of the Medical Records Department are delegated to the Medical Record Librarian, who reports to an Associate Administrator of the hospital. She should be registered by the American Association of Medical Record Librarians, and qualified to use the professional designation of Registered Record Librarian (RRL). Her staff may be very small, or consist of a full complement of assistant librarians, clerical workers, medical stenographers, and—if the hospital uses data processing and computer equipment for storage and retrieval—computer technicians.

It is recommended that hospitals unable to employ a full-time Medical Record Librarian obtain the part-time services of an RRL as consultant.

MEDICAL RECORDS DEPARTMENT

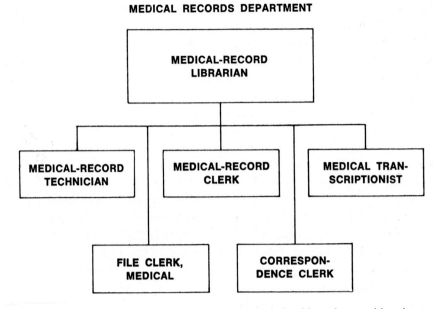

NOTE: This chart is for illustrative purposes only and should not be considered a recommended pattern of organization.

MEDICAL RECORD LIBRARIAN

Medical Record Librarians are responsible for the acquisition, analysis, storage, and retrieval of the complete, permanent, written case histories of every patient treated in the hospital and its clinics.

These records, which provide a vital medical profile of each patient's unique medical history, are extremely valuable to the patient, the community, the hospital administration and the professional members of its medical staff, and to medical researchers. The patient may need the information his record contains to expedite diagnosis and treatment in the event of future illness, and as verification of insurance claims, or evidence in legal actions. Public health officials and community planning groups need the information in order to plan wisely for community health care. The hospital administration also needs the statistics extrapolated from records to aid future planning, while the medical staff relies on the accumulation of data in records as a basis for evaluating techniques of diagnosis and treatment. The permanence of records makes it possible for research scientists to compare the effectiveness of new methods against those previously used; and the standardization of terminology in records allows valid comparison of series of studies on the same subject made in different institutions, or even in different countries.

In short, realization of the hospital's full potential in health care, and its contribution to the advancement of medical science, depend to a considerable extent upon the accuracy and thoroughness with which the Medical Records Department does its work.

The key individual in this department is the Administrator, who should be a

Many hospitals and other health care facilities use some form of automation for storage and retrieval of medical records. A number of large institutions use computerized systems. A common method is storage on microfilm, which allows Librarians to recover important data quickly in an emergency.

Photo courtesy of the American Medical Record Association

Registered Record Librarian. The need for personnel trained in this capacity is urgent. In more than 30,000 United States hospitals and other medical installations that need one or more medical record personnel, there are fewer than 5,000 Registered Record Administrators, and only about 4,000 Accredited Record Technicians. Salary ranges compare favorably with positions in other professions requiring equivalent training.

Job opportunities exist in clinics, neighborhood health centers, medical research organizations, health departments, nursing homes, and government agencies, as well as hospitals.

Important qualities in a Medical Record Administrator are orderliness, accuracy, and precision. Poise and patience are assets, since the duties involve working with very busy physicians, and occasionally with worried patients and their families. The obligation to keep medical records confidential requires a strong sense of discretion, and integrity.

In large institutions, the head of the Medical Records Department may have a staff that includes other Registered Record Librarians, Medical Record Technicians, Medical Record Clerks, Medical Transcriptionists, and Medical Secretaries. In small hospitals, one person may constitute the entire staff, and perhaps carry out the duties of the Medical Librarian as well. Several small hospitals in a vicinity may attain the quality of service they need by sharing a qualified administrator.

JOB DUTIES

The Medical Record Librarian who acts as Administrator coordinates the activities of personnel engaged in analyzing, compiling, coding, indexing, and filing permanent medical records of patients. She assists the medical staff in research. She prepares periodic statistical reports, and provides information to authorized persons.

She reviews records for completeness, accuracy, and conformity with accepted hospital accreditation standards of the Joint Commission on Accreditation of Hospitals of the American Hospital Association. If there is any discrepancy or omission in the record, she seeks out the attending physician, surgeon, or other responsible authority for rectification.

She brings unusual or interesting material to the attention of the medical staff, and assists in planning monthly conferences and conducting research studies.

She selects and tabulates data from patients' charts as requested by proper authorities, transcribes notes and reports, and searches bibliographies to assist in completion of research projects. She provides guidance in preparation of the final document according to requirements for conference or publication.

She prepares periodic reports on such subjects as morbidity, birth and death rates; analysis of utilization of hospital beds according to professional services and percentage of beds occupied; outpatient services rendered; and related data. She compiles statistical reports, such as analyses of types of surgery performed; types of diseases treated; and types of cases receiving special forms of therapy. In all of these tasks, she utilizes her knowledge of medical terminology, embracing accepted nomenclature and classification of diseases and operations.

She answers properly authorized inquiries for information contained in patients' charts by correspondence or telephone. On occasion, she represents the hospital in court cases involving subpoena of medical or clinical records, using her knowledge of principles of medical jurisprudence and the laws of the state governing use of clinical records in court actions.

She arranges for the training of department personnel in indexing and filing, preparation and arrangement of medical information, medical terminology, nomenclature, and classification of diseases. She outlines medical records, methods and procedures, and instructs personnel in medical ethics, hospital organization and management, and policies and practices. In a teaching hospital, she participates in teaching interns, by giving lectures in nomenclature, classification of diseases, and uses of records.

She performs related administrative duties, such as preparing budgets for the department; designing systems and methods to make data more accessible, and work sheets to adapt methods for compilation of data to the needs of the hospital; and selecting office equipment and supplies to be purchased.

She may serve as librarian for the hospital medical library.

EDUCATION, TRAINING, AND EXPERIENCE

Qualification as a Medical Record Librarian requires high school graduation, plus a four-year course in an approved college, leading to a bachelor's degree in Medical Record Library Science; or a two-year (60 semester hours) course in an approved college of liberal arts and sciences, plus a one-year approved hospital course in Medical Record Library Science. Registration entails passing an examination given by the American Association of Medical Record Librarians.

At present there are 29 schools for Medical Record Librarians approved by the American Medical Association. In addition to scholarships that are available from them, and other student loan programs, the Foundation of Record Education of the American Medical Records Association offers loans to students who have been accepted in approved programs.

JOB RELATIONSHIPS

Workers supervised: All personnel assigned to the department.
Supervised by: Administrator or an Associate Administrator.
Promotion from: No formal line of promotion.
Promotion to: No formal line of promotion. Some hospitals employ several levels of Medical Record Librarians and promotion is from lower to higher level through addition of administrative and supervisory duties.

PROFESSIONAL AFFILIATIONS

American Association of Medical Record Librarians
211 East Chicago Avenue
Chicago, Illinois 60611

Foundation of Record Education
American Medical Record Association
875 North Michigan Avenue, Suite 1850
Chicago, Illinois 60611

State and local organization.

Medical Record Librarian: (DOT) 100.388-018

MEDICAL RECORD TECHNICIAN
Chart Analysis Clerk
Coding Clerk

Without accurate, comprehensive medical records, much of the effectiveness of modern health care would be sacrificed. These permanent records—which furnish a medical profile of every patient treated—give the patient's doctor valuable information the next time he is ill; they provide his present doctor with a means for evaluating the benefits of a given treatment by allowing him to compare a series of patients who received it against a series of patients who did not; they aid the hospital administrator in laying future plans for the hospital; they aid community health groups in judging the needs in public health; and they furnish the basis for research projects by providing accumulations of similar cases from which judgments can be made.

The Medical Record Technician is an important member of the health care team, in that it is her work that makes all of the necessary information available permanently, and she can retrieve any part of it, or combinations of it, instantly. Her task is professional in the truest sense. Like physicians and nurses, she is entrusted with confidential information, which she must process efficiently and discreetly.

In the ideal medical records department, the Medical Record Technician works under the supervision of a Medical Record Librarian or Medical Record Administrator. Due to the critical shortage of trained medical record personnel, however, she often has the entire responsibility of the department in a small hospital, clinic, or nursing home.

There are few fields, in or out of health care, that offer as much long-term security and opportunity for rapid advancement as does work in medical records. Personnel is needed everywhere, and the young person who enters this field finds much encouragement, including financial assistance, to continue her training and improve her skills.

JOB DUTIES

In a small institution, the Medical Record Technician may perform many of the duties outlined in the job description of the Medical Record Librarian.

In larger departments, she prepares statistical reports, codes diseases and operations according to accepted classifications, maintains indexes according to established plans and procedures, and answers requests for medical information when they are made on proper authority.

She reviews the reports submitted by physicians and surgeons on methods of treatment they have used for a given case, or the surgery that was performed. The Medical Record Technician codes these according to the International Classification of Diseases and Operations, for the purpose of indexing them. When she has finished indexing and cross-indexing, a single case will be filed under several headings, such as the disease suffered, method of treatment, type of surgery, if any, and other distinctions. By this means, when a public health official wants to know how many cases of pneumonia have been hospitalized in the past month, or a physician wants to see all the cases of a certain type of cancer that the hospital has treated in the last ten years, or the hospital administrator wants to know what percentage of hospital beds are occupied by overflow from the Pediatric Service, the information is readily retrievable.

She may do her own typing and filing, or she may supervise the filing area and Medical Record Clerks who do this work, and train new employees.

She may be called upon to record the minutes of medical staff committees.

In the absence of a Medical Record Librarian or Administrator, she may be called upon to represent the hospital in court actions when medical records are subpoenaed, and testify regarding information in the records, according to hospital policy and state laws governing release of medical information.

EDUCATION, TRAINING, AND EXPERIENCE

High school graduation is required, plus graduation from an accredited school for Medical Record Technicians conducted by the hospital (a nine-month course), or successful completion of the appropriate correspondence course conducted by the American Association of Medical Record Librarians.

For accreditation, one or two years of junior college and hospital training in the technical aspects of the functions performed in the medical record department are required; that, plus successful examination, establishes eligibility for the designation Accredited Record Technician (ART).

Scholarship funds are available from schools, and student loans from the Foundation of Record Education of the American Medical Record Association.

JOB RELATIONSHIPS

Workers supervised: May supervise file clerks and Medical Record Clerk.
Supervised by: Medical Record Librarian.
Promotion from: No formal line of promotion.
Promotion to: No formal line of promotion. Some hospitals employ several levels of Medical Record Technicians and promotion is from lower to higher level through addition of administrative and supervisory duties.

PROFESSIONAL AFFILIATIONS

American Association of Medical Record Librarians
211 East Chicago Avenue
Chicago, Illinois 60611

Foundation of Record Education
American Medical Records Association
875 North Michigan Avenue—Suite 1850
Chicago, Illinois 60611

Medical Record Technician: (DOT) 249.388-033

MEDICAL RECORD CLERK
JOB DUTIES

The Medical Record Clerk assembles medical records—the various parts of which originate in different sections of the hospital—after each patient has been discharged. He reviews the records for completeness, and compiles data from them for periodic and statistical reports.

He assembles the content of the medical record into established order, for permanent filing. He reviews inpatient and emergency room records, to insure that required reports and signatures are included. He notes any deficiencies which must be corrected by the physician or other professional staff.

He insures receipt of all records of patients discharged from the hospital by checking the list of discharged patients daily. He corrects daily census reports if there are errors on the discharge listing.

He maintains surveillance of incomplete records, and prepares reports of delinquent physicians; he follows up until records are completed and received.

He compiles periodic and statistical reports from records and other data, such as census reports, and discharge service analysis.

He may assist with coding. He records diagnosis and operations on specified forms for use in completing hospital insurance billing forms. He may prepare and process birth certificates.

EDUCATION, TRAINING, AND EXPERIENCE

High school graduation with commercial course, including courses in typing, filing, office methods, and business English is required.

Related office experience may be substituted for one to two months' on-the-job training.

Three to six months' on-the-job training to become familiar with hospital record-keeping system and to comprehend pertinent medical terminology is required.

JOB RELATIONSHIPS

Workers supervised: None.
Supervised by: Medical Record Librarian.
Promotion from: No formal line of promotion. This may be an entry job.
Promotion to: No formal line of promotion. If hospital is large enough, may be promoted to a Section Superivsor.

PROFESSIONAL AFFILIATIONS

None.

Medical Record Clerk: (DOT) 249.388-034

MEDICAL TRANSCRIPTIONIST
JOB DUTIES

The Medical Transcriptionist transcribes medical reports on diagnostic workups, therapeutic procedures, and clinical records for inclusion in medical records and for transmission to physicians or other medical care facilities.

Her skills are welcomed in extended care facilities, nursing homes, research organizations, pharmaceutical firms, and government agencies as well as hospitals.

Among her accomplishments is sufficient familiarity with medical terminology and abbreviations that she can take much of her copy from dictaphone belts and spell medical words correctly.

JOB DUTIES

The Medical Transcriptionist operates a transcribing machine through the use of dials and pedals to control the quality of voice reproduction and speed of dictation, and uses ear devices to listen. She follows prescribed procedures for the use of various forms with one or more carbon copies in typing particular reports. She follows specified procedures for dispatching finished reports to designated persons for signature and approval of dictator, and for dispatching carbon copies to designated persons and offices.

She is responsible for verifying the accuracy of the dictator in identifying the patient by name, hospital number, location in the hospital, and any address that may involve the use of patient name files. She makes entries on prescribed control forms in regard to which report was transcribed for a particular patient, dates the dictation was received and transcribed, and name of the dictator.

Job performance may involve the use of electric or manual typewriter, as well as disk, belt, or tape-driven dictating and transcribing equipment.

EDUCATION, TRAINING, AND EXPERIENCE

High school graduation with business courses that include typing, business English, and office procedures is required, plus on-the-job training in medical terminology, anatomy, and use of reference texts; or completion of an approved vocational training program for medical transcribers.

A home-study correspondence course leading to a Certificate of Completion is offered by the American Medical Record Association, which is also the examining and accrediting agency for Medical Record Administrators and Technicians.

JOB RELATIONSHIPS

Workers supervised: None.
Supervised by: Medical Record Librarian or by Transcribing Operator, Head (General Clerical Department).
Promotion from: No formal line of promotion. This may be an entry job.
Promotion to: No formal line of promotion. May be promoted to other clerical job for which ability is demonstrated.

PROFESSIONAL AFFILIATIONS

None.

Transcribing Machine Operator: (DOT) 208.588-026

FILE CLERK, MEDICAL RECORDS

The File Clerk files and retrieves medical records and loose reports of hospital and clinic patients. He maintains a signout system of records, and an updated index file of patients. He services patients' index for identifying patient by record number.

JOB DUTIES

The File Clerk routinely checks for the existence of any prior medical record of every patient admitted as an inpatient or an outpatient. He retrieves any prior record for inclusion with the current record.

He may type the index card from the source reference sheet. He updates patients' index file by filing new cards or recording additional data on existing cards, and audits patients' index for any misfiles. He notes on the index card when the record is pulled, and to which medical unit or physician it is being sent. He files cards according to the established filing system.

He files medical records by the established numbering system, and rechecks filing for proper location on filing shelves.

He answers inquiries from hospital departments regarding existence and whereabouts of medical records on specified patients. He repairs or replaces worn or torn folders, and may issue file folders on new admissions and dispatches them to patient care areas. He routinely retrieves records of patients scheduled for admission to clinic or hospital.

He follows established procedures for dispatching medical records to other areas of the hospital.

EDUCATION, TRAINING, AND EXPERIENCE

High school or vocational school graduation with some business training is preferred, however employers will accept applicants without experience.

Up to one month's on-the-job training in exact details of medical record procedures is provided.

JOB RELATIONSHIPS

Workers supervised: None.
Supervised by: Medical Record Librarian.
Promotion from: No formal line of promotion. This may be an entry job.
Promotion to: If hospital is large enough, to a File Supervisor or to Medical Record Clerk.

PROFESSIONAL AFFILIATIONS

None.

File Clerk II: (DOT) 206.388-022

CORRESPONDENCE CLERK

The Correspondence Clerk processes requests for the release of information contained in medical records. A significant part of his responsibility is to protect the confidentiality of records, and assure that they are released only to properly authorized persons.

JOB DUTIES

The Correspondence Clerk receives requests for information from medical records of patients by mail or telephone from such sources as physicians, patients, lawyers, insurance companies, or health and welfare agencies. He processes requests for delivery of records for use in answering correspondence, and checks for properly executed authorization to release medical information on designated patients. He follows specified procedures for abstracting or copying specified portions of medical records. He compares signatures and types standard letters to requesting parties, following established policies and procedures on the release of medical information.

He performs related duties, such as answering and routing telephone calls, and receiving people requesting information and services in the department.

EDUCATION, TRAINING, AND EXPERIENCE

High school graduation is required, with courses in typing, business English, and office procedures. One year of general office experience and/or experience as Medical Transcriptionist is preferred.

Approximately three months' on-the-job training is provided, to become familiar with medical record procedures.

JOB RELATIONSHIPS

Workers supervised: None.
Supervised by: Medical Record Librarian.
Promotion from: Medical Record Clerk; File Clerk, Medical Records; or Medical Transcriptionist.
Promotion to: Sectional Supervisor.

PROFESSIONAL AFFILIATIONS

None.

Correspondence Clerk: (DOT) 204.288-010

Nursing Education Department

According to a survey by the National League for Nursing (the agency that grants national accreditation to nursing schools), there were 1,362 schools of nursing in

At the University of Texas School of Nursing at San Antonio, Clinical Nursing Students enjoy a break between classes and hospital duty.

the United States in late 1972, offering 1,372 state-approved courses leading to the designation of Registered Nurse (R.N.). Almost 60 per cent of these schools had gained national accreditation, but by no means all of them offer the four-year diploma, professional nurse degree. No doubt there are now more schools, and more nationally accredited schools, and the numbers of both will continue to increase.

The academic aspects of many schools of nursing are centered in colleges and universities, with associated hospitals providing the laboratory on-the-job training. In such schools, the organizational pattern may vary with the manner of its integration into the general structure of the educational institution.

In schools that are hospital-centered, the basic structure is relatively simple, and its elements obtain—perhaps with elaborations—in all schools of nursing. The essential positions are described in the following pages.

For professional nurses who have a bent for teaching, particularly those who have attained advanced degrees, nursing education offers many opportunities.

DIRECTOR, SCHOOL OF NURSING

The Director of the School of Nursing should be a professional nurse (graduate of a four-year diploma course in an accredited school), who has had practical experience in nursing, and has attained a master's degree in nursing education.

She may report to the Administrator of the hospital, or to the Director of the Department of Nursing; but she is responsible for the planning and conduct of the

NURSING EDUCATION DEPARTMENT

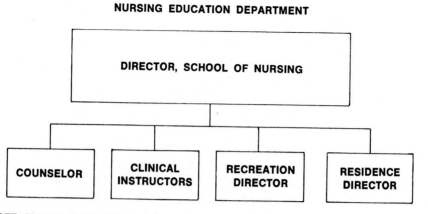

NOTE: This chart is for illustrative purposes only and should not be considered a recommended pattern of organization.

school. Her faculty will consist of qualified part-time and full-time Clinical Instructors, and a Student Counselor, a Residence Director, and a Recreation Director.

Together with the faculty, the Director plans standards of admissions for students, designed to assure so far as possible that prospective nurses are scholastically, physically, and temperamentally suited to the profession. To this end, the Director may personally interview student nurse applicants, and may utilize standardized intelligence tests and the comprehensive testing program developed by the National League of Nursing as means of determining students' aptitude for nursing.

Similarly, the Director, with faculty counsel, determines a curriculum that not only fulfills the needs of the students, but meets all the legal requirements for the practice of nursing in a particular state and, hopefully, requirements for national accreditation. The curriculum will include courses in the biological, physical, social, behavioral, medical, and nursing sciences, plus clinical practice in nursing.

The Director has many organizational responsibilities: establishing procedures for registration; planning orientation programs for students; providing for healthful, attractive living accommodations for students, with cultural and social activities, and health services; preparing class schedules; and arranging rotation of students through the various nursing services.

JOB DUTIES

The Director arranges for lectures and discussions by specialists in technical phases of nursing, and provides for classroom, laboratory, library, and other essential facilities. She negotiates with other institutions for training students in specialties not provided in the home institution.

She analyzes, evaluates, revises, and maintains an educational program consistent with current nursing practices and procedures. She holds periodic conferences with instructors and students, to interpret objectives and policies of the school, indicate changes in methods or procedures, and coordinate all phases of the educational process.

She devises and maintains a record system showing credit hours of academic instruction and clinical experience, grades, and general background information for every student. She prepares periodic reports concerning department activities, progress, and achievement of the students. She advises the student council, and individual counseling to students regarding professional, personal, or educational problems.

She confers with staff members, and observes work of student nurses, to evaluate instructors' effectiveness and teaching methods. She plans and directs inservice training for faculty; and interviews, appoints, and terminates employment of faculty members and nonprofessional nursing school personnel.

The Director assists in establishment of policies on tenure and remuneration of faculty members, working conditions, and qualifications of instructors; and conducts periodic staff conferences to resolve general faculty problems.

In cooperation with the Public Relations Department, she plans and organizes recruitment program for qualified students and assembles and edits materials promoting recruitment for newspapers, other publications, radio, and television. She contacts officials of schools, churches, and clubs to enlist support in encouraging potential applicants; and addresses civic, educational, and other public groups to explain the educational program. She contacts the alumnae association to enlist cooperation of members and promote the school's interests.

The Director prepares and administers nursing education budget.

She may conduct classes in human relations, professional ethics, or technical phases of nursing training, using lecture and demonstration methods.

EDUCATION, TRAINING, AND EXPERIENCE

Graduation from an accredited college or university, and a master's degree in nursing education and current licensure by the state Board of Nursing are required. Experience as an assistant director for a period of time sufficient to demonstrate competence is desirable and often required.

JOB RELATIONSHIPS

Workers supervised: All personnel in school of nursing.
Supervised by: Director, Nursing Service or Administrator.
Promotion from: No formal line of promotion. May be promoted from Assistant Director of Nursing, Clinical Instructor, or Counselor.
Promotion to: No formal line of promotion.

PROFESSIONAL AFFILIATIONS

American Nurses' Association
10 Columbus Circle
New York, New York 10019

National League for Nursing Association
10 Columbus Circle
New York, New York 10019

State and local nursing associations.

Director, School of Nursing: (DOT) 075.118-030

CLINICAL INSTRUCTOR

Clinical Instructors, who make up the main body of the faculty in a school of nursing, may serve either full- or part-time. They teach the theoretical and clinical aspects of nursing to nursing students.

They participate with the Director and administrative staff members in planning and preparing curriculum content, and drafting course outlines in conformity with the objectives of the program and accreditation standards.

JOB DUTIES

The Clinical Instructor conducts a teaching schedule that integrates classroom activities with clinical experience. She lectures to students on medical-surgical, obstetric, rehabilitation, or operating room subjects, and illustrates her lectures with motion pictures, slides, and models. In the clinical units of the hospital, she instructs and demonstrates the nursing care of patients such as those in surgical, medical, psychiatric, obstetrical, and pediatric wards. She may appoint members of the hospital supervisory staff to lecture and demonstrate their particular specialties to her class.

She assigns and supervises students in giving nursing care to selected patients, renders individual training assistance wherever needed, and observes the students' performance in actual nursing situations. She cooperates with related departments, and coordinates the student nurses' clinical assignments with the Nursing Service. She conducts clinical conferences with students, to discuss their assignments and experiences, and to evaluate their performance.

She develops study assignments and prepares, administers, and scores examinations to determine students' progress. She maintains various records to indicate the amount and type of instruction and progress. She counsels and provides guidance on academic problems.

The Clinical Instructor cooperates with other faculty members and student committees in planning and coordinating extracurricular projects—such as social, religious, and athletic activities—to promote cultural, physical, and personal development of the students. She may participate in the school's program of recruitment.

She makes recommendations relative to improving teaching and nursing techniques. She researches technical subjects in professional journals and texts, and recommends publications to be added to the hospital library, or information to be duplicated for appropriate personnel.

She requisitions equipment and facilities required for instruction, and maintains an inventory of supplies.

Instructors usually specialize in a nursing area such as medical-surgical, pediatrics, or psychiatric, and spend a major portion of their time in the clinical environment.

EDUCATION, TRAINING, AND EXPERIENCE

Graduation from an accredited school of nursing with current licensure by State Board of Nursing, with at least a bachelor's and preferably a master's degree from a recognized college or university, with advanced study in area of specialization are required.

Sufficient experience to have demonstrated competence in area of specialization is essential.

JOB RELATIONSHIPS

Workers supervised: Student nurses during instruction periods.
Supervised by: Director, School of Nursing.
Promotion from: No formal line of promotion.
Promotion to: No formal line of promotion. May be promoted to Assistant Director, School of Nursing.

PROFESSIONAL AFFILIATIONS

National League for Nursing
10 Columbus Circle
New York, New York 10019

American Nurses' Association
10 Columbus Circle
New York, New York 10019

State and local nursing organizations.

Nurse, Instructor: (DOT) 075.128-022

COUNSELOR

The Student Counselor provides a guidance program in the school of nursing. Because these students after graduation as qualified nurses, will have much closer association with patients than any other medical personnel, it is imperative that they develop as stable, empathetic, and competent adults. The Counselor does not wait to be approached, as she might in other college situations, but takes the initiative in becoming well-acquainted with each student.

JOB DUTIES

The Counselor interviews students to obtain information about their interests, aptitudes, personality characteristics, and achievement levels. If standardized tests, such as the comprehensive aptitude tests developed by the National League for Nursing Association, were not administered prior to admission, she may use them, along with others. She gains further information from personal history forms, and cumulative records. She also confers with instructors, regarding students with special abilities or problems, and compares students' grades with the results of intelligence and achievement tests, to determine which student needs particular help. She evaluates all of this information, and assists students to understand their own qualifications and personality characteristics in terms of educational and occupational alternatives.

She creates a climate in which students feel free to express themselves, and bring specific problems to her. When these arise, she renders such help as may be needed. She initiates and directs group guidance programs to instruct students in mental hygiene; principles of educational, vocational, and personal-social adjustment; and informs them of available guidance services. She advises instructors in methods of dealing with specific problems.

If a student develops a severe emotional problem, the Counselor performs therapy within the limits of interview techniques. This may include conferring with parents, instructors, and other students regarding the problem, and recommending specific corrective action. When necessary, she refers students to specialized agencies.

The Counselor follows each student's progress during training and after placement, to study and assist in educational, occupational, and social adjustment; and to evaluate and modify her counseling techniques. She interviews graduating students to determine their self-sufficiency, and dropouts to determine and analyze the causes of their failure and withdrawal.

She maintains records of all counseling, and makes periodic reports. She prepares and maintains cumulative records.

She may direct programs of extracurricular activities, and act as consultant to the teaching staff and administration on curricular and educational problems.

EDUCATION, TRAINING, AND EXPERIENCE

A master's degree in education, psychology, or personnel administration from a recognized college or university is usually required. Credits should include courses in tests and measurements, the counseling process, understanding the individual, educational and occupational information, research and evaluative procedures, statistics, psychology, economics, and sociology.

At least one year's counseling experience, in addition to six months' supervised counseling experience, is required. Teaching experience and group work practice are desirable.

JOB RELATIONSHIPS

Workers supervised: May supervise clerical assistants.
Supervised by: Director, School of Nursing.
Promotion from: No formal line of promotion.
Promotion to: No formal line of promotion.

PROFESSIONAL AFFILIATIONS

American Personnel and Guidance Association
1605 New Hampshire Avenue, NW.
Washington, D.C. 20009

Counselor II: (DOT) 045.108-014

RECREATION DIRECTOR

Exigencies and variations of clinical duties in combination with academic schedules make a normal social life difficult for students in nursing schools. Recreation Director, by supervising and helping to plan cultural, social, and recreational activities, helps toward maintaining a healthy balance.

JOB DUTIES

The Recreation Director meets with student and faculty groups to organize such activities as dances, receptions, and cultural programs, and schedule them to avoid interference with students' work schedules. She confers with administrative officials on specific recreational problems. She contacts entertainers, caterers, decorators, and others to make arrangements for scheduled events. She also organizes group activities, such as dramatics.

She assists in orientation of incoming students, and interprets hospital and school policies. She may provide individual counseling on selection of social activities and proper use of leisure time. When necessary, she refers individuals to the Counselor.

She promotes student participation in recreational activities through bulletins and publications. She attends school functions to evaluate their success, and may act as chaperone.

In small institutions, this job may be combined with that of Counselor or Residence Director.

EDUCATION, TRAINING, AND EXPERIENCE

College graduation with major in psychology, sociology, personnel or business administration, social education, or recreational leadership is preferable.

Experience in group social or recreational work, guidance, or personnel work is essential.

JOB RELATIONSHIPS

Workers supervised: Student nurses during recreational activities.
Supervised by: Director, School of Nursing.
Promotion from: No formal line of promotion.
Promotion to: No formal line of promotion.

PROFESSIONAL AFFILIATIONS

None.

Group Worker: (DOT) 195.108-038

RESIDENCE DIRECTOR

The Residence Director supervises and coordinates activities of a student nurses' residence, acting as house mother.

JOB DUTIES

She interviews and counsels students in the nursing residence on health, personal, social, housing, and financial problems, and suggests remedial or corrective action, assisting students to improve their adjustment.

She investigates reports of disturbances or misconduct, and attempts to resolve the causes of any conflicts. She may schedule interviews with all the resident students, to become acquainted with them and determine whether there is need for guidance.

She initiates and conducts group conferences to discuss residence regulations, plan social and recreational activities, and provide group counseling on dress, conduct, mental hygiene, and social activities. She serves as hostess and receptionist for the students.

She inspects all areas of the residence to assure that it is operating efficiently and meeting sanitary regulations. She plans for upkeep and maintenance of facilities, to provide proper conditions for group living and study. She supervises the housekeeping personnel assigned to the residence.

She maintains records, such as time sheets and inventory records, and submits periodic reports on activities in the residence.

She attends to the needs of occupants who are ill.

EDUCATION, TRAINING, AND EXPERIENCE

Some experience in teaching, counseling, student personnel work, or group activities is preferred. On-the-job orientation to become familiar with school of nursing regulations for housing of student nurses is desirable.

JOB RELATIONSHIPS

Workers supervised: None.
Supervised by: Director, School of Nursing.
Promotion from: No formal line of promotion.
Promotion to: No formal line of promotion.

PROFESSIONAL AFFILIATIONS

None.

House Mother: (DOT) 187.138-010

Nursing Service Department

When people think of nursing, they usually think of the Registered Nurse (R.N.), or so-called "professional nurse," although the latter term properly applies only to

A Pediatric Nurse takes a moment to play with a young epileptic patient. Nurses have closer contact with patients than any other hospital personnel, and their personalities and attitudes toward patients influence the quality of patient care.
Photo courtesy of the Epilepsy Foundation of America

nurses who have had four or more years of training. However, there are others who work with the professional nurse in caring for the sick, among them licensed practical nurses, nurses' aides, orderlies, and attendants.

The Registered Nurse heads the team, assisted by the other categories of personnel. This permits her to concentrate on the specialized services that only she is qualified to perform, while other members of the team undertake routine patient-care responsibilities like bathing, feeding, bed-making, etc.

REGISTERED NURSES

In 1970, according to the United States Department of Labor Bureau of Labor Statistics, 700,000 registered nurses were employed in the United States. Almost 500,000 worked in hospitals, nursing homes, and related institutions. Approximately 60,000 were private duty nurses, who care for individual patients in hospitals or private homes, and about 50,000 were office nurses. School nurses, visiting nurses, nurses in clinics and public health agencies numbered more than 50,000, while nurses teaching in nursing schools accounted for about 31,000, and nurses in industry numbered 20,000. Most of the remainder were staff members of professional nurse and other organizations, or state boards of nursing, or were employed by research organizations. About 25 per cent of all nurses worked part-time. Only about one per cent were men, although the demand for male nurses has activated efforts to recruit them into the profession.

In the intervening years, more registered nurses have been graduated, but the demand for their services in all of the areas in which they serve is far from satisfied.

NURSING EDUCATION

With the rapid advances in medical-surgical science and technology over recent years, the education and training of registered nurses who are to engage in more than general duty nursing necessarily have been upgraded.

Standards for education and training leading to the designation of Registered Nurse (R.N.) are set state-by-state, with graduation from a state-approved course within the state a prerequisite for examination and licensing in each state.

Three levels of training still obtain: (1) the associate degree program, usually offered in junior or community colleges, and requiring two years of education and training beyond the high school diploma. (2) diploma programs, usually conducted by hospitals and independent schools, which require three years of education and training beyond high school graduation. (3) baccalaureate, or bachelor's degree programs, which usually require four years of study and clinical training following high school graduation, but occasionally require five years.

All lead to the designation of Registered Nurse, but only the graduate of a bachelor's degree program can be called a professional nurse.

In the same space of time that demand for improved preparation of nurses was increasing, Americans became excessively mobile. There was need for some system of national accreditation of schools that would make it possible for Registered Nurses to be licensed in more than one state. The National League of Nursing Association (NLN) fulfills the accrediting function; and while its standards are higher than might be demanded locally in each of the three nursing programs, and reciprocity between states is voluntary, almost 60 per cent of the 1,362 nursing schools in the United States were accredited by NLN in late 1972.

Programs of nursing education include classroom instruction and supervised nursing practice in a clinical setting. Students take courses in anatomy, physiology, microbiology, nutrition, psychology, and basic nursing care. Under close supervision in hospitals and health facilities, they receive clinical experience in caring for patients who have different types of health problems and illnesses. Students in colleges offering the bachelor's degree program, and in some of the other schools, are also assigned to public health agencies, to learn how to care for patients in clinics and in their homes. General education is combined with nursing education in bachelor's and associate degree programs, and in some diploma programs.

Following graduation from any of the three nursing programs, a state licensing examination is required before an R.N. can practice. Except where states recognize each other's licenses, a similar examination must be taken in each additional state in which the nurse wishes to practice.

FINANCIAL ASSISTANCE

Due to many factors, such as extension of prepayment plans for hospitalization and medical care (including Medicaid and Medicare), expansion of medical services resulting from new techniques and drugs, and increased public information and interest in preventive medicine and rehabilitation, the demand for nurses has become sufficiently critical that a considerable number of plans for scholarships and loans have now been made available.

There are scholarships offered for beginning nursing students, those who are part way through school, and for graduate study; and for all three types of programs for Registered Nurses, as well as for Licensed Practical Nurses. (Short courses for Aides, Orderlies, and Attendants are low-cost through vocational schools, or no-cost or on-the-job basis through local hospitals or community programs.)

Local service clubs, such as the Rotary, Lions, Altrusa, etc., offer scholarships, as do hospitals and schools of nursing. Many voluntary agencies have scholarships available, as do churches, professional organizations, nurses' associations, foundations, fraternal organizations, and a myriad other groups.

A number of states have scholarship and loan programs for which the state appropriates funds. State departments of education keep files of these.

At the national level, there are Merit Scholarships; special scholarships for veterans, veterans' children, blacks, and American Indians; United Public Health

Service scholarships; Army and Navy scholarships; and loans available under Title II of the Health Manpower Act of 1968.

In some loan programs, part or all of the debt may be "forgiven" in accordance with years spent in service following graduation. In most loan programs, neither payment of interest nor repayment of principle begins until a reasonable time after graduation.

The National League for Nursing maintains updated listings of sources, which may be obtained on request. These note many specific sources, and suggest other categories which the nursing student or prospective student can investigate.

Registered Nurses in Hospital Employment

The newly graduated R.N.—regardless of the program from which she has graduated—usually begins her career as a general duty nurse, caring for patients under the direction of a head nurse. However, the quality of her education, coupled with her ability and the experience she acquires, determine how far and how fast she is able to move up the career ladder.

The professional nurse, who already has her bachelor's degree, is most able to continue her education, obtaining advanced degrees that allow her to take full advantage of all opportunities. (When graduates of two- or three-year courses wish to continue, they do not ordinarily get full credit for the work they have done, and in transfer usually have to make up more than a full year before earning the baccalaureate degree that allows them to continue toward advanced degrees.) Positions in advanced fields of nursing are most open to Registered Nurses who do continue their education and earn a master's degree or doctorate in nursing.

The graduate of a four-year, professional program also has an advantage in administrative promotions, and in choice of a clinical specialty.

Double-checking to be sure that all details of every patient's condition and treatment are recorded on his chart is a responsibility of the Head Nurse.

Photo courtesy of the New York State Health Department

CLINICAL SPECIALTIES

The special nursing units in the Nursing Service Department usually include medical, surgical, pediatric, obstetric, and psychiatric. In addition to the overall responsibilities and functions of nursing service, the units also carry more specific responsibilities and functions of patient care, varying with each nursing unit. The establishment and execution of educational programs for staff and student nurses are functions of these special nursing units.

- *Medical and Surgical:* Nursing care is provided in medical and surgical units in accordance with physician's instructions and recognized techniques and procedures. While medical conditions are not easily divided into distinct categories, medical nursing is considered a specialty in that normal and abnormal reactions or symptoms of diagnosed diseases must be recognized and reported. The patient with a stroke or a cardiac condition requires a much different type of nursing from that given the patient with an ulcer or diabetes. Surgical patients also require special preoperative and postoperative care.
- *Pediatrics:* This service embraces the care of children. Care of the newborn is usually in a separate unit located in the obstetric unit. The activities of the pediatric unit require understanding of the unique needs, fears, and behavior of children, which is reflected in the type and degree of nursing care given. Where illnesses require protracted convalescence, educational and occupational therapy become concerns of the nursing service. Relationships with parents pose further important responsibilities.
- *Obstetrics:* Prenatal care, observation, and comfort of patients in labor, delivery room assistance, and care of mother after delivery, as well as nursing care of newborn, are important responsibilities of this unit. Obstetric nurses assist in instructing new mothers in postnatal care and care of the newborn. Care of the newborn, particularly the premature, requires special nursing skills dictated by their unique requirements.
- *Psychiatric:* While most emotionally disturbed patients are treated in specialized hospitals, the general hospital also recognizes a responsibility and provides facilities for the mentally ill. Nursing care of the mentally ill requires a knowledge of their various behavior patterns and how to cope with them. Techniques must be learned for dealing with all types of problem behavior, so that skilled, therapeutic care is given to such patients. Family and community education is also an important function of the psychiatric unit.

Other special units within the Nursing Service Department are Operating Room, Recovery Room, Emergency Room, and an Intensive Care Unit.

- *Operating Room:* This unit has primary responsibility for comforting patients in the O. R.; maintaining aseptic techniques; scheduling all operations in cooperation with surgeons; and determining that adequate personnel, space, and

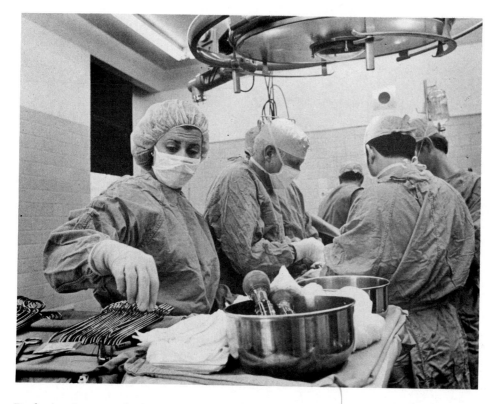

Professional nurses who have specialized in operating room techniques are a valuable part of the surgical team.

Photo courtesy of Emory University, Atlanta, Georgia

equipment are available. Nursing personnel assist the surgeon during operations and are part of the surgical team. Preparation for operations includes sterilization of instruments and equipment; cleaning up after operations is also part of the unit's responsibility.

- *Recovery Room:* In many hospitals, the Recovery Room unit is an adjunct responsibility of the Operating Room unit. Special nursing attention must be given patients after an operation until they have completely recovered from the effects of anesthesia.

- *Emergency Room:* This unit is responsible for emergency care, and for arrangements to admit the patient to the hospital, if necessary. The unit completes required records; makes reports to police and safety and health agencies; handles matters of payment, and notification of relatives; and refers patients to other services within the hospital or community, as needed.

- *Intensive Care:* Many hospitals have an Intensive Care Unit; some hospitals have several. These Units usually accommodate a limited number of patients whose conditions are very critical or who require specialized care and equipment such as electronic instruments for observation, signaling, recording, and

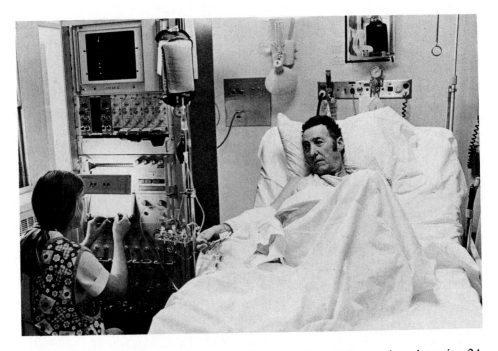

Patients in Stanford University Hospital's Coronary Care Unit are given intensive 24-hour-a-day care by a team including physicians, residents, interns, and specially trained nurses. Here, the Nurse measures the patient's intra-cardiac pressures with the aid of electronic instruments.

measuring physiological functions. In addition to providing continuous recording of cardiac function, bedside systems may monitor temperature, blood pressure, respiration rate, and other measurements. More nurses are assigned per number of patients and they are continuously in the room or within sight of the patient under care. This makes it possible to give close attention to the critically ill or postoperative patient requiring intensive care and to concentrate special equipment where it is most likely to be needed. There have now emerged an increasing number of specialized "teams" consisting of one or more physicians and other medical specialists, nurses, and ancillary personnel who respond to emergency situations. They are known by the specialized function they perform such as "cardiac team," kidney failure team," "respiratory therapy team," etc. .

• *Nurse-Midwife:* Far from being a throw-back to pioneer days, nurse-midwifery as a profession is growing in the United States. The qualified Nurse-Midwife, under supervision of the Obstetrician, works with patients throughout their pregnancies, through delivery, and in the postpartum period. She provides continuing, close relationship with patients, giving them support and assurance. She does not attempt to manage unusual situations, but refers these to the Obstetrician.

WORKING CONDITIONS

Most professional nurses work a 40-hour week, but they cannot always expect to have a conventional nine-to-five day. The daytime schedules in hospitals begin early in the morning—usually at 7:00 A.M.—and proceed by eight-hour shifts round the clock. Some nurses prefer to work the evening or night shift, but all nurses must expect to work whatever shift is assigned. Similarly, not everyone can have her two days off on every weekend, or holiday leave always on the exact holiday.

Although nursing service personnel may be subject to various physical strains in moving and lifting patients, this hazard, as well as danger to the patient, is minimized by training in proper lifting techniques, and the uses of various devices and equipment.

Possibility of exposure to various communicable diseases or infections is minimized by strict routines of isolation, asepsis, and utilization of sterilized clothing.

Personnel who must attend patients receiving radiological treatments are protected against over-exposure by film badges that register exposure. These are periodically analyzed, to insure safe levels. Additionally, such personnel are specially trained in safe procedures in management of these patients.

STANDARDS FOR NURSING SERVICE DEPARTMENTS

Standards for this department have been defined by the American Nurses' Association, National League for Nursing, and the Joint Commission for Accreditation of Hospitals of the American Medical Association and the American Hospital Association.

DIRECTOR, NURSING SERVICE

The Director of the Nursing Service organizes and administers the Department of Nursing.

She establishes objectives for the department, and the organizational structure for achieving these objectives. She interprets, and puts into effect, the administrative policies established by the governing authority of the hospital.

JOB DUTIES

The Director of the Nursing Service assists in preparing and administering budget for the department. She selects and recommends personnel for appointment on the nursing staff.

She directs and delegates management of professional and ancillary nursing personnel. She plans and conducts conferences and discussions with administrative

NURSING SERVICE DEPARTMENT

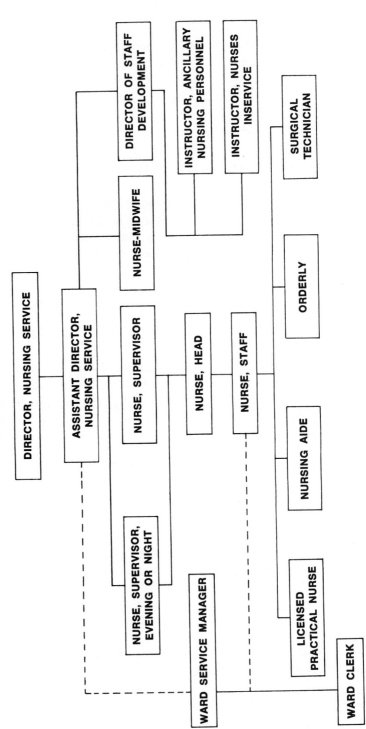

DIRECTOR, NURSING SERVICE

ASSISTANT DIRECTOR, NURSING SERVICE

DIRECTOR OF STAFF DEVELOPMENT

NURSE-MIDWIFE

INSTRUCTOR, ANCILLARY NURSING PERSONNEL

INSTRUCTOR, NURSES INSERVICE

NURSE, SUPERVISOR

NURSE, HEAD

NURSE, STAFF

SURGICAL TECHNICIAN

ORDERLY

NURSE, SUPERVISOR, EVENING OR NIGHT

WARD SERVICE MANAGER

NURSING AIDE

LICENSED PRACTICAL NURSE

WARD CLERK

NOTE: This chart is for illustrative purposes only and should not be considered a recommended pattern of organization.

and professional nursing staffs to encourage participation in formulating departmental policies and procedures, promote initiative, solve problems, and interpret new policies and procedures.

She coordinates the activities of the various nursing units, promoting and maintaining harmonious relationships among nursing personnel, and with medical staff, patients, and public.

She plans and directs orientation and inservice training programs for professional and paraprofessional nursing staff.

She analyzes and evaluates nursing and related services rendered, to improve the quality of patient care, and plan better utilization of staff time and activities.

She participates in community educational health programs.

EDUCATION, TRAINING, AND EXPERIENCE

Graduation from an accredited school of nursing is required, with a bachelor's degree preferred, and a master's degree desirable. Current licensure by the State Board of Nursing is required, and also demonstrated administrative ability.

The Director of Nursing Service should have five to ten years of nursing experience, including satisfactory experience as an instructor or supervisor, or as Assistant Director in a school of nursing.

JOB RELATIONSHIPS

Workers supervised: General supervision of all nursing personnel in the hospital.
Supervised by: Administrator.
Promotion from: Assistant Director, Nursing Service.
Promotion to: No formal line of promotion.

PROFESSIONAL AFFILIATIONS

American Nurses' Association
10 Columbus Circle
New York, New York, 10019

National League for Nursing
10 Columbus Circle
New York, New York 10019

American Society for Nursing Service Administrators
840 North Lake Shore Drive
Chicago, Illinois 60611

State and local nursing associations.

Director, Nursing Service: (DOT) 075.118-018

ASSISTANT DIRECTOR, NURSING SERVICE

The Assistant Director of the Nursing Service assumes the responsibilities delegated by the Director in organizing and administering the department.

JOB DUTIES

She conducts conferences and discussions with personnel to encourage participation in formulating departmental policies, promote initiative, solve problems, and present new policies and procedures.

She analyzes nursing and auxiliary services to improve quality of patient care and to obtain maximum utilization of the staff's time and abilities. She coordinates activities of the nursing service units, to achieve and maintain efficient and competent nursing service, and to promote and maintain harmonious relationships among personnel supervised, medical staff, patients, and others.

She assists in establishing lines of authority and responsibility, and defining the duties of nursing service personnel, consistent with good administrative techniques, to assure that department objectives are accomplished.

She assists in review and evaluation of budget requests against current and projected needs of the nursing service.

The Assistant Director interviews applicants, and recommends appointments of staff personnel, outlining their duties, scope of authority, and responsibilities. She participates in establishing and administering orientation and inservice training programs for both professional and paraprofessional personnel.

She assures proper and economic use of equipment, supplies, and facilities for maintaining patient care. She maintains personnel and other records, and directs maintenance of patient care records.

She cooperates with medical staff performing research projects or studies, as they affect nursing. She works with agencies and groups in the community to promote the growth and broaden knowledge and skills of the professional staff, and improve the quality of hospital services.

EDUCATION, TRAINING, AND EXPERIENCE

Graduation from an accredited school of nursing with bachelor's degree preferred, and master's degree is desirable. Current licensure by State Board of Nursing is required, plus demonstrated administrative ability.

Experience in a supervisory capacity with demonstrated executive ability and leadership is essential.

JOB RELATIONSHIPS

Workers supervised: Direct supervision of Nurse, Supervisors and indirect supervision of all professional and ancillary nursing staff in the department.
Supervised by: Director, Nursing Service.
Promotion from: May be promoted from a nursing position in which administrative ability has been demonstrated.
Promotion to: Director, Nursing Service.

PROFESSIONAL AFFILIATIONS

American Nurses' Association
10 Columbus Circle
New York, New York 10019

National League for Nursing
10 Columbus Circle
New York, New York 10019

State and local nursing associations.

Director, Nursing Service: (DOT) 075.118-018

NURSE, SUPERVISOR, EVENING OR NIGHT
Assistant Director of Nursing, Evening or Night

The Evening or Night Supervisor coordinates the activities of nursing personnel on evening or night duty, to maintain continuity for round-the-clock nursing care.

JOB DUTIES

The Evening or Night Supervisor visits nursing units to oversee nursing care, and to ascertain the condition of patients. She advises and assists nurses in administering new or unusual treatments, gives advice for treatments, medications, and narcotics, in accordance with medical staff policies, in the absence of physicians.

She arranges for emergency operations, and reallocates personnel during emergencies. She admits, or delegates admission, of new patients, and arranges for the services of private duty nurses. She determines the necessity for calling physicians. She may perform some bedside nursing services.

She delegates preparation of reports covering such items as critically ill patients, new admissions, discharges or deaths, emergency situations encountered, and private-duty nurses employed. She informs supervisory personnel on ensuing tour of duty of patients' condition and hospital services rendered during her work period.

She interprets hospital policies and regulations to staff members, patients, and visitors, and insures conformance.

She evaluates work performance, and assists in preparing performance reports for the nursing staff. She participates in staff education, and conferences for formulating policies and program plans, and the integration of various nursing services.

EDUCATION, TRAINING, AND EXPERIENCE

Graduation from an accredited school of nursing and current licensure by State Board of Nursing are required. Experience as Nurse Supervisor, during which executive ability has been demonstrated is desirable.

JOB RELATIONSHIPS

Workers supervised: Professional and ancillary nursing personnel assigned to evening or night service.
Supervised by: Director, Nursing Service or Assistant Director, Nursing Service.
Promotion from: Nurse, Supervisor.
Promotion to: Director, Nursing Service.

PROFESSIONAL AFFILIATIONS

American Nurses' Association
10 Columbus Circle
New York, New York 10019

National League for Nursing
10 Columbus Circle
New York, New York 10019

State and local nursing associations.

Nurse, Supervisor: (DOT) 075.128-034

NURSE, SUPERVISOR

The Nursing Supervisor coordinates the activities of nursing personnel engaged in specific nursing services, such as obstetrics, pediatrics, or surgery, or for two or more patient care units.

She supervises the Head Nurses in carrying out their responsibilities in the management of nursing care. She evaluates the performance of the Head Nurses, and nursing care as a whole, and suggests modifications. She inspects unit areas, to verify that patient needs are being met.

She participates in planning the work of her own units, and coordinates activities with other patient care units and with those of related departments.

JOB DUTIES

She consults with the Head Nurses on specific nursing problems and interpretation of hospital policies. She supervises maintenance of personnel and nursing records.

She plans and organizes orientation and inservice training for unit staff members, and participates in guidance and educational programs. She interviews prescreened applicants, and makes recommendations for employing or for terminating personnel. She assists the Director of the Nursing Service in formulating her unit's budget. She engages in studies and investigations related to improving nursing care. She performs the specialized duties of her section.

The Nurse, Supervisor is usually known by the name of the nursing section to which she is assigned, or in which she has specialized, such as Nurse, Supervisor, Medical and Surgical; or Nurse, Supervisor, Pediatrics.

EDUCATION, TRAINING, AND EXPERIENCE

Graduation from an accredited school of nursing and current licensure by State Board of Nursing is required. Advanced education is desirable. The Nurse, Supervisor should have experience as Nurse, Head in which administrative, supervisory, and teaching abilities have been demonstrated.

JOB RELATIONSHIPS

Workers supervised: Nurses, Head directly, and indirectly other professional and nursing personnel.
Supervised by: Assistant Director, Nursing Service.
Promotion from: Nurse, Head.
Promotion to: Assistant Director, Nursing Service.

PROFESSIONAL AFFILIATIONS

American Nurses' Association
10 Columbus Circle
New York, New York 10019

National League for Nursing
10 Columbus Circle
New York, New York 10019

State and local nursing associations.

Nurse, Supervisor: (DOT) 075.128-034

NURSE-MIDWIFE

A Nurse-Midwife is a registered professional nurse who has completed a recognized program of study and experience leading to a certificate in nurse-midwifery (C.N.M.). She never practices independently, but functions as part of an obstetrical team. She manages and provides prenatal, intrapartum, postpartum, and family planning care geared to individual patients, with delegated medical authority in municipal and voluntary hospitals, or with obstetrical groups for private patients.

Many Nurse-Midwives have used this training as background for positions as maternal and child health consultants in health departments, as supervisors and administrators of maternity care services, in parent education relating to childbirth, as professors and instructors of maternity nursing, and as teachers of midwifery.

JOB DUTIES

The Nurse-Midwife gives each patient personal care throughout her pregnancy, during delivery, and in the days following childbirth. She performs all prenatal examinations, including breast examination, abdominal palpation, complete pelvic examination, and is even assigned the responsibility of taking Papanicolaou smear when such an investigation is indicated.

She handles the delivery, providing warmth and reassurance to the patient. She encourages her to participate in the birth process so far as she is able. She consults the Obstetrician who is her supervisor if anything unusual occurs. She administers any treatments, infusions, or medications needed during delivery, in accordance with the hospital's approved orders for nurse-midwifery service.

She administers necessary immediate care to the infant, including giving the Apgar test, and she signs the birth certificate.

She performs the postpartum examinations of the mother, and offers support and reassurance at times of infant feeding, emphasizing an early positive mother-newborn relationship. She counsels, instructs and administers methods of birth control to mothers who desire such help.

EDUCATION, TRAINING, AND EXPERIENCE

Schools of nurse-midwifery are approved by the American College of Nurse-Midwives, which means that their graduates are eligible to take certification examinations, and apply for licenses in the 20 states in which they can now practice. There are now about ten approved colleges in the United States and Puerto Rico.

Nurse-midwifery education is offered at the post R. N. level and the master's degree level. Post R. N. level programs are about eight months in duration, and provide an intensive course of both training and clinical experience. Master's degree programs are twelve to 20 months in duration, and offer the student both certification and a master's degree. Scholarships are available in almost all nurse-midwifery programs.

JOB RELATIONSHIPS

Workers supervised: None.
Supervised by: Obstetrician.
Promotion from: Registered Professional Nurse.
Promotion to: No formal line of promotion.

PROFESSIONAL AFFILIATIONS

American College of Nurse-Midwives
50 East 92nd Street
New York, New York 10028

Nurse-Midwife: (DOT) 075.378-030

NURSE, HEAD

The Head Nurse directs nursing activities, including the preparation of nursing care plans, and instructs nurses in an organized hospital patient care unit.

JOB DUTIES

The Head Nurse assigns duties to professional and ancillary nursing personnel, based on patients' needs, available staff, and unit needs. She supervises and evaluates work performance in terms of patient care, staff relations, and efficiency of service. She provides for nursing care in the unit, and cooperates with other members of the medical-care team in coordinating patients' total needs.

She identifies and studies nursing service problems and assists in their solution. She observes nursing care and visits patients to insure that nursing service is carried out as directed, and treatment is administered in accordance with physicians' instructions, and to ascertain need for additional or modified services.

She maintains a safe environment for patients. She operates, or supervises the operation, of specialized equipment assigned to the unit, and provides assistance and guidance to the nursing team as required.

The Head Nurse accompanies physicians on rounds, to answer questions, receive instructions, and note patients' requirements.

She reports to her replacement on the next tour of duty on the condition of patients, and any unusual actions taken. She may render professional nursing care and instruct patients and members of their families in techniques and methods of home care after discharge.

She directs preparation and maintenance of patients' clinical records, including nursing and medical treatments and related services provided by the nursing staff. She compiles daily reports on staff hours worked, and care and condition of patients. She investigates and adjusts complaints or refers them to the Supervisor.

She insures established inventory standards for medicines, solutions, supplies, and equipment. She accounts for narcotics.

She provides orientation for new personnel to job requirements, equipment, and unit personnel. She instructs unit personnel in new nursing care techniques, procedures, and equipment. She presides over unit personnel meetings to discuss patient care needs. She evaluates individual work performance through observation, spot-checking work completed, and conferences. She promotes individual staff development.

She attends meetings of supervisory and administrative staff, to discuss unit operation and staff training needs, and to formulate programs to improve these areas. She may assist in developing and administering budget for the nursing unit to which she is assigned. She assists with studies related to improvement of nursing care.

Nurse, Head is usually identified by the nursing unit to which she is assigned or in which she has specialized, such as Nurse, Head, Medical and Surgical; or Nurse, Head, Pediatrics.

In smaller hospitals, the duties and responsibilities of this job may be combined with those of Nurse, Supervisor.

EDUCATION, TRAINING, AND EXPERIENCE

Graduation from an accredited school of nursing and current licensure by the State Board of Nursing are required. Advanced preparation in the clinical specialty, ward management, principles of supervision, and teaching is preferred.

The Nurse, Head should have had experience as a professional nurse, in which potential administration and supervisory competence has been demonstrated.

JOB RELATIONSHIPS

Workers supervised: Nurses, Staff and ancillary nursing personnel assigned to the unit.
Supervised by: Nurse, Supervisor, assigned unit.
Promotion from: Nurse, Staff.
Promotion to: Nurse, Supervisor.

PROFESSIONAL AFFILIATIONS

American Nurses' Association
10 Columbus Circle
New York, New York 10019

National League for Nursing
10 Columbus Circle
New York, New York 10019

State and local nursing associations.

Nurse, Head: (DOT) 075.128-018

NURSE, STAFF

The Staff Nurse renders professional nursing care to patients within an assigned unit of a hospital, in support of medical care as directed by the medical staff, and in accordance with the objectives and policies of the hospital.

JOB DUTIES

She performs nursing techniques for the comfort and well-being of the patient. She prepares equipment and assists physicians during examination and treatment of patients. She administers prescribed medicines, orally and by injection; provides treatments, using therapeutic equipment; observes patients' reactions to medications and treatments; observes progress of intravenous infusions and subcutaneous infiltrations; changes, or assists the physician in changing dressings, and cleaning wounds or incisions; takes temperature, pulse, respiration rate, blood pressure, and heart beat to detect deviations from normal and gauge progress of the patient, following physicians' orders and approved nursing care plan. She observes, records, and reports to supervisor or physician, the patients' condition and reaction to drugs, treatments, and significant incidents.

The Staff Nurse maintains patients' medical records on nursing observations and actions taken, such as medications and treatments given, reactions, tests, intake and emission of liquids and solids, temperature, pulse, and respiration rate. She records nursing needs of patients on nursing care plan to assure continuity of care.

She observes the emotional stability of patients, expresses interest in their progress, and prepares them for continuing care after discharge. She explains procedures and treatments ordered, to gain patients' cooperation and allay apprehension.

Staff Nurses rotate on day, evening, and night tours of duty, and may be asked to rotate among various clinical and nursing services of the hospital. Each service will have specialized duties, and the Staff Nurses may be known by the section to which each is assigned, such as Nurse, Staff, Obstetrics; or Nurse, Staff, Pediatrics. She may serve as a team leader for a group of personnel rendering nursing care to a number of patients.

The Staff Nurse assists in planning, supervising, and instructing Licensed Practical Nurses, Nursing Aides, Orderlies, and students. She demonstrates nursing techniques and procedures, and assists nonprofessional nursing care personnel in rendering nursing care in the unit.

She may assist with operations and deliveries by preparing rooms; sterilizing instruments, equipment, and supplies; and handing them, in order of use, to the surgeon or other medical specialist.

EDUCATION, TRAINING, AND EXPERIENCE

Graduation from an accredited school of nursing and current licensure by State Board of Nursing are required.

The Staff Nurse must have orientation training in specific unit only; no experience is required beyond that obtained in school of nursing.

JOB RELATIONSHIPS

Workers supervised: May supervise ancillary nursing personnel of unit.
Supervised by: Nurse, Head.
Promotion from: No formal line of promotion.
Promotion to: Nurse, Head.

PROFESSIONAL AFFILIATIONS

American Nurses' Association
10 Columbus Circle
New York, New York 10019

National League for Nursing
10 Columbus Circle
New York, New York 10019

State and local nursing associations.

Nurse, General Duty: (DOT) 075.378-014

DIRECTOR OF STAFF DEVELOPMENT
Inservice-Education Coordinator

The Director of Staff Development plans, develops, and directs the program of education for all hospital nursing service personnel, and coordinates staff development with the nursing service program.

JOB DUTIES

The Director of Staff Development organizes, schedules, and directs the orientation program for professional and auxiliary nursing service personnel. She develops instructional materials to assist new personnel in becoming acquainted with hospital operational techniques. If the Personnel Department has not done so, she schedules hospital tours and addresses by administrative staff, to introduce the overall operation and interrelationships of the hospital services to new personnel. She determines the effectiveness of orientation materials and procedures through practice sessions. She sets up demonstrations of nursing service equipment to acquaint hospital staff with new equipment, and make 'them more familiar with established equipment.

She plans, coordinates, and conducts regular and special inservice training sessions for the hospital nursing staff, to acquaint them with new procedures and policies, and new trends and developments in patient care techniques; and to provide opportunity for individual members to develop their full potential.

She keeps abreast of latest developments by attending professional seminars and institutes, and reading professional journals. She assists Supervisors and Head

Nurses in planning and implementing staff development programs in their units. She keeps bulletin boards current by listing information on seminars and institutes, and promotes appropriate staff attendance at these professional meetings. She plans training sessions for supervisory staff members.

She may participate with committees in writing and maintaining policies-and-procedures manuals and nursing service forms. She reviews suggestions submitted by the nursing service staff for changes or clarification of policies and procedures.

She writes annual reports on her activities, and prepares plans for future activities, as well as budget requests.

EDUCATION, TRAINING, AND EXPERIENCE

Graduation from an accredited school of nursing and current licensure by State Board of Nursing are required, as well as graduation from a recognized college or university with specialization in education and bachelor's degree. Experience as Nurse, Head; Nurse, Supervsor; or Nurse, Educator is a prerequisite for appointment.

JOB RELATIONSHIPS

Workers supervised: Supervises other training personnel in Nursing Service Department.
Supervised by: Assistant Director, Nursing Service or Head of Training Department.
Promotion from: Nurse, Supervisor or Nurse, Head.
Promotion to: No formal line of promotion.

PROFESSIONAL AFFILIATIONS

American Nurses' Association
10 Columbus Circle
New York, New York 10019

National League for Nursing
10 Columbus Circle
New York, New York 10019

State and local nursing associations.

Director of Staff Development: (DOT) 075.118-

INSTRUCTOR, ANCILLARY NURSING PERSONNEL

The Instructor, Ancillary Nursing Personnel, plans, coordinates, and carries out educational programs in the theoretical and practical aspects of nursing directed primarily to the Licensed Practical Nurses, Aides, Orderlies and Attendants who assist the Registered Nurses in patient care.

JOB DUTIES

The Instructor prepares and issues training manuals that describe the duties and responsibilities of nursing assistants, which serve as training guides. She familiarizes new employees with the physical layout of the hospital, hospital policies and procedures, organizational structure, hospital etiquette, and employee benefits.

She plans and conducts classes in basic patient care procedures, such as bedmaking, blood pressure and temperature taking, and feeding of patients. She demonstrates nursing procedures for the Nurses' Aides and Orderlies in classrooms and clinical situations, and lectures on techniques, using films, charts, and slides by way of illustration.

She observes the trainees in their practical application of procedures.

She secures the cooperation of the Supervisors and Head Nurses in the performance of their teaching responsibilities with a view to:

   (i) coordinate training with all nursing service units
   (ii) maintain consistency in the practice of ancillary nursing
   (iii) establish interdependent relationship
   (iv) give adequate scope to the program
   (v) point out variations of duties required by different units and on different shifts.

She prepares, administers, and scores examinations to determine trainees' suitability for jobs, and makes recommendations to the nursing service regarding placement of trainees according to test scores and practical application performance. She evaluates trainees' progress during and following the training period, and submits her report to the nursing service for further action.

She conducts meetings with trainees and supervisors to discuss problems and ideas for improving nursing service training program.

EDUCATION, TRAINING, AND EXPERIENCE

Graduation from an accredited school of nursing and current licensure by State Board of Nursing; advanced training in teaching methods and supervision are required plus one year's experience as Nurse, Head or Nurse, Supervisor.

JOB RELATIONSHIPS

Workers supervised: Trainees during training period.
Supervised by: Director of Staff Development.
Promotion from: Nurse, Head or Nurse, Supervisor.
Promotion to: Director of Staff Development.

PROFESSIONAL AFFILIATIONS

American Nurses' Association
10 Columbus Circle
New York, New York 10019

National League for Nursing
10 Columbus Circle
New York, New York 10019

State and local nursing associations.

Nurse, Instructor: (DOT) 075.128-022

INSTRUCTOR, NURSE, INSERVICE

The Instructor of Nurses, Inservice plans, directs and coordinates inservice orientation and educational programs for the professional nursing personnel.

JOB DUTIES

She assists the Director of Staff Development in planning and scheduling training programs for nurses on the staff, orientation programs for new nursing personnel, and refresher programs for professional nurses who are returning to hospital service.

She lectures to nurses, and provides demonstrations of procedures and improved methods of nursing, using motion pictures, charts, and slides.

She instructs volunteer workers in routine procedures, such as aseptic practices, and blood pressure and temperature taking.

EDUCATION, TRAINING, AND EXPERIENCE

Graduation from an accredited school of nursing and current licensure by State Board of Nursing are required, plus advanced training in teaching methods and supervision. One year's experience as Nurse, Head or Nurse, Supervisor is necessary.

JOB RELATIONSHIPS

Workers supervised: None.
Supervised by: Director of Staff Development.
Promotion from: Nurse, Head or Nurse, Supervisor.
Promotion to: Director of Staff Development.

PROFESSIONAL AFFILIATIONS

American Nurses' Association
10 Columbus Circle
New York, New York 10019

National League for Nursing
10 Columbus Circle
New York, New York 10019

State and local nursing associations.

Nurse, Instructor: (DOT) 075.128-022

LICENSED PRACTICAL NURSE

The Licensed Practical Nurse (L.P.N.) performs a wide variety of patient care activities and accommodative services for hospital patients in the unit to which she is assigned. She works under the direction of the Head Nurse and/or the team leader in her unit.

JOB DUTIES

She performs assigned nursing procedures for the comfort and well-being of the patients in her unit, such as assisting in the admission of new patients, bathing and feeding patients, making beds, helping patients get into and out of bed.

She takes patients' blood pressure, temperature, pulse, and respiration, and records the results on patients' charts.

She collects specimens, such as urine and sputum, and labels the containers before sending them to the clinical laboratory for analysis.

She dresses wounds, administers prescribed procedures, such as enemas, douches, alcohol rubs, and massages. She applies compresses, ice bags, and hot water bottles. She observes patients for reactions to drugs and treatments, such as cyanosis, weak pulse, excessive respiratory rate, or other unusual conditions, and reports adverse reactions to the Head Nurse or Staff Nurse.

She administers specified medication, and notes time and amounts on the patients' charts. She assembles and uses such equipment as catheters, tracheotomy tubes, and oxygen supplies.

She drapes or gowns patients for various types of examinations. She assists patients to walk about the unit as permitted, or transports patients by wheelchair to various departments as needed.

She records food and fluid intake and emission. She answers patients' call signals, and assists the Staff Nurse or the Physician in advanced medical treatments. She assists in the care of deceased persons.

She sterilizes equipment and supplies, using germicides, sterilizer, or autoclave.

She may specialize in the work of a particular patient unit, and be known by its name, such as Licensed Practical Nurse, Recovery Room; or Licensed Practical Nurse, Psychiatrics.

She may be required to work rotating shifts.

High school graduation plus graduation from a recognized one-year practical nurse program are required. The Licensed Practical Nurse must pass state Board of Nursing licensing examination.

JOB RELATIONSHIPS

Workers supervised: None.
Supervised by: A member of professional nursing staff, depending upon organization of the hospital and nursing unit to which assigned.
Promotion from: No formal line of promotion.
Promotion to: No formal line of promotion.

PROFESSIONAL AFFILIATIONS

National Federation of Licensed Practical Nurses
250 West 57th Street
New York, New York 10019

National Association for Practical Nurse Education and Service, Inc.
535 Fifth Avenue
New York, New York 10017

Nurse, Licensed, Practical: (DOT) 079.378-026

NURSING AIDE
Nurse Aide
Nursing Assistant

The Nursing Aide performs various patient care activities and related nonprofessional services necessary to satisfy the personal needs and minister to the comfort of patients.

JOB DUTIES

The Nursing Aide answers patients' signal lights and bells, to determine patients' needs. She bathes, dresses and undresses patients, and assists with personal hygiene to increase their comfort and well-being. She may serve and collect food trays, feed patients who need that help, and provide between-meals nourishment and fresh drinking water.

She transports patients to various units of the hospital for treatments, using a wheelchair or wheeled carriage, or assisting the patient to walk. She drapes the patient for examinations and treatments, and stays with him, performing such duties as holding instruments, or adjusting lights.

She takes and records temperatures, pulse and respiration rates, and food intake and output as directed.

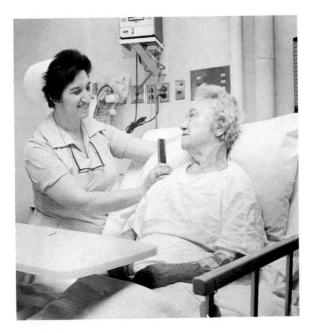

Nursing Aides do many of the small, personal, time-consuming things that make patients' hospital stay more comfortable and pleasant.

Photo courtesy of the New York State Health Department

She may apply icebags and hot water bottles, and give alcohol rubs.

She reports all unusual conditions or reactions of patients to the nurse in charge.

She may assemble equipment and supplies in preparation for various diagnostic or treatment procedures, which are to be performed by a physician or nurse.

She tidies patients' rooms, and cares for flowers, changes bed linen, runs errands, directs visitors, and answers telephone. She collects and bags soiled linen, and stores clean linen. She collects charts, records, and reports, and delivers them to authorized personnel.

She may clean, sterilize, store, and prepare treatment trays and other supplies used in the unit.

She may be required to work rotating shifts.

The Nursing Aide may be known by the unit in which she works, as Nursing Aide, Psychiatric; or Nursing Aide, Nursery.

EDUCATION, TRAINING, AND EXPERIENCE

High school graduation is preferred. The Nursing Aide takes hospital-conducted on-the-job training programs. To work in some departments, additional training is given.

JOB RELATIONSHIPS

Workers supervised: None.

Supervised by: A member of nursing staff, depending on organization of hospital and unit to which assigned.

Promotion from: This is an entry job in the department of nursing.
Promotion to: No formal line of promotion.

PROFESSIONAL AFFILIATIONS

None.

Nurse Aide: (DOT) 355.878-034

ORDERLY
Nursing assistant, male

JOB DUTIES

Orderlies assist nursing personnel by performing a variety of duties for patients (usually for male patients), and certain heavy duties in the care of patients, including persons who are mentally ill or mentally retarded.

Their jobs are the same as those of the Nursing Aides.

EDUCATION, TRAINING, AND EXPERIENCE

High school graduation is preferred. The Orderly completes hospital-conducted on-the-job training programs. For work in some departments, additional training is given.

JOB RELATIONSHIPS

Workers supervised: None.
Supervised by: A member of nursing staff, depending on organization of hopsital unit to which assigned.
Promotion from: This is usually an entry job in the department of nursing.
Promotion to: No formal line of promotion.

PROFESSIONAL AFFILIATIONS

None.

Orderly: (DOT) 355.878-038

SURGICAL TECHNICIAN
Scrub Technician

The Surgical Technician performs a variety of duties in the operating room, to assist the surgical team.

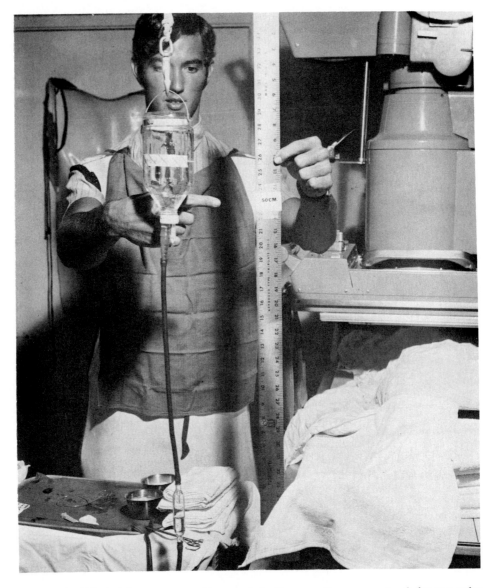

The Surgical Technician gets everything ready in the operating room, stands by to render any help the surgeon asks for during the operation, helps the Orderly get the patient to the recovery room, and puts the operating room back in order.

JOB DUTIES

She changes into operative clothing, scrubs hands and arms, and puts on a sterile gown, mask, and gloves. She arranges the sterile setup for the operation, and assists the circulating nurse in positioning the patient for the type of surgery to be performed. She may assist in preparing the operative area of the patient.

She may assist the Anesthesiologist in administration of the anesthetic. During surgery, she passes instruments, sponges, and sutures to the surgeon and surgical assistants. She adjusts lights and equipment as directed. She may count sponges, needles, and instruments used during the operation. She may prepare operative specimens, place them in preservative solution, and deliver them to the laboratory for analysis. She may record data on patients' record data sheets.

Upon completion of surgery, she assists in moving the patient onto the wheeled carriage for transport to the recovery room.

She assists in the cleanup of the operating room, including disposal of used linen, gloves, instruments, utensils, equipment, and waste.

She may be required to work rotating shifts.

EDUCATION, TRAINING, AND EXPERIENCE

High school graduation or equivalent is required. Some employers prefer graduation from a recognized one-year practical nurse program. The candidate must take a hospital-conducted on-the-job training course in operating room techniques.

JOB RELATIONSHIPS

Workers supervised: None.
Supervised by: Nurse, Staff.
Promotion from: No formal line of promotion.
Promotion to: No formal line of promotion.

PROFESSIONAL AFFILIATIONS

None.

Surgical Technician: (DOT) 079.378-042

WARD SERVICE MANAGER
Unit Manager
Ward Supervisor

The Ward Service Manager supervises and coordinates administrative management functions for one or more patient care units.

JOB DUTIES

He supervises the clerical staff and assures accomplishment of administrative functions on a 24-hour-a-day basis, by scheduling working hours and arranging for coverage of nursing care unit by non-nursing personnel. He performs personnel-management tasks by orienting and training new personnel, and evaluating the performance of assigned workers by checking for quality and quantity.

He inventories and stores patients' personal effects, either within the unit, or in the hospital vault.

He establishes and maintains an adequate inventory of drugs and supplies for the unit.

He coordinates with other departments, such as housekeeping and maintenance, to assure that the unit is hygienically safe and functional. He checks for cleanliness of the units, and reports discrepancies to the appropriate supervisor. He performs daily maintenance inspection, and through proper channels initiates minor facility improvement projects.

He maintains close contact with medical and surgical reservations in regard to admissions, transfers, discharges, and other services. He serves as liaison between the specific patient care unit and other departments. He reviews special tests at the end of the shift.

He insures that the medical record is completed, in accordance with the standards of the Joint Commission on Accreditation of Hospitals. He insures hospital compliance with Medicare requirements insofar as certification and related administrative matters are concerned. He checks charts of patients scheduled for surgery, or other special procedures, to verify completeness of orders of consent, preparation orders, and lab results, and for necessary signatures.

He greets, directs, and gives nonprofessional factual information to patients, visitors, and personnel from other departments.

He participates in projects, surveys, and other information-gathering activities approved by the hospital management.

EDUCATION, TRAINING, AND EXPERIENCE

One year of college or equivalent is required, plus a minimum of one year's supervisory experience.

On-the-job training is provided in coordinating nonnursing services for the assigned nursing units.

JOB RELATIONSHIPS

Workers supervised: Ward Clerk and other nonnursing personnel assigned to the unit.
Supervised by: Assistant Director, Nursing Service or Administrator.
Promotion from: No formal line of promotion.
Promotion to: No formal line of promotion.

PROFESSIONAL AFFILIATIONS

None.

Ward Service Manager: (DOT) 187.—T

WARD CLERK
Floor Clerk
Nursing Station Assistant

The Ward Clerk performs clerical duties by preparing, compiling, and maintaining records in a hospital nursing unit.

JOB DUTIES

The Ward Clerk records the name of patient, address, and name of attending physician on medical record forms. He copies information, such as patient's temperature, pulse rate, and blood pressure, from nurses' records. He writes requisitions for laboratory tests and procedures such as basal metabolism, X-ray, EKG, blood examinations, and urinalysis. Under supervision, he plots temperature, pulse rate, and other data on appropriate graph charts. He copies and computes other data as directed, and enters on patients' charts. He may record diet instructions. He keeps the file of medical records on patients in the unit. He routes charts when patients are transferred or discharged, following specific procedures. He may compile the census of patients.

He keeps record of absences and hours worked by unit personnel. He types various records, schedules, and reports, and delivers them to appropriate offices. He may maintain records of special monetary charges to patients, and forward them to the business office. He may verify stock supplies on the unit, and prepare requisitions to maintain established inventories. He dispatches messages to other departments, and makes appointments for services to patients from other departments as requested by the nursing staff. He makes posthospitalization appointments with patients' physicians. He delivers mail, newspapers, and flowers to patients.

EDUCATION, TRAINING, AND EXPERIENCE

High school graduation or equivalent, including courses in English, typing, spelling, and arithmetic, or high school graduation supplemented by commercial school course in subjects indicated, are required.

No previous experience is required.

On-the-job training in practices and procedures of the hospital and certain medical terminology is provided.

JOB RELATIONSHIPS

Workers supervised: None.
Supervised by: Ward Service Manager or nurse in charge of unit or ward in which work is performed.
Promotion from: This is usually an entry job.

Promotion to: No formal line of promotion. May be promoted to higher grade clerical job for which ability is demonstrated.

PROFESSIONAL AFFILIATIONS

None.

Ward Clerk: (DOT) 219.388-286

Outpatient Department

For many low-income city families, the Outpatient Department of the hospital takes the place of the family physician. They come to the department as they would go to a doctor.

The Outpatient Department also serves to continue treatment of patients who no longer need to stay in hospital, but still need regular attention. Other patients who do not need hospitalization may be referred to the Outpatient Department for special services by physicians who are on its staff and also in private practice.

The Outpatient Department needs all the facilities of the hospital in general, and its organization parallels that of the hospital.

The department bears a major responsibility for instructing its patients in disease prevention, and in guidance during convalescence. Accurate and complete records must be maintained, covering all social and medical data bearing on each case. These records are necessary for group studies, medical research, and accounting purposes, and for adequate care of each patient. Many patients are "regular customers" of the department, and their records may be ongoing for a period of years.

The department is headed by a Director, Outpatient Services, who reports directly to the Administrator or a designated Associate Administrator, and to the Chief of the Medical Service where professional matters are concerned. The Direc-

In an Outpatient Clinic a Therapeutic Dietitian explains a prescribed diet to a patient.

tor has full authority for operation of the department, and for coordinating its work with that of other hospital departments.

Other staff members who are unique to this department are the Clinic Coordinator, Ambulance Attendant, and Ambulance Driver.

Physicians and nurses staffing the Outpatient Department are members of the regular medical staff of the hospital. This staff holds periodic conferences to review and analyze clinical work and present selected cases at hospital general clinical conferences.

In hospitals having schools of nursing, students are assigned to the Outpatient Department as part of their training. Interns and residents also receive training in this department. The medical records of outpatients should be the same as those for inpatients and should follow patients from one place to another. This involves a system for procuring and returning all outpatient records to the Medical Record Department.

Instructions on health matters may be carried on in cooperation with community organizations, and the department should participate with local agencies regarding health education, hygiene, preventive medicine, contagious and venereal diseases, and similar subjects.

Unless the department serves a great many patients with a great variety of services requiring on-the-premises diagnostic and treatment facilities, the regular facilities and services of the hospital will be used by this department. Personnel from diagnostic and adjunct services, such as laboratory, pharmacy, dental, and technical services, may be assigned to the Outpatient Department for specified periods. Although their work will be supervised by their respective department heads, close working relationships between heads of departments and the Director, Outpatient Services are imperative.

Departments such as laundry, housekeeping, engineering and maintenance, business, and social service are included in services rendered to the Outpatient Department.

DIRECTOR, OUTPATIENT SERVICES

The Director of Outpatient Services supervises and directs all activities of the Outpatient clinic, and coordinates its work with inpatient facilities, to insure adequate and competent outpatient care.

JOB DUTIES

He establishes clinic policies and procedures in cooperation with inpatient department heads and administrative personnel. He interprets and administers personnel policies established by the Board of Governors according to national standards. He reviews clinic activities, and makes recommendations for changes in, or better utilization of, facilities, services and staff. He plans clinic sessions and supervises staff and patient scheduling to meet community needs. He selects personnel, and supervises clerical, medical, nutritional, nursing, medical-social, and medical records personnel. He authorizes purchases of supplies and equipment. He prepares the department's budget. He also prepares statistical data concerning department activities.

He participates in community activities designed to promote health education, and meets with personnel of other local institutions and organizations (such as public health and public welfare) to establish policies and services for community health problems.

He may administer physical examinations, and diagnose and treat ambulatory patients having illnesses that respond quickly to treatment. He refers patients requiring prolonged or specialized treatment to other facilities. He may act as consultant to clinic physicians and interns on difficult cases.

EDUCATION, TRAINING, AND EXPERIENCE

Where a physician is required as head of the clinic, he must have an unrestricted state license to practice medicine or osteopathy.

Five to 10 years' hospital supervisory experience may be required, depending upon administrative policies.

JOB RELATIONSHIPS

Workers supervised: All personnel assigned to the clinic.
Supervised by: Associate Administrator or Administrator.
Promotion from: No formal line of promotion.
Promotion to: No formal line of promotion.

PROFESSIONAL AFFILIATIONS

American Medical Association
535 North Dearborn Street
Chicago, Illinois 60610

Director, Outpatient Services: (DOT) 187.168

CLINIC COORDINATOR

The Clinic Coordinator acts as liaison between clinic patients and the medical, nursing, clerical, and social service staffs. She coordinates the clerical functions between these staffs.

JOB DUTIES

She sets up and opens the clinic by obtaining appointment books and requisitioning patients' cards. She greets patients upon arrival, checks appointment sheets against patients' cards, and makes sure that the patients' records are on hand and available to the physician. She assigns patients to doctors in accordance with the regulations of the clinic. She has the responsibility for making patients' appointments and reappointments.

She reviews patients' medical records, recommendations, and referrals for each patient. She relays a variety of information to the patient regarding preparation for various types of examinations, and location of laboratory, pharmacy, and other treatment areas.

She makes minor entries in patients' records and fills out forms for treatments, tests, diets, and various other forms that may be used in specific clinics. She checks the accuracy of the work of volunteers, and assists and guides them in their duties.

She checks doctors' time sheets; computes and compiles statistics for clinic attendance; and tallies the number of patients seen by each doctor.

She attends meetings of coordinator groups and social service committees to discuss mutual problems, review old procedures, and implement new procedures.

EDUCATION, TRAINING, AND EXPERIENCE

The Clinic Coordinator should have two years of college, supplemented by courses in psychology, social sciences, and general science. She should have some experience in dealing with the general public, either in a hospital or office situation.

On-the-job training in coordination of services is rendered by the clinic.

JOB RELATIONSHIPS

Workers supervised: Clerical personnel and volunteers assigned to the department.
Supervised by: Director, Outpatient Services.
Promotion from: No formal line of promotion.
Promotion to: No formal line of promotion.

PROFESSIONAL AFFILIATIONS

None.

Clinic Coordinator: (DOT) 187.—T

AMBULANCE ATTENDANT

JOB DUTIES

The Ambulance Attendant accompanies and assists the Ambulance Driver in lifting patients into and out of ambulance, wheelchair, or stretcher, and renders first aid in emergencies.

He bandages, splints, or administers oxygen to patients at home or during the trip in the ambulance. He covers patients with blankets, and exercises care in moving patients to avoid aggravating injury or disease.

He assists the Ambulance Driver in maintaining the ambulance in efficient operating condition by helping with minor mechanical repairs and adjustments. He replaces the linen on the stretcher, and collects clean linen for each trip.

He may be required to have a Red Cross first aid training certificate.

Some hospitals today have mobile cardiac and maternity units, as well as emergency ambulances staffed with medical or paramedical personnel capable of administering to patients on the scene, under supervision of medical personnel at the hospital via radio communication. Training for these attendants is comparable to that of medics in the military.

EDUCATION, TRAINING, AND EXPERIENCE

Grammar school education with courses in first aid is required.

On-the-job training in methods and procedures is provided.

JOB RELATIONSHIPS

Workers supervised: None.
Supervised by: Director, Outpatient Services.
Promotion from: No formal line of promotion. This may be an entry job.
Promotion to: No formal line of promotion. May rotate with Ambulance Driver.

PROFESSIONAL AFFILIATIONS

None.

Ambulance Attendant: (DOT) 355.878-010

AMBULANCE DRIVER

JOB DUTIES

The Ambulance Driver transports, sick, injured, or convalescent patients to and from the hospital.

He is assisted by the Ambulance Attendant in carrying or helping patients in and out of the ambulance, using stretcher or wheelchair. He covers patients with blankets, and exercises care in moving them in order not to aggravate injury or disease. He administers first aid, such as bandaging, splinting, and giving oxygen.

He maintains the ambulance in efficient operating condition, making minor repairs and adjustments. He checks gas, oil, water, and tire pressures after each trip. He mops and cleans the inside of the ambulance to keep it neat and orderly.

He prepares reports indicating departures, destinations, and arrivals on calls.

He uses knowledge and skill in driving, to avoid sudden motions that might be detrimental to patients.

He may be required to have a Red Cross first aid training certificate.

EDUCATION, TRAINING, AND EXPERIENCE

High school graduation is preferred with courses in first aid and auto mechanics. One year's driving experience is required.

On-the-job training in methods and procedures of ambulance driving is provided. The Driver may be required by the state to have a chauffeur's license.

JOB RELATIONSHIPS

Workers supervised: None.
Supervised by: Director, Outpatient Services.
Promotion from: No formal line of promotion. This may be an entry job.
Promotion to: No formal line of promotion.

PROFESSIONAL AFFILIATIONS

None.

Ambulance Driver: (DOT) 913.883-010

Pharmacy

The Pharmacy Department is responsible for storing and dispensing all drugs and pharmaceutical preparations used in the hospital for patient medication, and for filling outpatient prescriptions.

The Pharmacists compound some medications and sterile solutions from ingredients purchased in bulk from reputable wholesalers and manufacturers. Other compounds are purchased ready for use from pharmaceutical companies, since today this procedure is often more economical.

The Pharmacy Department is the repository for all drugs, chemicals, pharmaceuticals, and narcotics used in the hospital. Separate stocks of most commonly used medications and narcotics are maintained within treatment areas for convenience, but the Pharmacy still is responsible for their maintenance and distribution, and for control of such products as narcotics, barbiturates, and alcohol. It is also responsible for seeing that biologicals, vaccines, and any other drugs that are subject to deterioration are stored under proper refrigeration, and inventory-controlled, to prevent use after the recommended expiration dates.

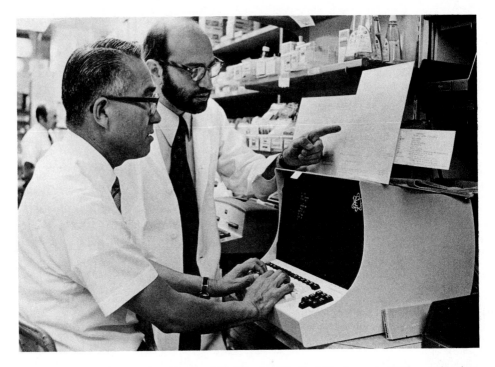

In the Hospital Pharmacy at Stanford University Medical Center, scientists are developing a new computer-based system to prevent drug mixtures in prescriptions that might cause harmful reactions in hospitalized patients. Here, Dr. Stanley N. Cohen, Director of the Division of Clinical Pharmacology (standing), and Director of Pharmacy Hiram Silva respond to a series of question prompts at the computer television unit.

Each year many new drugs come on the market, and while the Pharmacist must know how to compound any pharmaceutical preparation, he must also be aware of new products, their advantages and disadvantages, and disseminate this information to the medical and nursing staff.

New and replacement drugs are purchased directly by the department, and bills submitted to the Purchasing or Financial Management Department.

The department must be headed by a licensed pharmacist, and standards for its operation are those recommended by the Committee of Pharmacy of the American Hospital Association and the American Pharmaceutical Association. Legally, all pharmacies must retain a record of physicians' orders for drugs. Only drugs, chemicals, and pharmaceutical preparations of at least the quality indicated by the United States Pharmacopeia, National Formulary, and New and Nonofficial Remedies may be used in treatment of patients.

In very small hospitals, there may be only one licensed pharmacist, and he may be working only part-time. In very large hospitals, the department may be extensively staffed. If there is a school of pharmacy in conjunction with the hospital, pharmacy interns may help under supervision, and may be used to handle the voluminous paperwork of the department.

PHARMACY DEPARTMENT

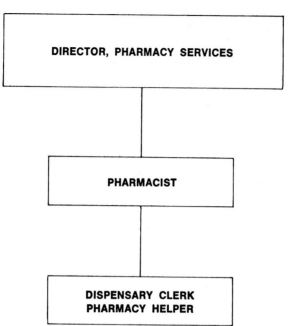

NOTE: This chart is for illustrative purposes only and should not be considered a recommended pattern of organization.

DIRECTOR, PHARMACY SERVICES
Chief Pharmacist

The Director of Pharmacy Services must be a licensed pharmacist. He supervises and coordinates the activities of personnel in the hospital pharmacy, and compounds and dispenses medications by means of standard chemical and physical procedures, to fill written medication and prescription requests issued by physicians, dentists, and other qualified prescribers.

JOB DUTIES

The Director of Pharmacy Services plans, organizes, and supervises activities in the hospital pharmacy in accordance with hospital policies, standard practices of the profession, and state and Federal laws.

He interviews, employs, and orients trained Pharmacists; and establishes their work schedules, assigning them to specific areas of responsibility in the administration, preparation, or dispensation functions of the department. He supervises the work performance of his staff and related personnel to insure adherence to established standards.

As necessary, he assists Pharmacists in compounding and dispensing medications.

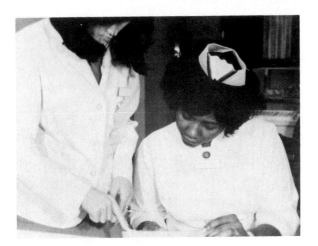

A Pharmacist in the hospital reviews a patient's chart, in order to be able to advise on drug therapy.
Photo courtesy of the American Association of Colleges of Pharmacy

He reviews written prescriptions, to determine that overdoses or toxic compounds will not result from the prescribed ingredients.

In preparing compounds, he weighs, measures, and mixes ingredients; or uses such procedures as blending, filtering, distilling, emulsifying, and titrating. He selects prepackaged pharmaceuticals from company's stock when available. When he compounds his own medications, he bottles and labels them, with instructions for use. He completes written records of each prescription filled, for the pharmacy files; for control file on narcotics, poisons, and habit-forming drugs; and for billing purposes by the Financial Department.

He supervises inventory of pharmaceutical stocks periodically, to determine stock needed and assure use of stock before expiration date recommended by the manufacturer. He places orders for supplies with salesmen or drug wholesalers, verifies receipt of the merchandise, and approves bills for payment.

He maintains formularies, sources of information on preparations, standard compendia on pharmaceuticals, reference texts, and journals in the department for use by qualified personnel. He consults with and advises medical staff concerning information obtained on medications, such as warnings issued on drugs currently on the market, incompatibility of certain drugs, or contraindications of drugs or other pharmaceuticals.

He initiates, develops and carries out rules and regulations pertaining to administrative and professional policies of the department with the approval and cooperation of hospital administration, and the Pharmacy and Therapeutic Committee, respectively. He establishes and maintains a system of records and bookkeeping in accordance with hospital policy for recording patients' charges for prescriptions and pharmaceutical supplies, and for maintaining adequate controls over dispensing and requisitioning all pharmaceuticals, including control file of narcotics, barbiturates, habit-forming drugs, and poisons received and issued.

He may serve as a member of the hospital Pharmacy and Therapeutic Committee in formulating departmental policies. He may serve on community committees to inform the public on uses and abuses of drugs.

He prepares the departmental budget.

Graduation from an accredited School of Pharmacy with five-years' college program in pharmacy. Completion of one year pharmacy internship and licensure as Registered Pharmacist by passing examination of State Board of Pharmacy are required.

Two to five years' experience in the hospital pharmacy field is usually required.

JOB RELATIONSHIPS

Workers supervised: Pharmacist and all other workers assigned to the pharmacy.
Supervised by: Associate Administrator.
Promotion from: Pharmacist.
Promotion to: Associate Administrator.

PROFESSIONAL AFFILIATIONS

American Pharmaceutical Association
2215 Constitution Avenue, N.W.
Washington, D.C. 20037

American Society of Hospital Pharmacists
4630 Montgomery Avenue
Washington, D.C. 20014

American Society for Pharmacology and Experimental Therapeutics, Inc.
9650 Rockville Pike
Bethesda, Maryland 20014

State and county pharmaceutical associations.

Director, Pharmacy Services: (DOT) 074.131T

PHARMACIST
Hospital Pharmacist

The hospital Pharmacist compounds and dispenses medications and other pharmaceuticals, using standard physical and chemical procedures to fill written prescriptions issued by physicians, dentists, and other qualified prescribers.

He reviews written prescriptions, to determine ingredients needed, and to be sure that overdoses or toxic compounds have not been prescribed. According to standard

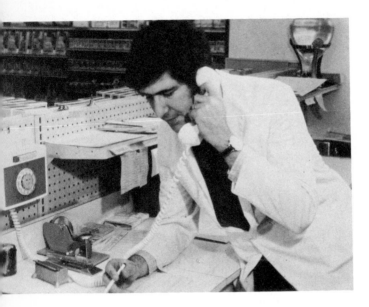

The hospital Pharmacist confers with a patient's physician about suitable drug therapy.
Photo courtesy of the American Association of Colleges of Pharmacy

formulas, he weighs, measures, and mixes ingredients; or he may compound ingredients by filtering, distilling, emulsifying, or titrating. He frequently fills prescriptions from bulk stock.

He sterilizes injectable preparation if it is made up in the pharmacy or purchased in nonsterile prepared form. He fills bottles, capsules, or other package forms with measured amounts of medication to prescription specifications. He types and affixes the label to the container, with identifying data and instructions for use. He may orally explain prescription use to outpatients.

He maintains records on all prescriptions filled for department files, computes and records prescription charges, and collects money from outpatients, or forwards charges for inpatients to the hospital's Financial Management Department for posting on patients' accounts. He maintains control records on narcotics, poisons, barbiturates, and habit-forming drugs as required by state and Federal laws.

He maintains inventory of pharmaceuticals and supplies, storing them under proper conditions of refrigeration and security. He may compound bulk emulsions, liquids, powders, and ointments for pharmacy and nursing-unit stocks.

He provides information to physicians and other staff members on availability of new drugs, warnings on currently marketed drugs, incompatibility of certain drugs, and contraindications of drugs and other pharmaceuticals.

If the hospital is small and there is no Director, Pharmacy Services, he may perform many of those activities.

EDUCATION, TRAINING, AND EXPERIENCE

Graduation from an accredited School of Pharmacy with a 5-year college program in pharmacy plus completion of one year's pharmacy internship and licensure as

Registered Pharmacist by passing examination of State Board of Pharmacy are required.

Short break-in period to become acquainted with specific hospital procedure and policy is provided.

JOB RELATIONSHIPS

Workers supervised: Pharmacy Helper, Dispensary Clerk, and clerical help.
Supervised by: Director, Pharmacy Services.
Promotion from: Pharmacist Intern.
Promotion to: Director, Pharmacy Services.

PROFESSIONAL AFFILIATIONS

American Pharmaceutical Association
2215 Constitution Avenue, N.W.
Washington, D.C. 20037

American Society of Hospital Pharmacists
4630 Montgomery Avenue
Washington, D.C. 20014

American Society for Pharmacology and Experimental Therapeutics, Inc.
9650 Rockville Pike
Bethesda, Maryland 20014

State and county pharmaceutical associations.

Pharmacist, Hospital: (DOT) 074.181-010

DISPENSARY CLERK
Pharmacy Clerk-Typist

JOB DUTIES

The Dispensary Clerk types labels for medications issued by the hospital pharmacy, and records transactions in pharmacy log to assist staff Pharmacist.

He receives written prescription and medication requests, after they are reviewed by the Pharmacist, and he types the suitable labels. In recording the log, he enters prescription number, patient's name and physician's name, and the description or name of the medication. He types a secondary label, listing patient's name, physician, prescription or pharmacy number, and hospital nursing unit to which pre-packaged and labeled medications are to be sent for inpatients. He types labels for other inpatient medications showing additional data concerning name, form, strength, and expiration date of drug. He clips typed labels to recorded medication requests and delivers them to the Pharmacist for affixing to drug containers.

He types labels for outpatient prescriptions after recording the prescription in the log by assigned prescription number, listing all identifying data such as patient's name, physician's name, and prescription number. He copies the physician's instructions for use of the medication onto the label from the prescription form. He returns the label and prescription form to the pharmacist for affixing to the filled prescription.

He types billing slips for prescriptions issued to welfare patients and mails to appropriate agency to obtain payment. He enters pharmacy charge on medication forms from price list; files one copy and forwards one copy to Financial Management Department for posting to patient's account. He compiles periodic reports from logbook on number and types of prescriptions filled for use of Pharmacist.

He maintains daily time and attendance records on pharmacy personnel for payroll use.

EDUCATION, TRAINING, AND EXPERIENCE

High school graduation with 1 year of typing, plus one to two years' experience as clerk-typist is desirable but not necessary. Up to three months' on-the-job training to learn routine of the department is provided.

JOB RELATIONSHIPS

Workers supervised: None.
Supervised by: Pharmacist.
Promotion from: No formal line of promotion. This may be an entry job.
Promotion to: No formal line of promotion. May be promoted to a responsible clerical position.

PROFESSIONAL AFFILIATIONS

None.

Dispensary Clerk: (DOT) 209.588-018

Physical Medicine and Rehabilitation

Until World War II, the practice of physical medicine in the United States was confined largely to applying heat, cold, water, electricity, and massage for relief from a few ailments.

During the War, Dr. Howard A. Rusk, then a Colonel in the Air Force, was stationed at Jefferson Barracks in St. Louis. As casualties streamed into the hospital, Dr. Rusk was not content to stop with whatever medicine and surgery could do for these young men, who represented the best of our youth. Amputees, paraplegics—whatever their disability, he wanted them restored to as active, independent, and full lives as possible. He began to apply the techniques of physical medicine, coupled with exercise and development of a wide variety of prostheses, toward rehabilitation of his patients. His experiments were so successful that he was soon

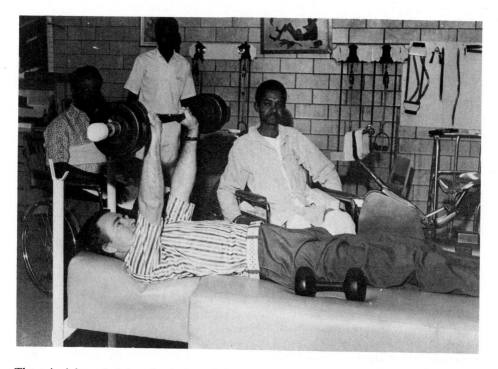

The principle underlying physical medicine and rehabilitation is to make the most of the abilities patients have, however discouraging they may seem at first diagnosis. At the Veterans Administration Hospital at Houston, Texas, men wounded in Vietnam gather in the gymnasium, to work out under the direction of a Physical Therapist.

transferred to the Pentagon, for the purpose of establishing similar programs in other hospitals.

After the War, Dr. Rusk was eager to make the same services available to the hundreds of thousands of disabled American civilians. He began with a few beds in New York City's Bellevue Hospital, and immediately set about raising funds to build a center specifically designed for, and exclusively devoted to rehabilitation. Within five years his dream was realized, in the Institute for Physical Medicine and Rehabilitation, affiliated with New York University Medical Center.

In a very short space of time, similar centers were established in other cities, and most hospitals developed departments of physical medicine and rehabilitation.

Staffing these centers and units with qualified personnel has not been an easy task, and the demand for trained physical, corrective, occupational, recreational, and other therapists continues. The demand is expected to exceed the supply for years to come. Although about 75 per cent of therapists are women, there are also ample opportunities for men in this field.

The scope of employment for physical therapists is not limited to hospitals alone; their service is also in great demand in other institutions, industral firms, schools, in the Armed Forces, and in public health services. The field offers long-term security, and unusual satisfaction in that workers know the value of the help they give.

The scope of physical medicine and rehabilitation today covers work with children who have congenital defects, accident victims who have been hurt in traffic or at work, older persons who have suffered strokes, patients who have suffered nerve injuries, amputees, victims of fractures, arthritis, and certain chest conditions. The techniques are also employed with patients recovering from almost any illness that has entailed bed rest, in order to keep muscles strong, and make the patient ambulatory as soon as possible. Its use in this manner results in shorter hospital stays for many patients.

The methods used in physical therapy include exercise and massage, and various applications of heat, cold, water, light, and electricity.

The Director of the Physical Medicine Department is a Doctor of Medicine or Osteopathy, who has specialized in this field, and is called a Physiatrist. Preferably, he is a diplomat of the American Congress of Physical Medicine or of the American Osteopathic Board of Physical Medicine and Rehabilitation.

Whether the patient suffering from paralysis is a veteran or a civilian, the road back to health is often long and difficult. The Therapist uses both encouragement and discipline to keep patients trying to do all they can . . .

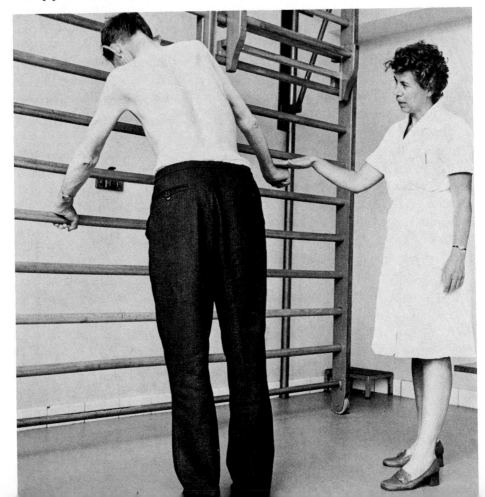

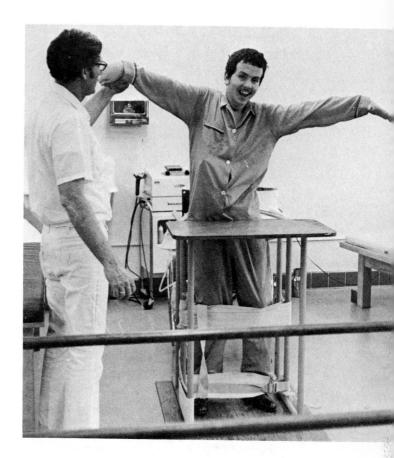

. . . But moments of triumph
prove the effort worthwhile.

The staff should consist of well-trained therapists who have passed certification examinations and are registered with their professional associations. They may also have to pass state examinations.

Attendants, aides, and volunteers perform many routine tasks in this department. These workers need only high school diplomas and brief on-the-job training.

PHYSIATRIST

The Physiatrist supervises and directs the activities of his staff in performing various types of therapy. He also makes diagnoses, and evaluates patient care.

JOB DUTIES

He establishes department policies and methods of operation in accordance with accepted national standards and criteria of the hospital.

He participates with personnel of other departments in planning joint administra-

PHYSICAL MEDICINE AND REHABILITATION DEPARTMENT

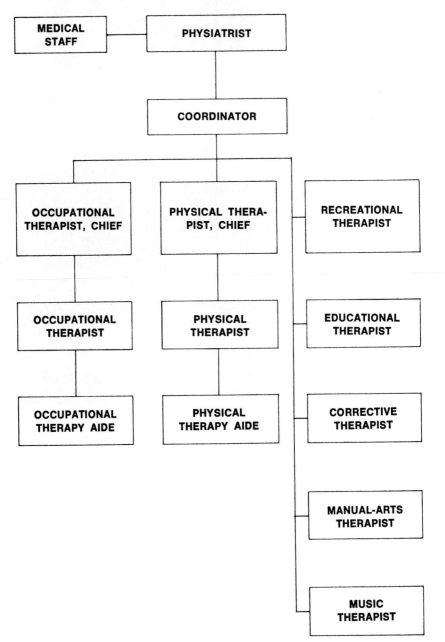

NOTE: This chart is for illustrative purposes only and should not be considered a recommended pattern of organization.

tive and technical programs, and recommends methods and procedures for co-ordination of physical medicine with related patient care services. He may develop new techniques and equipment, and conduct experimental studies on their effectiveness. He may serve as consultant in cooperative public health planning, and address public health, medical, educational, and civic groups, and conferences.

The Physiatrist specializes in clinical, diagnostic, and therapeutic use of physical agents and exercises of the various types of therapies to provide physical medicine and rehabilitation to patients. He consults with the referring physician, and plans a therapy program according to diagnosis and therapeutic problems. He prepares a prescription for the patient, to be followed by the appropriate therapist. He directs physical therapy, occupational therapy, counseling, social service, and other necessary services to provide assistance in rehabilitation of disabled patients. He instructs technicians on the nature and duration of dosage of treatments, and insures that they are administered properly. He reexamines patients at intervals to determine progress, and whether to change or discontinue treatment.

He prescribes therapeutic exercises designed to develop function of a specific anatomical part or muscle group.

He recommends and supervises occupational and vocational counseling for patients whose convalescence will be long, or whose physical disability demands change of occupation, and who may require therapies and adaptive devices to achieve the greatest possible independence and self-care. He correlates the physical, occupational, and recreational therapy activities.

He keeps a complete record of services rendered and patient reactions. He counsels patients' relatives in patient care and needs. He directs the training of resident physicians, interns, and technicians in the department.

He requisitions needed supplies and equipment.

EDUCATION, TRAINING, AND EXPERIENCE

The Physiatrist should have graduated from a medical school recognized by the Council on Medical Education and Hospitals of the American Medical Association or the Committee on Hospitals of the Bureau of Professional Education of the American Osteopathic Association, and be licensed to practice medicine or osteopathy in the state where he is practicing.

A residency in physical medicine and rehabilitation is desirable.

JOB RELATIONSHIPS

Workers supervised: All workers assigned to the department.
Supervised by: Associate Administrator for administrative purposes, and Chief of Medical Staff for professional practice.
Promotion from: No formal line of promotion.
Promotion to: No formal line of promotion.

PROFESSIONAL AFFILIATIONS

American Medical Association
535 North Dearborn Street
Chicago, Illinois 60610

American Academy of Physical Medicine and Rehabilitation
30 North Michigan Avenue
Chicago, Illinois 60602

American Osteopathic Board of Physical Medicine and Rehabilitation
212 East Ohio Street
Chicago, Illinois 60611

American Osteopathic College of Physical Medicine and Rehabilitation
2235 Spring Garden
Philadelphia, Pennsylvania 19130

Physiatrist: (DOT) 070.108-062

COORDINATOR

The Coordinator organizes all the efforts of occupational, physical, and other therapists in the Physical Medicine and Rehabilitation Department.

Through staff conferences and inservice training programs, he insures that the staff understands the practical significance of the various techniques employed in all therapies. With his staff, he analyzes the physical and mental requirements of each patient, so that objectives can be set for maximum development of the patient's potential, and possible capability for performance of a job, or of work in a sheltered environment.

JOB DUTIES

The Coordinator reviews notes to keep aware of patients' progress in overall rehabilitation, and to insure that therapy prescription is understood and applied. He counsels patients so that they have confidence in the therapy programs formulated for them.

He participates with personnel of other departments (such as Nursing and Social Service Departments) to plan joint technical progress and to coordinate physical medicine with related patient care. He works with patients' families, industry, employers, and community as a whole as an advisor on rehabilitation problems.

He organizes and engages in research projects and studies pertaining to rehabilitation approaches.

He plans most efficient use of personnel, space, and equipment, to afford most effective treatment to the greatest possible number of patients.

He performs all necessary details of administration for the department, thus releasing the Physiatrist to give maximum attention and supervision to treatment.

He recommends patient fees, prepares budget, and maintains supplies and equipment.

EDUCATION, TRAINING, AND EXPERIENCE

A Master of Science or Bachelor of Science degree in physical medicine from an approved college or university is required.

Four to five years' experience as a therapist in a hospital is preferred.

Brief on-the-job training in the administrative aspects of the department should be provided.

JOB RELATIONSHIPS

Workers supervised: Administrative supervision of Occupational Therapist, Physical Therapist, Recreational Therapist, any other specialized therapists assigned to the department, clerical, and volunteer staff.
Supervised by: Physiatrist or Associate Administrator.
Promotion from: Occupational Therapist, Physical Therapist, or Recreation Therapist.
Promotion to: No formal line of promotion.

PROFESSIONAL AFFILIATIONS

The American Physical Therapy Association
1790 Broadway
New York, New York 10019

The American Occupational Therapy Association
250 West 57th Street
New York, New York 10019

National Therapeutic Recreation Society
1700 Pennsylvania Avenue, N.W.
Washington, D.C. 20006

Coordinator: (DOT) 079.128T

OCCUPATIONAL THERAPIST, CHIEF

The Chief of the Occupational Therapy section establishes its goals and policies, and standards for patients' participation in its activities, as well as reporting and record-keeping procedures in accordance with those of the department.

JOB DUTIES

She confers with physicians regarding referral procedures, and schedules patients for treatment in accordance with available personnel and equipment, and assigns

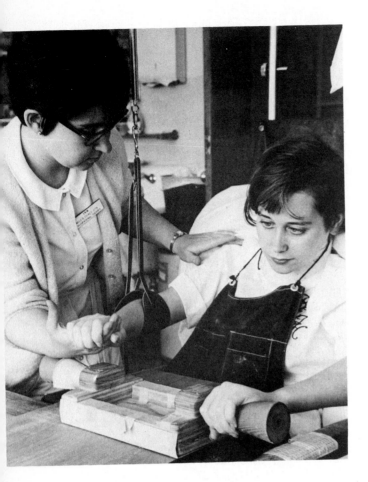

For patients who can use their hands independently, occupational therapy is likely to consist of handcrafts, or other activity that results in a product or a skill. This boy at New York University Medical Center does not yet have enough strength or coordination to do things himself, so the Occupational Therapist works with him in an exercise to strengthen his hands and arms.

cases to the therapists. She supervises and observes therapists engaged in instructing patients in such activities as practice in prevocational or homemaking skills; or activities of daily living: or activities to promote physical function, perceptual-cognitive motor abilities, adjustment to disability, upper extremity prosthetic training; or family orientation. She evaluates the therapists' efficiency, skill, abilities, and attitudes toward patients and fellow workers, for use in recommending personnel actions, and determining program effectiveness.

She is responsible for personnel policies in the section, and appraises, employs, and dismisses staff as necessary. She trains new personnel, and lectures on phases of occupational therapy to medical students and nurses.

She attends case conferences with physicians and nurses to discuss and evaluate individual patients' conditions, progress, and plans for therapy.

She performs related duties, such as supervision of treatment charges, annual reports, budget requests, and requisitioning of equipment and facilities.

EDUCATION, TRAINING, AND EXPERIENCE

The Occupational Therapist, Chief, must have graduated from an accredited college with a four- or five-year course leading to a Bachelor of Science degree in occupational therapy, and be certified by the Board of Registry of the American Occupational Therapy Association. She must also have three years of hospital experience as an Occupational Therapist. Advanced postgraduate training is desirable.

JOB RELATIONSHIPS

Workers supervised: Occupational Therapist, Occupational Therapy Aide, and volunteers engaged in instructing patients in various crafts.
Supervised by: Physiatrist, Coordinator, or physician in charge of patient.
Promotion from: Occupational Therapist.
Promotion to: No formal line of promotion.

PROFESSIONAL AFFILIATIONS

American Occupational Therapy Association
250 West 57th Street
New York, New York 10019

Occupational Therapist, Chief: (DOT) 079.128-018

OCCUPATIONAL THERAPIST

The Occupational Therapist plans programs involving such activities as manual arts and crafts, practice in fundamental prevocational and homemaking skills, and activities of daily living. She participates in a variety of sensorimotor, educational, recreational and social activities designed to help patients regain physical or mental function, or adjust to their handicaps.

JOB DUTIES

The Occupational Therapist consults with other members of the rehabilitation team to determine the most appropriate activity program for each patient, and to coordinate this with the other activities in the department. She selects activities suited to the patient's physical capacity, intelligence, and interest, in order to upgrade him to maximum independence, prepare him for return to some form of employment eventually, assist in restoring muscular and articular functions, improve general physical condition, and aid in adjustment. She teaches the patients the skills and techniques needed for participation in activities, and evaluates their progress, attitudes, and behavior as related to their rehabilitative potential.

She adapts programs to each patient's situation, so that cardiac or stroke pa-

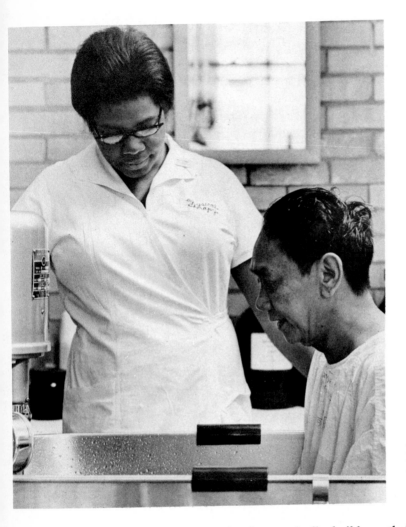

At Johns Hopkins Medical Institutions, Baltimore, an elderly patient enjoys the gentle massage provided by a whirlpool bath.

tients are assigned tasks that gradually build up their physical tolerance, while patients who must be bedridden for long periods are given hobbies and crafts to utilize their time constructively, and disabled patients may be given tasks to develop substitute skills.

In neuropsychiatric hospitals, the Occupational Therapist selects games and handcrafts, or narrates stories, to redirect antisocial tendencies into constructive channels. She provides routine sedentary tasks for overactive patients, and stimulating ones for depressed patients. She attempts to create a normal social atmosphere to aid recovery and lessen disciplinary problems.

She judges the program's interest value by studying patients' reactions to activities, and reports these for review by other members of the rehabilitation team.

She requisitions supplies and equipment, and cleans and repairs tools after each session. She may direct one or more assistants or volunteer workers, and she may conduct training programs for them and for medical and nursing students. She may also design and fit adaptive devices, such as splints and braces, for patients' use.

EDUCATION, TRAINING, AND EXPERIENCE

The Occupational Therapist must be a graduate of a four-year accredited college with a Bachelor of Science degree in occupational therapy, and must be certified by the Board of Registry of the American Occupational Therapy Association. When educational requirements are met, no previous experience is required. Hospitals provide up to six months of training on the job, for familiarity with the hospital facilities and regulations, doctors' techniques, and department procedures.

JOB RELATIONSHIPS

Workers supervised: Occupational Therapy Aide and volunteers engaged in instructing patients in various crafts.
Supervised by: Occupational Therapist, Chief or Coordinator.
Promotion from: May be promoted from Occupational Therapy Aide after additional training and experience.
Promotion to: Occupational Therapist, Chief.

PROFESSIONAL AFFILIATIONS

American Occupational Therapy Association
250 West 57th Street
New York, New York 10019

Occupational Therapist: (DOT) 079.128-018

PHYSICAL THERAPIST, CHIEF

The Chief of the Physical Therapy section establishes its goals and policies, standards for patients' participation, and the reporting procedures and types of records to be maintained.

JOB DUTIES

The Chief of the section confers with physicians regarding treatments for individual patients, and schedules them for treatment in accordance with available personnel and equipment. He assigns cases to therapists, indicating the type and specifications of treatment to be given, and the type of equipment or therapeutic devices required.

He observes the therapists in performance of their duties, to evaluate efficiency, skill, abilities, and attitudes toward patients and fellow workers, in order to recommend personnel actions, and determine the effectiveness of the program. He introduces and demonstrates new techniques, and observes patients' reactions to prescribed treatments, and evaluates their progress.

He trains new personnel, and lectures students and nurses on phases and effects of physical therapy. He instructs and demonstrates to outpatients and parents of pediatric patients, so that they know how to do the prescribed exercises at home.

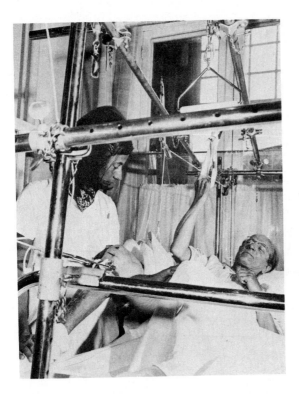

Mechanical contrivances sometimes help patients to help themselves. This patient proudly
shows his daughter how he can
lift himself in bed.

He attends case conferences with doctors and nurses to discuss and evaluate patients' conditions, progress, and future therapy.

He prepares treatment charges, submits budgets, requisitions supplies and equipment, and submits records and reports.

EDUCATION, TRAINING, AND EXPERIENCE

The Physical Therapist, Chief must have graduated from an accredited institution with a Bachelor of Science degree in physical therapy, plus a supervised clinical internship of about four months' duration to prepare for professional registration. An individual who holds a bachelor's degree in a related field may enroll in a certificate course offered by some schools, for a period of 18 months to two years. Most states now require examination before granting a license to practice physical therapy. Master's degree programs are available in some schools, and short courses are offered for specialized training in specific techniques and procedures.

The Chief of the section should have three to five years of experience as a Physical Therapist.

One to three months is usually allowed for on-the-job training.

JOB RELATIONSHIPS

Workers supervised: Physical Therapist, Physical Therapy Aide, volunteers, and clerical assistants.
Supervised by: Physiatrist or physician in charge of patient.
Promotion from: Physical Therapist.
Promotion to: No formal line of promotion.

PROFESSIONAL AFFILIATIONS

American Physical Therapy Association
1740 Broadway
New York, New York 10019

Physical Therapist, Chief: (DOT) 079.378-034

PHYSICAL THERAPIST
Physiotherapist

Physical Therapists employ exercise, massage, heat, water, light, and electricity in treating patients to prevent disability following disease or injury, or loss of a body part; and to help patients reach their maximum performance and assume a place in society while learning to live within the limits of their capabilities.

JOB DUTIES

The Physical Therapist applies diagnostic and prognostic tests of each patient's ability in the function of muscles, nerves, and joints, and plans an individualized therapy program for him. She directs and aids patients in active and passive exercises, muscle reeducation, and walking; and offers functional training, utilizing pulleys and weights, steps, and inclined surfaces. She uses equipment, including ultraviolet and infrared lamps, low-voltage generators, diathermy, and ultrasonic machines. She gives whirlpool and contrast baths, and applies moist packs. She directs patients in the care and use of wheelchairs, braces, canes, crutches, and prosthetic and orthoptic devices. She gives instruction in posture control and therapeutic procedures to be continued by the patient. She adapts conventional physiotherapeutic techniques to meet the needs of patients unable to comprehend verbal commands, or voluntarily carry out a regime of exercise.

She evaluates records, and reports patients' progress for review by other members of the rehabilitation team. She requisitions supplies and equipment. She may direct and supervise the activities of assistants or volunteer workers. She may conduct teaching programs or participate in training of medical and nursing personnel, students, and other workers in physical therapy techniques and objectives.

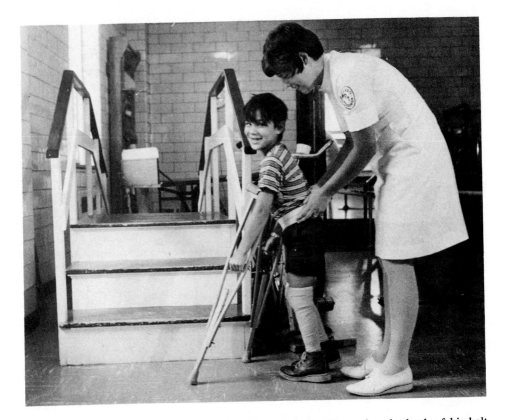

The Therapist steadies her small patient with a gentle hand grasping the back of his belt as he prepares to climb the practice stairs. They look as tall as Mount Everest, but he will come down safely on the other side.

Photo courtesy of the University of Wisconsin Center for Health Sciences

EDUCATION, TRAINING, AND EXPERIENCE

The Physical Therapist should have acquired a Bachelor of Science degree from an accredited institution offering training in this specialty, plus a supervised clinical internship of approximately four months to prepare for professional registration. Individuals holding a bachelor's degree in a related field may enroll in a certificate course, offered by some schools, for a period of 18 months to two years. Most states now require an examination before granting a license to practice physical therapy. Master's degree programs are offered by some universities. Short courses are available for specialized training in specific therapeutic skills.

When educational requirements are met, no additional experience is necessary. Up to six months of on-the-job training is usually provided, to gain familiarity with the hospital equipment and regulations, doctors' techniques, and department procedures.

JOB RELATIONSHIPS

Workers supervised: Physical Therapy Aide and volunteer and clerical assistants.
Supervised by: Physical Therapist, Chief.
Promotion from: No formal line of promotion. May be promoted from Physical Therapy Aide after additional formal training.
Promotion to: Physical Therapist, Chief.

PROFESSIONAL AFFILIATIONS

American Physical Therapy Association
1740 Broadway
New York, New York 10019

Physical Therapist: (DOT) 079.378-034

RECREATIONAL THERAPIST

The Recreational Therapist organizes and directs such activities as sports, dramatics, nature study, social activities, games, and arts and crafts in accordance with patients' needs, capabilities, and interests as determined by discussion with them and with other members of the rehabilitation team.

JOB DUTIES

The Recreational Therapist prepares reports on patients' actions and reactions during recreational periods, as these reflect progress or regression, and these reports are evaluated by the rehabilitation team in planning future therapy.

The Therapist surveys and evaluates the therapeutic recreation program, and recommends changes or modifications. She prepares budgets and periodic reports of activities, and orders supplies of recreation apparatus and equipment.

She assigns duties, and delegates responsibilities to her assistants and volunteer workers.

She may specialize in one or more aspects of recreation, such as sports, or arts and crafts.

She may make arrangements for movies, live entertainment for special programs, and group outings such as picnics, ball games, shopping, or sightseeing.

She attends professional meetings and conventions and reads various journals and periodicals to keep abreast of her field. She may write articles. She maintains a close relationship with therapeutic recreation departments in other community agencies.

EDUCATION, TRAINING, AND EXPERIENCE

The Recreation Therapist must have a college degree, preferably in recreation or recreation therapy, although a degree in physical education, social science, job guidance, art, dramatics, or related subjects may be acceptable. When educational requirements are met, no previous experience is required.

Brief on-the-job training is usually provided for orientation.

JOB RELATIONSHIPS

Workers supervised: May supervise an aide and volunteers participating in therapy program.

Supervised by: Physiatrist, Coordinator, or physician in charge of patient.

Promotion from: No formal line of promotion. May be promoted from aide after additional formal training and experience.

Promotion to: No formal line of promotion. Advancement is through addition of supervisory, administrative, or teaching duties.

PROFESSIONAL AFFILIATIONS

National Therapeutic Recreation Society
1700 Pennsylvania Avenue, N.W.
Washington, D.C. 20006

Recreational Therapist: (DOT) 079.128-022

EDUCATIONAL THERAPIST

The Educational Therapist instructs patients in prescribed academic subjects, to prevent mental deterioration, and aid in attainment of knowledge and skills that will meet patients' vocational objectives.

JOB DUTIES

The Educational Therapist collaborates with other members of the rehabilitation team in planning such courses as English, mathematics, botany, geography, typing, painting, bookkeeping, or mechanical drawing. She selects subjects and teaching methods that are most suitable to the patients' attitudes, capabilities, and interests. She employs academic courses of study, business equipment and methods, and holds group discussions. She utilizes psychological techniques and personal qualities to gain the patients' confidence, motivate acceptance of hospital services, maintain interest, and relieve tensions and frustration.

She instructs patients at various educational levels, and administers graded educational activities to develop and evaluate patients' mental and physical capacities. She administers accreditation tests and transmits results to school authorities or state departments of education for grading, and certification of each patient's educational level.

She prepares reports of patients' emotional reactions to, and progress in, individual and group training situations, to provide clinical data for evaluation by the rehabilitation team.

EDUCATION, TRAINING, AND EXPERIENCE

The Educational Therapist should have graduated from an accredited college or university, with emphasis on subject matter to be taught. She should be a certified teacher. A special education teacher with a degree at the master's level is desirable. She must also have undergone a clinical training period of two to seven months.

JOB RELATIONSHIPS

Workers supervised: None.
Supervised by: Physiatrist, Coordinator, or physician in charge of patient.
Promotion from: No formal line of promotion.
Promotion to: No formal line of promotion.

PROFESSIONAL AFFILIATIONS

National Education Association
1201 16th Street, N.W.
Washington, D.C. 20036

Educational Therapist: (DOT) 091.228-010

CORRECTIVE THERAPIST

The Corrective Therapist provides a medically prescribed program of physical exercises and activities designed to prevent muscular deterioration, and to achieve fullest mental and physical rehabilitation.

JOB DUTIES

The Corrective Therapist confers with the physician, and collaborates with other members of the rehabilitation team to plan and organize each patient's course of treatment. She establishes rapport with patients to motivate them, choosing physical exercises and activities that are in accordance with the medical prescription, but which will sustain interest and insure continued participation. She employs any one or combination of assistive, resistive, or free movement exercises, utilizing equipment, devices and aids such as stationary bicycles, weights, pulleys, rowing machines, walking bars, and hydrogymnastics.

She directs patients in the use, function, and care of braces, artificial limbs, and other devices designed to assist in walking. She instructs amputees and partially paralyzed patients in ambulatory techniques, and use of specially equipped automobiles. She guides blind persons in foot travel during initial stages of training, to help them achieve self-confidence and independence. She directs patients in self-care activities, including personal hygiene.

She adapts physical education and recreation programs to suit children, old people, and other special groups.

She observes patients during exercises and activities, to evaluate emotional reactions, strength, endurance, and self-care ability, to determine the patient's rate of progress and recovery. She prepares progress reports on each patient, for evaluation by the physician and the rest of the rehabilitation team.

EDUCATION, TRAINING, AND EXPERIENCE

The Corrective Therapist must have graduated from an approved college or university, with a degree in physical education and courses in the basic sciences. She should have had two to seven months of clinical experience under the direction of a licensed physician, and be certified by the American Board of Corrective Therapists.

JOB RELATIONSHIPS

Workers supervised: None. May supervise volunteers who assist the program.
Supervised by: Physiatrist, Coordinator or physician in charge of patient.
Promotion from: No formal line of promotion.
Promotion to: No formal line of promotion. Advancement is through addition of supervisory, administrative, or teaching responsibilities.

PROFESSIONAL AFFILIATIONS

Association for Physical and Mental Rehabilitation
1265 Cherry Road
Memphis, Tennessee 38117

Corrective Therapist: (DOT) 079.368-014

MANUAL ARTS THERAPIST

The Manual Arts Therapist instructs patients in medically prescribed manual arts activities, to assist in maintaining or improving or developing work skills, within the limits of the patients' abilities.

JOB DUTIES

The Manual Arts Therapist collaborates with other members of the rehabilitation team in planning and organizing work activities. He utilizes industrial or agricultural work activities in actual work situations, in the hospital building, or on the grounds. He may set up work situations, making conditions as realistic as possible to determine whether a patient can perform in a real-life situation, and to instill self-confidence.

He selects activities, following medically prescribed instructions related to the patient's vocational goals, such as metalworking, printing, woodworking, or radio and television repair. He may give bedfast patients instruction in leathercraft or other handcrafts. He instructs patients in technical aspects of whatever work they are doing, and in use and care of tools and equipment. He coordinates his activities with other therapy programs.

He prepares reports showing the development of each patient's work tolerance and emotional and social adjustment, to aid medical personnel in evaluation of the patient's progress, and his ability to meet the physical and mental demands of employment.

EDUCATION, TRAINING, AND EXPERIENCE

The Manual Arts Therapist should have graduated from an approved college or university with a major in industrial arts, agriculture, or a related field. His courses should include education, psychology, and anatomy. Two to seven months of clinical training is required.

JOB RELATIONSHIPS

Workers supervised: None. May supervise volunteers who assist the program.
Supervised by: Physiatrist, Coordinator, or physician in charge of patient.
Promotion from: No formal line of promotion.
Promotion to: No formal line of promotion. Advancement is through addition of supervisory, administrative, or teaching responsibilities.

PROFESSIONAL AFFILIATIONS

American Association for Rehabilitation Therapy
Veterans Administration Hospital
Hines, Illinois 60141

Manual Arts Therapist: (DOT) 079.128-010

MUSIC THERAPIST

The Music Therapist plans, organizes, and conducts medically prescribed musical activities intended to change or improve patients' mental outlook, to assist in their rehabilitation from mental or physical illness or disability.

JOB DUTIES

The Music Therapist plans her work in collaboration with other members of the rehabilitation team. She selects musical activities and methods of application suitable to patients' needs, capabilities, and interests. She contacts musicians and arranges concerts or solo appearances.

She conducts and participates in instrumental and vocal musical activities based upon individual patient's needs, such as chorus, group, and solo singing: or orchestra, rhythm training; listening to selected music and musical quiz programs; and attending patients' or visiting musicians' concerts. She instructs patients in playing instruments, singing, reading music, and music appreciation.

She observes and studies patients' reactions to various musical activities for signs of progress or regression. She prepares periodic reports containing data on patient's reactions and progress and submits them to the physician or rehabilitation team for evaluation. She confers with the physician and rehabilitation team to determine the effectiveness of the program. She prepares individual records of patients' musical activities.

She may conduct or participate in other activities, such as dancing, or games to the accompaniment of music, in concert with volunteer workers, teachers, or other therapists.

EDUCATION, TRAINING, AND EXPERIENCE

The Music Therapist must have a bachelor's degree in music therapy, plus a six-month internship in an approved psychiatric institution affiliated with an accredited school offering a degree in music therapy. A college graduate with a degree in music may qualify by taking additional postgraduate courses, or sometimes by substituting relevant qualifying experience.

JOB RELATIONSHIPS

Workers supervised: None. May supervise volunteers who assist the program.
Supervised by: Physiatrist, Coordinator, or physician in charge of patient.
Promotion from: No formal line of promotion.
Promotion to: No formal line of promotion.

PROFESSIONAL AFFILIATIONS

National Association for Music Therapy, Inc.
P.O. Box 15
Lawrence, Kansas 66044

Music Therapist: (DOT) 079.128-014

Radiology-Nuclear Medicine Department

Except in large research or teaching hospitals, the Departments of Radiology and Nuclear Medicine are usually combined. This is due to the complexity of nuclear medicine techniques, the cost of the equipment, the scarcity of highly skilled technologists, and the relatively small proportion of patients who require such special services. However, nuclear medicine is a rapidly advancing segment of medical science, and will be receiving increasing emphasis in the future. The Society of Nuclear Medicine estimates that an additional 1,000 technologists will be needed each year, and that this number is likely to rise with continuing development and application of nuclear medicine technology.

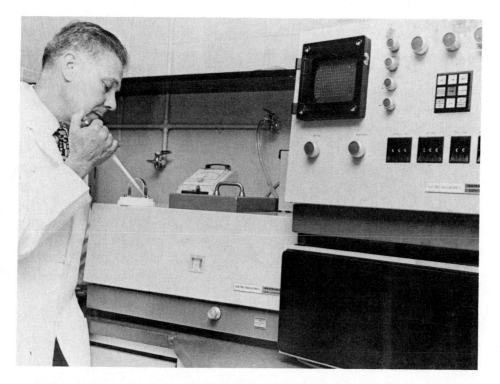

A physician-scientist at work with a radioactive material, which must be handled with extreme care and caution. The radioactive element is stored in thick-walled lead containers and is to be moved only with special tools.

In the field of radiology, which is also expanding, the United States Bureau of Labor Statistics reports that in 1970 there were 80,000 radiologic technologists employed in this country, and about two-thirds of them are women. About one-third of them work in hospitals; most of the remainder work in medical laboratories, physicians' or dentists' offices, clinics, Federal and state health agencies, and public school systems. A few work as members of mobile X-ray teams, engaged in detection of tuberculosis.

In hospitals, the Radiology-Nuclear Medicine Department aids physicians in diagnosis of disease by taking, processing, examining, and interpreting radiographs and fluorographs. Fluorographs are taken when it is necessary to study the action of internal physiologic processes, or locate foreign bodies. Technologists in the department also administer radioisotopes, which indicate the course of compounds introduced into the human body. They employ X-ray, radium, and radioactive substances in treatment of disease, most notably various forms of cancer. In addition, the department is responsible for planning and carrying out policies and procedures to protect all hospital personnel who have contact with the radioactive materials; provide consultation and advice to physicians in interpreting diagnostic findings; plan diagnostic X-ray procedures and other pertinent matters; participate in research projects, and in the hospital's educational program.

Authority for the department rests with the Director of Radiology, who should be a physician who has specialized in radiology, and who reports to the Administrator on business matters and the Chief of the Medical Staff on professional matters. In smaller institutions, the department is often headed by a Radiologic Technologist.

In large hospitals, where Nuclear Medicine is a separate department, the Chief of Nuclear Medicine heads that staff, and supervises workers concerned with theory, research, techniques, and procedures.

Standards for departments of radiology are set by the American College of Surgeons and American College of Radiology.

DIRECTOR OF RADIOLOGY
Chief of Radiology

The Director of Radiology administers the programs of the department, and directs and coordinates its activities in accordance with accepted national standards and administrative policies.

JOB DUTIES

The Director confers with the hospital administrators, heads of other departments, and medical staff to determine the hospital's needs, and plans the scope, emphasis, and objectives of the radiology programs to meet them. He participates with per-

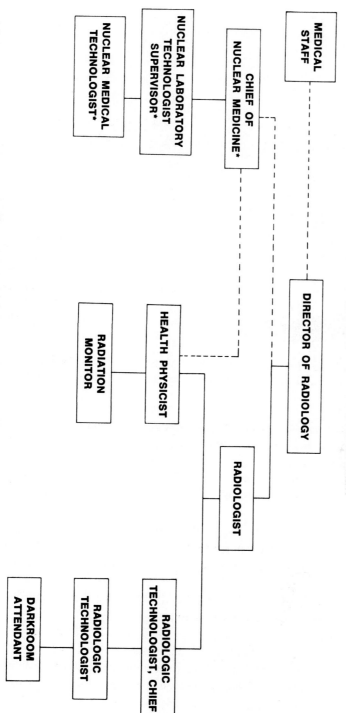

RADIOLOGY-NUCLEAR MEDICINE DEPARTMENT

MEDICAL STAFF

CHIEF OF NUCLEAR MEDICINE*

NUCLEAR LABORATORY TECHNOLOGIST SUPERVISOR*

NUCLEAR MEDICAL TECHNOLOGIST*

DIRECTOR OF RADIOLOGY

HEALTH PHYSICIST

RADIATION MONITOR

RADIOLOGIST

RADIOLOGIC TECHNOLOGIST, CHIEF

RADIOLOGIC TECHNOLOGIST

DARKROOM ATTENDANT

* This job may be found in the Radiology Department or separate in a Department of Nuclear Medicine.
NOTE: This chart is for illustrative purposes only and should not be considered a recommended pattern of organization.

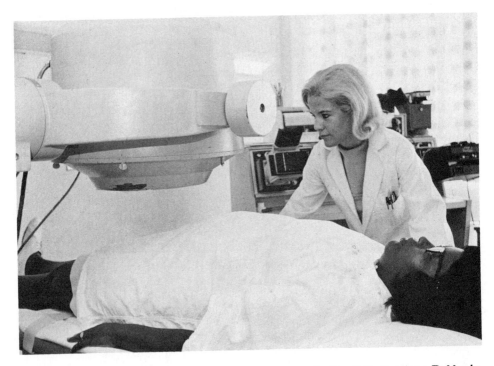

A patient is carefully positioned for radiologic treatment by Dr. Sally Jacobsen DeNardo, Assistant Clinical Professor of Radiology at the University of California at Davis School of Medicine.

sonnel of other departments in planning joint administrative and technical programs, and recommends methods and procedures for coordination of radiological services with other patient care services.

He investigates and studies trends and developments in radiologic practices and techniques, and develops manuals for his staff that outline methods, procedures, and techniques to be used.

He establishes, and enforces through subordinate supervisors, safety regulations to insure that both patients and hospital personnel receive maximum protection from hazardous effects of roentgen rays and radioactive materials used in diagnosis and therapy.

The Director handles all the administrative chores of the department, including budgeting, hiring, reports, and recommendations.

He instructs students and interns in the theory and practice of radiology, conducting diagnostic seminars, or providing individual instruction and on-the-job training.

The Director's personal involvement in providing diagnostic and therapeutic radiology service for patients depends on the size of the radiology staff, and the hospital's organization. In a small hospital, he may be the only person in the department, while in a large institution he may confine his clinical activities to one specialty, such as radiation therapy, nuclear medicine, or diagnosis.

The Director may limit his activity to furthering a specific research project, or act solely as a consultant to assist staff radiologists and the medical staff with unusual or complex cases. He may also decide what research is to be undertaken, and assign staff members to specific projects.

EDUCATION, TRAINING, AND EXPERIENCE

Graduation from a medical school recognized by the Council on Medical Education and Hospitals of the American Medical Association or Committee on Hospitals of the Bureau of Professional Education of the American Osteopathic Association and a license to practice medicine or osteopathy in state where located are required.

For certification by the American Board of Radiology, applicant must have three years' special training in radiology in clinics, hospitals, or dispensaries recognized and approved by the Board and by the Council on Medical Education and Hospitals of the American Medical Association.

Four to six years' radiology specialization, one or more of which was in supervisory or administrative capacity are necessary.

JOB RELATIONSHIPS

Workers supervised: All persons assigned to Radiology Department (professional, technical, clerical, and paramedical).
Supervised by: Associate Administrator for administrative purposes, and Chief of Medical Staff for professional practice.
Promotion from: Radiologist.
Promotion to: No formal line of promotion.

PROFESSIONAL AFFILIATIONS

American Medical Association
535 North Dearborn Street
Chicago, Illinois 60610

American Osteopathic Association
212 East Ohio Street
Chicago, Illinois 60611

American College of Radiology
20 North Wacker Drive
Chicago, Illinois 60606

Director of Radiology: (DOT) 070.118T

RADIOLOGIST
Roentgenologist

A Radiologist diagnoses and treats abnormalities of the human body, using radiant energy. She determines, on the basis of patients' physical condition, history, and symptoms what radiologic examinations are necessary for accurate diagnosis.

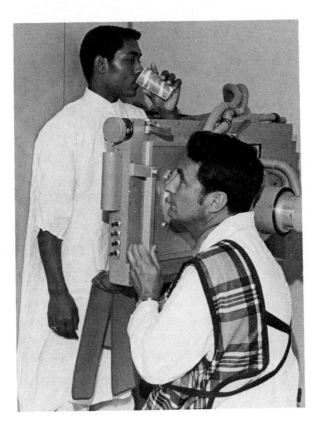

At Duke University Medical Center, a physician examines a patient by fluoroscope.

JOB DUTIES

The Radiologist prescribes X-rays for specific body areas; she administers any radiopaque substances that a patient cannot take orally; or injects radioisotope-tagged compounds to render internal structures and organs visible to diagnostic X-ray or the fluoroscope screen.

After study of the developed X-rays or fluoroscope, she evaluates her findings, and correlates them with other examinations and tests. She records her diagnosis and recommendations and includes them in the patient's record, to be forwarded to the attending physician.

She serves as a consultant to other department heads, to interpret radiologic findings, and assist in determining the nature and extent of treatment that will be needed.

The Radiologist supervises treatment of internal or external growths and diseases that are amenable to the effects of radiation. She evaluates each patient's condition, stage of development of the disease, and its severity. She determines the best radiologic therapy, and prescribes the kind, amount, and frequency of radiation to be administered. She reviews each patient's chart, and interprets each subsequent X-ray to evaluate the effectiveness of the treatment, and to verify the technologist's adherence to the prescription.

Where surgery is involved, the Radiologist participates as a member of the medical team.

She conducts training courses for medical students, interns, nurses, and radiology staff in the science and technology of radiology and its application in medicine. She designs practical exercises to implement the knowledge gained in the classroom.

She attends local and regional seminars, conferences, and equipment exhibits, to keep her own skills up-to-date.

She may be called upon to take some administrative responsibilities. She may also participate in research projects.

Some radiologists specialize in such fields as diagnostic radiology, radiation therapy, or nuclear medicine.

EDUCATION, TRAINING, AND EXPERIENCE

Graduation from a medical school recognized by the Council on Medical Education and Hospitals of the American Medical Association or Committee on Hospitals of the Bureau of Professional Education of the American Osteopathic Association and license to practice medicine or osteopathy in the state where located, are required.

For certification by the American Board of Radiology, applicant must have three years' special training in radiology in clinics, hospitals, or dispensaries recognized and approved by the Board and by the Council on Medical Education and Hospitals of the American Medical Association.

JOB RELATIONSHIPS

Workers supervised: All persons assigned to Radiology Department (professional, technical, clerical, and paramedical).
Supervised by: Director of Radiology.
Promotion from: No formal line of promotion.
Promotion to: Director of Radiology.

PROFESSIONAL AFFILIATIONS

American Medical Association
535 North Dearborn Street
Chicago, Illinois 60610

American Osteopathic Association
212 East Ohio Street
Chicago, Illinois 60611

American College of Radiology
20 North Wacker Drive
Chicago, Illinois 60606

Radiologist: (DOT) 070.108-086

HEALTH PHYSICIST
Radiological Physicist

The Health Physicist devises and directs research, training, and monitoring programs, to protect hospital personnel and patients from radiation hazards. His work may include the design of the hospital radiation facilities, the specification and calibration of equipment, development of instrument and radiation standards, and supervision of the safety and quality control program in the department.

JOB DUTIES

The Health Physicist conducts research to develop inspection standards, radiation exposure limits for personnel, safe work methods, and decontamination procedures. He tests surrounding areas to insure that radiation is not in excess of permissible standards, as established by regulations of the Atomic Energy Commission.

He designs and modifies such health physics equipment as detectors and counters. He directs the testing and monitoring of equipment, and the recording of personnel and plant-area radiation exposure data. He requests bioassay samples from persons believed to have been exposed. He may assist in developing standards of permissible concentrations of radioisotopes in liquids and gases which will be administered to patients.

He instructs personnel in principles and regulations related to radiation standards, and assigns film badges and dosimeters to personnel; and recommends changes in assignments for health reasons. He demonstrates equipment operation, decontamination techniques, and emergency procedures.

He writes instructional aids on fundamentals of radiological science and discipline, legal requirements of radiation control, and the services of the department. He prepares reports on radiation hazards, and recommends improved methods of control when needed.

EDUCATION, TRAINING, AND EXPERIENCE

Graduation from an accredited college or university with a Bachelor of Science in physics, chemistry, or engineering or, two years' college with qualifying courses in physical and radiological sciences plus two years' experience as a Radiation Monitor are acceptable.

On-the-job training is minimal.

JOB RELATIONSHIPS

Workers supervised: Radiation Monitor.
Supervised by: Head of Department or Associate Administrator.
Promotion from: May be promoted from Radiation Monitor.
Promotion to: No formal line of promotion.

PROFESSIONAL AFFILIATIONS

Health Physics Society
194 Pilgrim Road
Boston, Massachusetts 02215

Health Physicist: (DOT) 079.021-010

RADIATION MONITOR
Health Physics Technician
Personnel Monitor

The Radiation Monitor operates various radiation detectors and counters to locate and identify sources of stray radiation, and determine hazards to the health of hospital personnel and patients from X-ray machines and other equipment and materials.

JOB DUTIES

The Radiation Monitor uses portable radiation detection instruments on planned rounds of the hospital area where radiographic examinations and nuclear therapy are performed. When contamination is detected, he cleans it up, and disposes of radioactive waste. He responds to emergency calls from institutional personnel.

He instructs hospital personnel in safe handling of equipment and materials, and demonstrates techniques to be employed in the event of a radioactive hazard.

He maintains records, as required by the Atomic Energy Commission. He receives, stores, and issues certain radioactive materials, and maintains inventory of these supplies.

He studies radiochemistry laboratory techniques and maintains current knowledge of routine and emergency decontamination procedures through reading Atomic Energy Commission and public health literature.

EDUCATION, TRAINING, AND EXPERIENCE

The Radiation Monitor should have a high school diploma, with courses in mathematics, physics, and chemistry as the minimum requirement. Completion of some college courses in physical or biological sciences is preferred.

Some employers will hire without direct experience, provided the applicant has worked one or two years with laboratory equipment and has college-level science courses. Others prefer 1 to 2 years' experience with radiation monitoring.

Up to 30 days' on-the-job training to become acquainted with the layout of the institution and location of equipment and to learn hospital rules and regulations is desirable.

JOB RELATIONSHIPS

Workers supervised: None.
Supervised by: Health Physicist.
Promotion from: No formal line of promotion.
Promotion to: No formal line of promotion.

PROFESSIONAL AFFILIATIONS

None.

Radiation Monitor: (DOT) 199.187-010

RADIOLOGIC TECHNOLOGIST, CHIEF
Chief X-ray Technologist

The Chief Radiologic Technologist supervises the other Technologists in the department, and directs all the technical aspects of its services. She maintains these services in accordance with standards established by the hospital, and also by local, state, and Federal standards. She is responsible for the technical aspect of radiological safety, recommending programing, monitoring, and the location of warning

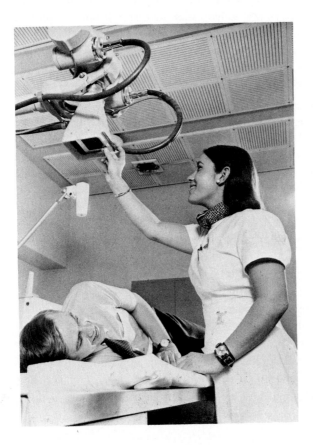

Radiologic Technician focuses X-ray equipment to expose only the area of the patient's body that must be photographed.

or identifying devices necessary to carry out the recommendations of the Health Physicist.

JOB DUTIES

The Chief Radiologic Technologist may operate X-ray machines and fluoroscopes under the direction of the Radiologist; she may administer opaque chemicals to patients, to make organs visible on X-ray film or the fluoroscope screen and assist the Radiologist in difficult radiologic procedures, and also assist Technologists on the staff with any unusual procedures.

Her administrative duties include recommendation of modifications in equipment, purchase of new equipment, and essential construction within the department, and for maintaining stock levels, as well as for storage and utilization.

She prepares reports, payroll records, statistical surveys, and other data as required. She provides for recruitment, selection, training, supervision and other personnel matters in the department. She makes work assignments, and coordinates requests for radiologic service with hospital routine.

She evaluates the accuracy and technical quality of X-ray films taken in the department, and explains difficult or new technical procedures to the technical staff.

EDUCATION, TRAINING, AND EXPERIENCE

The Radiologic Technologist must be a high school graduate who has completed a formal radiologic technology training course in an American Medical Association-approved school, of which there are about 1,200. Training can also be secured in the Armed Forces. Courses are usually 24 months in length, although some schools offer three- and four-year courses, and bachelor's degrees.

The Radiologic Technologist must be certified by the American Registry of Radiologic Technologists (ARRT).

The Chief Radiologic Technologist must also have at least five years of experience within the department, to be familiar with all aspects of its procedures.

JOB RELATIONSHIPS

Workers supervised: Darkroom Attendant, Radiologic Technologist, Nuclear Medical Technologist, clerical assistants, and student technologists.
Supervised by: Radiologist.
Promotion from: Radiologic Technologist, Nuclear Medical Technologist.
Promotion to: No formal line of promotion.

PROFESSIONAL AFFILIATIONS

American Society of Radiologic Technologists
645 North Michigan Avenue
Chicago, Illinois 60611

American Registry of Radiologic Technologists
2600 Wayzata Boulevard
Minneapolis, Minnesota 55404

Radiologic Technologist, Chief: (DOT) 078.168-010

RADIOLOGIC TECHNOLOGIST
X-ray Technologist

Medical X-rays play a major role in the diagnostic and therapeutic fields of medicine. Radiologic Technologists take these X-rays, working under the direction of a physician who has specialized in radiology. Most Radiologic Technologists perform diagnostic work, using X-ray equipment to take pictures of internal parts of the patient's body.

Some Radiologic Technologists also perform radiation therapeutic work. They assist physicians in treating diseases, such as certain cancers, by administering pre-

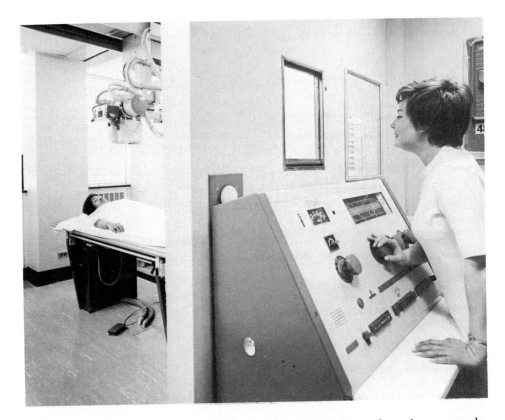

Continual exposure to even small amounts of radiation could cause hazardous accumulation for workers unless properly protected. Here, a Technologist at New York University Medical Center speaks reassuringly to the patient from behind a protective control panel.

scribed doses of X-ray or other forms of ionizing radiation to the affected area of the patient's body. They also may assist the Radiologist in measuring and handling radium and other radioactive materials.

JOB DUTIES

The Radiologic Technologist may prepare chemical mixtures, such as barium salts, which the patient swallows to make specific organs visible on the X-ray film.

In handling the X-ray machines and other radioactive materials, the Technologist must exercise extreme care to protect herself and the patient from excessive radiation. Every hospital has definite, strict procedures that she must follow.

The Technologists adjusts the X-ray equipment to the correct setting for each examination or treatment, positions and instructs the patient, and determines the proper voltage, current, and desired exposure time for each radiograph. She arranges, attaches, or adjusts immobilization and supportive devices, such as sandbags, binders, and angleboards, to obtain the precise position of the patient and prevent him from moving. She adjusts a lead shield to protect unaffected parts of the patient's body from exposure to X-ray. She selects the proper film and puts it in the holder, positions the X-ray equipment to the precise distance and angle desired, and adjusts the cone for direct concentration of rays on the affected area. She then steps behind a protective shield, and flips the switch that activates the machine and cuts it off at the exact exposure time. She repeats this procedure for every radiograph she takes.

The Technologist places the exposed film and patient's identification in a wall safe, for processing by the Darkroom Assistant. In some situations, such as a doctor's or dentist's office, she may develop the film herself.

She follows the same procedures when using mobile equipment in the operating room, emergency room, or at bedside.

She prepares and maintains records and files as directed, and cleans and may make minor repairs on equipment. She may also give on-the-job training to new employees.

EDUCATION, TRAINING, AND EXPERIENCE

The Radiologic Technologist must be a high school graduate who has completed a formal radiologic technology training course in an American Medical Association-approved school, of which there are about 1,200. Training can also be secured in the Armed Forces. Courses are usually 24 months in length, although some schools offer three- and four-year courses, and 11 offer bachelor's degrees.

The Radiologic Technologist must be certified by the American Registry of Radiologic Technologists (ARRT).

JOB RELATIONSHIPS

Workers supervised: None. May supervise student technologists.
Supervised by: Radiologic Technologist, Chief; Radiologist.
Promotion from: No formal line of promotion. May be promoted from a student technologist.
Promotion to: Radiologic Technologist, Chief or other senior staff member.

PROFESSIONAL AFFILIATIONS

American Society of Radiologic Technologists
645 North Michigan Avenue
Chicago, Illinois 60611

American Registry of Radiologic Technologists
2600 Wayzata Boulevard
Minneapolis, Minnesota 55405

Radiologic Technologist: (DOT) 078.368-030

CHIEF OF NUCLEAR MEDICINE
Director of Radioisotope Laboratory

The Chief of Nuclear Medicine must be a licensed physician or osteopath who has had extensive additional training and experience in radiology and nuclear medicine.

He coordinates and directs the activities of the radioisotope laboratory; instructs students and interns in theory and techniques of nuclear medicine; serves as specialist in diagnostic, internal, and nuclear medicine; and performs nuclear medical research.

JOB DUTIES

The Chief of Nuclear Medicine interviews, selects, and hires the staff of the radioisotope laboratory, and is responsible for establishing policies and standards of procedure, to provide the best possible patient care, and protect personnel and patients from hazards of radiation.

He acts as liaison between the radioisotope laboratory and medical staff from other departments of the hospital. He formulates and conducts seminars, conferences, and teaching programs on nuclear medicine for students and interns. He attends nuclear medicine seminars and reads technical journals to keep his own knowledge up-to-date.

He examines new patients, and discusses diagnoses with attending physicians to determine courses of treatment, and makes his recommendations on the basis of the tissues to be treated and the type of radioisotope that is applicable. Having prescribed treatment, he follows each case, to be certain that his orders are adhered to, and to check on each patient's progress. He records data for hospital records, and confers with other physicians as necessary.

He conducts research to discover more ways and means of using radioisotopes in diagnosis and treatment of disease. He studies current unsolved medical problems, or observes patients' needs, to determine areas of research that might prove advantageous. He studies all available isotopes to select the one most suitable to the proposed research. He delegates technical responsibilities to members of his staff, but assembles the final data, evaluates the results for application to patient care, and writes and publishes findings at the end of each experiment.

EDUCATION, TRAINING, AND EXPERIENCE

The Chief of Nuclear Medicine must be a graduate of a medical school recognized by the Council on Medical Education and Hospitals of the American Medical Association, or the Committee on Hospitals of the Bureau of Professional Education of the American Osteopathic Association, and be licensed to practice in the state where the hospital is located.

For certification by the American Board of Radiology, he must have three years of special training in radiology in clinics, hospitals, or dispensaries recognized and approved by the above authorities.

To qualify as Chief, he must have four to six years' experience in nuclear medicine or radiology, of which one or more years was in a supervisory or administrative capacity.

JOB RELATIONSHIPS

Workers supervised: All persons assigned to Nuclear Medical Laboratory (professional, technical, clerical, and paramedical).
Supervised by: Director of Radiology and Chief of Medical Staff.
Promotion from: No formal line of promotion.
Promotion to: No formal line of promotion.

PROFESSIONAL AFFILIATIONS

American College of Radiology
20 North Wacker Drive
Chicago, Illinois 60606

American Medical Association
535 North Dearborn Street
Chicago, Illinois 60610

American Osteopathic Association
212 East Ohio Street
Chicago, Illinois 60611

Chief of Nuclear Medicine: (DOT) 070.118T

NUCLEAR LABORATORY TECHNOLOGIST SUPERVISOR
Radioisotope Laboratory Supervisor

In many diagnostic and therapeutic nuclear medicine procedures, a radioisotope–tagged pharmaceutical is injected directly into a patient, where it accumulates in specific tissues or a specific organ, and provides a way of measuring both the structure and function of that part of the body. Sometimes a simple measurement of the amount of radioactivity yields all the information needed: more often, pictures of the organ are made with the help of instruments called scanners, or gamma ray cameras. In some instances, nuclear medicine studies provide information that could not be obtained by X-rays.

In special circumstances, large amounts of radioactivity are administered to a patient for treatment purposes. Because of the affinity of certain isotopes for specific organs or tissues, certain cancers can be treated in this way without exposing normal tissues to radiation. Sometimes these substances can be taken orally, and need not be injected.

In some diagnostic procedures, radioisotopes are not given to the patient, but a sample of his blood or urine is mixed with radioactive material to measure the presence of hormones, drugs, blood constituents, and other components.

JOB DUTIES

The Supervisor of Nuclear Laboratory Technology directs the activity of personnel in the laboratory, instructs medical students in nuclear medical technology, and performs the technical aspects of nuclear medical research.

She assigns work schedules, explains duties, and interprets policies and regulations. She reviews appointment schedules, suggesting or effecting changes to provide for maximum use of facilities and staff, and best service to patients and their physicians. She demonstrates and explains procedures and equipment operation in training new technologists and improving the performance of the regular staff.

She evaluates staff performance, and recommends personnel actions.

She performs assigned phases of nuclear research, under direction of the Chief of Nuclear Medicine; she assists him in difficult procedures; and she guides and assists other Technologists as necessary.

She takes responsibility for maintaining the inventory of radioisotopes, by weekly review of appointment schedules, estimating needs, and checking on potency of the materials in stock.

EDUCATION, TRAINING, AND EXPERIENCE

The Chief Technologist usually has a number of years of experience in nuclear medicine technology, and may also have a bachelor's degree in one of the sciences, as well as a minimum 24-month period of training in nuclear medicine at a school approved by the American Medical Association. An increasing number of programs leading to certification as Nuclear Medicine Technologist (NMT) are developing. Certification is by the American Registry of Radiologic Technologists or by the Register of Medical Technologists of the American Society of Clinical Pathologists.

JOB RELATIONSHIPS

Workers supervised: Nuclear Medical Technologists.
Supervised by: Chief of Nuclear Medicine.
Promotion from: Nuclear Medical Technologist.
Promotion to: No formal line of promotion.

PROFESSIONAL AFFILIATIONS

Registry of Medical Technologists
P.O. Box 2544
Muncie, Indiana 47304

American Society of Radiologic Technologists
645 North Michigan Avenue
Chicago, Illinois 60611

Registry of Medical Technologists of the American Society
of Clinical Pathologists
2100 West Harrison Street
Chicago, Illinois 60612

American Registry of Radiologic Technologists
2600 Wayzata Boulevard
Minneapolis, Minnesota 55405

Society of Nuclear Medicine
305 East 45th Street
New York, New York 10017

Nuclear Laboratory Technologist Supervisor: (DOT) 078.221T

NUCLEAR MEDICAL TECHNOLOGIST
Nuclear Laboratory Technician, Magna Scanner
Nuclear Laboratory Technician, Spectrometer
Radioisotope Technician

Under the supervision of a physician who has specialized in nuclear medicine, and often of a Nuclear Medical Technologist Supervisor, the Nuclear Medical Technologist (NMT) performs the technical tasks that permit the hospital to offer up-to-date patient care in this field.

JOB DUTIES

When a radioisotope-tagged chemical is administered to a patient, it is the Technologist's job to carefully verify the patient's records, prepare the radiopharmaceutical, administer the drug in exact dosage, place the patient in the correct position under the scanner or gamma ray camera, operate the equipment correctly, and present the results of the study to the physician for interpretation.

When large amounts of radioactive materials are administered for therapeutic purposes, the Technologist has the responsibility for protecting herself, other laboratory personnel, the nursing staff, and the patient from the hazards of excessive radiation. To do this requires strict adherence to the hospital's regulations on handling radioactive materials, coupled with considerable training and experience.

When she is conducting a test that does not require administration of radioactive materials to the patient, the Technologist collects the necessary blood or other specimens from the patient; prepares the radioactive material; conducts laboratory studies and tests, such as measurement of blood volume, red cell survival, and fat absorption studies, utilizing a variety of scientific detection equipment.

She computes the results of her tests, possibly using an electric calculator and nomograms, following specified statistical procedures. She posts test results to appropriate forms, and routes them to the physician for interpretation.

She performs miscellaneous duties, such as assaying the quality of isotopes purchased from local suppliers, using a vibrating-reed electrometer and ion chamber. Occasionally she monitors contaminated articles and bed linens of patients, to insure that radioactivity does not spread to unaffected persons.

She keeps records showing the use and disposition of isotopes, and body products containing isotopes.

EDUCATION, TRAINING, AND EXPERIENCE

The Nuclear Medical Technologist must be a high school graduate who has completed a minimum two-year course in nuclear medicine technology in an American Medical Association-approved school, and is certified by either the American Registry of Radiologic Technologists or by the Registry of Medical Technologists of the American Society of Clinical Pathologists.

JOB RELATIONSHIPS

Workers supervised: None.
Supervised by: Nuclear Laboratory Technologist Supervisor or Chief of Nuclear Medicine.
Promotion from: No formal lines of promotion.
Promotion to: Nuclear Laboratory Technologist Supervisor or Radiologic Technologist, Chief.

PROFESSIONAL AFFILIATIONS

American Society of Radiologic Technologists
645 North Michigan Avenue
Chicago, Illinois 60611

Society of Nuclear Medicine
305 East 45th Street
New York, New York 10017

American Registry of Radiologic Technologists
2600 Wayzata Boulevard
Minneapolis, Minnesota 55405

Registry of Medical Technologists of the American Society
   of Clinical Pathologists
2100 West Harrison Street
Chicago, Illinois 60612

Nuclear Medical Technologist: (DOT) 078.381-014

Social Service Department

When a person is ill, or there is illness in a family, other existing problems are likely to be aggravated, and new problems arise at the very time that the patient and his family are least able to handle them. Tension—resulting from disruptions of life-style, job and economic dislocations, social and family difficulties—increase the patient's anxiety, and often serve to prolong his illness.

The Social Service Department of the hospital is designed to assist patients and their families in coping with these very immediate and destructive forces. The department fulfills its function by assignment of case workers, who counsel patients and their families, and gain information about them as total individuals in the social and economic environment in which they live and work. A Social Worker also evaluates each patient's ability to understand and cooperate with a program of medical or psychiatric treatment; and by learning the patient's obligations, and material and personal resources, she contributes to the attending physician's understanding of the social elements in the patient's life, and indirectly to more suitable diagnosis and plan for treatment. Similarly, the Social Worker is able to interpret and explain treatment to the patient and his family, as well as to relieve anxiety by utilizing community agencies, if necessary, to solve urgent problems. Often, the Social Worker makes followup visits to patients' homes following discharge from the hospital, or sees them as outpatients in the clinic, to insure continued treatment in an atmosphere conducive to recovery.

Social workers are assigned to duty in various clinics and services of the hospital, and patients are referred to them by the medical staff, or other persons and agencies.

In addition to individual counseling and group work, the Social Service Department of the hospital participates in development of social and health programs in the community, in educational programs for professional personnel, and in medical–social research. Social Service records, incorporated with patients' permanent files in the Medical Records Department, furnish data that is valuable in planning future patient services.

Standards for Social Service Departments in hospitals are set by the National Association of Social Workers, which also certifies qualified workers by registry in the Academy of Certified Social Workers (ACSW).

Employment for qualified social workers is not limited to hospitals. They are in great demand by public and private health centers, local, state, and Federal public health departments, military and veterans' hospitals, voluntary health agencies, and as teachers in schools of medicine, public health, and social work. The need, in all of these places, increases year by year.

As in other professions, opportunities for advancement are greater for workers who have completed graduate studies and attained at least a master's degree in social work.

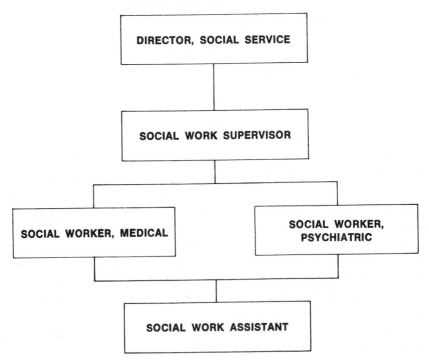

SOCIAL SERVICE DEPARTMENT

DIRECTOR, SOCIAL SERVICE

SOCIAL WORK SUPERVISOR

SOCIAL WORKER, MEDICAL

SOCIAL WORKER, PSYCHIATRIC

SOCIAL WORK ASSISTANT

NOTE: This chart is for illustrative purposes only and should not be considered a recommended pattern of organization.

DIRECTOR, SOCIAL SERVICE

The Director, Social Service heads the department, and is responsible for its internal operation; but plans for treatment and procedures with patients must be made in collaboration with the attending medical staff of the hospital.

The Director must be professionally educated in social work, and should have had extensive experience in the field. His department may function in a purely medical or purely psychiatric setting, or in a combination of both.

JOB DUTIES

The Director develops and maintains working relationships with other department heads.

He selects, promotes, or dismisses staff members according to standards agreed upon with hospital administrators. He develops personnel practices with staff participation, and administers the personnel policies of the social service staff. He devises and directs office routine. He guides progams for staff development.

In conjunction with the Administrator, he develops the department's budget, and supervises its programs within the budgetary framework.

The Director prepares and presents reports on the department's services and patient needs. He assists in development of hospital policies in regard to social agencies, and participates in community planning of health and welfare services, and in educational programs for other professional personnel.

He assists in planning cooperative research programs with heads of other departments, and with community agencies. He may initiate research projects within the Social Service Department.

He utilizes and directs the work of social service volunteers.

In a small hospital this job may be combined with Social Work Supervisor.

EDUCATION, TRAINING, AND EXPERIENCE

The Director must have a master's degree from an accredited school of social work; plus five years of experience, of which at least two years were in a health setting, and two years in an administrative, supervisory, or consulting capacity in a social agency having acceptable standards. The size of the hospital and its case load may dictate requirements for more experience.

JOB RELATIONSHIPS

Workers supervised: Social Work Supervisor; Social Workers; Social Work Assistants; and clerical workers.
Supervised by: Associate Administrator or Administrator.
Promotion from: Social Work Supervisor or Senior Social Worker.
Promotion to: No formal line of promotion.

PROFESSIONAL AFFILIATIONS

National Association of Social Workers
2 Park Avenue
New York, New York 10017

American Society for Hospital Social Work Directors
840 North Lake Shore Drive
Chicago, Illinois 60611

Director, Social Service: (DOT) 195.118-010

SOCIAL WORK SUPERVISOR
Associate Director, Social Service
Chief Social Worker

The Social Work Supervisor directs a staff of caseworkers and group workers, and takes part in planning programs and formulating services for the hospital.

JOB DUTIES

The Supervisor assists members of the Social Work staff to increase their professional knowledge and skills. She plans staff development programs, including conferences, recommendation of attendance at institutes, and seminars. She supervises, plans, and arranges for the orientation of new workers; and participates in the selection of personnel and evaluation of work.

She reviews information from staff members concerning the needs and effects of current policies, and makes recommendations for change when needed.

She works closely with government, volunteer, and other community social agencies, to keep informed of potential sources of assistance in resolving patients' problems, to avoid overlapping services, and to use available services to the full. She familiarizes the staff with community services that can be used as resources.

She participates in the teaching program of the department, particularly in regard to social work students.

She assists in recording and reporting social data, and may aid in research projects. In the Director's absence, she may act as head of the department.

EDUCATION, TRAINING, AND EXPERIENCE

The Supervisor must have a master's degree in social work from an accredited school of social work; plus a period of satisfactory supervisory experience under direction. With these qualifications, a person not previously so employed would be given from one to three months of orientation in the hospital setting.

JOB RELATIONSHIPS

Workers supervised: Social Workers, both casework and group work.
Supervised by: Director, Social Service.
Promotion from: Social Worker.
Promotion to: Director, Social Service.

PROFESSIONAL AFFILIATIONS

National Association of Social Workers
2 Park Avenue
New York, New York 10017

Casework Supervisor: (DOT) 195.168-010

SOCIAL WORKER, MEDICAL

The Medical Social Worker is an essential member of the patient care team, which is headed by the attending physician. She is trained to understand people and their personal and social needs, particularly as these are associated with illness or disability. She views each patient as a total human being, whatever his creed, color, economic or cultural level, personality, or type of problem.

To serve the wide diversity of needs that patients present, she must be thoroughly familiar with services available from all community agencies, for she frequently will have to call on one or more of them to get the help a patient needs.

The Medical Social Worker has become an important link between hospitalization of a patient and his return to normal life in the community. Her planning allows him to convalesce and pick up his life again with a minimum of stress. Often the Worker makes followup home calls, or sees the patient regularly when he comes to the outpatient clinic. Her work helps him to be discharged from hospital earlier than he might be otherwise.

Her success depends to a large extent on the quality of her professional training. Some 200 accredited colleges in the United States now offer bachelor's degrees in social work, and 73 offer master's degree programs; doctorates can be earned in 23 accredited institutions. The Council on Social Work Education is the accrediting agency in the United States and Canada.

JOB DUTIES

Patients are referred to the Social Worker by medical staff members, nurses, or community agencies.

She interviews both patients and family members to learn about the home environment, family relationships, health history, and the patient's personality traits. She confers with each patient's attending physician and other staff members who are part of his health team in the hospital; she evaluates all the information she has gathered in terms of the medical plan of treatment, available social service programs, and her knowledge of casework or group work, and plans a suitable therapy program.

She helps patients and their families understand, accept, and follow medical recommendations; and provides services to aid in meeting their problems. This may entail arranging for home care after discharge, placement in an institution or nursing home, arrangements for care of children, financial assistance, housing, and a myriad other services.

The Worker prepares and keeps patient's records, and makes case reports on his progress. She also makes summaries of information received from other persons or agencies who have knowledge of the patient.

She takes part in planning hospital policies and procedures; works with community agencies related to health and welfare; helps in the hospital's educational program, particularly in supervision of students and beginning social workers.

She may take part in research projects, or prepare statistical reports of numbers of patients to whom service has been given, as an aid in planning further programs, evaluating the department's performance, or as a basis for research projects.

EDUCATION, TRAINING, AND EXPERIENCE

A master's degree from an approved school of social work is required.

Social workers without work experience will work under close supervision for approximately two years before being considered fully qualified. Two years' casework experience in health institutions, child welfare agencies, psychiatric clinics, and family counseling services is preferred.

One to three months' orientation in an individual hospital's methods and policies is required for all new employees regardless of prior experience.

JOB RELATIONSHIPS

Workers supervised: Social Work Assistants.
Supervised by: Social Work Supervisor or Director, Social Service.
Promotion from: No formal line of promotion.
Promotion to: Social Work Supervisor or Director, Social Service.

PROFESSIONAL AFFILIATIONS

National Association of Social Workers
(Medical Social Work Section)
2 Park Avenue
New York, New York 10017

Social Worker, Medical: (DOT) 195.108-046

SOCIAL WORKER, PSYCHIATRIC

Psychiatric social workers are employed in mental hospitals, mental wards of general hospitals, mental health clinics, child guidance clinics, institutions for the mentally retarded, Federal hospitals providing psychiatric care, courts, community centers, and rehabilitation organizations. Demand vastly exceeds supply.

Persons with mental or emotional problems usually have job, family, or financial problems, too. When a patient enters the mental hospital or mental health clinic, the psychiatrist needs to learn all about him—his family background, relationships, early life, education, work experience, and social interests. He also needs to know the patient's immediate symptoms and the events leading to his breakdown. The Psychiatric Social Worker, who is almost the first person the patient sees, is professionally trained to elicit this information.

Patients admitted to mental hospitals or clinics often continue treatment for long periods of time, and the Social Worker serves as a continuing contact between patients and their families. Later, she smooths the way to discharge, and follows up afterward, to assure adequate adjustment to the outside world.

JOB DUTIES

The Psychiatric Social Worker interviews the patient, his relatives, friends, and others, to obtain data on his personal, job, social, and emotional history. She prepares a complete case history to provide a starting point for diagnosis and plan of treatment. She presents the case history at staff conference, and assists the psychiatrist, psychologist, and other members of the health team in planning a program of therapy.

She may interpret the patient's illness and the prescribed course of treatment to him and his family, and suggest methods of helping him to recovery. She attempts to overcome attitudes of fear and prejudice that make it difficult for patients and families to accept psychiatric care and treatment.

She assists with problems arising from hospitalization, and in working out the patient's discharge and posthospital care plans. In this, she may utilize the resources of several community agencies. She helps the patient to determine his vocational abilities and goals, and to secure suitable opportunities to pursue them.

She maintains complete, detailed case records, including followup on each case, as a basis for comparative research on the effectiveness of various forms of therapy. She cooperates with parole officers, law-enforcement agencies, military personnel, government bureaus, and clergy, and lends them requested records when the hospital administration authorizes her to do so.

She may assist in establishing hospital policies on admission and referral of patients; participate in community activities concerned with health and welfare; address lay groups on the functions of hospital psychiatric service; and help to develop favorable community attitudes toward recognition and treatment of mental disorders.

EDUCATION, TRAINING, AND EXPERIENCE

Training for the Psychiatric Social Worker is comparable to that of the Medical Social Worker, but with some differentiation in courses, to stress psychologic and psychiatric aspects of work.

A master's degree from an approved school of social work is required.

Social workers without experience will work under close supervision until considered fully qualified.

One to three months' orientation in an individual hospital's methods and policies is required for all new employees, regardless of prior experience.

JOB RELATIONSHIPS

Workers supervised: Social Work Assistants.
Supervised by: Social Work Supervisor or Director, Social Service.
Promotion from: No formal line of promotion.
Promotion to: Social Work Supervisor or Director, Social Service.

PROFESSIONAL AFFILIATIONS

National Association of Social Workers
(Psychiatric Social Work Section)
2 Park Avenue
New York, New York 10017

Social Worker, Psychiatric: (DOT) 195.108-050

SOCIAL WORK ASSISTANT
Case Aide
Social Service Assistant

The Social Work Assistant needs only a bachelor's degree, and receives on-the-job training. She works on the simpler aspects of cases, and provides services to less complex cases, under close and regular supervision.

JOB DUTIES

The Assistant may interview patients to obtain medical and other history; help with environmental difficulties that are hindering recovery; arrange for postdischarge care of patients who are chronically ill; assess the adequacy of home care facilities; help patients secure needed hearing, optical, or orthopedic appliances; compile medical-social history summaries and statistical reports; and collect and revise information on community health and welfare resources.

She confers with hospital personnel on behalf of patients as this is needed, and serves as liaison between medical and nursing staffs, patients, relatives, and appropriate outside agencies.

EDUCATION, TRAINING, AND EXPERIENCE

A bachelor's degree in social work or any of the humanities is required.

No previous experience is required.

The worker will receive on-the-job training in social work tasks and assignments under supervision of a graduate social worker.

JOB RELATIONSHIPS

Workers supervised: None.
Supervised by: Social Worker, Medical or Social Worker, Psychiatric.
Promotion from: No formal line of promotion.
Promotion to: No formal line of promotion.

PROFESSIONAL AFFILIATIONS

None.

Case Aide: (DOT) 195.208-010

Speech and Hearing Therapy Department

Speech pathology and audiology (speech and hearing therapy) are comparatively new professions, but they constitute a vital part of any total program of rehabilitation. It is reliably estimated that one out of 20 persons in the United States has a speech problem that requires treatment.

Like many other young health services, this field is in great need of additional personnel. Some of the types of disabilities with which the Speech Pathologist and Audiologist work are lisping, cleft palate, impaired hearing, speech difficulties resulting from cerebral palsy, or from emotional or physical disturbance, or retardation.

In speech disabilities that have a physical cause, the pathologist may need to work with physicians and dentists. When the disorder is emotional, he may need to cooperate with a psychiatrist or psychologist. He may consult a vocational counselor if the speech problem is a handicap in employment.

In patients having multiple disabilities, often nothing else can be done until communication can be established. In children, overcoming whatever difficulty exists is doubly important, since without communication the intelligence level of the patient is very difficult to evaluate, and progress in school is impossible.

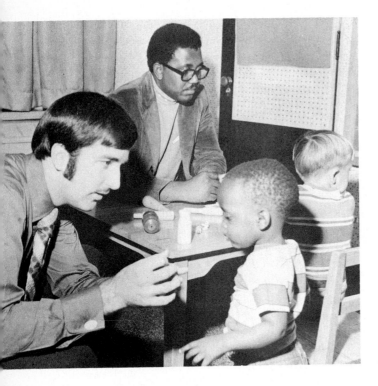

Speech pathology and audiology students at Memorial Baptist Hospital in Houston, Texas, observe and study the language behavior of normal young children.

In 1970, only about 22,000 persons were employed in speech and hearing therapy in this country. Three-fourths of them were women. The majority worked in public school systems, while colleges and universities employed the next largest number in classrooms, clinics, and research. The remainder were distributed among hospitals, rehabilitation and community health centers, state and Federal government agencies, industry, and private practice.

Qualification requirements for these professions are high. In terms of personality, workers who treat exceptional children, retarded adults, and older persons recovering from strokes, must be sensitive, patient, genuinely fond of people, and emotionally stable. Increasingly, educational requirements include a master's degree. However, many scholarships, fellowships, assistantships and traineeships are available, particularly at the graduate level, in colleges and universities. The United States Rehabilitation Services Administration, the Maternal and Child Health Service, the United States Office of Education, the National Institutes of Health, and the Veterans Administration all allocate funds for these purposes.

In a hospital setting, the Speech and Hearing Therapy Department must meet standards set by the American Speech and Hearing Association, which also grants certificates of Clinical Competence to candidates in speech pathology and audiology who have completed academic training at the master's degree level, plus one year of experience in the field, and pass a national examination.

SPEECH AND HEARING DEPARTMENT

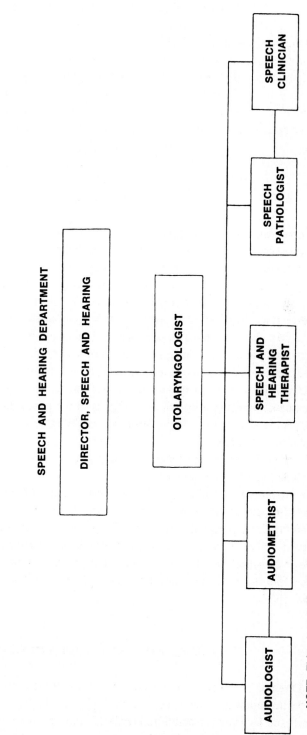

```
            DIRECTOR, SPEECH AND HEARING
                         │
                 OTOLARYNGOLOGIST
                         │
        ┌────────────────┼────────────────┐
        │                │                │
  AUDIOLOGIST    SPEECH AND HEARING   SPEECH
        │            THERAPIST      PATHOLOGIST
  AUDIOMETRIST                           │
                                    SPEECH
                                    CLINICIAN
```

NOTE: This chart is for illustrative purposes only and should not be considered a recommended pattern of organization.

DIRECTOR, SPEECH AND HEARING

The Director of Speech and Hearing, who is responsible for both the administrative and professional activities of the department, is not a Doctor of Medicine, but is a highly trained and thoroughly experienced audiologist and speech pathologist.

In speech and hearing therapy, the two fields are so closely related that to be proficient in either area, a worker must be familiar with both. This is particularly true of the Director, who must coordinate, supervise, and evaluate activities in both areas.

JOB DUTIES

The Director consults with patients, students, staff, and physicians from various hospital services and from other speech and hearing centers, to instruct, advise, or inform them of audiometric procedures and tests. He plans various clinical programs, schedules and assigns testing and treatment activities, and prepares time schedules for seminars and classes for student nurses and resident students.

He reviews diagnosis and test evaluations of patients as prepared by therapists, and makes further recommendations for medical or social assistance. He may work with a patient and make an analysis of his condition. He keeps constant check on the progress of patients, to ascertain program effectiveness.

He recruits and trains departmental personnel, and develops the content of the department's training program as it applies to the particular hospital department or clinic. He evaluates the job performance of the staff, and recommends promotion, transfer, or discharge.

He attends meetings to keep up-to-date on ideas and techniques in the fields of speech and hearing therapy.

He prepares financial and statistical reports and estimates budgets. He supervises the keeping of case records, and reviews them. He directs preparation of brochures explaining the department's function. He confers with staff members to inform them of new developments and new hospital policies, or to solve problems.

He is constantly alert to all phases of department operation and objectives, and takes action to implement any changes that will result in more effective treatment for patients.

EDUCATION, TRAINING, AND EXPERIENCE

The Director of the Speech and Hearing Department is required to have a master's degree in audiology and speech pathology, and to be certified by the American Speech and Hearing Association. He should have as much as ten years of experience as an audiologist and speech pathologist.

One to three months of on-the-job training is needed for him to gain familiarity with the policies of a specific establishment.

JOB RELATIONSHIPS

Workers supervised: Audiologist, Speech Pathologist, Speech and Hearing Therapist, Audiometrist, Speech Clinician, and clerical and volunteer staff.
Supervised by: Associate Administrator.
Promotion from: Audiologist or Speech Pathologist.
Promotion to: Associate Administrator.

PROFESSIONAL AFFILIATIONS

American Speech and Hearing Association
1001 Connecticut Avenue, N.W.
Washington, D.C. 20036

National Association of Hearing and Speech Agencies
919 18th Street, N.W.
Washington, D.C. 20006

Director, Speech and Hearing: (DOT) 079.108-038

OTOLARYNGOLOGIST
Laryngologist
Otologist
Rhinologist

The Otolaryngologist is a medical physician who has specialized in diagnosis and treatment of diseases and deformities of the ear, nose, and throat. He is qualified to perform surgery in these areas.

He is accountable to the hospital Administrator, and to the Chief of its Medical Staff, and his status is on a part with that of the department Director.

JOB DUTIES

The Otolaryngologist examines the affected organs of all patients, using such equipment as audiometers, prisms, nasoscopes, microscopes, X-ray, and fluoroscopes. He determines the nature and extent of disorders, and prescribes or administers medication or therapy. He performs surgery as indicated.

He discusses cases with heads of other departments involved in treatment of given patients, in order to set up cooperative techniques. He checks tests and evaluations made by clinicians, and makes the final diagnosis in questionable cases. When a patient needs services beyond those of the Speech and Hearing Department, he refers him to the appropriate department of the hospital.

The Otolaryngologist lectures on techniques and procedures to students, staff, and community organizations. He attends conventions and professional meetings to secure new ideas and exchange points of view. He contacts community agencies for cooperation in hospital-school programs involving hearing and speech therapies.

EDUCATION, TRAINING, AND EXPERIENCE

The Otolaryngologist must graduate from a medical school or school of osteopathy recognized by the Council on Medical Education and Hospitals of the American Medical Association, or the Committee on Hospitals of the Bureau of Professional Education of the American Osteopathic Association, and be licensed to practice medicine or osteopathy in the state where the hospital or clinic is located. He must have completed an internship and four-year residency in otolaryngology.

His qualifications must include demonstrated administrative or research experience.

JOB RELATIONSHIPS

Workers supervised: All members of speech and hearing clinic, through Director, Speech and Hearing.
Supervised by: Chief of Medical Staff for professional purposes and Associate Administrator for administrative purposes.
Promotion from: None.
Promotion to: None.

PROFESSIONAL AFFILIATIONS

American Medical Association
535 North Dearborn Street
Chicago, Illinois 60610

National Association of Hearing and Speech Agencies
919 18th Street, N.W.
Washington, D.C. 20006

American Academy of Ophthalmology and Otolaryngology
15 Second Street, S.W.
Rochester, Minnesota 55901

State and local organizations.

Otolaryngologist: (DOT) 070.108-054

AUDIOLOGIST

The Audiologist deals with hearing problems in children and adults. He is particularly concerned with hearing disabilities caused by certain otologic or neurologic disturbances. There are some kinds of hearing loss that science cannot yet overcome; but if a patient has any residual hearing, the Audiologist evaluates it, and plans a program to give the patient the highest degree of hearing possible.

JOB DUTIES

The Audiologist administers a variety of tests, such as pure-tone and speech audiometers, and galvanic skin response, to find out precisely how much hearing a patient has, and then to determine the most likely site of damage to the auditory system, and predict potential benefits from the use of a hearing aid and/or special training. He differentiates between organic and inorganic loss, through evaluation of total response, and use of such acoustic tests as Stenger and delayed-speech feedback. He coordinates the audiometric results he obtains with other diagnostic data, such as educational, medical, social, and behavioral information about the patient.

He assists in selection and use of suitable hearing aids, in helping the patient develop good listening habits, and in use of visual clues to "fill in the blanks" of hearing. When a patient has a hearing loss of a type that can be treated surgically, the Audiologist assists the surgeon preoperatively by describing the extent and kind of hearing loss; postoperatively, he conducts studies to see whether surgery has brought about improvement.

He plans, directs, and participates in programs to build or rebuild hearing through counseling, guidance, auditory training, lip reading, and speech conversation. He writes reports on his diagnostic findings, the therapy used, and the progress made.

He conducts research in the physiology, pathology, biophysics, or psychophysics of auditory systems, to increase understanding of the complex processes of speech and hearing, to increase basic knowledge of the essential nature of various disorders, and to develop improved methods for evaluation and treatment of patients.

He may design and develop clinical procedures and research methods, and apparatus. He may act as consultant to educational, medical, and other professional groups. He may teach audiology to physicians, nurses, teachers, and other professional personnel. He may perform some of the duties of the Speech Pathologist.

EDUCATION, TRAINING, AND EXPERIENCE

The Audiologist is required to have a master's degree in audiology and speech pathology, with sufficient credits in speech and hearing to be certified by the American Speech and Hearing Association. This may include four years of supervised experience, plus passing a written examination. Some employers require a doctor's degree in audiology.

If the above training experience requirement is met, no additional experience is demanded.

JOB RELATIONSHIPS

Workers supervised: Audiometrist.
Supervised by: Director, Speech and Hearing.
Promotion from: No formal line of promotion.
Promotion to: Director, Speech and Hearing.

PROFESSIONAL AFFILIATIONS

American Speech and Hearing Association
1001 Connecticut Avenue, N.W.
Washington, D.C. 20036

National Association of Hearing and Speech Agencies
919 18th Street, N.W.
Washington, D.C. 20006

Audiologist: (DOT) 079.108-010

AUDIOMETRIST
Hearing-Test Technician

The Audiometrist administers tests prescribed by the Audiologist to children and adults who have a hearing disability, in order to measure the amount of hearing which the patient still possesses. This aids in diagnosis, and in planning a program of treatment to build or rebuild hearing ability, or to compensate for its loss.

A little girl who has hearing loss raises her hand to signal the Audiometrist that she can hear the pure tone emitted by the machine at a certain level. Her hearing loss is measured by the volume at which she can hear.

Photo courtesy of Johns Hopkins Medical Institutions, Baltimore, Maryland

JOB DUTIES

The Audiometrist interviews each patient whenever possible, and explains the test that is to be given. She fits earphones on the patient's head, and instructs him to raise a hand, repeat words, press a button, or otherwise indicate specified responses during the test—the purpose of which is to determine at exactly what volume the patient can hear a so-called "pure-tone."

She monitors a control panel similar to those in radio stations, as tones of increasing volume are transmitted to the patient. She records the subject's responses and enters specified data on a standard form, and in the patient's medical record. By interpretation of these test results, the Audiologist or physician is aided in determining whether more definitive hearing examination is needed.

She may give instructions to students on operation of the audiometric equipment.

EDUCATION, TRAINING, AND EXPERIENCE

The Audiometrist must have a bachelor's degree in speech and hearing, one year's experience in a speech and hearing department, and be certified by the American Speech and Hearing Association. The hospital or clinic should provide three months' familiarity with the apparatus and equipment.

JOB RELATIONSHIPS

Workers supervised: None.
Supervised by: Audiologist or Director, Speech and Hearing.
Promotion from: No formal line of promotion.
Promotion to: No formal line of promotion.

PROFESSIONAL AFFILIATIONS

American Speech and Hearing Association
1001 Connecticut Avenue, N.W.
Washington, D.C. 20036

National Association of Hearing and Speech Agencies
919 18th Street, N.W.
Washington, D.C. 20006

Audiometrist: (DOT) 078.368-010

SPEECH AND HEARING THERAPIST

The Speech and Hearing Therapist has a close and continuing relationship with patients and their families. She is the person who works with each patient day after day, sharing both frustrations and successes. Her job requires a genuine liking for

Bubble-blowing motivates children who have speech and language difficulties.
Photo courtesy of Stanford University Medical Center

people, infinite patience, and emotional stability. However, its rewards are great for young persons who want to feel that their work has value.

JOB DUTIES

The Speech and Hearing Therapist examines and tests the patient, diagnoses his complaints, and administers appropriate remedial treatment.

She interviews patients, discusses their cases with family members, and reads physicians' reports to obtain data on each patient's condition. She prepares case histories, and schedules tests and treatments.

She tests patients for hearing acuity by use of the audiometer, which registers intensity of sound. She records the hearing test results, and may refer patients with severe hearing loss to the otolaryngologist for treatment.

She obtains and records speech samples of patients on tape, through conversations, reading, and other devices. She makes a phonetic analysis of the speech, by testing for articulation of all sounds in various positions occurring in pronunciation of words, vowels, and consonants. She measures the flexing of throat and mouth muscles, observes action and condition of lips, teeth, tongue, hard and soft palate, and nasal cavities, to determine the efficiency of speech articulation.

She records her interpretation of test results, and recommendations for remedial treatment; and determines whether there is need for referral to a specialist in medicine, dentistry, education, psychology, sociology, or related areas. She interprets her findings to parents, teachers, and others who have association with the patient. She confers with physicians, other therapists, and social workers as needed to provide the best therapy possible for the patient.

She treats patients with speech defects that can be remedied, such as stuttering, and articulatory problems associated with such impairments as cleft palate, cerebral palsy, and aphasia, by use of corrective methods and techniques designed to improve diction and breathing. She uses oral exercises, such as sounding alphabet letters, reading, singing songs, playing toy instruments, blowing balloons, or using special equipment. She fingers patients' mouths, lips, and jaws to assist in movement of muscles and formation of sounds. She directs patients in listening exercises, such as reproducing sounds from a tape recorder, while observing themselves in a mirror. She advises on home care, and care after treatment.

She may teach lip reading and use of hearing aids to hard-of-hearing patients.

She may visit local schools, to conduct speech therapy clinics, and transmit findings on students to parents and physicians for remedial action. She may distribute information about the school-hospital program to outlying communities, to encourage participation. She may visit discharged patients' homes to evaluate the effectiveness of the course of treatment, obtain reference material for future use, or advise patients' families.

EDUCATION, TRAINING, AND EXPERIENCE

Minimum training for the Speech and Hearing Therapist includes a bachelor's degree from a college offering specialized work in speech and/or hearing. Course emphasis should be in the physical and social sciences. Often the first two years' training can be obtained in a college offering basic courses, after which the student may transfer to a school where graduate training may be obtained.

Possession of a master's degree enables the individual to meet requirements for certification of the American Speech and Hearing Association.

If training requirements are met no additional experience is required.

JOB RELATIONSHIPS

Workers supervised: None.
Supervised by: Director, Speech and Hearing.
Promotion from: No formal line of promotion.
Promotion to: No formal line of promotion. Advancement is through addition of supervisory, administrative, or teaching duties.

PROFESSIONAL AFFILIATIONS

American Speech and Hearing Association
1001 Connecticut Avenue, N.W.
Washington, D.C. 20036

National Association of Hearing and Speech Agencies
919 18th Street, N.W.
Washington, D.C. 20006

Speech and Hearing Clinician: (DOT) 079.108-042

SPEECH PATHOLOGIST

The position of the Speech Pathologist in his field is comparable to that of the Audiologist in hearing therapy. The Speech Pathologist diagnoses, treats, and performs research related to speech and language problems. He evaluates the causes of disorders, and tests the results of therapies. He interprets his findings to parents, teachers, and others concerned with patients.

JOB DUTIES

The speech disabilities with which he is concerned include functional articulatory disorders, stuttering, voice problems, delayed speech, and organic disorders such as cleft palate, polio, aphasia, and impaired hearing. He determines need for referral to specialists in medicine, dentistry, education, psychology, sociology, and related areas. He counsels preoperative and postoperative patients to prepare them for surgery, and the treatment to follow.

He plans, directs, or conducts remedial programs designed to restore or improve communicative efficiency. He trains patients with functional or organic speech disorders to produce, improve, or conserve proper speech. He trains patients in techniques of esophageal voice, or in use of an artificial larynx. He provides counseling and guidance to speech- and language-handicapped persons, both children and adults. He writes reports on his diagnostic findings, therapy used, and results obtained.

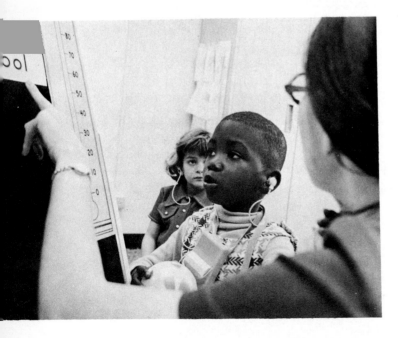

After blowing bubbles, it's easy to say "cool."

The Speech Pathologist acts as consultant to educational, medical, and other professional groups. He instructs physicians, nurses, teachers, and other professional personnel in basics of speech therapy.

He directs scientific projects concerned with investigation of biophysical and biosocial phenomena associated with voice, speech, and language; and may conduct research related to development of diagnostic and remedial techniques or procedures, or design of apparatus.

EDUCATION, TRAINING, AND EXPERIENCE

A master's degree in audiology and speech pathology is required, with adequate course credits in speech and hearing to be certified by the American Speech and Hearing Association. This may include four years' supervised experience plus passing a written examination. Some employers require a doctorate in speech pathology.

If the above requirements are met, no additional experience is required except for supervisory positions.

JOB RELATIONSHIPS

Workers supervised: Speech Clinician.
Supervised by: Director, Speech and Hearing.
Promotion from: No formal line of promotion.
Promotion to: Director, Speech and Hearing.

PROFESSIONAL AFFILIATIONS

American Speech and Hearing Association
1001 Connecticut Avenue, N.W.
Washington, D.C. 20036

National Association of Hearing and Speech Agencies
919 18th Street, N.W.
Washington, D.C. 20006

Speech Pathologist: (DOT) 079.108-038

SPEECH CLINICIAN
Speech Therapist

The Speech Clinician treats only speech disorders. In smaller hospitals and clinics, her work is combined with that of the Speech and Hearing Therapist, and the personal qualifications listed in that occupation also apply to the more specialized job classification.

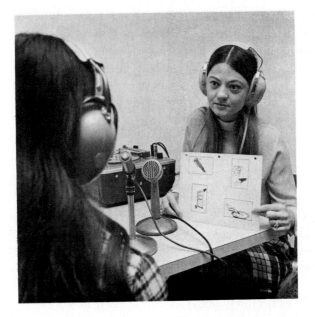

The Speech Therapist uses pictures of familiar objects, to encourage children with speech and hearing disabilities to associate the correct word with each picture.

JOB DUTIES

The Speech Clinician examines patients with speech and language disorders, and provides remedial treatment for such conditions as stuttering, voice disorders, and articulatory and speech problems associated with impairments, such as cleft palate, cerebral palsy, and aphasia.

She instructs speech-handicapped persons in development of desirable speech by training in control of articulation and voice. She assists patients to say simple words or sentences, using color cards, pictures, children's books, or toys. She demonstrates the position of lips, jaws, and tongue for forming sounds to produce words. She uses word games and tape recordings to aid children in overcoming articulation difficulties, and devises vocal exercises to overcome stuttering and nasal, harsh, or hoarse tones.

She teaches laryngectomees the techniques of speaking with the esophageal voice, using tape recordings. She teaches proper breath control, to conserve powers of speech, and prepares exercises that can be practiced away from the clinic.

The Speech Clinician prepares patients' progress reports, describing the therapy used.

She may participate in research, and counsel patients' families.

EDUCATION, TRAINING, AND EXPERIENCE

The Speech Clinician must have a master's degree in audiology and speech pathology with adequate course credits in speech and hearing to be certified by the American Speech and Hearing Association. This may include four years' supervised experience plus passing a written examination.

If training and educational requirements are met, no additional experience is necessary.

JOB RELATIONSHIPS

Workers supervised: None.
Supervised by: Speech Pathologist or Director, Speech and Hearing.
Promotion from: No formal line of promotion.
Promotion to: No formal line of promotion.

PROFESSIONAL AFFILIATIONS

American Speech and Hearing Association
1001 Connecticut Avenue, NW.
Washington, D.C. 20036

National Association of Hearing and Speech Agencies
919 18th Street, NW.
Washington, D.C. 20006

Speech Clinician: (DOT) 079.108-034

Technical Services

As medicine and surgery embrace the many advances of technology to improve health care services, the need for technicians whose basic skills can be adapted to operate and manipulate complex machines and materials increases in a geometrical proportion. A device created to implement one procedure makes another procedure possible, which, in turn, leads to another device, *ad infinitum.* Some of the most exciting jobs in health care are within these categories of expanding horizons.

The individual job classifications listed do not constitute a department of the hospital in the sense of line-staff organization. They are likely to be distributed among other departments, in accordance with the service for which they are suited. However, their common denominator is that they all have evolved from technology, and require technicians: and technicians are in such short supply that many hospitals are forced to train medical technologists, radiologic technologists, or nurses to perform these functions.

Representative classifications include:

- Cardio-Pulmonary Technician
- Catheterization Technician
- Dialysis Technician
- Electrocardiograph Technician
- Electroencephalograph Technician
- Heart-Lung Machine Operator

- Orthoptist
- Prosthetist-Orthotist
- Pulmonary Function Technician
- Respiratory Therapist
- Therapy Technician
- Thermograph Technician

In large research and teaching hospitals, additional technical classifications are constantly developing, and in future many more can be expected.

CARDIO-PULMONARY TECHNICIAN

The Cardio-Pulmonary Technician operates a number of devices, among them recording oscilloscope, vectorcardiograph, vasograph, spirometer, and artificial kidney equipment. Inclusion of kidney equipment in the list of devices used by a heart-lung technician comes about because deficient functioning of the heart affects the kidneys. Similarly, kidney damage affects the heart.

The Technician conducts tests of the heart and blood vessels, lungs, and kidneys, to provide medical specialists and surgeons with information they need to diagnose heart, vascular, and lung diseases.

The Technician may also assist in the operating room, handing instruments to the surgeon, applying the defibrillator to restore normal heartbeat, and administering oxygen to the patient in case of cardiac arrest.

JOB DUTIES

In cardiologic, vascular, and pulmonary diagnostic tests, the Technician places the patient in suitable position, and positions whatever instruments are to be used in proper relation to him, or in contact with him. As the various machines or devices are operated, variations in heartbeat, blood pressure, or air pressure are registered on an oscilloscope, and the impulses are either traced on graph paper or photographed. When each test is complete, the Technician computes the recorded data, using tables and formulas, and enters the test results on the patient's chart.

In treating kidney disorders, he fills the tank of the artificial kidney machine with water and the prescribed amount of chemicals to form a solution that absorbs uremic particles. After connecting the rubber tubing to the coil of the machine and the venous and arterial shunts of patients, the Technician starts the machine, observing pressure gauges, monitoring the patient's blood pressure, and changing the chemical solution at prescribed intervals. He also draws a blood sample periodically, to test clotting time, and gives the patient the prescribed amount of anticoagulant medication through the tubing.

The Technician records and reports all procedures.

Graduation from an accredited school of nursing and current licensure by the State Board of Nursing is required. Usually one year of experience in performing general nursing duties is needed to qualify for this position. One year of on-the-job training is necessary to develop skills in operating the various types of cardiologic, pulmonary, and vascular test equipment.

JOB RELATIONSHIPS

Workers supervised: None.
Supervised by: Physician or surgeon in charge of patient.
Promotion from: No formal line of promotion.
Promotion to: No formal line of promotion. Promotion may be through increased supervisory and administrative duties.

PROFESSIONAL AFFILIATIONS

American Nurses' Association
10 Columbus Circle
New York, New York 10019

National League for Nursing
10 Columbus Circle
New York, New York 10019

Cardio-Pulmonary Technician: (DOT) 078.—T

CATHETERIZATION TECHNICIAN
Cath Lab Technician

A catheter is a small tubular instrument, varying in shape according to its purpose, which, when attached to thin plastic tubing, can be passed through a body orifice to reach an internal organ. Once inserted, fluids or gases can be pumped through it into the organ, or withdrawn from it. At the same time that this is done, X-rays, X-ray movies, fluoroscope or closed circuit television pictures can be obtained, so that the attending physician or surgeon can track the catheter's progress and control it.

In the cardiac catheterization laboratory, catheters are inserted into a vein or artery, depending on the part of the heart that is under study, and guided into the heart itself. This may be done for purposes of diagnosis; or as a supportive measure, to assist a weakened heart.

JOB DUTIES

The Catheterization Technician does not make the insertion of the catheter, but his work is vital to the success of the attending physician or surgeon who does so.

The Technician makes all of the necessary preparations, such as mixing any dyes that are to be injected in order to get clear pictures, attaches the tubing to the catheter, readies sterile instruments, and sets up whatever monitoring equipment is to be used.

When the patient is brought into the laboratory, the Technician reassures him, explaining the nature of the procedure to be done. He positions the patient in the manner prescribed for the procedure, and fastens the immobilization straps. He prepares the area of the patient's body where the insertion is to be made, and double checks his equipment, making any necessary adjustments.

During the surgery, he operates and monitors the photographic and other equipment, keeping the surgeon advised of the progress of the catheter at all times, and indicates the degree of manipulation needed to position it accurately. He remains with the patient and physician throughout the operation, and removes the equipment and materials upon its completion. He either develops any film, or has it developed, and attaches all films and machine readings to the patient's chart. He also keeps records in the cardiac logbook, giving full information and technical data.

If oscilloscope is used rather than fluoroscope, he loads the machine with sensitized graph paper and attaches electrodes to the patient's skin with gauze or special paste at specified points, and connects wires to the equipment. He aids the physician as directed during the surgery, and advises him of any abnormal conditions. He may perform emergency resuscitation measures, such as applying the defibrillation device to heart muscle, or giving oxygen.

He calculates all data gained from the graphs, such as blood volume rates of flow, various blood pressures, and the exact area of cardiac defect, using a slide rule and desk calculator, and following established formulas. He enters this data in the patient's chart.

EDUCATION, TRAINING, AND EXPERIENCE

The Catheterization Technician must have a high school diploma or equivalent, and have satisfactorily completed formal radiologic technology training in an American Medical Association-approved school, and he must meet requirements for registry by the American Registry of Radiologic Technologists (ARRT). This will usually involve at least two years of nursing or other training in an approved college course.

JOB RELATIONSHIPS

Workers supervised: None.
Supervised by: Physician in charge of patient.
Promotion from: No formal line of promotion.
Promotion to: Radiologic Technician, Chief.

PROFESSIONAL AFFILIATIONS

American Society of Radiologic Technologists
645 North Michigan Avenue
Chicago, Illinois 60611

American Registry of Radiologic Technologists
2600 Wayzata Boulevard
Minneapolis, Minnesota 55405

Radiologic Technologist: (DOT) 078.368-030

DIALYSIS TECHNICIAN
Kidney Machine Operator

Today many patients who have kidney disorders or kidney failure are able to lead reasonably normal lives because of dialysis treatment, in which an external, artificial kidney machine cleanses waste from the body. Until this machine became available, these patients were doomed.

JOB DUTIES

The Dialysis Technician assembles the artificial kidney machine, attaching the coil, tubing and connectors. She mixes the formula prescribed for the solution, and primes the coil with saline solution, heparinized solution, and whole blood obtained from the blood bank.

When the machine is in readiness, she aids the Orderly in positioning the patient on the cart. She takes and records his predialysis weight, temperature, blood pressure, pulse rate, and respiration rate. She removes the dressing from the patient's arm, where permanent shunts have been placed in a vein and an artery. She takes a sample of arterial blood from the shunt, then connects the kidney coil tubes to the artery shunt and the vein shunt in the patient's arm, to start blood circulating through the coil. She reads the patient's diet, to determine foods that may be eaten during the dialysis procedure, which may last for a period of several hours.

During dialysis, the Technician takes periodic readings of the patient's blood pressure, and performs hematocrit and clotting time tests on the patient's blood samples. She continually observes the patient, and monitors the solution in the machine. She administers oxygen or gives a blood transfusion if needed.

At the close of the treatment, the Technician again takes the patient's weight, temperature, blood pressure, pulse rate and respiration rate, and records these readings on his chart. When she disconnects the shunts, she inspects them for any sign of leakage before bandaging the patient's arm. She returns the patient to his room, with help of the Orderly, and transfers the daily chart data to the patient's permanent data sheet. She delivers a final blood sample to the laboratory. She files all necessary charge slips, specimen requisitions, and pharmacy charges.

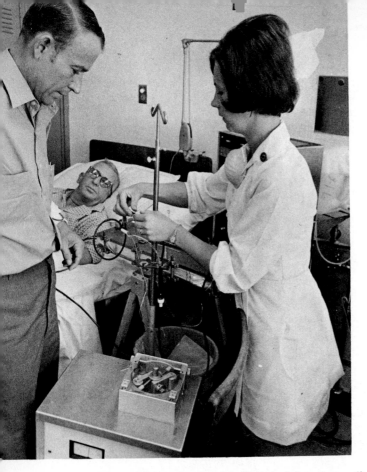

A Dialysis Technician instructs patients in procedures for self-dialysis at the Atlanta Regional Nephrology Center in Grady Hospital.

Photo courtesy of Emory University, Atlanta

She then returns to the dialysis laboratory, dismantles, drains, and cleans the machine ready for reuse.

She orders and maintains inventory of expendable supplies in the dialysis laboratory.

She assists the physician during surgical insertion of the shunts in kidney patients' arms.

She explains the dialysis procedure to patients and emphasizes aseptic care that must be taken to protect the shunts against contact with infection. She provides outpatients with necessary aseptic dressings for use at home.

EDUCATION, TRAINING, AND EXPERIENCE

The Dialysis Technician must be a graduate of an accredited school of nursing, and currently licensed by the Board of Nursing in the state where she practices. One to three months of on-the-job training is given by the physician.

JOB RELATIONSHIPS

Workers supervised: None.
Supervised by: Physician responsible for patient.
Promotion from: No formal line of promotion.
Promotion to: No formal line of promotion.

PROFESSIONAL AFFILIATIONS

American Nurses' Association
10 Columbus Circle
New York, New York 10019

National League for Nursing
10 Columbus Circle
New York, New York 10019

Dialysis Technician: (DOT) 078.—T

ELECTROCARDIOGRAPH TECHNICIAN
E.K.G. Technician

The Electrocardiograph Technician records electromotive variations in action of the heart muscle on an electrocardiograph, for diagnosis of heart ailments.

JOB DUTIES

The Technician studies each patient's medical records to obtain and record information required for electrocardiograph (EKG) records.

She positions the patient on the table or in bed, with chest, arms, and legs exposed. She attaches electrodes to specified areas of ankles and wrists, and connects leads from the EKG machine to them. She turns on the machine and records pulse from the electrodes. She moves another electrode around the chest in a specific pattern to record variations in different parts of the heart muscle. She identifies sections of the recording by pushing a marker button to signify electrode positions. She may ask the patient to perform physical exercise, as specified by the physician, and record his heart's electrical response to exertion.

She removes the electrodes from the patient, and the tracings from the machine. She studies the tracings, to be sure they are clear and to detect any abnormality. When the physician has studied them, she cuts standard lengths of the tracings and mounts them for filing with the patient's record. She fills in the identifying information on these cards. She may duplicate tracings, using a duplicating machine.

She keeps the machine in order, and replenishes supplies. She may type diagnoses, and may need ability to type for other tasks, such as billing, if she is working in a private physician's office.

EDUCATION, TRAINING, AND EXPERIENCE

High school graduation, including courses in the physical sciences, is required.

Three to six months' on-the-job training under supervision of an experienced technician or cardiologist is the usual way in which this technique is learned.

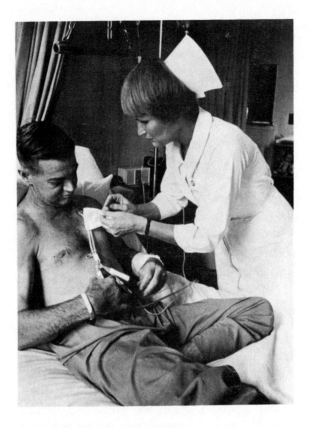

The Electrocardiograph Technician attaches electrodes from the machine to a patient's ankles, wrists, and chest.

JOB RELATIONSHIPS

Workers supervised: None.
Supervised by: Physician in charge of patient.
Promotion from: No formal line of promotion. This is usually an entry job.
Promotion to: No formal line of promotion.

PROFESSIONAL AFFILIATIONS

None.

Electrocardiograph Technician: (DOT) 078.368-018

ELECTROENCEPHALOGRAPH TECHNICIAN
E.E.G. Technician

The Electroencephalograph Technician measures, by means of an electroencephalograph (EEG) machine, so-called "brain waves" of patients, by detecting impulse frequencies and differences in electrical potential between various areas of the brain, to obtain data for use in diagnosis of brain disorders.

JOB DUTIES

The EEG Technician analyzes the patient's medical record to obtain such information as history of head injury or epilepsy, and to be alert for the development of any symptoms during the test. She positions the patient on table or cot, and attaches the EEG electrodes to predetermined positions on forehead, scalp, and ears; or she inserts needle electrodes into specified areas of the scalp. She checks her machine, and instructs the patient on relaxing during test.

She turns on the machine, which produces continuous graphs of a number of irregular waves, indicative of differences between different parts of the brain. She studies the graph for wave characteristics that might indicate brain disorders, and may mark the graphs accordingly. She detects and eliminates all irrelevant waves. She may ask the patient to do some simple activity, such as breathing rapidly, and measure the differences in his reactions as shown by the waves. If the EEG machine is equipped with oscilloscope and camera, she may photograph the wave patterns.

After the test, she removes the tracing from the machine, marks it for identification, and with the name of the physician who had ordered it. The skill in this job is the ability to distinguish curve characteristics caused by brain disorders, and recognize those that are not relevant. She does not interpret the wave pattern.

She takes care of her machine and maintains supplies.

EDUCATION, TRAINING, AND EXPERIENCE

The EEG Technician must be a high school graduate, and have taken courses in the physical sciences. Some college work in such subjects as neuroanatomy is desirable.

Three months' formal training in electroencephalography at a hospital having an EEG department is generally considered adequate. However, an informal apprenticeship requiring three to six months, depending upon the trainee's background, is the usual way to learn this technique.

JOB RELATIONSHIPS

Workers supervised: None.
Supervised by: Physician in charge of patient.
Promotion from: No formal line of promotion.
Promotion to: No formal line of promotion.

PROFESSIONAL AFFILIATIONS

None.

Electroencephalograph Technician: (DOT) 078.368-022

HEART-LUNG MACHINE OPERATOR

The advent of the heart-lung machine, which takes over the functions of these organs temporarily, has made all of modern open-heart surgery possible.

The Heart-Lung Machine Operator works under the direction of the surgeon during such operations.

JOB DUTIES

The Operator confers with surgeons to learn the nature of the surgery to be performed, and prepares for it by assembling the machine, fastening tubing to pumps and filters. He may also prepare the sterilization equipment to be used in surgery. He attaches the sterilized oxygenator equipment to the base of the machine, and connects tubing to form a circulatory system.

He primes the pump preparatory to operation, using standard procedures, with specified type and quantity of blood and other solutions. He sets the machine into operation to double check its action, and to remove any air bubbles in the solution.

On direction from the surgeon, he operates the machine to achieve the condition ordered, such as total bypass, coronary perfusion, recirculation, or partial bypass. During surgery, he maintains the supply of blood in the system, and makes adjustments to changes in the patient's blood balance or blood temperature, the oxygen/carbon dioxide ratio in blood. He monitors the machine at all times, and may operate it manually in case of malfunction. Frequently two Operators work as a team.

When surgery is completed, the Operator dismantles, cleans, and stores the equipment in readiness for future use.

He may train new operators in use of the machine, and make modifications in the system to improve its efficiency.

EDUCATION, TRAINING, AND EXPERIENCE

The Heart-Lung Machine Operator is required to have a high school diploma, with courses in biology, physiology, and physics preferred. Usually he must have one year of experience as a Surgical Technician before he can start training to become a machine operator. About three months of intensive on-the-job training, including formal classroom study is required; and about one year of experience beyond the training period is necessary for the Operator to be fully competent.

JOB RELATIONSHIPS

Workers supervised: None.
Supervised by: Anesthesiologist or surgeon in charge.
Promotion from: No formal line of promotion. May be promoted from Surgical Technician (Nursing Service Department).
Promotion to: No formal line of promotion.

PROFESSIONAL AFFILIATIONS

None.

Heart-Lung Machine Operator: (DOT) 078.—T

ORTHOPTIST

The Orthoptists works with patients who are unable to achieve normal binocular vision because of their inability to focus both eyes together. In children, since this defect makes reading almost impossible, it is likely to brand them with the stigma of being retarded. In adults, in whom it sometimes happens following illness or stroke, it is a most distressing condition.

JOB DUTIES

The Orthoptist studies the physician's referral slip, to learn the patient's medical diagnosis and history, and the instructions for testing or treatment.

He administers tests that measure visual acuity, focusing ability, binocular co-operation, and eye motor movement of eyes. He uses such equipment as telebinoculars, tachistoscopes, disparators, amblyscopes, and prisms.

He positions, instructs, and assists the patient during tests and therapy. He develops visual skills in eye-hand coordination, near-visual discrimination, and depth perception, using developmental glasses.

He instructs adult patients, or parents of children, in use of corrective exercises and methods at home.

He maintains patients' case histories and hospital records, and confers with physicians in regard to patients' progress.

EDUCATION, TRAINING, AND EXPERIENCE

The Orthoptist must have at least two years of college, with courses in biology, physics, and child psychology, plus one year of theoretic and practical training at an approved training center, after which he is eligible to take the examination for certification given by the American Orthoptic Council. Some schools now require that applicants for special training be college graduates or registered nurses before acceptance.

Brief on-the-job training, to acquaint the worker with physicians' techniques and hospital procedures, is desirable.

JOB RELATIONSHIPS

Workers supervised: None.
Supervised by: Physician in charge of patient.
Promotion from: No formal line of promotion.
Promotion to: No formal line of promotion.

PROFESSIONAL AFFILIATIONS

American Orthoptic Council
4200 North Woodward Avenue
Royal Oak, Michigan 48072

Orthoptist: (DOT) 079.378-030

PROSTHETIST-ORTHOTIST

The Prosthetist-Orthotist designs, writes specifications for, and fits artificial limbs, braces, and appliances for body deformities and disorders, following prescription of a physician or other qualified medical practitioner. The actual making of the appliances is done by an Orthopedic-Appliance-and-Limb Technician, under his supervision.

JOB DUTIES

The Prosthetist-Orthotist examines the patient, noting any deformities that may require special fitting. He takes measurements, and plans an appliance that will give the patient maximum function. In the course of doing this, he may make a plaster cast. He selects suitable materials, and gives specifications for the appliance to the Technician.

When the appliance is delivered, he fits it on the patient, making any necessary adjustments. He confers with physicians, therapists and others on the rehabilitation team to evaluate the success of the appliance. He may instruct the patient on how to use and care for it.

EDUCATION, TRAINING, AND EXPERIENCE

The Prosthetist-Orthotist must complete a four-year training course following high school graduation. In high school, he should have taken courses in physics, chemistry, biology, and mathematics, as well as shopwork in metal, wood, and plastics. Some universities now offer a four-year course leading to a Bachelor of Science degree, which includes courses in functional anatomy, physiology, and principles of biomechanics. It is preferred that the worker have a six- to ten–week course in engineering as related to prosthetic and orthotic appliances, and actual shop experience in appliance construction. He must be certified by the American Board of the Prosthetic and Orthotics Appliance Industry, Inc.

For other workers, such as the Orthopedic-Appliance-and-Limb Technician, and the Orthopedic-Cast Specialist, high school graduation plus short courses or on-the-job training satisfy requirements.

JOB RELATIONSHIPS

Workers supervised: May supervise Orthopedic-Appliance-and-Limb Technician and trainees.
Supervised by: None. (Follows prescription of a physician.)
Promotion from: No formal line of promotion.
Promotion to: No formal line of promotion.

PROFESSIONAL AFFILIATIONS

American Orthotics and Prosthetics Association
919 18th Street, NW.
Washington, D.C. 20006

Prosthetist-Orthotist: (DOT) 078.368-026

Orthopedic-Appliance-and-Limb Technician: (DOT) 712.281-018

Orthopedic-Cast Specialist: (DOT) 712.884-046

PULMONARY-FUNCTION TECHNICIAN

The Pulmonary-Function Technician operates a variety of electromechanical equipment, such as respirometer, radiometer, and intermittent positive pressure breathing machines, to obtain data about patients' respiratory efficiency. This information is of value to physicians in diagnosing and determining treatment of pulmonary disorders.

JOB DUTIES

The Technician explains tests to patients, to allay anxiety and assure cooperation.

He may then fasten the nose clip to patient, assuring breathing through the mouth only. He performs tidal volume and oxygen-consumption test, maximum-inspiratory-capacity test, expiratory-reserve-volume test, maximum breathing-capacity test, and forced expiratory vital-capacity test. When he has completed the pulmonary mechanics test, he calculates results, using an electric calculator, or posting valves recordings on kymographs to computerized work sheets for processing.

He performs anticongestion tests, using intermittent positive pressure breathing machine and bronchodilator medications, to determine the effect of medication on pulmonary function.

He analyzes specimens of patients' blood to determine the saturation of oxygen, percentage of red cells, and other content. He notes scale readings of equipment, following specified statistical procedures to correct findings for temperature, and barometric pressure, age, height, and weight of the patient. He routes all findings to the attending physician for interpretation.

EDUCATION, TRAINING, AND EXPERIENCE

Two years of college-level courses with a major in science is required. A bachelor's degree is highly preferred. Usually prior experience is not necessary, but six months' on-the-job training is required.

JOB RELATIONSHIPS

Workers supervised: None.
Supervised by: Physician in charge of patient.
Promotion from: No formal line of promotion.
Promotion to: No formal line of promotion.

PROFESSIONAL AFFILIATIONS

None.

Pulmonary-Function Technician: (DOT) 078.—T

RESPIRATORY THERAPIST
Inhalation Therapist
Inhalation Technician
Oxygen-Therapy Technician

The field of respiratory therapy is expanding so rapidly that the old terms "Inhalation Therapist" and "Inhalation Technician" are no longer adequate, and decreasing in day-to-day usage. Instead, the broader terms "Respiratory Therapist" and "Respiratory Technician" are more frequently used.

Respiratory therapy is employed in the diagnosis, treatment, management, control, and preventive care of patients with heart and lung problems. Life-threatening respiratory problems may arise in the newborn nursery, among asthmatic, stroke, and emphysematous patients, drowning victims, and among head- and chest-injured patients in the emergency room, in the cardiac intensive care unit, the operating room, the geriatric ward, or the outpatient department of the hospital.

Some cases are life-and-death emergencies, when the respiratory team converts to one part of the cardiopulmonary arrest team, working in coordination with doctors and nurses.

While this kind of care is essential, day-to-day respiratory care is just as crucial, if not more so. Respiratory therapy personnel, working from the written orders of physicians, carry out specific therapeutic treatments to support life in patients who are in cardiopulmonary distress.

Respiratory therapy employs a variety of diagnostic techniques, such as use of radioactive gases or aerosols administered to the patient so that various portions of the lungs may be screened for obstructions and abnormalities.

Respiratory therapy in the form of hyperbaric oxygen is also utilized to treat gangrene, carbon monoxide poisoning, tetanus, and other disorders. Its importance

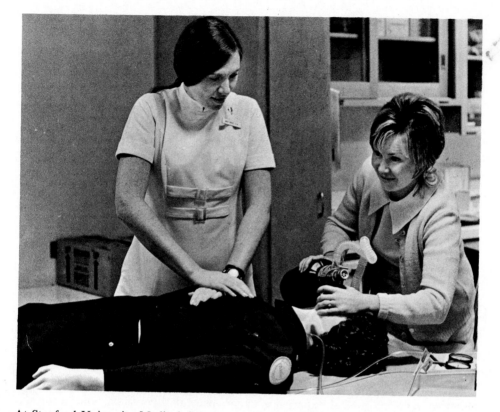

At Stanford University Medical Center, two Teaching Nurses demonstrate procedure to start emergency cardiac resuscitation, using "Resuscie-Annie," a dummy made for this purpose. All nurses preparing to work in the Coronary Care Unit must learn this technique.

increases as medical science strives to meet problems associated with cigarette smoking, and industrial and traffic pollution.

While hospitals are the major employers of respiratory therapy personnel, employment opportunities also exist in clinics, physicians' offices, nursing homes, industry, and the Armed Forces.

JOB DUTIES

There are three levels of professional accreditation in this field: the Respiratory Therapist, the Certified Respiratory Therapy Technician, and the Respiratory Therapy Assistant.

The *Respiratory Therapist* is most highly trained, and acts as supervisor of the team. He is able to administer gas therapy, aerosol therapy, and intermittent positive pressure breathing (IPPB) treatments, as well as oxygen, humidification, bronchopulmonary drainage and exercises, cardiopulmonary resuscitation, mechanical ventilation, airway management, pulmonary function studies, blood-gas analysis, and physiological monitoring. However, much of his time may be occupied with administrative duties, teaching, working on unusual or difficult diagnostic problems, or research.

The *Certified Technician* is responsible for the bulk of patient care, and is capable of carrying out most or all of the techniques. He is also responsible for sterilizing and maintaining equipment, and keeping adequate patient and departmental records.

The *Assistant* on the team works under the direction of the Therapist or Technician, and is most concerned with cleaning, disinfecting, sterilizing, and maintenance of equipment. He may perform only limited patient care, but may have responsibility for the bulk of clerical duties.

EDUCATION, TRAINING, AND EXPERIENCE

The *Respiratory Therapist* must have a high school diploma, and have completed a two-year course of respiratory therapy approved by the American Medical Association Council on Medical Education. At this point, the candidate may apply for a written registry examination. Before taking the oral section of the examination, he must complete one year of clinical experience under licensed medical supervision. Following successful oral examination, he is then designated a Registered Respiratory Therapist, by the American Registry of Inhalation Therapists.

The *Certified Respiratory Therapy Technician* must have a high school diploma, plus two years of clinical experience under medical supervision, and successful passage of a certifying examination. However, as of January 1, 1975, applicants for examination are required to have completed one year of an approved respiratory training program, plus one year of supervised clinical experience approved by the American Medical Association, or to be a graduate of a similarly approved two-year program.

The *Respiratory Therapy Assistant* qualifies by high school graduation, plus on-the-job training in basic clinical skills.

JOB RELATIONSHIPS

Workers supervised: The Respiratory Therapist supervises the Technician and Assistant. The Technician supervises the Assistant.

Supervised by: The Respiratory Therapist is supervised by the physician in charge; the Technician and Assistant by the Therapist.

Promotion from: Technician to Therapist.

Promotion to: Technician to Therapist.

PROFESSIONAL AFFILIATIONS

American Association of Inhalation Therapists
332 South Michigan Avenue
Chicago, Illinois 60604

American Registry of Inhalation Therapists
University of Rochester Medical Center
Rochester, New York 14642

American Association for Respiratory Therapy
7411 Hines Place
Dallas, Texas 75235

Inhalation Therapist: (DOT) 079.368-018

THERAPY TECHNICIAN
Cobalt Technician
Hyperbaric Chamber Technician
Radiotherapy Technician
Therapy Technologist

The Therapy Technician works in specialized facets of radiology, utilizing specialized X-ray equipment, radioactive cobalt, and a plastic hyperbaric chamber. (A hyperbaric chamber is one in which air, gases, or solutions can be controlled at pressures greater than normal. Its principle can be understood by recalling that deep sea divers, men in submarines, or "sandhogs" who dig deep tunnels, cannot come to the surface all at once, but must be maintained under pressure long enough for their bodies to adjust to the change gradually.)

A few buildings constructed entirely as hyperbaric chambers exist in the United States, but in general control of pressure has to be achieved within a small space defined by plastic walls. The Therapy Technician usually works within these limits.

Hyperbaric pressure in combination with radioisotopes has been shown to be effective against certain types of cancer. Hyperbaric pressure is also a useful treatment in extreme infections such as gangrene.

JOB DUTIES

The Technician studies the patient's chart to learn the type of treatment prescribed, location of affected area, history of previous radiation treatment, and the amount of radiation exposure that is to be given.

The Technician is careful to wear protective garments, and to follow all standardized procedures in handling radioactive material. All of the regulations for the Nuclear Medical Technologist apply to her, and her work may overlap that job classification.

When using the hyperbaric chamber, the Technician positions the patient, and explains the procedure. She adjusts the equipment to expose only the body area to be irradiated, and protects the patient with the plastic enclosure. She attaches monitoring devices, such as earphones and microphone, so that the patient can communicate with her throughout the treatment. She attaches the electrodes of the electro-cardiograph and pulse amplifier. When all is in readiness, the Technician leaves the chamber, secures the door, and goes into the control room, from which she can monitor the patient in all aspects throughout the treatment. If anything untoward occurs, she notifies the Radiologist.

At the end of treatment, she removes the patient, and records the treatment data in the logbook and the patient's record.

EDUCATION, TRAINING, AND EXPERIENCE

High school graduation or equivalent is required, plus satisfactory completion of formal radiologic technology training in an American Medical–approved school, and ability to meet the requirements of the American Registry of Radiologic Technologists for certification as ARRT. One to two years of training in operation of specific equipment is preferred.

JOB RELATIONSHIPS

Workers supervised: None.
Supervised by: Physician in charge of patient.
Promotion from: No formal line of promotion.
Promotion to: Radiologic Technologist, Chief.

PROFESSIONAL AFFILIATIONS

American Society of Radiologic Technologists
645 North Michigan Avenue
Chicago, Illinois 60611

American Registry of Radiologic Technologists
2600 Wayzata Boulevard
Minneapolis, Minnesota 55405

Radiologic Technologist: (DOT) 078.368-030

THERMOGRAPH TECHNICIAN

The job classification of Thermograph Technician is a relatively easy way for a young person with a high school education to enter the health care field, where he can observe health techniques at work, and have time enough to decide where his particular talents might lead.

The job classification of Thermograph Technician is one that a young person with a high school education might consider to enter the health care field. Here he can observe health techniques at work, and have time to decide where his particular talents might lead.

The Technician uses a machine called a thermograph, mirrors, and various devices to increase body warmth of specified areas, then scans the areas, and films them. He monitors both the patient and the equipment, and records all data. When the film exposed has been developed, he attaches it to patients' records, writing notes on the variables in the procedures he has employed, so that the attending physician has his evaluation to use in making diagnosis.

EDUCATION, TRAINING, AND EXPERIENCE

The Thermograph Technician must have a high school education, plus three to six months of on-the-job training.

JOB RELATIONSHIPS

Workers supervised: None.
Supervised by: Physician in charge of patient.
Promotion from: No formal line of promotion. This may be an entry job.
Promotion to: No formal line of promotion.

PROFESSIONAL AFFILIATIONS

None.

Thermograph Technician: (DOT) 078.—T

5

HOSPITAL AND HEALTH CARE ADMINISTRATION

As hospitals have increased the scope of their activities, and become more responsive to the needs of their communities, they have evolved into very complex institutions. Their primary function is the care of bed patients, toward which they provide special facilities and trained personnel to assist physicians. However, this function has been expanded in recent years to care of the sick or potentially sick persons in their normal living situations. Increasingly, hospitals have assumed responsibility for programs of preventive medicine, and serve as a medium in many communities through which physicians and nurses, along with voluntary and official health agencies, pool their efforts for improvement of public health. In addition, they also serve as teaching institutions, providing education of both professional and para-medical personnel.

The coordination of all these diverse activities is one task of the hospital administration. Further, it is responsible for all financial and personnel management; for the upkeep and functioning of buildings, equipment, and grounds; and for the smooth operation of the hospital as a health care institution.

In some aspects, a hospital resembles and incorporates activities normal in commercial enterprises; but it also includes several activities that would be unusual in most businesses, such as its own power plant and laundry, a dietary service, a paint shop, and a large maintenance staff.

Hospital administration differs from that of other businesses in such mundane matters as daily schedules. In business or industry schedules for production are set up, and workers' hours are specific and binding. A hospital must function at full efficiency 24 hours a day, and weekends, and holidays.

Industries produce tangible goods and services, which the public can accept or reject. Hospitals provide facilities and personnel for services the patient must have, whether he likes it or not, and at a cost that is not always predictable. Thus, hospital employees deal with people who are emotionally and physically upset, so that even technical and mechanical skills must be fitted into a framework of quiet persuasion and full understanding of abnormal human behavior.

Again, businesses and industries usually have a clear line of established authority. In contrast, hospital and health care workers are responsible to two major authorities: One involves the administrative, financial, and management aspects of the hospital. The other is the professional medical authority.

In consequence of all these factors, hospital and health care administration must achieve a working climate in which there is strong awareness of teamwork, and mutual respect among professional staff, technical workers, and all of the many workers who do the basic humdrum tasks.

However, in some job classifications in administration, plant operation, and plant maintenance of hospitals (particularly low-echelon clerical or laborer jobs) the contrasts between the requirements of hospitals and those of businesses and industries are largely demands for personality traits and attitudes appropriate to the hospital situation, rather than differences in education or training. Consequently, some jobs appear in the organizational charts of various departments, but are not described fully. In these cases, the Dictionary of Occupational Titles (DOT) classifications are given for use by employment and guidance counselors. It may be assumed that they require only high school graduation or less, possibly plus short–course or on-the-job training.

Executive Department

All hospitals and health care institutions are responsible to some sort of governing authority which represents the community it serves, or the institution's founders. This may be a municipal, state, or other Hospital Board, Board of Governors, or Board of Trustees. Members of these boards are usually unsalaried. Their purpose is to maintain the policies and quality of the hospital as a continuum, regardless of staff changes.

The Chief of Medical Staff, the Administrator, and the Chaplain of the hospital are directly responsible to this board. In day-to-day operation, the Administrator heads the Executive Department.

ADMINISTRATOR
Executive Director
Executive Vice President
Hospital Administrator

In 1970, there were about 17,000 hospital administrators employed in the United States. About two-thirds of them worked in nonprofit or private hospitals and institutions, and most of the rest in local, state, or Federal institutions. About 15 per cent of them were women.

The Administrator holds the highest executive position in the hospital, working under general guidance from its Governing Board. In small hospitals, he may have to assume all the management functions. In large hospitals, he is assisted by specialists trained in various aspects of hiring and training workers; preparing and admin-

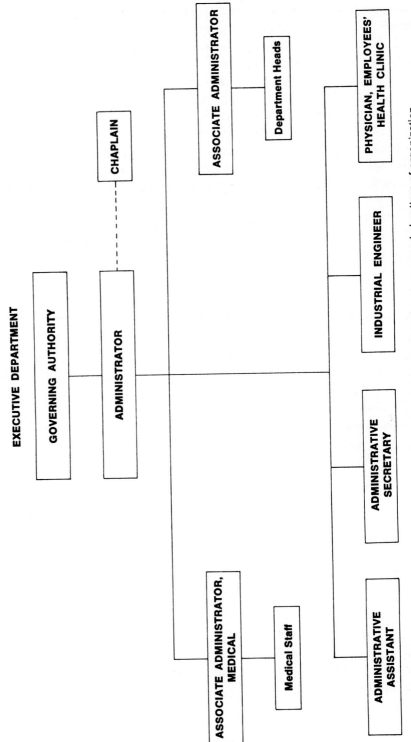

EXECUTIVE DEPARTMENT

GOVERNING AUTHORITY

ADMINISTRATOR

CHAPLAIN

ASSOCIATE ADMINISTRATOR

Department Heads

ASSOCIATE ADMINISTRATOR, MEDICAL

Medical Staff

ADMINISTRATIVE ASSISTANT

ADMINISTRATIVE SECRETARY

INDUSTRIAL ENGINEER

PHYSICIAN, EMPLOYEES' HEALTH CLINIC

NOTE: This chart is for illustrative purposes only and should not be considered a recommended pattern of organization.

istering the budget; raising funds; establishing accounting procedures; planning current and future space needs; insuring proper maintenance and operation of buildings and equipment; purchasing supplies and equipment; providing for laundry, mail, telephone and other communications, information, and necessary services for both patients and staff.

The Administrator may or may not be a physician. As the complexities of health care administration have grown, there is an increasing tendency to employ persons trained as executives in the health field for these positions. In 1970, there were 29 colleges and universities in the United States that offered courses leading to a master's degree in hospital administration.

JOB DUTIES

The Administrator coordinates all activities of the hospital. He organizes its functions through appropriate departmentalization and the delegation of duties. He schedules regular staff meetings, and acts as liaison between the medical staff and other departments.

He prepares reports for, and attends meetings of, the Governing Board of the hospital, in regard to hospital activities, and also concerning such matters as legislation affecting health care.

He provides personnel policies and practices that adequately support good patient care, and maintains accurate and complete personnel records.

He reviews and acts upon the reports of authorized inspecting agencies.

The Administrator implements the control and effective use of the physical and financial resources of the hospital, and sets up a system of responsible accounting, including budget and internal controls.

He participates in, or is represented at, community, state, and national hospital associations and professional meetings that define the delivery of health care services and aid in short- and long-range planning. He provides an acceptable public relations program.

He pursues a continuing program of formal and informal education in health care, administrative, and management areas to maintain, strengthen, and broaden his concepts, philosophy, and ability as a health care administrator.

EDUCATION, TRAINING, AND EXPERIENCE

The Administrator should have graduated from an accredited college or university, with graduate work in an accredited program in hospital administration.

Education and experience requirements may vary according to individual background, size of hospital, and section of the country. However, a minimum of three years of serving in subordinate administrative positions is required by most hospitals. Larger hospitals may require one year of resident or administrative internship experience.

JOB RELATIONSHIPS

Workers supervised: All employees of hospital through Associate Administrators and department heads.
Supervised by: Governing authority of hospital.
Promotion from: Associate Administrator.
Promotion to: No formal line of promotion. This is the highest occupation level in the hospital.

PROFESSIONAL AFFILIATIONS

American College of Hospital Administrators
840 North Lake Shore Drive
Chicago, Illinois 60611

Association of University Programs in Hospital Administration
1642 East 56th Street
Chicago, Illinois 60637

Local, state, and national hospital associations.

Local and State civic and services organizations.

Superintendent, Hospital: (DOT) 187.118-062

ASSOCIATE ADMINISTRATOR

The Associate Administrator directs, supervises, and coordinates the functions of one or more hospital departments. He acts as the Administrator when the latter is away.

JOB DUTIES

The Associate Administrator confers with and advises the Administrator on many problems related to hospital operation. He may recommend changes in policies, assist in preparation of budgets, make studies of costs, review departmental budget estimates, and direct the accounting of hospital funds.

He may recommend improvement of hospital facilities, including construction or renovation of buildings, and purchase of new equipment. He bases such recommendations on personal inspection of the premises, consideration of hospital policies, and his knowledge of community needs and resources.

He interprets hospital and departmental policies, objectives, and operational procedures to department heads, and resolves problems concerning such matters as staffing, utilization of hospital facilities, equipment and supplies.

He meets with members of the community to promote good public relations for the hospital; and attends meetings of professional, civic, and service organizations for a similar purpose. He may direct public relations, and engage in fund-raising.

EDUCATION, TRAINING, AND EXPERIENCE

The Associate Administrator should have graduated from an accredited college or university, with graduate work in hospital administration in an accredited program or in a specialty such as accounting, business administration, or public health.

Education and experience requirements may vary according to combined background of the individual, size of the hospital, and section of the country. However, a minimum of three years' progressively responsible administrative work is required. Experience as head of a major hospital department may be acceptable.

JOB RELATIONSHIPS

Workers supervised: All workers in department for which he is responsible.
Supervised by: Administrator.
Promotion from: May be promoted from head of any department.
Promotion to: Administrator.

PROFESSIONAL AFFILIATIONS

American College of Hospital Administrators
840 North Lake Shore Drive
Chicago, Illinois 60611

Association of University Programs in Hospital Administration
1642 East 56th Street
Chicago, Illinois 60637

Local, State, and national hospital associations.

Local and State civic and service organizations.

Superintendent, Hospital: (DOT) 187.118-062

ASSOCIATE ADMINISTRATOR, MEDICAL
Medical Director

The Associate Administrator, Medical directs and coordinates all medical and related activities in the hospital, with the exception of the nursing service.

He is the hospital's authority in questions of professional ethics, and of policy. He is a physician, licensed to practice in the state where the hospital is located, and has had considerable experience in one or more branches of medicine and surgery, as well as administrative or supervisory experience.

JOB DUTIES

The Associate Administrator, Medical advises the Administrator on medical and administrative problems, and assists in establishing standards of medical service, and on problems of policy and public relations as they relate to medical practice.

He supervises the heads of the various medical departments, and recommends appointments, promotions, and transfers of physicians and supervisory personnel of medical units. He initiates and directs staff conferences for instructional purposes and discussion of administrative and medical problems. He acts as consultant in difficult or unusual cases, and advises the clinical staff on a wide variety of problems. He plans for, and participates in, instruction of interns and residents. He investigates and studies new developments in medical practices and techniques, and adapts them to the needs of the hospital.

He plans the hospital medical program, and determines facilities and personnel required to carry them out within budgetary limits.

He represents the hospital in professional groups. He reviews all medical reports released for publication under the name of the hospital. He also determines that relationships between the various medical departments and the community reflect established hospital policies.

Among the hospital department heads that he supervises are those of anesthesiology, clinical laboratory, dentistry, medical records, pharmacy, physiatrics, radiology, and speech and hearing.

EDUCATION, TRAINING, AND EXPERIENCE

The Associate Administrator, Medical must have graduated from a medical school approved by the Council on Medical Education and Hospitals of the American Medical Association or the Committee on Hospitals of the Bureau of Professional Education of the American Osteopathic Association, or be a diplomate of the National Board of Medical Examiners or National Board of Osteopathic Examiners, and be licensed to practice in the state where the hospital is located.

Training and experience requirements may vary according to combined background of the individual, size of the hospital, and the section of the country.

JOB RELATIONSHIPS

Workers supervised: Physicians and surgeons who are members of the hospital staff.
Supervised by: Administrator.
Promotion to: No formal line of promotion. May be promoted to Administrator.
Promotion from: Physician in charge of any of the medical departments.

PROFESSIONAL AFFILIATIONS

American Medical Association
535 North Dearborn Street
Chicago, Illinois 60610

American College of Hospital Administrators
840 North Lake Shore Drive
Chicago, Illinois 60611

Local, State, and national hospital and medical associations.

Local and State civic and service organizations.

Medical Director: (DOT) 070.—T

ADMINISTRATIVE ASSISTANT

The Administrative Assistant (of whom there may be several in a large hospital) carries out specific work projects assigned by the Administrator, relative to operation of the total hospital or specific patient services. He reports to the Administrator, providing information for evaluation and revision of regulations, practices, and procedures.

JOB DUTIES

The Administrative Assistant may be assigned to investigate and report on patient or visitor complaints; analyze admission procedures and suggest plans for more efficient methods; study the relationship between various departmental records, with a view toward consolidation and reduction of clerical staff; gather data on consumption of utilities, and make a comparative survey with other institutions; investigate advisability, in terms of cost and service, of using commercial laundry, dietary, maintenance, or other services rather than maintaining them within the hospital framework; determine operating costs, distribution of personnel, and work schedules for specified departments; or assist department heads in assembling data relative to specific problems.

He prepares statistical and other reports, to complete his work assignments, and performs related duties as directed.

EDUCATION, TRAINING, AND EXPERIENCE

The Administrative Assistant should have graduated from an accredited college, university, medical school, or school of nursing. Completion of a course in hospital administration is preferred.

Some hospital administrative experience is desirable, but this job is usually considered an administrative trainee position. The worker receives on-the-job training in hospital administration and procedures through specific work assignments.

JOB RELATIONSHIPS

Workers supervised: None.
Supervised by: Administrator or Associate Administrator.
Promotion from: No formal line of promotion. This is considered a trainee position.
Promotion to: May be promoted to Associate Administrator.

PROFESSIONAL AFFILIATIONS

None.

Administrative Assistant: (DOT) 169.168-014

ADMINISTRATIVE SECRETARY

The Administrative Secretary performs both secretarial and minor executive functions. She provides the logistic support that the Administrators need to coordinate all their work.

JOB DUTIES

The Administrative Secretary keeps records of appointments and meetings, reminds the Administrator of them, and sends notices to staff and members of Governing Board. She takes the minutes of board, staff, and executive committee meetings, and distributes minutes to designated personnel.

She assembles material for reports, such as those of the American Hospital Association, American Medical Association, and American College of Surgeons, and also for annual reports on interns and residents, as well as special questionnaires.

She maintains files, handles mail, answers routine correspondence on her own initiative, and may perform clerical duties related to purchasing, personnel, and training programs. She may train and supervise clerical workers.

EDUCATION, TRAINING, AND EXPERIENCE

The Administrative Secretary should have graduated from high school, or commercial school, with courses in typing, stenography, and business English. Two years of college education or more is preferred. She should have at least one year of experience as a stenographer or secretary, plus on-the-job training in the hospital or health care institution of at least one to three months.

JOB RELATIONSHIPS

Workers supervised: May supervise a number of clerical workers.
Supervised by: Administrator.
Promotion from: No formal line of promotion. May be promoted from Secretary; Medical Secretary; Stenographer; or other clerical job in which ability is demonstrated.
Promotion to: No formal line of promotion.

PROFESSIONAL AFFILIATIONS

National Secretaries Association
1103 Grand Avenue
Kansas City, Missouri 64106

Executive Secretaries Association, Inc.
1090 Ticonderoga Drive
Sunnyvale, California 94087

Secretary: (DOT) 201.368-018

INDUSTRIAL ENGINEER
Director, Management Engineering
Management Analyst
Management Engineer
Methods Analyst
Methods Engineer
Systems Analyst, Engineering

In a hospital or health care institution setting, the Industrial Engineer is an "efficiency expert," who plans and oversees the utilization of hospital buildings, facilities, equipment, and personnel. He conducts studies, and makes recommendations about the hospital's physical organization, programs, methods, and procedures. He helps in development of new work methods, and operational improvements. He evaluates major equipment purchases to determine their effectiveness in utilization of resources.

He conducts work analyses and measurement studies, standardizes and controls design for forms and other office supplies, and recommends regulations for their use.

JOB DUTIES

The Industrial Engineer assists the Administrator in: increasing the productivity of human and material resources; cost reduction; development of management information flow systems; design of new organizational systems; planning of data processing and computer control systems; coordination of hospital maintenance policies and programs; and development of communications and reporting systems.

He formulates and recommends corporate inventory management policies and procedures, and verifies the feasibility of capital expenditures. He conducts office methods and processing surveys, and identifies and solves distribution problems. He furnishes liaison services between hospital management and outside consultants and vendors. He assists in management decision-making through use of computers or development of mathematical models simulating complex hospital problems.

Educational background and professional training vary widely in this field and depend upon the local situations and needs of the institution.

Generally speaking, the minimum educational requirement is a bachelor's degree in industrial engineering. A master's degree is highly desirable and the Industrial Engineer should be a Registered Professional Engineer. Industrial engineering curricula accredited by the Engineers' Council for Professional Development require (a) courses common to all branches of engineering in physics, chemistry, mathematics through integral calculus, and engineering sciences such as statistics, dynamics, strength of materials, thermodynamics, and fluid mechanics; (b) humanistic social studies; and (c) specialized subjects characteristic of industrial engineering, such as organization planning, motion study, materials handling, and engineering economy.

Two or three years of progressive experience in industrial engineering, industrial management, or business administration, some of which should be hospital oriented, are usually required.

JOB RELATIONSHIPS

Workers supervised: Technical or clerical personnel.
Supervised by: Administrator.
Promotion from: No formal line of promotion.
Promotion to: No formal line of promotion.

PROFESSIONAL AFFILIATIONS

Hospital Management Systems Society
840 North Lake Shore Drive
Chicago, Illinois 60611

Industrial Engineer: (DOT) 012.188-030

PHYSICIAN, EMPLOYEES' HEALTH CLINIC
Employees' Physician
Health Service Physician

JOB DUTIES

The Physician in the Employees' Health Clinic examines prospective employees in regard to fitness for duty, and reexamines employees who are returning to duty after illness. He treats minor illness or injury of employees when these occur on-the-job.

He confers with the administration and governing board in planning employee health programs, and makes recommendations.

He examines employees at specified intervals, and may make recommendation for correction of defects, or further examinations or tests to be performed by other hospital services, such as the clinical laboratory, radiology, or other technical service. He gives anti–flu and other injections.

He supervises nurses and other personnel assigned to the infirmary, and oversees maintenance of case histories and other medical records of employees.

He inspects the institution and makes recommendations for sanitation and elimination of health hazards. He may visit employees who are confined to their homes, and may also visit employees on the job to insure that their working conditions are satisfactory.

He may be employed full- or part-time.

EDUCATION, TRAINING, AND EXPERIENCE

The physician must have graduated from a medical school approved by the Council on Medical Education and Hospitals of the American Medical Association, or the Committee on Hospitals of the Bureau of Professional Education of the American Osteopathic Association, or a diplomate of National Board of Medical Examiners or National Board of Osteopathic Examiners. State license where located to practice medicine or osteopathy.

He should have had three to four years' experience as a general practitioner. Special training or experience in the physical, mental, and social requirements of hospital jobs.

JOB RELATIONSHIPS

Workers supervised: Nursing service and clerical personnel assigned to the infirmary.
Supervised by: Administrator.
Promotion from: No formal line of promotion.
Promotion to: No formal line of promotion.

PROFESSIONAL AFFILIATIONS

American Medical Association
535 North Dearborn Street
Chicago, Illinois 60610

Physician, Occupational: (DOT) 070.108-070

CHAPLAIN
Pastoral Counselor

The hospital Chaplain provides religious counseling and guidance to patients, family members, hospital employees, and students, as part of total patient care.

JOB DUTIES

The Chaplain meets with the Administrator and staff to plan religious services for patients, employees, and attending families. He coordinates pastoral care with activities of other departments, to avoid interrupting medical care, yet insure adequate spiritual help for patients.

He visits newly admitted patients on a social and friendly level, and makes routine visits to rooms, wards, and other areas, making counseling and advice available. He may arrange for interpreters to assist with non-English-speaking patients and families. He acts as liaison between the hospital and patients' families and friends in times of crisis. He also contacts patients' own pastors, to notify them of hospitalizations. He performs religious rites, as requested by patients or families.

He participates in discussion groups for patients in the psychiatric wards, and may develop inservice training programs for pastoral students. He speaks at civic and service organizations, to explain the pastoral care programs.

EDUCATION, TRAINING, AND EXPERIENCE

The Chaplain must have a Bachelor of Arts degree from an accredited institution, preferably in psychology or sociology. Must also have a Bachelor of Divinity degree and Master of Theology degree in psychology from a recognized seminary, divinity school, or college of theology.

A minimum of three years of general pastoral care and two years of hospital pastoral care experience is required for entry on this job.

Up to six months is required to attain adequate proficiency in the administrative, pastoral, and educational aspects of the position, and in the relating of pastoral care to the medical well-being of patients.

JOB RELATIONSHIPS

Workers supervised: May have an assistant and clerical help.
Supervised by: Administrator.
Promotion from: May be promoted from a pastoral care student.
Promotion to: No formal line of promotion.

PROFESSIONAL AFFILIATIONS

None.

Chaplain: (DOT) 120.108-010

Communications Department

In hospitals and health care centers, where minutes or even seconds are often critical, there must be efficient communication systems, both within the institution and into the community. In addition, the persons who operate these systems must be capable, calm, and able to think clearly under pressure.

These communication systems consist of telephone connections and in some instances, short wave radio, between the outside world and staff personnel; of page service over a public address system; and, in some hospitals, the light and sound signals that indicate malfunction of engineering equipment such as heating and air-conditioning, fire alarms and sprinkler systems, and a critical status of oxygen and nitrous oxide levels.

Job classifications in a large communications department may consist of a Communications Coordinator, who supervises the Chief Telephone Operator, who in turn supervises all the other Telephone Operators.

In all of these, the general qualifications are the same as they would be for similar positions in an efficient industry, or a hotel. The exception lies in the fact that personnel in charge of hospital communications must keep accurate records of all calls, both local and long distance, incoming and outgoing; and they must also be aware of the working schedules of staff physicians, and their whereabouts at all times. Both the Coordinator and all Operators must be more dedicated and responsible than might be required in comparable employment elsewhere.

In all categories, high school graduation is a minimum requirement, plus familiarity with PBX equipment. The Communications Coordinator should have from three to five years of total switchboard experience, including some hospital experience, and supervisory training. The Chief Telephone Operator should have similar experience, and may be required to hold a radio operator's license. Operators need only three months of experience with PBX equipment. Orientation programs are usually provided to provide familiarity with the hospital's personnel and procedures.

Communications Coordinator: (DOT) 235.138-010

Telephone Operator, Chief: (DOT) 235.138-014

Telephone Operator: (DOT) 235.862-010

DATA PROCESSING

The amount of paperwork involved in operation of a modern hospital is enormous. Few businesses or other activities have needs equal to those of a hospital for speed and accuracy in communication, recording, processing, analysis, and retrieval of vital information. For this reason, many hospitals have established electronic data processing systems to manage the business aspects of their operation, and some are utilizing such systems for management of medical records, and for data essential to medical research.

In terms of educational and training requirements, and the competencies needed in workers, there is little or no difference between hospitals and organizations in business and industry. No special scientific medical education or experience is

COMMUNICATIONS DEPARTMENT

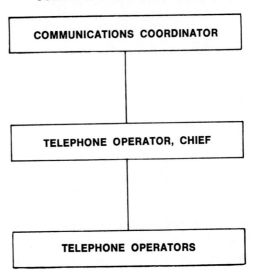

NOTE: This chart is for illustrative purposes only and should not be considered a recommended pattern of organization.

necessary. Except for the Manager of the department, the Chief Programer, and the Systems Analyst, college education is not usually a prerequisite, and when it is, emphasis is on business administration, computer programing, data processing, statistics, and mathematics. All other job classifications require high school education plus siutable technical training.

Manager, Electronic-Data Processing: (DOT) 169.168-058

Systems Analyst, Business-Electronic-Data Processing: (DOT) 012.168-022

Programer, Chief: (DOT) 020.168-010

Supervisor, Computer Operations: (DOT) 213.138-010

Supervisor, Machine-Records Unit: (DOT) 213.138-014

Programer, Business: (DOT) 020.188-026

Digital-Computer Operator: (DOT) 213.382-018

Computer-Peripheral-Equipment Operator: (DOT) 213.382-014
    (Tab Operator)

Key-Punch Operator: (DOT) 213.582-010

Coding Clerk: (DOT) 219.388-074

There are three stages in data processing: Planning, in which the Manager and Systems Analyst are involved: Programing, which is accomplished by the Chief and other Programers; and Processing, in which all other members of the department participate.

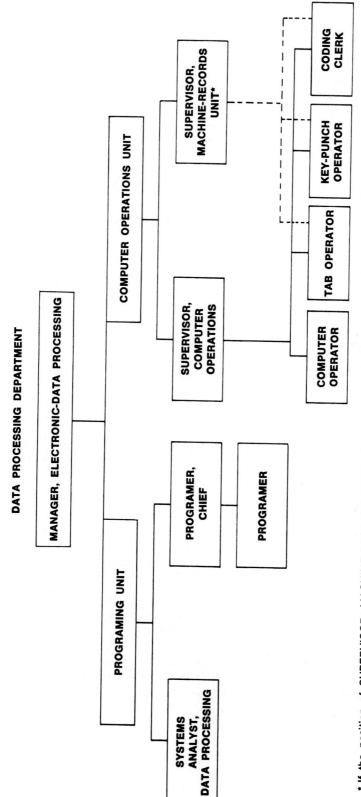

DATA PROCESSING DEPARTMENT

* If the position of SUPERVISOR, MACHINE-RECORDS UNIT exists, this worker supervises those jobs shown by dotted line.

NOTE: This chart is for illustrative purposes only and should not be considered a recommended pattern of organization.

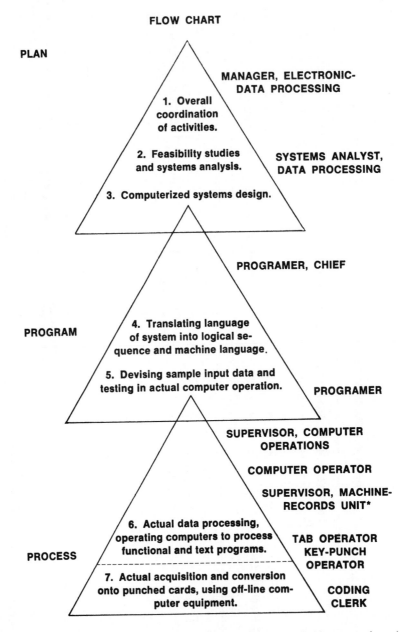

FLOW CHART

PLAN

MANAGER, ELECTRONIC-
DATA PROCESSING

1. Overall coordination of activities.

2. Feasibility studies and systems analysis.

SYSTEMS ANALYST, DATA PROCESSING

3. Computerized systems design.

PROGRAMER, CHIEF

PROGRAM

4. Translating language of system into logical sequence and machine language.

5. Devising sample input data and testing in actual computer operation.

PROGRAMER

SUPERVISOR, COMPUTER OPERATIONS

COMPUTER OPERATOR

SUPERVISOR, MACHINE-RECORDS UNIT*

6. Actual data processing, operating computers to process functional and text programs.

TAB OPERATOR
KEY-PUNCH OPERATOR

PROCESS

7. Actual acquisition and conversion onto punched cards, using off-line computer equipment.

CODING CLERK

* In some establishments this worker and the subdivision of this stage do not exist, in which case the SUPERVISOR, COMPUTER OPERATIONS, handles this entire stage and supervises all workers involved in data processing.

MANAGER, ELECTRONIC-DATA PROCESSING

JOB DUTIES

The Manager of Electronic–Data Processing confers with the hospital management to define boundaries and priorities of tentative projects, discuss equipment acquisitions, determine specific requirements of the management and medical staff, and to allocate operating time of the computer systems. He confers with department heads who are involved with proposed projects to insure cooperation and further define the nature of the project. He consults with the Systems Analyst to define equipment needs.

He reviews project feasibility studies, and revises computer operating schedules to introduce new program testing and operating runs. He reviews reports of computer and peripheral equipment production, malfunction, and maintenance to ascertain costs and plan operating changes in the department. He analyzes data requirements and flow to recommend reorganization or department changes. He prepares reports to inform the hospital administration of project development and any deviation from projected goals.

He establishes work standards, assigns schedules, and reviews the work of departmental personnel. He participates in decisions in regard to staffing of the department.

He contracts with management specialists or technical experts to solve development problems. He prepares proposals and solicits purchases of system analysis, programing, and computer services from outside firms. He participates in management conferences, giving information and advice on programing systems designed for more sophisticated applications in problems such as cost analysis and research activities. He may develop and test new programs; write manual for, and compile documentation, new programs.

EDUCATION, TRAINING, AND EXPERIENCE

The Manager, Electronic-Data Processing should have a college degree in business, mathematics, or accounting, with courses in business, computer operations, programing, and systems analysis. Two years of formal post-high school training is necessary for smaller installations.

From two to four years' experience as Supervisor, Computer, Operations; Programer, Chief; or other supervisory positions in data processing, with experience in systems analysis; or over one year of experience as manager of data processing department or assistant manager in a large data processing establishment.

JOB RELATIONSHIPS

Workers supervised: May supervise Supervisor, Computer Operations; Systems Analyst, Data Processing; Programer, Chief; Supervisor, Machine-Records Unit.
Supervised by: Administrator or Associate Administrator.
Promotion from: Supervisor, Computer Operations; Programer, Chief; or Supervisor, Machine-Records Unit.
Promotion to: Associate Administrator.

PROFESSIONAL AFFILIATIONS

Data Processing Management Association
505 Busse Highway
Park Ridge, Illinois 60068

Manager, Electronic-Data Processing: (DOT) 169.168-058

PROGRAMER, CHIEF
Coordinator, Computer Programing
Lead Programer
Senior Programer

JOB DUTIES

The Chief Programer plans, schedules, and directs preparation of programs to process business and medical data for the hospital, using electronic equipment.

He consults with the administration and Systems Analyst to clarify the program intent, indicate problems, suggest changes, and determine the extent of electronic techniques to use. He assigns, coordinates, and reviews the work of the programing personnel.

He develops his own programs and routines from workflow charts or diagrams, and consolidates segments of the program into a complete sequence of terms and symbols. He breaks down program and input data for successive computer passes, depending on such factors as computer storage capacity and speed, extent of peripheral equipment, and intended use of output data. He analyzes test runs on the computer to correct or direct correction of the coded program and input data. He revises or directs revision of existing programs, to increase operating efficiency or adapt to new requirements. He compiles documentation of program development and subsequent revisions.

He trains subordinates in programing and program coding, and prescribes standards of terminology and symbology to simplify the interpretation of programs. He collaborates with computer manufacturers and other users to develop new methods.

He prepares records and reports.

EDUCATION, TRAINING, AND EXPERIENCE

The Chief Programer must have graduated from a technical school or college. Training in business administration, computer programing, data processing mathematics, logic, and statistics is the usual educational requirement.

A minimum of two years experience in programing for the same or similar computer system, or broad and complex projects is usually required. Experience should indicate knowledge of organization structure and workflow, and also reflect proven ability to supervise others and coordinate work activities of the group supervised with that of other organizational units of hospital.

JOB RELATIONSHIPS

Workers supervised: Programer.
Supervised by: Manager, Electronic-Data Processing.
Promotion from: Programer.
Promotion to: Manager, Electronic-Data Processing.

PROFESSIONAL AFFILIATIONS

Data Processing Management Association
505 Busse Highway
Park Ridge, Illinois 60068

Programer, Chief: (DOT) 020168-010

SYSTEMS ANALYST, DATA PROCESSING
Commercial Systems Analyst and Designer
Data Methods Analyst
Methods Analyst
Procedures Analyst

The Systems Analyst works with projects such as inventory control, cost analysis, and medical projects, to formulate problems involved, and convert them to programable form for input into computers.

He confers with the Manager of Electronic-Data Processing, hospital administrative personnel, medical staff members, and heads of departments, regarding the specifics of their projects. He confers with personnel of operating departments to devise plans for obtaining and standardizing input data.

He studies current systems or devises new systems, and analyzes alternative methods of deriving input data to select the most feasible and economical method for each project. He develops process flow charts or diagrams in outline, then in detailed form for programing, indicating external verification points, such as audit–trial printouts.

He may work as a member of a team, applying specialized knowledge to one phase of the project. He may coordinate the activities of team members, and direct preparation of programs.

EDUCATION, TRAINING, AND EXPERIENCE

The Systems Analyst should be a college graduate, with the credits in business administration and accounting that are usually required for entrants without experience in data processing. Some employers, while requiring a college degree, may not require a specific major or specified courses. Many employers waive formal educational requirements for workers who have had several years of manual and machine experience prior to computer conversion.

Experience requirements range from none to two to four years of experience in system analysis, computer operation, or programing, including experience as a Programer or Programer, Chief. Institutions that require no experience usually have their own facilities for training.

On-the-job training of six months to one year is usually given.

JOB RELATIONSHIPS

Workers supervised: Generally none. May supervise one or more Programers.
Supervised by: Manager, Electronic-Data Processing.
Promotion from: Programer.
Promotion to: Manager, Electronic-Data Processing.

PROFESSIONAL AFFILIATIONS

Data Processing Management Association
505 Busse Highway
Park Ridge, Illinois 60068

Systems and Procedures Association of America
7890 Brookside Drive
Cleveland, Ohio 44138

Systems Analyst, Business-Electronic-Data Processing: (DOT) 012.168-022

SUPERVISOR, COMPUTER OPERATIONS
Supervisor, Data Processing
Supervisor, Electronic-Data Processing

JOB DUTIES

The Supervisor of Computer Operations coordinates the activities of workers who operate electronic data processing machines for the hospital. He assigns personnel and schedules workflow, directs the training of personnel in operation of computers and peripheral and off-line auxiliary equipment.

He works with programing personnel in testing new and revised programs, and develops methods to process data, such as wiring diagrams for peripheral equipment control panels, and making minor changes in standardized programs or routines, to modify output content or format. He directs insertion of program instructions and input data and observes operations.

He aids operators in locating and overcoming error conditions, and makes minor changes through the computer console. He notifies programing and maintenance personnel if he is unable to locate or correct the cause of error or failure. He revises operating schedules to adjust for delays.

He prepares or reviews records and reports of production, operating, and downtime. He recommends changes in programs, routines, and quality control standards. He consults with the Manager, Electronic-Data Processing about problems such as including new program testing and operating runs in the schedule, and arranging for preventive maintenance time. He coordinates the flow of work between shifts, to assure continuity. He may supervise personnel in key-punching, data typing, and tabulating.

EDUCATION, TRAINING, AND EXPERIENCE

High school graduation is the minimum requirement for the Supervisor of Computer Operation; however, some employers require a college degree. Training in business administration, mathematics, and accounting are regarded as particularly desirable. Usually a minimum of one to three years of experience in operating computers is required including operation of peripheral and offline equipment. Experience in supervision is also desirable.

JOB RELATIONSHIPS

Workers supervised: Computer Operator; Tab Operator; Key-Punch Operator; Coding Clerk.
Supervised by: Manager, Electronic-Data Processing.
Promotion from: Computer Operator or Programer.
Promotion to: Manager, Electronic-Data Processing.

PROFESSIONAL AFFILIATIONS

Data Processing Management Associations
505 Busse Highway
Park Ridge, Illinois 60068

Supervisor, Computer Operations: (DOT) 213.138-010

SUPERVISOR, MACHINE-RECORDS UNIT
Tabulating Supervisor

JOB DUTIES

The Supervisor of the Machine-Records Unit coordinates the activities of workers engaged in keeping and tabulating records in the hospital, using punchcard and off-line computer equipment, such as tabulating, key-punch, and sorting machines.

He schedules work assignments for operators, depending on workload and personnel available. He trains new employees in operation of key-punch, sorter, collater, interpreter, and other machines.

He sets up machines for new operations, and diagrams wiring connections according to machine function to be performed, following manual instructions. He wires control boards, making circuit connections according to wiring diagrams, or supervises workers who perform this function. He verifies the machine output to determine accuracy and detect malfunctions. He directs the care and cleaning of machines.

He develops logical sequence with use of the department's record machines, and writes operating instructions for Tab Operators. He keeps records and reports regarding production, equipment, operating costs, and personnel, and submits them to administrative personnel.

He may handle all personnel matters concerning operators.

He may adjust or repair machines in an emergency.

He may assist administrative officials in planning new accounting methods and design of cards and forms for new clerical processes.

EDUCATION, TRAINING, AND EXPERIENCE

Most employers accept applicants who are high school graduates. Some employers also require one or more of the following: A college course in accounting, a six-month course in data processing, or high school courses in general business or bookkeeping. In addition, continuing education after placement in the job is often required in order to keep up with changes in equipment and procedures.

Experience of one or two years in operating most all data processing equipment is required, with an additional one year's experience at supervisory level. On-the-job training lasting six months to one year is given.

JOB RELATIONSHIPS

Workers supervised: May supervise Key-Punch Operator, Tab Operator and Coding Clerk.

Supervised by: Manager, Electronic-Data Processing or by a supervisor in the Financial Management Department.

Promotion from: Key-Punch Operator, Tab Operator, or Coding Clerk.

Promotion to: Manager, Electronic-Data Processing or to a supervisory position in the Financial Management Department.

PROFESSIONAL AFFILIATIONS

Data Processing Management Association
505 Busse Highway
Park Ridge, Illinois 60068

Supervisor, Machine-Record Unit: (DOT) 213.138-014

Financial Management

Traditionally, the public correctly views hospitals as institutions of charity, mercy, and healing. These noble purposes, however, can be achieved only if hospitals are financially solvent. To keep them economically sound has become increasingly difficult in recent years, as scientific methods have grown more intricate, more demanding of specialized facilities, equipment, and personnel, while costs of both labor and goods have risen spectacularly. During the same period, with expanding insurance coverage and lengthening age span, patient loads have multiplied, compounding financial problems of the health care institutions.

The Financial Management Department, headed by the Controller, is charged with balancing income and expenditure, and conserving the hospital's assets, without lessening the services that it renders. The task is further complicated by the free services the hospital supplies to indigent patients, and the varying scales of payment it receives from such underwriters as Medicaid, Medicare, and private health insurance companies.

The department may be organized in a variety of ways, depending on the size of the hospital. It may be subdivided into a number of units, such as accounting, data processing, payroll, admitting, credit and collections, and purchasing. In smaller hospitals, several of these functions may be combined in a single job classification. Cashiers, Bookkeepers, Clerks, and Secretaries will be employed in most such departments.

No particular medical or scientific knowledge or background is required of personnel in this department. The emphasis is on general principles of business management, accounting, and good office practice, although experience in a hospital setting may be required. With the exceptions of the Controller, Business Office Manager, Accountant, and Admitting Officer, college degrees are not necessary for entrance into jobs. All other positions are open to high school graduates who have taken appropriate business courses, and who have varying amounts of suitable business experience.

Controller: (DOT) 186.118-014

Manager, Credit and Collection: (DOT) 168.168-050

FINANCIAL MANAGEMENT DEPARTMENT

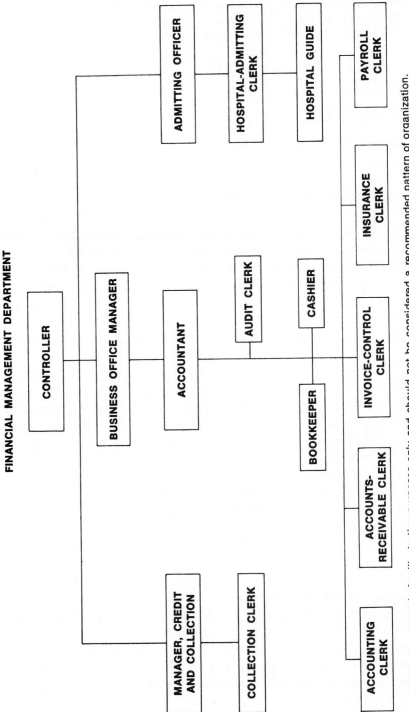

NOTE: This chart is for illustrative purposes only and should not be considered a recommended pattern of organization.

Collection Clerk: (DOT) 240.388-010

Manager, Office: (DOT) 169.168-062

Accountant: (DOT) 160.188-010

Audit Clerk: (DOT) 210.388-014

Bookkeeper I: (DOT) 210.388-022

Cashier I: (DOT) 211.368-010

Admitting Officer: (DOT) 237.368-010

Hospital-Admitting Clerk: (DOT) 237.368-014

Hospital Guide: (DOT) 355.878-030

Accounting Clerk: (DOT) 219.488-010

Accounts-Receivable Clerk: (DOT) 219.488-030

Invoice-Control Clerk: (DOT) 209.488-018

Insurance Clerk: (DOT) 210.368-146

Payroll Clerk: (DOT) 215.488-010

CONTROLLER

The Controller is responsible for directing and coordinating all hospital activities related to financial administration, general accounting, patient business services, and financial and statistical reporting. He may also have responsibility for the data processing function, and for administrative systems and procedures.

JOB DUTIES

The Controller devises and installs new or modified systems of accounting, to provide complete and accurate records of hospital assets, liabilities, and financial transactions. He evaluates accounting and patient business service procedures, in order to plan methods for insuring timely receipt of payments on patients accounts, reducing costs of accounting operations, and expediting flow of work. He compiles information about new equipment, such as cost and labor-saving features, application to hospital accounting procedures, and storage requirements.

He prepares, or directs subordinates in preparing, hospital budgets based on past, current, and anticipated expenditures and revenues. He directs compilation of data and preparation of financial and operating reports for planning effective administration of hospital activities by management. He prepares detailed analyses of financial statements to reflect variance in income, expenditures, and capital asset values from previous periods. He makes recommendations concerning means for reducing hospital operating costs and increasing revenues, based on his knowledge of market trends, financial reports, and industry operating procedures.

He participates in discussions with the finance committee on such matters as equipment purchases and construction of additional facilities. He arranges for audit of hospital accounts. He computes and records depreciation on buildings, equipment, and real estate holdings. He examines insurance policies to ascertain that hospital assets are properly insured against loss. He is responsible for cost reimbursement reports to government and private third party agencies.

In small hospitals, the Accountant or the Administrator may perform some of these functions.

EDUCATION, TRAINING, AND EXPERIENCE

The Controller should hold a Bachelor of Science degree in accounting or business administration, with a major in accounting, and may be required to be a Certified Public Accountant in the state where the hospital is located.

Usually three to five years of experience as Business Office Manager or Accountant is required. Six to nine months of on-the-job training is usually necessary.

JOB RELATIONSHIPS

Workers supervised: Accountant; Admitting Officer; Business Office Manager; and Manager, Credit and Collection. May also supervise Purchasing Agent and Manager, Electronic-Data Processing.
Supervised by: Administrator.
Promotion from: No formal line of promotion. May be promoted from Business Office Manager or Accountant.
Promotion to: No formal line of promotion. May be promoted to Administrator or Associate Administrator.

PROFESSIONAL AFFILIATIONS

National Association of Accountants
505 Park Avenue
New York, New York 10022

American Institute of Certified Public Accountants
666 Fifth Avenue
New York, New York 10019

Hospital Financial Management Association
840 North Lake Shore Drive
Chicago, Illinois 60611

Controller: (DOT) 186.118-014

BUSINESS OFFICE MANAGER
Manager, Business Office

JOB DUTIES

The Business Office Manager organizes office operations, such as typing, bookkeeping, preparation of payrolls, and other clerical services. He maintains a sufficient flow of work by evaluating office production, and revising procedures accordingly. He directs supervisors responsible for other clerical and administrative functions.

He standardizes office procedures, and initiates policy and procedural changes.

He directs department operations to prepare and retain records, files, and reports, in accordance with hospital standards.

He plans office layouts, requisitions office supplies and equipment, and initiates cost reduction programs. He reviews clerical and personnel records to insure completeness, accuracy, and timeliness. He coordinates his activities with those of other departments, and prepares activity reports to help guide management. He may participate in budget preparation.

He interviews and hires new business office employees, and assigns them to various sections of the department. He may arrange on-the-job training for these employees. He conducts periodic staff meetings to inform the staff of changes in policies or procedures. In some hospitals, the duties of the Manager of Credit and Collection are combined with this job.

EDUCATION, TRAINING, AND EXPERIENCE

Graduation from a recognized college or university with a degree in business or hospital administration is required.

Two years' experience in office management, preferably in a hospital or similar institution, is required.

Usually requires three to six months' on-the-job training.

JOB RELATIONSHIPS

Workers supervised: Bookkeeper; Audit Clerk; Cashier; Accounts-Receivable Clerk; Invoice-Control Clerk; Accounting Clerk; Payroll Clerk. May supervise Insurance Clerk and Collection Clerk.

Supervised by: Controller.

Promotion from: No formal line of promotion.

Promotion to: No formal line of promotion. May be promoted to Controller.

PROFESSIONAL AFFILIATIONS

Hospital Financial Management Association
840 North Lake Shore Drive
Chicago, Illinois 60611

Manager, Office: (DOT) 169.168-062

ACCOUNTANT

JOB DUTIES

The Accountant installs and maintains the general accounting system in the hospital, and prepares financial and operational reports from statistical data.

He evaluates existing procedures for recording assets, liabilities, and financial transactions to determine methods for reducing time and cost of accounting operations, applying knowledge of advanced accounting techniques, business systems, and approved tabulating and recording machines. He devises and installs new or modified bookkeeping and accounting procedures for use by accounting and business office personnel.

He organizes and directs the posting of entries to such ledgers as general, accounts payable, and accounts receivable; and examines entries posted for accuracy and compliance with established policies and procedures. He runs a trial balance of the general ledger, to insure that debits and credits balance. He verifies entries in ledger with source data to correct balance discrepancies. He audits cash receipts, disbursements, payroll timecards, and inventory records for accuracy and procedural requirements.

He prepares or directs preparation of hospital operating reports and financial statements from general and subsidiary ledger entries, for use in financial administration of the hospital. He computes net income, expenses, and profit or loss for each department of the hospital, based on such factors as patient revenue, material and supply costs, and staff salaries and wages. He prepares current and comparative analysis reports and statements, reflecting variations in costs and revenues, and financial condition of the hospital.

He compiles and prepares budget estimates from anticipated operating costs, revenues, and expenses submitted by hospital department heads, and submits this estimate to the Controller for approval. He computes and files tax returns, patient welfare and hospitalization insurance reports, and other regular or special reports to government and other third party agencies.

The position of Accountant varies with the size and organization of hospitals, as well as organization of the department. It may be combined with the job of Controller, or Business Office Manager. In small hospitals, the Accountant may handle details of general accounts, accounts payable, accounts receivable, and payroll.

Graduation from a recognized college or university with a degree in accounting, or a degree in business administration with a major in accounting may be required. Certification by State Board as Certified Public Accountant may also be required. A minimum requirement would be graduation from a recognized business college with an associate degree in accounting.

Up to three years' accounting experience is usually required.

Usually requires six to nine months' on-the-job training to become thoroughly acquainted with hospital administrative policies and accounting procedures.

JOB RELATIONSHIPS

Workers supervised: May supervise Bookkeeper; Audit Clerk; Cashier; Accounts-Receivable Clerk; Invoice-Control Clerk; Accounting Clerk; and Payroll Clerk.
Supervised by: Controller.
Promotion from: No formal line of promotion. May be promoted from Bookkeeper after additional formal training.
Promotion to: No formal line of promotion. May be promoted to Controller.

PROFESSIONAL AFFILIATIONS

American Institute of Certified Public Accountants
666 Fifth Avenue
New York, New York 10019

National Association of Accountants
505 Park Avenue
New York, New York 10022

Hospital Financial Management Association
840 North Lake Shore Drive
Chicago, Illinois 60611

American Association of Hospital Accountants
840 North Lake Shore Drive
Chicago, Illinois 60611

Accountant: (DOT) 160.188-010

MANAGER, CREDIT AND COLLECTION

Accounts Manager
Business Accounts Manager
Credit Manager
Patients' Accounts Manager

JOB DUTIES

The Manager of Credit and Collection interviews patients or persons responsible for them to arrange credit or methods of payment. He secures information relative to the patient's financial status, such as type of employment, salary, references, and financial obligations. He evaluates the patient's credit history, and determines payment dates based on ability to pay and policy of the hospital. He approves or disapproves extension of credit, and may secure assignment of benefits in cases where the patient carries insurance. He may confer with various welfare agencies in cases of patients who are unable to pay. In other cases he may recommend sources of credit, such as banks, insurance companies, or credit unions.

He collects accounts that are not paid in full up to the time of discharge or at the promised date. He supervises mailing of followup letters when statements do not bring response, and attempts to collect delinquent accounts himself, or turns them over to an attorney or collection agency. He recommends cancellation of accounts in hardship cases.

He supervises and trains personnel performing clerical tasks related to credit and collection. He initiates and answers pertinent correspondence. He prepares reports, showing number and amounts of collections, delinquent accounts, and related matters.

He participates in discussions with heads of other departments to resolve problems encountered in collections. He evaluates the collection procedures, and recommends changes to management.

In some hospitals, this job may be combined with that of Business Office Manager.

EDUCATION, TRAINING, AND EXPERIENCE

High school graduation is required. Employers strongly prefer, and in some cases require, at least two years' additional education in accounting or business administration.

Two years' experience in credit and collection work, preferably in a hospital or similar institution, is required.

Worker usually receives from three to six months' on-the-job training to become familiar with hospital policies and procedures.

JOB RELATIONSHIPS

Workers supervised: Collection Clerk; may also supervise Accounts-Receivable Clerk and Insurance Clerk.
Supervised by: Controller.
Promotion from: No formal line of promotion. May be promoted from Collection Clerk or Accounts-Receivable Clerk.
Promotion to: No formal line of promotion. May be promoted to Business Office Manager or Controller.

PROFESSIONAL AFFILIATIONS

Hospital Financial Management Association
840 North Lake Shore Drive
Chicago, Illinois 60611

Manager, Credit and Collection: (DOT) 168.168-050

ADMITTING OFFICER
Director of Admitting

The Admitting Officer makes reservations for patients, arranges for their admission to hospital, and directs and coordinates activities of hospital admitting office personnel.

JOB DUTIES

The Admitting Officer checks the hospital privileges of the physician making the reservation against the staff list. She records information identifying physician and patient, type of accommodation desired, insurance coverage, date of admission, and type and date of operation if the case is surgical. She reviews the list of unoccupied beds, and makes preadmission reservations, often forwarding the admission form to the patient to be filled out before coming to the hospital. She notifies the ward to expect the patient.

She interviews the patient, his relatives, or other persons who are responsible for him, to obtain biographical information. She interprets hospital regulations to the patient, as they apply to visitors, visiting hours, and disposition of clothing and valuables. In accordance with information previously received, she may request partial payment in advance.

She secures necessary information from patients who come to the emergency room, and assigns a bed; or, if the patient is to be sent home, explains charges and arranges for payment. She records information about the patient, and forwards cash payments to the business office.

She explains differences in rates and charges to patients who desire changes in accommodations.

She may obtain the necessary signature authorizing surgery from the patient or person responsible for him.

She may have clerks or assistants, who handle much of the typing and other detail in the admitting office, and whom she supervises.

In small hospitals, she may also handle the duties of the credit department.

EDUCATION, TRAINING, AND EXPERIENCE

The Admitting Officer must be a graduate of a recognized college or university, and should have courses in psychology, sociology, and personnel and business administration. Some employers prefer a graduate nurse.

One or two years of experience in an accredited hospital or social agency is usually required, plus three months of on-the-job training to become familiar with admitting office policies and procedures.

JOB RELATIONSHIPS

Workers supervised: Hospital-Admitting Clerk and Hospital Guide.
Supervised by: May be supervised by Controller; Associate Administrator; or Business Office Manager.
Promotion from: No formal line of promotion. May be promoted from Hospital-Admitting Clerk.
Promotion to: No formal line of promotion. May be promoted to Business Office Manager or Controller.

PROFESSIONAL AFFILIATIONS

Hospital Financial Management Association
840 North Lake Shore Drive
Chicago, Illinois 60611

Admitting Officer: (DOT) 237.368-010

General Clerical Department

General Clerical jobs are found in every department of the hospital, and do not constitute a formal department in themselves.

High school graduation plus appropriate business courses and experiences are the criteria for most of these jobs. A few do not require completion of high school. On-the-job training is provided.

Addressing-Machine Operator: (DOT) 234.582-010

Clerk, General: (DOT) 209.588-018

Clerk, General Office: (DOT) 219.388-066

Clerk-Typist: (DOT) 209.388-022

Duplicating-Machine Operator I: (DOT) 207.884-010

Duplicating-Machine Operator II: (DOT) 207.782-022

Duplicating-Machine Operator III: (DOT) 207.782-018

Duplicating-Machine Operator IV: (DOT) 207.885-010

File Clerk I: (DOT) 206.388-018

Mail Clerk: (DOT) 231.588-014

Medical Secretary: (DOT) 201.368-014

Medical Stenographer: (DOT) 202.388-014

Messenger: (DOT) 230.878-022

Receptionist: (DOT) 237.368-018

Information Clerk: (DOT) 237.368-022

Secretary: (DOT) 201.368-018

Transcribing Operator, Head: (DOT) 208.138-010

Transcribing-Machine Operator: (DOT) 208.588-026

Typist: (DOT) 203.588-018

Personnel Department

Personnel administration is characterized by the philosophy, motives, and methods of organizing and treating people so that they will consistently perform at the highest levels of which they are capable, while obtaining the greatest degree of satisfaction in their jobs.

The number and kinds of functions assigned the Personnel Department will vary greatly depending upon the needs, size, and goals of the hospital.

The department is responsible, within delegated authority, for planning and administering a comprehensive personnel program, including participation in development of an overall personnel policy. It is responsible for developing techniques and procedures to assist line supervisors in improving the personnel aspects of their jobs. It serves as advisor to the Administrator on personnel problems, proposes changes in established personnel policies, and consults with and assists supervisors on a continuing basis. The major functions of this department may be classified as (1) developing sources of qualified employees, (2) recruiting and retaining competent personnel, and (3) increasing employee productivity and job stability.

Specifically, the Personnel Department performs some or all of the following functions: Recruits and screens job applicants; inducts and orients new employees; advises on methods of training—and may plan and conduct training programs; develops procedures and policies to promote employee stabilization; develops procedures for position control through job analyses and job evaluations; establishes and maintains programs of wage and salary administration, and employee benefits; assists in planning and establishing lines of communication; may take part in collective bargaining procedures; establishes health and safety programs; advises the administration on legal problems relating to employment; does research to determine causes of and solution to personnel problems; advises on hospital organization and helps establish employee budgetary controls; maintains complete personnel files on all employees; and maintains organization charts and staffing patterns.

Sound employee relations tend to be reflected in employee contacts with the public; therefore, the Personnel Department is a key to good public relations. Through direct contact with other departments, job applicants, employment agencies, social agencies, schools, public officials, and many other groups and individuals, it is in a unique position to create a favorable impression of the hospital and promote effective public relations.

Both the professional and clerical staffs of this department are subject to combinations of job duties, depending upon the size and organizational makeup of the particular hospital.

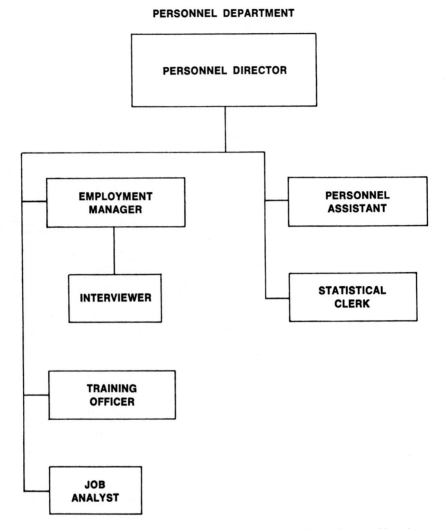

PERSONNEL DEPARTMENT

PERSONNEL DIRECTOR

EMPLOYMENT MANAGER

PERSONNEL ASSISTANT

INTERVIEWER

STATISTICAL CLERK

TRAINING OFFICER

JOB ANALYST

NOTE: This chart is for illustrative purposes only and should not be considered a recommended pattern of organization.

PERSONNEL DIRECTOR

Keeping the hospital staffed with highly qualified non-physician employees is the primary responsibility of the Personnel Director, and the quality of patient care depends heavily on how well he does his job.

JOB DUTIES

The duties of the Personnel Director include recruiting, screening, placing, processing, and orientation of new employees. He recommends transfers and promotions, and handles terminations. He manages such employee concerns as credit unions, vacation policies, insurance plans, and pension plans. He organizes on-the-job training programs, inservice training programs, and refresher courses for employees. He may be responsible for the hospital's employee safety programs, and employee food services.

The Director reports to the hospital Administrator, or a delegated Associate Administrator. He recommends changes in personnel policies and procedures, and may originate new practices, consistent with hospital policy.

As administrator of the salary and wage program, the Director is concerned with job analyses, job classifications, and review of employee performance. If the hospital is unionized, he may participate in collective bargaining or grievance arbitration sessions.

Since the Director is a significant link between the hospital and the community, as well as between hospital administration and staff, he must be a competent writer and speaker. If the hospital has no public relations department, he may be responsible for all inhouse communications.

EDUCATION, TRAINING, AND EXPERIENCE

The Personnel Director must be a graduate of a recognized college or university, with a degree in personnel management, industrial relations, or business administration. His course credits should include tests and measurements, statistics, applied psychology, personnel and business administration, economics, labor relations, and cost accounting. Experience as an Assistant Personnel Director is recommended.

JOB RELATIONSHIPS

Workers supervised: Employment Manager; Interviewer; Training Officer; Job Analyst; and clerical staff.
Supervised by: Administrator.
Promotion from: Assistant Personnel Director or Employment Manager.
Promotion to: No formal line of promotion. May be promoted to an Associate Administrator.

PROFESSIONAL AFFILIATIONS

American Society for Personnel Administration
52 East Bridge Street
Berea, Ohio 44017

Public Personnel Association
1313 East 60th Street
Chicago, Illinois 60637

American Personnel and Guidance Association
1605 New Hampshire Avenue, N.W.
Washington, D.C. 20009

American Society for Hospital Personnel Directors
840 North Lake Shore Drive
Chicago, Illinois 60611

State and local personnel associations and societies.

Manager, Personnel: (DOT) 166.118-022

EMPLOYMENT MANAGER

The Employment Manager supervises recruiting, interviewing, employing, and indoctrinating new employees of the hospital. He assigns duties to Interviewers for preliminary screening of applicants, and conducts interviews with those referred to him for final hiring.

JOB DUTIES

The Manager receives requests for additional or replacement personnel from department heads, and obtains approval or requisitions for unbudgeted positions from the Personnel Director. He reviews applications on file, or contacts various sources to find qualified applicants. These persons are then interviewed for additional information, and evaluated as to education, personality, and experience, against the requirements of the job vacancy.

The Manager administers, scores, and interprets psychological tests and skill tests pertinent to specific job openings. He provides orientation for qualified applicants in regard to hospital personnel policies, wages, hours, employee benefits, and duties and responsibilities of the position. He then refers applicants to department heads for final approval of those selected. He may suggest alternate positions for which an applicant is qualified. He checks references given by applicants, and arranges for physical examination of those accepted.

He confers with department heads in regard to their personnel needs and problems of individual employees. He recommends transfers of qualified employees to other positions, and reviews recommendations for discharge of employees. He interviews all terminated employees, to discover whether hospital screening, placement, or other practices require revision. He recommends changes in policies, procedures and benefits to maintain high employee and job stability.

He prepares periodic reports relative to employment activities, and develops and directs the use of personnel forms. He may arbitrate employee grievances, or refer problems to the Personnel Director.

The duties of this job may be combined with those of the Job Analyst, Interviewer, or Training Officer.

EDUCATION, TRAINING, AND EXPERIENCE

The Employment Manager should be a graduate of an approved college or university, with courses in personnel or business administration and psychology. Experience as an Interviewer is desirable. Inservice training in hospital policies and personnel procedures and routines is provided.

JOB RELATIONSHIPS

Workers supervised: Interviewers; clerical workers.
Supervised by: Personnel Director.
Promotion from: No formal lines of promotion. May be promoted from Interviewer.
Promotion to: Personnel Director.

PROFESSIONAL AFFILIATIONS

American Society for Personnel Administration
52 East Bridge Street
Berea, Ohio 44017

Public Personnel Association
1313 East 60th Street
Chicago, Illinois 60637

American Personnel and Guidance Association
1605 New Hampshire Avenue, N.W.
Washington, D.C. 20009

American Society for Hospital Personnel Directors
840 North Lake Shore Drive
Chicago, Illinois 60611

Manager, Employment: (DOT) 166.168-026

INTERVIEWER

JOB DUTIES

Interviewers conduct the initial screening of applicants for positions in the hospital. The Interviewer gives whatever help an applicant may need in filling out forms, and requests additional information as necessary. She answers questions and supplies information regarding employment policies and requirements. She notes the appearance, manner, and experience of applicants, and checks other requirements for employment in the specific job opening. She checks references on applications to verify work history, and refers qualified applicants to the Employment Manager.

She prepares reports supplying information on present employees or new employees, as requested; and maintains personnel records, making changes as necessary to keep them up to date. She may administer and score tests not requiring special education and training.

The duties of this job may be combined with those of Employment Manager, Job Analyst, or Training Officer.

EDUCATION, TRAINING, AND EXPERIENCE

The Interviewer must be a graduate of an approved college or university, with courses in personnel or business administration and psychology. She should be skilled in interviewing techniques. Inservice training is provided in hospital policies and personnel procedures and routines.

JOB RELATIONSHIPS

Workers supervised: None.
Supervised by: Employment Manager.
Promotion from: No formal line of promotion.
Promotion to: Employment Manager.

PROFESSIONAL AFFILIATIONS

None.

Employment Interviewer II: (DOT) 166.268-018

TRAINING OFFICER

The Training Officer assists in planning, organizing, and directing employee training programs designed to orient employees, improve skills, and develop potential capabilities.

JOB DUTIES

The Training Officer confers with supervisors and department heads to determine need for training in order to increase job proficiency or improve morale. He plans new or special training classes and demonstrations, writes training manuals, or adapts existing materials to immediate needs. He prepares and distributes pamphlets, memoranda, or manuals to be used by trainees. He schedules classes in cooperation with department heads, and arranges for lectures, demonstrations, or on-the-job training.

He instructs employees relative to nature and hazards of equipment and materials handled, responsibilities of specific positions, and hospital safety rules. He conducts or arranges for sessions to introduce new procedures or equipment, and follows up on programs, to evaluate effectiveness of training and to determine need for revision of methods or materials.

He institutes supervisory training programs to develop more effective relationships between supervisors and subordinates, and instructs supervisors in training methods and use of training material. He assists other members of the Personnel Department with specific training problems they encounter.

He selects and edits training materials such as educational films and books. He may prepare handbooks outlining personnel policies of the hospital, including information about salaries and promotion, insurance, vacation, sick leave and other benefits, and standards of what is expected of employees and what they can expect from the hospital.

The duties of this job may be combined with those of interviewer, Job Analyst, Employment Manager, or Personnel Director.

EDUCATION, TRAINING, AND EXPERIENCE

The Training Officer must be a graduate of an accredited college or university, with courses in educational methods, personnel administration, applied psychology, English, and possibly journalism. Teaching experience or experience in personnel work is essential. Inservice training is provided in regard to hospital procedures and routines.

JOB RELATIONSHIPS

Workers supervised: None.
Supervised by: Personnel Director.
Promotion from: No formal line of promotion. May be promoted from Interviewer.
Promotion to: No formal line of promotion. May be promoted to Personnel Director after additional training and experience.

PROFESSIONAL AFFILIATIONS

American Society for Personnel Administration
52 East Bridge Street
Berea, Ohio 44017

Public Personnel Association
1313 East 60th Street
Chicago, Illinois 60637

American Personnel and Guidance Association
1605 New Hampshire Avenue, N.W.
Washington, D.C. 20009

Supervisor, Training: (DOT) 166.228-022

JOB ANALYST

The Job Analyst collects, analyzes, and develops occupational data relative to jobs, including job requirements and workers' qualifications, to serve as a basis for selection and placement of workers, wage evaluation, counseling, and other personnel practices.

JOB DUTIES

The Job Analyst works with department heads and the Personnel Director to determine what aspects of job analysis are needed in the hospital, and the procedures to be followed.

He interviews workers and observes tasks being performed, in order to identify each job, describe its duties, and indicate requirements for workers. He includes such pertinent information as use of equipment and tools, working conditions, and requirements for physical skills and knowledge, degree of dexterity, special sensory acuteness, and personal characteristics.

He writes descriptions of each job, emphasizing points of information needed for personnel practices involving recruitment, placement, promotion, and transfer; job and employee evaluation; training and full utilization of workers; safety and health research; improved personnel policies; and counseling. He reviews his completed analyses with department heads and Personnel Director for verification.

The Job Analyst writes hiring specifications to aid in making valid selection of prospective employees, and reviews job duties to reveal duplication of effort and establish promotion sequence of jobs. He devises employee performance evaluation systems, and recommends changes in job classifications. He may use tests to determine occupational knowledge and skill of workers. He also determines interrelationships among jobs for purposes of transfer, promotion, and job redesign.

He assists in developing job analysis schedules and other personnel forms, and performs research to find improved personnel procedures.

The duties of this job may be combined with those of Interviewer, Training Officer, or Employment Manager.

EDUCATION, TRAINING, AND EXPERIENCE

The Job Analyst should be a graduate of an accredited college or university, with courses in statistics, tests and measurements, and personnel administration. Experience in job analysis or a similar phase of personnel work is essential. Inservice training in hospital routines and procedures is provided.

JOB RELATIONSHIPS

Workers supervised: None.
Supervised by: Personnel Director.
Promotion from: No formal line of promotion. May be promoted from Interviewer.
Promotion to: No formal line of promotion. May be promoted to Personnel Director after additional training and experience.

PROFESSIONAL AFFILIATIONS

American Society for Personnel Administration
52 East Bridge Street
Berea, Ohio 44017

Public Personnel Association
1313 East 60th Street
Chicago, Illinois 60637

American Personnel and Guidance Association
1605 New Hampshire Avenue, N.W.
Washington, D.C. 20009

Job Analyst: (DOT) 166.088-010

PERSONNEL ASSISTANT
Records Clerk

The Personnel Assistant maintains the personnel records of the hospital employees, and answers employment inquiries.

JOB DUTIES

The Assistant handles typing and filing chores, records changes in personnel situations, explains and answers questions about hospital policies, schedules job applicant appointments, and reviews departmental reports to determine vacancies, and to compile statistical data for monthly reports.

EDUCATION, TRAINING, AND EXPERIENCE

The Personnel Assistant must have a high school diploma with commercial courses: college courses in personnel administration and psychology are desirable. On-the-job training is provided. As she improves her skills and training, she may be promoted to Interviewer.

JOB RELATIONSHIPS

Workers supervised: None.
Supervised by: Personnel Manager.
Promotion from: No formal line of promotion. This may be an entry job.
Promotion to: No formal line of promotion. May be promoted to Interviewer.

PROFESSIONAL AFFILIATIONS

None.

Personnel Clerk: (DOT) 205.368-014

STATISTICAL CLERK

JOB DUTIES

The Statistical Clerk compiles data for reports in regard to hospital personnel, using such source material as number of job applicants, interviews, tests, hirings, transfers, promotions, absenteeism, injuries, and turnover records. He makes comparison reports by month and year. He also makes periodic wage and hour surveys, and comparisons with other hospitals in the area.

All of these are of value to the Personnel Director and the hospital administration in future planning.

EDUCATION, TRAINING, AND EXPERIENCE

High school graduation with courses in mathematics and use of business machines is required. No previous experience is necessary. On-the-job training is provided to learn particular statistical procedures.

JOB RELATIONSHIPS

Workers supervised: None.
Supervised by: Personnel Director.
Promotion from: No formal line of promotion. This may be an entry job.
Promotion to: No formal line of promotion.

PROFESSIONAL AFFILIATIONS

None.

Statistical Clerk: (DOT) 219.388-258

Public Relations Department

A hospital can be of most value in a community when it has public acceptance, confidence, and respect. To foster these attitudes is the responsibility of the Public Relations Department.

This department promotes and develops community understanding of hospital services, and stimulates the hospital staff to an active interest in the community's needs. It informs the public about hospital achievements, as well as its programs. It cooperates with other health agencies to fulfill the health and welfare needs of the community in delivery of health care. It clarifies controversial health and welfare needs for both the staff and the community, and stimulates willingness for voluntary contributions and endeavors, and for public and private endowments.

There are many ways in which this end is accomplished, beginning with careful selection of all personnel who come into contact with the public: telephone operators, receptionists, admitting office personnel, and others. Development of awareness of the value of good relationships with patients on the part of all medical, nursing, and nonmedical staff is often worth more than can be gained by newspaper and broadcast releases or public relations stories.

Regularly issued bulletins for the staff, bulletin boards, and special editions of annual reports, posters and exhibits, patients' handbooks, and similar written materials serve to keep patients, staff, and the public in contact with the hospital as an institution.

Public relations is a management function, and as such the department reports directly to the hospital Administrator. However, the department operates in a staff capacity, and has no authority over operating or line activities or personnel.

In some hospitals, the department is called the Office of Public Affairs, on the premise that this title carries more dignity than the public relations appellation, which is sometimes associated with commercial promotion.

DIRECTOR, PUBLIC RELATIONS
Community Relations Director

The Director of Public Relations writes news releases, reports, speeches, and articles and confers with the Administrator and the Governing Board to formulate public relations policies and to develop programs that will result in close community identification with the hospital and also comply with medical ethics.

JOB DUTIES

The Director of Public Relations writes news releases, reports, speeches, and articles for publication. He edits employee publications, newsletters, and management communications for both inhouse and general distribution. He produces leaflets and brochures that tell the hospital story. He places news stories and features with

PUBLIC RELATIONS DEPARTMENT

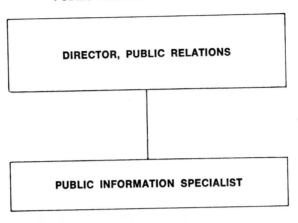

NOTE: This chart is for illustrative purposes only and should not be considered a recommended pattern of organization.

the media, and develops a reservoir of speakers who can appear at meetings or broadcast interviews on behalf of the hospital. He prepares any institutional advertising that is necessary. He keeps abreast of research and other achievements in the hospital, and arranges suitable forums through which these can be reported to the public. He arranges events that will bring the public into contact with the hospital, such as tours, an open house, a ground-breaking ceremony, or a dinner for civic leaders to launch a fund drive.

Fund-raising is frequently linked to the Department of Public Relations.

He cooperates with all departments, but particularly with the Personnel Director and the Director of Volunteers. He helps the Personnel Director set up training programs and refresher courses to assist employees in understanding hospital policies and interpreting them in their relationships with patients and the public. He is of great help to the Director of Volunteers in locating sources of volunteers in the community, making proper contacts, and providing explanatory and encouraging materials.

EDUCATION, TRAINING, AND EXPERIENCE

The Director of Public Relations should have a college degree with courses in English, social studies, and the humanities, plus five to ten years of experience in journalism and/or public relations. At least eight months of hospital orientation is desirable.

JOB RELATIONSHIPS

Workers supervised: Public Information Specialist. May have clerical help also.
Supervised by: Administrator.
Promotion from: None.
Promotion to: Associate Administrator.

PROFESSIONAL AFFILIATIONS

Public Relations Society of America, Inc.
845 Third Avenue
New York, New York 10022

American Society for Hospital Public Relations Directors
840 North Lake Shore Drive
Chicago, Illinois 60611

Director, Public Relations: (DOT) 165.038T

PUBLIC INFORMATION SPECIALIST
Editorial Assistant

The Public Information Specialist assists the Director of Public Relations, particularly in the capacities of writer and editor, although she may take responsibility for one or more continuing programs on the hospital public relations schedule.

JOB DUTIES

The Public Information Specialist confers with the Director of Public Relations to plan programs, including program limits, taking into account any hospital policies, involved, and determining format, media, and techniques to be used.

She writes news releases, stories, and feature articles for newspapers, radio, television, house organs, pamphlets, and brochures. She may compile the material for these by interviewing staff members, patients, and visitors, or by research in the medical library. She prepares layouts and edits departmental publications. She may write a daily news bulletin for distribution to visitors.

On occasion, she conducts visitors on hospital tours, assists families of patients, and explains hospital policies, procedures, and facilities to them. She answers queries about patients by letter or telephone.

She maintains historical records and scrapbook for future reference, and may obtain signatures authorizing release of information or photographs concerning patients.

She arranges facilities for conferences and other special events.

EDUCATION, TRAINING, AND EXPERIENCE

The Public Information Specialist should have a college degree with courses in English, social studies, and the humanities, plus two years' experience in public relations work.

Experience in journalism and group organization is desirable, and at least three months' orientation in hospital procedures is required.

JOB RELATIONSHIPS

Workers supervised: None.
Supervised by: Director, Public Relations.
Promotion from: None. This may be an entry job.
Promotion to: Director, Public Relations.

PROFESSIONAL AFFILIATIONS

Public Relations Society of America, Inc.
845 Third Avenue
New York, New York 10022

American Society for Hospital Public Relations Directors
840 North Lake Shore Drive
Chicago, Illinois 60611

Public Relations Man I: (DOT) 165.068-018

Purchasing and Receiving Department

The Purchasing and Receiving Department provides centralized procurement and control of all supplies, materials, and equipment used in the hospital; and is responsible for fulfilling hospital needs with goods of high quality, purchased as economically as possible.

The general functions of this department include: developing specifications for commonly used items; reviewing catalogs and other informational literature to discover sources of improved equipment; promoting standardization and use of labor-saving equipment and supplies; conducting inspections to insure that items are not overstocked; and maintaining numerous records.

Specifically, when a purchase order is to be placed, this department is responsible for editing orders for completeness and verifying orders against catalogs, previous orders, and manuals for specifications such as those established by the American Hospital Association and the National Bureau of Standards. A determination is then made of quantities to be ordered based upon such information as hospital finances, market conditions, time of delivery, storage space available, anticipated rate of consumption, and availability of hospital facilities for manufacture of certain required items as are necessary for some items of Central Supply. Competitive bids are then obtained, evaluated, and formal purchase orders issued.

The basis of all operations of the Purchasing Department is the requisition initiated by individual departments. These may be either stock or purchase requisitions, depending on whether desired supplies are stocked by the hospital or are to be purchased. Such forms indicate date, department, quantity of each item returned for exchange, and the quantity and specifications of each item needed. Requisitions are approved and signed by responsible departmental or administrative authority, and forwarded to stockroom or purchasing section for procurement. Supplies required before scheduled delivery dates are secured by *emergency requisitions* following similar procedures with an added notation stating reasons for emergency.

In most hospitals the Purchasing Department will receive, verify, store, and issue, as well as purchase, supplies and equipment; some hospitals assign this responsibility to the Business Office.

Since purchasing is a staff function, the department has no authority over operating personnel, but exerts line authority over employees within the department.

The department's standards are set by the Committee on Purchasing of the American Hospital Association.

The Purchasing Department deals directly with most other departments of the hospital. Particularly close coordination with the Business Department is necessary, in order to maintain effective accounting, auditing, and budgetary controls. In some hospitals, purchasing is a function assigned directly to the Business Department.

Purchasing Agent: (DOT) 162.158-102

Supervisor, Stock: (DOT) 223.138-038

Stock Clerk: (DOT) 223.387-094

PURCHASING AND RECEIVING DEPARTMENT

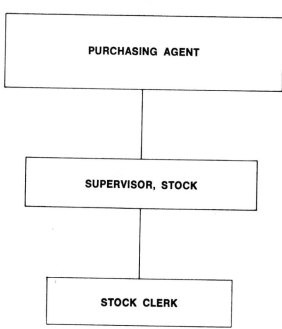

NOTE: This chart is for illustrative purposes only and should not be considered a recommended pattern of organization.

PURCHASING AGENT
Chief Buyer
Director of Purchases

While the educational requirements for a hospital Purchasing Agent are not unlike those for any other business, his work is highly specialized, and experience is of particular importance. Hospital purchasing involves a greater variety of materials than do most enterprises; the field is continually growing and changing, and many of the items purchased are for specialized use and significant in patient care.

In addition to technical knowledge concerning the products he buys, the Purchasing Agent must have full understanding of the broad program and goals of his hospital, be able to work well with department heads and the Business Department, and be a person of unquestioned integrity.

JOB DUTIES

The Purchasing Agent receives requisitions from department heads for medical equipment, furnishings, supplies, building materials, surgical instruments, linens, medications, oxygen, and a vast array of other commodities. He keeps abreast of market conditions through study of advertising literature, trade journals, and other publications, and may assist department heads in preparing requisitions for special items. The Agent then "comparison shops," to get the most favorable deal on each order. If a purchase is large, he may issue bid instructions to vendors, or may arrange for discount prices.

The Agent supervises the personnel in his department who are engaged in clerical work, inventory, receiving and storage, and issuance of purchased items to authorized departments. He examines all purchase orders, invoices, and other records for accuracy, and sees that complete files are maintained.

He compiles monthly reports on major purchases for inventory and budget purposes, and periodically reviews records to determine whether changes should be made in purchasing procedures.

In some hospitals, the Purchasing Agent may not buy the medicines or foodstuffs for patients, although he may purchase supplies for the hospital-operated employees' commissary. He may also direct the hospital's printshop and mailroom.

EDUCATION, TRAINING, AND EXPERIENCE

The Purchasing Agent should have a college degree in business administration or allied field, although some employers will accept lower educational standards if the applicant has had college courses and training in purchasing, merchandising, accounting, and marketing.

Usually two years of experience in some phase of purchasing is required, either at the hospital or a comparable institution. Some hospitals will select and train a promising young person from a lower classification on its staff, if he has acquired thorough knowledge of hospital policies, procedures, and the department's activities. One month of on-the-job training is usually required.

JOB RELATIONSHIPS

Workers supervised: Supervisor, Stock; Stock Clerk; and clerical workers.
Supervised by: Administrator, Associate Administrator or delegated authority.
Promotion from: No formal line of promotion.
Promotion to: No formal line of promotion. May be promoted to an Associate Administrator.

PROFESSIONAL AFFILIATIONS

American Association of Hospital Purchasing Agents
840 North Lake Shore Drive
Chicago, Illinois 60611

National Association of Hospital Purchasing Agents
840 North Lake Shore Drive
Chicago, Illinois 60611

Purchasing Agent: (DOT) 162.158-102

Training Department

The Training Department, headed by the Director of Training Programs, is responsible for coordinating all training programs within the hospital. These programs may encompass all phases of hospital job training, from the employee who needs only brief on-the-job training to perform satisfactorily, to the professional interns who need academic training as well as extensive practical experience to meet professional standards. If the hospital is connected with a teaching institution, then practical, theoretical, and technical training is provided to students. Refresher courses for returning professional personnel as well as advanced courses for personnel interested in upgrading and promotion are provided. This department is responsible for on-the-job training and orientation of every person employed by the hospital. Training of volunteers may also be a function.

While the personnel of the department may not take part in each training program, the department is responsible for planning, organizing, supervising, and carrying out all the programs for the hospital. It coordinates its policies and programs with community programs that may have resources for recruiting potential employees.

Headed by the Director of Training Programs, the department works through Training Officers of other departments in most instances. These may include the Training Officer of the Personnel Department, the Director of Staff Development in the Nursing Service, the Instructor of Ancillary Nursing Personnel, the Instructor of Inservice for Nurses, the Clinical Instructor in Nursing Education, and the Teaching Dietitian, among others. Each of these jobs has been described in its own classification.

The Director of Training Programs reports to the Administrator, or to an Associate Administrator.

DIRECTOR, TRAINING PROGRAMS
Educational Supervisor
Staff-Training Officer
Training Coordinator

JOB DUTIES

The Director of Training Programs confers with management and line supervisors to define the scope of programs, which include on-the-job training in various departments, orientation training, and inservice training.

He applies his knowledge of hospital procedures, job breakdowns, safety rules, supervision techniques, and related information to formulate a training curriculum. He makes sure that curricula for professional trainees adhere to standards established by professional organizations.

He organizes lectures, training manuals, examinations, visual aids, reference libraries, and other training implements. He trains instructors and supervisory personnel in proper methods and techniques to use in their departments, and assigns them to specific programs. He coordinates established training courses with technical and professional programs offered in public schools and universities.

He prepares the budget for training needs, and determines allocation of funds for staff, supplies, facilities, and equipment. He maintains records of training activities, and evaluates the effectiveness and application of programs.

He represents the hospital at vocational and educational meetings. He may screen, counsel, test, and recommend employees for inservice educational programs, or for promotion or transfer.

EDUCATION, TRAINING, AND EXPERIENCE

Graduation from an accredited college or university with courses in educational methods, personnel administration, applied psychology, English, and possibly journalism is required. Master's degree in education and personnel management is preferred.

Teaching and personnel management experience is essential.

Inservice training in hospital procedures, routines, policies, and organization.

JOB RELATIONSHIPS

Workers supervised: General supervision over instructors assigned to teach specific courses.
Supervised by: Administrator or an Associate Administrator.
Promotion from: An instructor with administrative ability.
Promotion to: No formal line of promotion.

PROFESSIONAL AFFILIATIONS

American Society for Training and Development
313 Price Place
P.O. Box 5307
Madison, Wisconsin 53707

Director, Educational: (DOT) 166.118-010

Volunteer Services Department

Personal involvement in community service is characteristic of Americans, and nowhere is this more evident than in the contribution made by volunteers in health care institutions. Hospitals, psychiatric institutions, extended care facilities, homes for the aged, and rehabilitation centers use the services of volunteers in almost every department.

To make their work effective, it must be organized to augment and supplement the regular hospital program. This is the task of the Volunteer Services Department, which is headed by a Director. In large hospitals, he may have one or more Assistants.

The Department recruits volunteers from the community, gives them orientation training, selects and assigns them, but does not supervise their work. Supervision is provided by the hospital departments to which they are assigned.

DIRECTOR, VOLUNTEER SERVICES

The Director of Volunteer Services consults with heads of other departments in the institution, to determine where volunteers can be used to advantage, and what qualifications each task requires.

He analyzes the social organization of the community, with a view to discovering where the workers needed may be obtained. Then, in cooperation with the hospital's Director of Public Relations, he sets about recruiting them from such sources as the hospital auxiliary; civic, professional, fraternal, and social organizations; church groups; senior centers and old-age clubs; industrial concerns and local labor unions; college groups; high school service clubs; and health career clubs. The Director of Public Relations prepares volunteer recruitment brochures, and obtains publicity

VOLUNTEER SERVICES DEPARTMENT

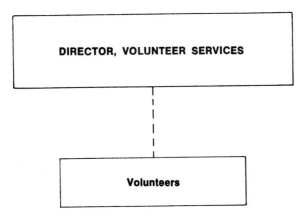

NOTE: This chart is for illustrative purposes only and should not be considered a recommended pattern of organization.

for the program through newspaper feature articles, releases, and radio and television interviews.

The Director of Volunteer Services makes himself and other qualified speakers available to programs on radio and television, interviews, and meetings of community groups. He arranges special events, such as receptions, and tours of the hospital.

JOB DUTIES

Before volunteers begin to apply, the Director develops a job description of each task that is to be performed, and also a variety of forms to go with it: application forms; record systems; forms for evaluating performance; forms for notifying department heads of assignments; and work-consent forms for junior volunteers.

He organizes a program of general orientation for the volunteers, to acquaint them with the hospital layout, policies, rules and regulations; and prepares information on ethics, standards, etiquette, uniforms, functions, training requirements, and conduct with patients. He may carry out on-the-job training himself, or provide training materials such as outline of course content, printed materials and audiovisual aids, to the heads of departments in which volunteers are to serve.

He handles recognition programs, evaluates volunteers' performance, and is responsible for complaints, promotions, and disciplinary actions.

He maintains records, and reports to the hospital Administrator, or an Associate Administrator assigned to supervise the department. Close contact with the Administrator is vital, since hospital cooperation is essential in encouraging volunteers and keeping them interested. The Director may ask for organization of an Advisory Committee, drawn from other departments, which can render assistance.

EDUCATION, TRAINING, AND EXPERIENCE

The educational requirement for the Director is usually a bachelor's degree, preferably with a major in sociology, psychology, or management. Other useful courses include personnel administration, community organization, public relations, business procedures, writing, and public speaking.

In addition to educational requirements, most hospitals and health care institutions prefer that the Director have three to five years of administrative or supervisory experience in a health care institution or community organization, as well as some experience as a volunteer. A good starting position is as assistant in the volunteer office, or in the public affairs office of a hospital or similar institution.

JOB RELATIONSHIPS

Workers supervised: All volunteer workers and departmental staff.
Supervised by: Administrator or Associate Administrator.
Promotion from: No formal lines of promotion.
Promotion to: No formal lines of promotion.

PROFESSIONAL AFFILIATIONS

American Society of Directors of Volunteer Services
American Hospital Association
840 North Lake Shore Drive
Chicago, Illinois 60611

Director, Volunteer Services: (DOT) 187.168-042

Engineering-Maintenance Department

The hospital Engineering and Maintenance Department creates a pleasant and comfortable physical environment, by supplying lights, heat, air-conditioning, and keeping up buildings and grounds. The job classifications required to do this are much the same as for any other large, self-sufficient institution, such as a resort hotel, or a college.

Director, Plant Operation (Superintendent, Building II): (DOT) 187.168-194

Engineering Foreman (Stationary-Engineer Foreman): (DOT) 950.131-014

Boiler Repairman (Boilerhouse Repairman): (DOT) 805.381-010

Fireman, Stationary Boiler: (DOT) 951.885-14

Stationary Engineer: (DOT) 950.782-054

Refrigerator Mechanic: (DOT) 637.281-034

Maintenance Foreman (Utilities-Maintenance Foreman): (DOT) 899.131-014

Dispatcher, Maintenance Service: (DOT) 239.388-010

ENGINEERING AND MAINTENANCE DEPARTMENT

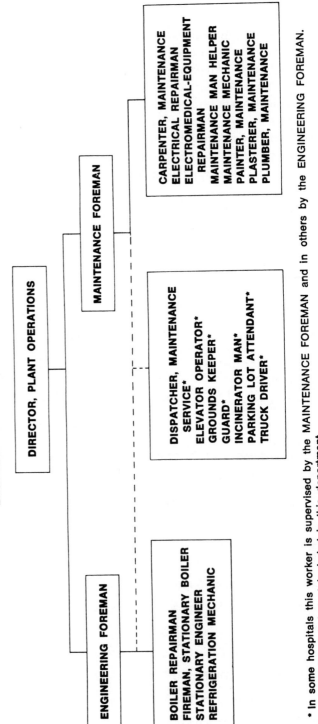

DIRECTOR, PLANT OPERATIONS

ENGINEERING FOREMAN

BOILER REPAIRMAN
FIREMAN, STATIONARY BOILER
STATIONARY ENGINEER
REFRIGERATION MECHANIC

MAINTENANCE FOREMAN

DISPATCHER, MAINTENANCE
SERVICE*
ELEVATOR OPERATOR*
GROUNDS KEEPER*
GUARD*
INCINERATOR MAN*
PARKING LOT ATTENDANT*
TRUCK DRIVER*

CARPENTER, MAINTENANCE
ELECTRICAL REPAIRMAN
ELECTROMEDICAL-EQUIPMENT
REPAIRMAN
MAINTENANCE MAN HELPER
MAINTENANCE MECHANIC
PAINTER, MAINTENANCE
PLASTERER, MAINTENANCE
PLUMBER, MAINTENANCE

* In some hospitals this worker is supervised by the MAINTENANCE FOREMAN and in others by the ENGINEERING FOREMAN.
Sometimes this job is not included in this department.

NOTE: This chart is for illustrative purposes only and should not be considered a recommended pattern of organization.

Elevator Operator: (DOT) 388.868-010

Grounds Keeper: (DOT) 407.884-010

Guard I: (DOT) 372.868-030

Incinerator Man: (DOT) 381.885T

Parking Lot Attendant: (DOT) 915.878-014

Truck Driver, Light: (DOT) 906.883-026

Truck Driver, Heavy: (DOT) 905.883-022

Carpenter, Maintenance: (DOT) 860.281-014

Electrical Repairman: (DOT) 829.281-022

Electro-Medical-Equipment Repairman: (DOT) 729.281-034

Maintenance Man Helper (Factory or Mill): (DOT) 899.884-030

Maintenance Mechanic II: (DOT) 638.281-026

Painter, Maintenance: (DOT) 840.781-010

Plasterer, Maintenance: (DOT) 842.781-018

Plumber, Maintenance: (DOT) 862.381-082

Plumber, Steamfitter: (DOT) 862.381-090

Housekeeping Department

The Housekeeping Department keeps the hospital clean, sanitary, and pleasant, and does so as economically as possible.

Institutional housekeeping is a complex activity, requiring constant attention to many different details, yet adhering to an overall plan that makes effective use of personnel, procedures, and material.

More specifically, responsibilities of the Housekeeping Department are to:

- Establish and maintain a regularly scheduled cleaning program throughout the hospital complex. Patient-care areas, intensive care units, surgical suites, and other specialized areas require that a high level of sanitation and sterilization be maintained.
- Recruit, select, and train personnel for this purpose.
- Study new techniques for improving housekeeping services; and evaluate, select, and provide proper equipment and supplies for efficient and economical operation of the housekeeping services.
- Provide qualified supervision and direction to scheduled work activities resulting in the most effective utilization of manpower.
- Establish and maintain procedures that will insure acceptable standards of quality. This includes routine cleaning of windows, walls, floors, fixtures, and

furnishings as well as responsibility for disposal of ordinary and contaminated refuse; disinfection of contaminated areas; pest and rodent control; taking bacteriologic surface samplings; and carrying out procedures for sterilization as needed.

- Utilize good interior design principles with regard to decorating and choice of furniture and furnishings; and attend to furniture repairs, refinishing, and upholstering, or replacement of equipment and supplies.
- Maintain linen selection, distribution, control, and repair.
- Be aware of common safety precautions, and correct or report safety hazards to the proper authority.
- Coordinate department activities with those of all other departments.
- Report building repair needs to the Engineering and Maintenance Department.

The Housekeeping Department may also be responsible for hospital security, elevator operation, operation of the laundry, and control of service contracts for work provided by outside vendors.

At present college training is not required for any of the job classifications in this department, and for some of them, ability to read, write, and understand orders is all that is needed for entrance, with training being given on the job. However, an effort is being made to professionalize the supervisory positions, and to raise standards of personnel. Special curricula have been drafted, and some scholarship help is available through professional associations.

PROFESSIONAL AFFILIATIONS

Institute of Sanitation Management
1710 Drew Street
Clearwater, Florida 33515

National Executive Housekeepers Association
204 Business and Professional Building
Second Avenue
Gallipolis, Ohio 45631

Director, Housekeeping Services (Executive Housekeeper): (DOT) 187.168-050

Housekeeping Supervisor (Housekeeper): (DOT) 321.138-010

Housekeeping Crew Leader (Porter, Head): (DOT) 381.137-014

Housekeeping Attendant (Porter I): (DOT) 381.887-026

Wall Washer: (DOT) 389.887-030

Window Washer (Window Cleaner): (DOT) 389.887-034

Housekeeping Aide (Maid, Hospital): (DOT) 323.887-018

Linen-Room Aide (Linen-Room Attendant): (DOT) 223.387-034

Seamstress (Seamstress, Linen-Room): (DOT) 785.381-022

HOUSEKEEPING DEPARTMENT

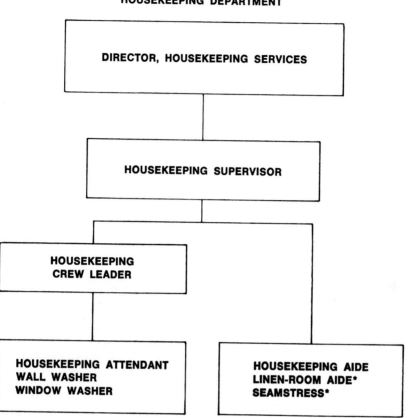

* This job may be assigned to the Laundry Department.

NOTE: This chart is for Illustrative purposes only and should not be considered a recommended pattern of organization.

Laundry Department

Many hospitals maintain their own laundries, which work in close cooperation with the Housekeeping Department.

Standards for such laundries are set by the National Association of Institutional Laundry Managers, the American Institute of Laundering, and the Laundry Manual of the American Hospital Association. Periodic bacteriologic counts are taken, and in some hospitals a Sanitarian periodically reviews the laundering and distribution process.

None of the positions in the laundry require more than grammar school education, although in supervisory positions preference is given to applicants who have graduated from a laundry school or hold certificates as professional laundry managers.

The Laundry Manager may be required to have one year of supervisory laundry

LAUNDRY DEPARTMENT

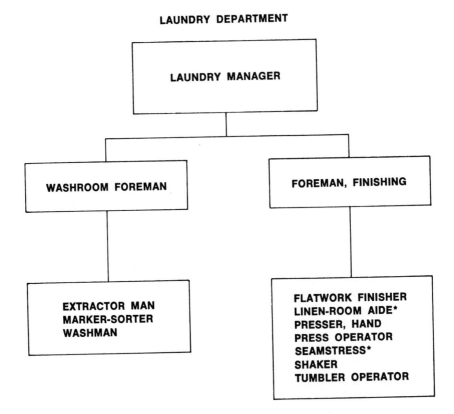

* See Housekeeping Department.

NOTE: This chart is for illustrative purposes only and should not be considered a recommended pattern of organization.

experience, and five years of general laundry experience. The Foremen may be required to have one year of experience.

PROFESSIONAL AFFILIATIONS

National Association of Institutional Laundry Managers
P.O. Box 11486
Philadelphia, Pennsylvania 19111

American Institute of Laundering
Doris and Chicago Avenues
Joliet, Illinois 60434

Laundry Manager (Laundry Foreman): (DOT) 361.138-010

Washroom Foreman: (DOT) 361.138-010

Extractor Man (Extractor Operator): (DOT) 581.885-

Marker-Sorter (Marker): (DOT) 369.887-018
    (Classifier): (DOT) 361.687-019

Washman (Washer, Machine): (DOT) 361.885-034

Foreman, Finishing (Flatwork Foreman): (DOT) 361.138-010

Flatwork Finisher: (DOT) 363.886-010

Linen-Room Aide (Linen-Room Attendant): (DOT) 223.387-034

Presser, Hand: (DOT) 363.884-022

Press Operator: (DOT) 363.885-014

Seamstress (Seamstress, Linen-Room): (DOT) 785.381-022

Shaker (Shaker, Flatwork): (DOT) 363.886-010
    (Shaker, Wearing Apparel): (DOT) 361.887-018

Tumbler Operator: (DOT) 369.885-034

6

VOLUNTARY HEALTH AGENCIES

Voluntary health agencies occupy a prominent place on the American scene. They express the health concerns of ordinary citizens, and provide avenues through which everyone in the community participates in advancing health care.

Even though many of them have huge "memberships" and are national in scope, they share a common function in recognizing and taking action on emerging community needs. Local units, with the needs of their own communities at heart, joining together in statewide and countrywide associations, are able to accomplish tasks none of them could do alone—such as conducting basic research, establishing treatment centers, and rallying eminent authorities to assist in educational campaigns.

The national headquarters of major voluntary agencies have medical advisory committees, drawn from outstanding specialists in the fields, and administrative and educational staffs of highly skilled professionals. In addition, many organizations have Boards of Directors and officers representing their membership. The national headquarters office gives leadership to local units, and serves their needs by providing consultation and materials.

Nevertheless, local units must have their own organization, tailored to the individual community's needs, and while much of the work can be done by volunteers, almost all units in communities of any size have one or more paid executives to coordinate their activities.

EXECUTIVE DIRECTOR

The Executive Director of a local chapter of a voluntary health agency works closely with the people in the community. He seeks to involve them in combatting the particular health hazard with which the organization is concerned.

Together with the chapter's Board of Directors, all of whom are volunteers, he sets the course of activities, develops the program, and organizes citizen committees.

In very small communities, the Executive Director may be the only paid employee, but in larger centers he usually has a small staff to assist in administration and public information, and possibly several staff members who render professional health services to the community in the area of the organization's special concern.

JOB DUTIES

The Executive Director, with such assistants as may be provided, is responsible for keeping the community accurately informed with regard to the health problem with which he is involved, and what the community resources are for meeting it.

He utilizes all the guidance and resources the national headquarters offers, in order to strengthen the local unit and make it effective in the community.

He works closely with comprehensive health-planning organizations and other agencies in the community, to bring their services into accord without overlapping or duplication.

He works with all kinds of community groups—civic, church, labor, government, farm, schools, newspapers, radio and television stations—to reach the most people possible, and enlist them in the agency's support.

He supervises recruitment, selection, and training of volunteers; and carries out personnel functions in hiring, training, and supervising his own staff. He runs the office.

He usually takes responsibility for local fund-raising, within the policies of the national organization. He develops a budget for consideration by the Board of Directors, and administers the funds.

EDUCATION, TRAINING, AND EXPERIENCE

The Executive Director of a local voluntary agency needs both maturity and stability, as well as managerial skills. Usually he has at least a bachelor's degree, preferably in social sciences, public or business administration, psychology and human relations, or in journalism and other subjects relating to communications. He also has had several years of experience in lower echelon jobs in the organization.

Some young people go directly into voluntary organization work when they finish college, beginning as junior assistants or part of the general office staff, and work their way up. However, the trend is toward gaining an advanced degree in public health, health education, or related fields. A master's degree is usually required in an agency of any size.

JOB RELATIONSHIPS

Workers supervised: Assistant Executive, Public Information Officer, office staff, professional employees, volunteers.
Supervised by: Board of Directors.
Promotion from: Assistant Executive or Public Information Officer.
Promotion to: No formal line of promotion, but may go to larger unit, or staff of state or national organization.

PROFESSIONAL AFFILIATIONS

National Health Council
1740 Broadway
New York, New York 10019

Director, Community Organization: (DOT) 187.118-014

FIELD REPRESENTATIVE

The Field Representative is the link between the national headquarters of a voluntary health agency and its local chapters. He may work directly out of national headquarters, or be assigned a section of the country in which he lives. In either case, the national Field Representative travels over a fairly large geographical area, making regular visits to each of the local chapters.

JOB DUTIES

The Field Representative brings the resources of the national organization to its affiliates, and helps the local Executive Director utilize them in solving problems. He may do this by consultation and advice, by suggesting programs that have worked elsewhere, or providing printed materials or visual aids.

He is usually adept at fund-raising, and gives assistance by suggesting techniques in this area. He may attend a local chapter meeting, or accompany the Director or President in calling on a prospective donor. He may appear as a speaker at a local service club.

In communities where his organization does not have units, he contacts community leaders for the purpose of setting up a local chapter, and helps with its organization.

EDUCATION, TRAINING, AND EXPERIENCE

A national Field Representative must have at least a bachelor's degree, and preferably a master's, in social sciences, health education, public health administration, or other suitable field, plus extensive experience in the public health or voluntary health field.

JOB RELATIONSHIPS

Workers supervised: None.
Supervised by: National headquarters.
Promotion from: No formal line of promotion.
Promotion to: No formal line of promotion.

PROFESSIONAL AFFILIATIONS

National Health Council
1740 Broadway
New York, New York 10019

Field Representative: (DOT) 187.268-010

7

PUBLIC HEALTH DEPARTMENTS

A Health Department is a government agency, supported by tax funds. It serves an entire community, usually a city or county, and has special responsibilities. It carries out its duties by programs of service, law enforcement, health education, and information. It has as objectives: promotion of health protection for all the people in the community; development and maintenance of a healthy environment; and an aggressive attack on major causes of disease and disability.

All government health agencies—whether local, state, or Federal—have similar characteristics. The differences between them result from the size of their jurisdictions. The state health department enforces state health laws, and provides guidance and assistance to local health departments. The United States Public Health Service has a similar relationship to state departments. In addition it represents the nation as a whole in interstate and international matters related to health. Both Federal and state health departments are deeply involved in initiating and supporting training of health personnel and in research. They offer many career opportunities in a wide range of occupations.

The American Public Health Association defines the following specialty areas as within the province of public health departments: community health planning, dental health, environment, epidemiology, food and nutrition, health administration, injury control and emergency health services, laboratory, maternal and child health, medical care, mental health, new professionals, occupational health, public health education, public health nursing, podiatric health, radiological health, school health, social work, statistics, and veterinary public health.

In so broad a framework, it is easy to see that many public health interests today are shared by industry, schools, and a vast diversity of professions.

For example, in the days when environmental threats to health were limited to infectious diseases and their carriers, public health departments were exclusively charged with protecting water and food supplies from contamination, and extermination of vermin.

But industrial development in the past fifty years has exposed mankind to air pollution; water pollution; pesticides in foods; injurious chemicals, fumes, and dusts in industry; and radioactivity from X-ray, radioactive isotopes, fissionable ma-

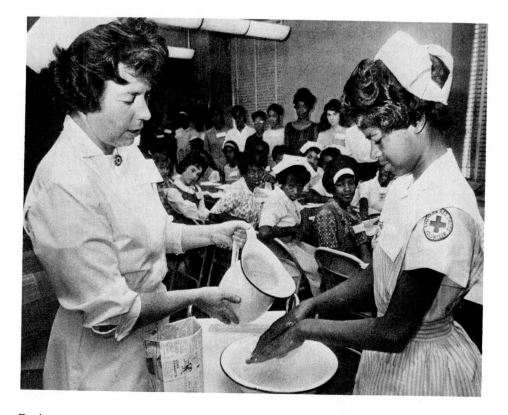

During summer vacation, teen-age girls like these in Washington, D.C. attend Home Nursing courses conducted by local chapters of the American Red Cross. Here, the District of Columbia Red Cross's Assistant Director of Nursing and a "Candy-striper" demonstrate proper washing of hands to prevent carrying infection. Many of the Youth Red Cross Volunteers in the class will become Candy-stripers, and, in their pink-and-white aprons, donate their spare time to helping nurses in the local hospitals.

Photo courtesy American Red Cross

terial and atomic and nuclear fallout on such an overwhelming scale that industry and other segments of society must augment public health efforts. Consequently, programs of environmental control are not limited to health departments. In some cities they constitute a department in themselves.

Many different health professions are needed to combat environmental health hazards, and often these specialists work together as a team to solve a particular problem.

There are only nineteen accredited full-scale schools of public health in the United States (Berkeley, UCLA, Columbia, Harvard, Hawaii, Illinois, Johns Hopkins, Loma Linda, Michigan, Minnesota, North Carolina, Oklahoma, Pittsburgh, Puerto Rico, Texas at Houston, Tulane, Washington at Seattle, and Yale). However, there are public health departments in arts and sciences divisions of universities and preventive medicine divisions of medical schools. The latter, while valuable, offer various degrees other than the master's or doctor's of public health. These variations, in face of the intense demand for personnel, make standardization of educational requirements difficult in many job classifications.

PUBLIC HEALTH ADMINISTRATOR
Health Commissioner
Medical Officer

Regardless of the size of the community, its local health department is almost always headed by a physician, and in most cases one who has had specialized training and experience in public health.

JOB DUTIES

The Chief Medical Officer has responsibility for analyzing the health situation in his community. This requires compiling health statistics and keeping them up-to-date. It also involves periodic appraisal of the community's health needs and their social and economic causes. With these facts in hand, the Medical Officer calls community attention to what is needed, and initiates plans to provide it. In carrying out plans, the community takes action, with leadership from the health department.

The Chief Medical Officer seeks to bring together the organizations and individuals in the community that are concerned with public health, including his own department, members of the health professions, the hospitals, voluntary health agencies, service clubs, public schools and universities or professional schools, labor, industry, and individual citizens.

The Chief Medical Officer is responsible for overall administration of the department. His staff usually includes several other public health physicians whose training is similar to his own. These Medical Officers may head separate divisions in the health department's programs. Other specialists—such as those responsible for environmental health, health statistics, public health nursing, health education, or public information—may serve on his immediate staff or head divisions of the department.

EDUCATION, TRAINING, AND EXPERIENCE

The Administrator of a Public Health Department should be a physician who has specialized in Public Health. Before reaching the top administrative post, he will have had extensive experience as a staff member or division head.

JOB RELATIONSHIPS

Workers supervised: All personnel of the department.
Supervised by: Governing body of the locality.
Promotion from: Staff Medical Officer.
Promotion to: No formal line of promotion.

PROFESSIONAL AFFILIATIONS

American Public Health Association
1015 Eighteenth Street N.W.
Washington, D.C. 20036

Public Health Service Officer: (DOT) 187.118-042

Medical Officer: (DOT) 070.108-038

MANAGEMENT SPECIALIST
Administrative Assistant

The complexity of modern public health agencies has necessitated the inclusion of management specialists to assist the chief public health officer. Some of the work roles of these specialists may be described as program analyst, program representative, or administrative assistant. In larger agencies, these may be separate jobs.

JOB DUTIES

As a program analyst, the Management Specialist is involved in planning the department's program. As a program representative, he goes out into the community to interpret, implement, and expedite the program. This might include fact-gathering, or interpretation of complex economic or social research data, or promotion of public participation in new health services.

He may work as a "contact man," either with community agencies or with individual members of the health professions and other civic leaders. He may represent the department in dealings outside the community, such as the state health department, local health agencies in other communities, or committees of the state legislature.

He functions as administrative assistant in such basic duties as preparing the budget and keeping budget records; accounting; personnel administration; and inventory, purchasing, and supply room services. In a small department, he may have secretarial and clerical duties. In a very large department, each of these functions may be handled by one or more persons, and brought together under the supervision of the Management Specialist.

EDUCATION, TRAINING, AND EXPERIENCE

A Management Specialist should have a bachelor's degree, preferably with a major related to the job duties to be undertaken, such as psychology, statistics, public administration, and social sciences, for the prospective program representative. Administrative assistants would find business administration helpful. Advancement to an executive level requires a year of postgraduate study in health, public or hospital administration, plus several years of management experience in a health department.

JOB RELATIONSHIPS

Workers supervised: Possible staff Management Specialists, clerical personnel.
Supervised by: Chief Public Health Officer.
Promotion from: Staff Management Specialist.
Promotion to: No formal line of promotion.

PROFESSIONAL AFFILIATIONS

American Public Health Association
1015 Eighteenth Street N.W.
Washington, D.C. 20036

Administrative Assistant: (DOT) 169.168-014

HEALTH STATISTICIAN

The Statistician in the health field is concerned with facts of disease and health as they occur in different populations, at different times, at different ages, and under different conditions. His most familiar work is exemplified by such tables as those showing the incidence of a specific disease, at what ages, and percentage of fatalities for an extended number of years; tables showing decline of infant and maternal mortality; tables showing lengthening life span; or those for incidence of heart disease among smokers and nonsmokers.

JOB DUTIES

The statistics the Health Statistician analyzes and organizes usually originate in records kept by local health departments, from which they flow to state health departments, and on to Federal agencies. The Health Statistician may work at any of these levels, or he may use the analyses made by others in different combinations to cast light on new problems, or compare local conditions with those in other areas.

A special aspect of his work is called biostatistics, or biometrics, in which the Statistician designs original research projects and techniques to answer such questions as whether one polio vaccine is more effective than another; whether fluoridation of the city's water supply will be beneficial; or whether past history indicates a regular cycle of recurrence of a certain infectious disease.

EDUCATION, TRAINING, AND EXPERIENCE

The Health Statistician should have a bachelor's degree with a major in statistics, and courses in mathematics, and the physical, biological, and/or social sciences. Students who are interested in careers in analytic statistics are advised to get a few years of practical experience in the field as a Statistical Clerk, before going on to take a master's or doctor's degree in a school of public health. For those looking toward careers in biostatistics, graduate training should stress statistics as related to biology and other medical or physical sciences. Some training or experience with computers is highly desirable.

JOB RELATIONSHIPS

Workers supervised: Possible assistants, Statistical Clerks.
Supervised by: Chief Health Officer or Management Specialist.
Promotion from: No formal line, though promotion may be made from Statistical Clerk.
Promotion to: No formal line of promotion.

PROFESSIONAL AFFILIATIONS

National Center for Health Statistics
U.S. Public Health Service
Department of Health, Education and Welfare
5600 Fishers Lane
Rockville, Maryland 20852

Public Health Statistician: (DOT) 020.188-048

Statistical Clerk: (DOT) 219.388-258

Environmental Health

All creatures, everywhere, at all times, have responded to their environment. Plants flourish only in conditions favorable to their growth. Animals migrate when food supplies grow short in the area they inhabit. People in cold climates devise warm clothing and shelters.

All species, if they survive, have adapted to nature (which is their environment). Only man has developed both the intelligence and manual skills to change it; and even he, in placing patch-upon-patch to alter immediate conditions, has failed to comprehend the effect of his work on environment as a whole.

In the last decade, when space flights gave all the people in the world a vantage point from which to view the earth in god-like perspective, it became appallingly

Environmental Technicians apply a new type of lightweight synthetic fibrous sheets at water's edge to absorb oil spill. Different forms of the new material are used to clean up oil spills in large areas.

Photo courtesy National Environmental Health Association and the 3M Company

evident that the environment in which we live is finite, and may be unique in the universe.

This exalted recognition coincided with painful realizations that even now much of earth's environment and resources may have been destroyed, and that industrially developed nations that have pillaged the environment for so-called "progress" are paying the penalty, along with more primitive cultures, in polluted air, polluted water, and food shortages.

Following rude awakening to these facts, the public has exerted pressure for protection of the environment to a sufficient extent that business and industry, as well as government, are concerned about reversing the situation while there is still time.

In consequence, many of the following job classifications that previously would have been found only in public health or other governmental agencies now appear with increasing frequency in many sectors of society. In many governmental units, environmental health departments are now separate entities. In economic units, they may be termed industrial health. Whatever the terminology, all of the jobs herein listed are outgrowths of public health activities, and are therefore listed under that general heading.

EPIDEMIOLOGIST
Environmental Health Specialist

The catalog of Yale University's school of public health defines epidemiology as "the study of all factors (and their interdependence) which affect the occurrence and course of health and disease in a population . . . Thus it is the study of man in relation to his total environment or the study of human ecology . . . not only does it cover the biological aspects of non-communicable as well as communicable disease in populations, but it also includes the environmental, social, and behavioral factors which play major roles in the health of populations."

Epidemiology draws upon other medical specialties, and upon biological and social sciences.

JOB DUTIES

In older concepts, it was the task of the Epidemiologist to track epidemics to their source and control or contain them; and to anticipate conditions that might give rise to infectious disease and eradicate them before epidemics occurred. In the latter connotation, rodent, parasite, and mosquito control furnish examples. In tracking epidemics to their source, the work of the Epidemiologist was (and is) frequently as exciting as a detective story.

In the modern, broader sense, epidemiologists may concentrate on such specialties within the field as tropical medicine, microbiology, cancer, human genetics, abnormalities of reproduction and development, causes of aging, and mental disorders.

EDUCATION, TRAINING, AND EXPERIENCE

The Epidemiologist is a physician who has specialized in this field through graduate work, preferably in a school of public health. Courses should include the biological sciences, statistics, and epidemiologic principles and methods.

JOB RELATIONSHIPS

Workers supervised: All persons assigned to the division.
Supervised by: Chief Medical Officer.
Promotion from: No formal line of promotion.
Promotion to: No formal line of promotion.

PROFESSIONAL AFFILIATIONS

American Public Health Association
1015 Eighteenth Street N.W.
Washington, D.C. 20036

Environmental Health Service, PHS
Department of Health, Education and Welfare
Room 18–81 Parklawn Building
5600 Fishers Lane
Rockville, Maryland 20852

Epidemiologist: (DOT)

RADIOLOGICAL HEALTH SPECIALIST

Artificial sources of radiation are widely used today in medicine, industry, agriculture, and utilities as well as in public health departments. With the benefits that radiological substances bring to man comes danger of overexposure. The Radiological Health Specialist and other radiological health personnel are increasingly in demand to maintain a safe balance and to assure adequate protective measures.

JOB DUTIES

The profession of radiological health applies many scientific and professional disciplines, among them biology, chemistry, physics, engineering, and medicine. In a large industrial program, specialists in several of these fields may work together. In smaller programs, a Radiological Health Specialist may work alone, and use information and skills from all these fields to solve the problems that face him.

In addition to scientists, engineers, and physicians who become Radiological Health Specialists, the programs draw upon the cooperation of nurses, pharmacists, and veterinarians.

EDUCATION, TRAINING, AND EXPERIENCE

Physicians intending to go into the radiological health field must complete medical school and internship, plus specialized training. College graduation in one of the basic sciences or engineering is the prerequisite for entrance to graduate training. There is increasing need for individuals with training in two or more related areas, such as biochemistry, biophysics, and engineering physics. A strong background in mathematics, and ability to speak and write clearly, are also important.

JOB RELATIONSHIPS

No standard pattern.

PROFESSIONAL AFFILIATIONS

American Registry of Radiologic Technologists
2600 Wayzata Boulevard
Minneapolis, Minnesota 55405

Radiological Society of North America
713 East Genesee Street
Syracuse, New York 13210

Radiation Monitor: (DOT) 199.187-010

Radiographer: (DOT) 199.381-010

SANITARY ENGINEER

The Sanitary Engineer maintains clean safe conditions in the community, and attempts to get the best environmental benefits in public health. He is usually employed by a municipality or public health department. The profession is advancing rapidly, in order to keep abreast of technological progress.

JOB DUTIES

The Sanitary Engineer designs and operates water supply systems and water purification processes, waste disposal systems, milk pasteurization plants, plans for control of rodents and insects, and standards for safe and healthful public housing. He may be called upon for special projects, such as protection of oyster beds from pollution, or noise abatement in the community. As nuclear power plants replace fossil fuel plants, air pollution will become less of a problem for the Sanitary Engineer, but he will have to cope with the possibility of air and water pollution by radioactive contamination.

Other future problems which he may be called upon to solve are changes in composition of sewage, due to use of detergents and garbage grinders. This may necessitate changes of design in sewage plants. The effect of today's use of chemicals in insecticides, pesticides, and herbicides; use of chemicals in food production; increased use of synthetic materials in clothing and buildings; and the need for better city planning, will all make demands on the Sanitary Engineer.

EDUCATION, TRAINING, AND EXPERIENCE

The Sanitary Engineer must hold an engineering degree and practice one of the professional engineering specialties. The distinctive mark of this specialty is that it combines engineering training and ability with a broad knowledge of the health sciences, and familiarity with the social sciences.

A four-year course in electrical, chemical, civil, public health, mechanical, or sanitary engineering plus specialized training in the sanitary sciences, including chemistry, physics, and biology is the minimum requirement for entrance into the

Sanitary Engineers survey a garbage dump, studying best method of future disposal in terms of location, economic and sanitary operation, and long-range usefulness.

Photo courtesy of the National Association of Sanitarians, and the National Environmental Health Association

field. Further specialized training is generally required for advancement to higher level positions. Scholarships and fellowships are available from government and other sources.

Sanitary Engineers should be registered or licensed according to the laws of the state in which they practice. Certification is made by the American Academy of Sanitary Engineers.

JOB RELATIONSHIPS

Workers supervised: Possibly other Sanitary Engineers and clerical help.
Supervised by: Depends on the work situation.
Promotion from: No standard line of promotion.
Promotion to: No standard line of promotion.

PROFESSIONAL AFFILIATIONS

American Public Health Association
1015 Eighteenth Street N.W.
Washington, D.C. 20036

Sanitary Engineer: (DOT) 005.081-046

Purification-Plant Operator: (DOT) 005.081-038

Sewage-Disposal Engineer: (DOT) 005.281-050

Public Health Service Officer: (DOT) 187.118-042

SANITARIAN

The Sanitarian's basic duty is interpretation and enforcement of city, state, and Federal laws regarding sanitary standards in food, water supply, garbage disposal, sewage disposal, and housing maintenance. Another duty involves an important role in obtaining community action for better health through environmental health control. The Sanitarian is usually employed by cities, counties, or public health departments.

JOB DUTIES

The Sanitarian must be alert to new sanitary problems created when communities grow. It is his responsibility to detect health hazards and bring them to the attention of the proper authorities, with his recommendations for correction.

In larger cities, the Sanitarian analyzes reports of inspections and investigations made by other environmental health specialists, and he advises on difficult or unusual sanitation problems. He may give evidence in court cases involving public health regulations, and he may promote laws and engage in health education activities. The Sanitarian works closely with the Public Health Officer, Sanitary Engineer, Public Health Nurse, and other health specialists to investigate and prevent outbreaks of disease, plan for civil defense and emergency disaster aid, make public health surveys, and conduct health education programs.

In large local public health departments, or in state or Federal departments, the Sanitarian may specialize in such areas as milk and other dairy products, food sanitation, refuse and other waste control, air pollution, occupational health, housing, institutional sanitation, or insect and rodent control. In rural areas and small towns, he must be responsible for a wide range of environmental health services.

EDUCATION, TRAINING, AND EXPERIENCE

A bachelor's degree in environmental health is the preferred requisite for a beginning job, although a degree in a basic science is generally acceptable. High level positions usually require a graduate degree in some aspect of public health. In some cases, Technicians who have entered the field with only two years of college but have amassed experience may be promoted to professional positions. Beginning Sanitarians usually work at a trainee level for at least a year under supervision. Many states now have laws requiring registration and certification of sanitarians.

Recommended undergraduate courses for sanitarians include mathematics, biology, chemistry, physics, elementary bacteriology, advanced bacteriology, medical entomology, and a series of public health courses.

JOB RELATIONSHIPS

Workers supervised: The Chief Sanitarian may supervise other Sanitarians, Technicians, and Trainees, as well as clerical help.
Supervised by: Varies with the working situation.
Promotion from: Sanitarian or Sanitary Technician.
Promotion to: No standard line of promotion.

PROFESSIONAL AFFILIATIONS

American Public Health Association
1015 Eighteenth Street N.W.
Washington, D.C. 20036

Sanitarian: (DOT) 079.118-014

GOVERNMENT FOOD AND DRUG INSPECTOR AND ANALYST

Government Inspectors and Analysts protect the public health by enforcing the laws set up by local communities, states, or the Federal Government in regard to foods and drugs. They ensure the safety of foods, drugs, household products, toys, cosmetics, and other goods that reach the consumer.

JOB DUTIES

Government Inspectors not only test the products; they also examine labels and packaging, and the conditions under which the foods or drugs are processed. They guard against improper sale of drugs that should be available only on doctor's prescription. They enforce the laws against bogus "health devices." When drugs or foods violate the law, they are seized by court action. The Inspector's work takes him wherever food and drugs travel on their way to the consumer—into mills, factories, processing plants, dairies, farms and ranches, packing plants, shipyards, transportation industries, storage warehouses, restaurants, and drug stores.

Behind the Inspector stands the Analyst, who works in a laboratory testing the samples of foods and drugs collected by the Inspectors. The Analyst checks them for purity, and compliance with claims on labels. He also does intensive research work on the safety and effectiveness of products, and development of methods for analyzing them, thus improving ways and means of determining their composition, and measuring degrees of spoilage or contamination. This combination of analysis and research requires chemists, biochemists, microbiologists, pharmacologists, food technologists, physiologists, and laboratory technicians.

At the Federal level, Inspectors and Analysts are employed by the United States Food and Drug Administration, and by the United States Department of Agriculture, which administers the Meat Inspection Act. Qualifications of Meat Inspectors are

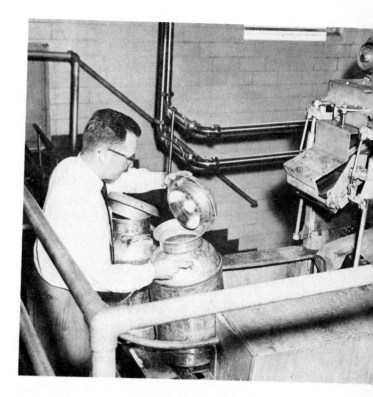

A Government Food Inspector visits a dairy. As part of his work he checks milk cans for cleanliness after they have been washed.
Photo courtesy of the National Environmental Health Association

described under the heading of Veterinarian. At state and local levels, Inspectors and Analysts may be employed by the public health service.

EDUCATION, TRAINING, AND EXPERIENCE

The Food or Drug Inspector should have at least a bachelor's degree in science, and be able to use scientific instruments for on-the-spot testing during inspections.

The Food or Drug Analyst should have four years of college, with a sound base of science courses, and a major in chemistry, bacteriology, zoology, physiology, or medical technology in some allied field. A master's or doctor's degree in the field of specialization is often required for top research jobs.

A degree in Veterinary Medicine is usually the basic requirement for Meat Inspectors.

JOB RELATIONSHIPS

Varies with the employment situation.

PROFESSIONAL AFFILIATIONS

Division of Personnel Management
Food and Drug Administration
U.S. Department of Health, Education and Welfare
Rockville, Maryland 20852

Food and Drug Inspector: (DOT) 168.287-042

Drug Analyst: (DOT) 029.281-018

FOOD TECHNOLOGIST

The Food Technologist applies the principles of science and engineering to the production, processing, packaging, distribution, preparation, evaluation, and utilization of foods. He solves the technological problems that arise in development of products, processes and equipment; the selection of raw materials; fundamental changes in the physical condition of any food where industrial processing is involved; or changes in the nutritional value of processed foods.

JOB DUTIES

Food technology is a pioneering field that offers exceptional opportunities. Depending on where he works, and the size of the organization, the Food Technologist may be concerned with improving the nutritive value of food, preventing spoilage, producing more acceptable food, or improving processing methods. He is also concerned with containers that protect the food, and in the effects upon it of warehousing and distribution. Another of his interests is quality control, and in this connection he tests both raw and finished products for purity and safety, and for accurate labeling.

The Food Technologist may be employed by industry, to assure quality in food processing; or by government agencies as a Food Analyst, whose duty is to protect the public against low-quality or harmful food products.

EDUCATION, TRAINING, AND EXPERIENCE

Because the field is new, avenues to professional positions are not well-defined. A recommended approach is graduation from college with a degree in chemistry or bacteriology, followed by work as a process engineer in a canning factory and later employment in the research department, where new products and processes are developed.

Some colleges offer programs leading to a bachelor's degree in food technology. A few have graduate programs, leading to a master's or doctor's degree. These are highly desirable for a career in research or teaching.

In the first two years of college, courses should include such basic sciences as chemistry, bacteriology, physics, nutrition, biology, and mathematics. The total program should include a thorough understanding of the fundamentals of science, engineering, and agriculture, together with their application to the manufacture and processing of food.

JOB RELATIONSHIPS

Vary with the employment situation.

PROFESSIONAL AFFILIATIONS

Career Guidance Committee
Institute of Food Technologists
221 North LaSalle Street
Chicago, Illinois 60601

Food Technologist: (DOT)

ENVIRONMENTAL TECHNICIAN

JOB DUTIES

Environmental Technicians assist the Environmental Health Specialist, Epidemiologist, and Medical Officers in the technical aspects of their work. They engage in a wide range of activities, which may include obtaining samples of air, water, and food, and assisting in performing tests to determine quality; operating, or assisting in operation of, water and waste-water treatment plants and solid-waste disposal facilities; and inspecting and evaluating various business establishments to determine whether health laws and regulations are being complied with.

Environmental Technicians are employed in public health departments at all levels, in air pollution control organizations, water purification plants, waste-water treatment plants, solid-waste collection and treatment plants, radiation protection units, consulting firms, and a variety of business and industrial firms concerned with environmental control.

Since this is a new field, job specifications have not yet been completely defined.

EDUCATION, TRAINING, AND EXPERIENCE

Most people working as Environmental Technicians have had at least two years of college or technical school training, with stress on courses concerned with the technical aspects of the field they planned to enter. Liberal arts courses are necessary for skill in communication, plus sociology, political science, psychology, economics, and basic science. Since not all of the desired skills can be gained in undergraduate education, field training is necessary.

JOB RELATIONSHIPS

Workers supervised: May supervise Environmental Aides.
Supervised by: Environmental Health Specialist.
Promotion from: No standard line of promotion.
Promotion to: No standard line of promotion.

PROFESSIONAL AFFILIATIONS

Environmental Health Service, PHS
Department of Health, Education and Welfare
Room 18–81, Parklawn Building
Washington, D.C. 20852

Environmental Technician: (DOT)

Environmental Aide: (DOT)

SAFETY ENGINEER

The Safety Engineer serves both employer and employee by detecting and correcting health hazards which might cause injury in industrial settings. He also promotes safe work practices.

His secondary goal is to prevent damage to machinery or equipment, and reduce losses in personnel and insurance costs related to industrial accidents.

JOB DUTIES

The Safety Engineer investigates every mishap to learn whether the cause is in human failure, failure of the worker to use necessary precautions, mechanical error, or structural defect. He does this by inspecting working conditions, materials, and equipment; and by watching workers at their jobs. He analyzes accident statistics, and consults with the Industrial Physician, Industrial Hygienist, Personnel Director, union representative, and workers.

Having gathered all the facts, he can recommend equipment changes, new safety rules, or perhaps an expanded safety education program.

He is expected not only to keep management informed of safety problems, but to carry out an effective program of accident prevention education, training, and compliance with industrial safety laws and standards.

EDUCATION, TRAINING, AND EXPERIENCE

A bachelor's degree in engineering, the physical sciences, or business administration offers the basic preparation for this profession, plus specialized training in special courses or one year of graduate study for a thorough grounding in all facets of this work.

JOB RELATIONSHIPS

Workers supervised: No standard pattern.
Supervised by: Top management.
Promotion from: No standard pattern.
Promotion to: No standard pattern.

PROFESSIONAL AFFILIATIONS

American Society of Safety Engineers
850 Busse Highway
Park Ridge, Illinois 60068

Safety Engineer: (DOT) 012.081-010

Air Analyst: (DOT) 012.281-010

Industrial Health Engineer: (DOT) 102.188-034

INDUSTRIAL HYGIENIST

Industrial hygiene is still a small field, but one that is growing. Industrial hygienists are most often found in industries that have full-scale occupational health programs, but also in public health offices, transportation and utilities companies, mining companies, large agricultural operations, and insurance and commercial businesses.

JOB DUTIES

The Industrial Hygienist battles conditions that were unknown or of little importance until recently. Radiation, fungi, air pollution, noise, vibration, and poor lighting are all considered as conditions that must be overcome. The Industrial Hygienist is also concerned with protection of workers from discomfort, fatigue, and other influences that may contribute to low morale and inefficiency.

The Industrial Hygienist must recognize hazards, evaluate their seriousness, and prescribe methods of eliminating or controlling them. It may be necessary to make drastic changes, even in an entire plant, and at great cost, in order to correct conditions. The Industrial Hygienist makes such recommendations, and in emergencies may have the authority to shut a plant down until a condition is corrected.

In large industries, the occupational health program is usually headed by a physician, and may consist of a dozen or more persons, including nurses, industrial hygienists, chemists, physicists, bacteriologists, laboratory testers, and industrial engineers. In small companies, the Hygienist may work alone, and also handle problems of safety engineering or work in personnel.

Young persons looking toward industrial hygiene as a career should have a strong sense of responsibility, since the comfort, health, and even lives of workers may depend on his judgment. He must also be a tactful, patient person, because his decisions may not please either labor or management when a costly change in equipment or work patterns must be made.

EDUCATION, TRAINING, AND EXPERIENCE

The basic educational requirement for an Industrial Hygienist is a college degree in engineering or one of the physical sciences. The trend is toward requiring a master's degree in one of the basic disciplines or in an area of categorical program specialization. Courses in biology and biochemistry are highly desirable, as are courses in psychology, personnel management, and business administration.

JOB RELATIONSHIPS

Depends upon the employment situation.

PROFESSIONAL AFFILIATIONS

American Industrial Hygiene Association
25711 Southfield Road
Southfield, Michigan 48075

Industrial Hygienist: (DOT) 079.188-010

Careers in the United States Public Health Service

Since 1798, the United States Public Health Service has made increasingly important contributions to the nation's health. The Service's Commissioned Corps is open to American citizens of suitable age and qualifications. Appointments correspond to ranks in the military services, and through the years that the Selective Service Act was in effect, provided an alternative to active military duty.

Student and career appointments are made in the following professions:

- Medicine
- Osteopathy
- Nursing
- Dietetics
- Nutrition
- Engineering
- Sanitary Science

- Pharmacy
- Veterinary Medicine
- Dentistry
- Health Services
- Physical Sciences
- Biological Sciences
- Physical Therapy

Opportunities are open equally to men and women.
Salaries and allowances are commensurate with corresponding military ranks.
Additional specific information may be secured from:

Department of Health, Education and Welfare
Office of the Secretary, Commissioned Personnel Operations Division
Employment Operations Branch
Parklawn Building—Room 4–35
5600 Fishers Lane
Rockville, Maryland 20852.

8

RESEARCH IN DELIVERY OF HEALTH CARE

Provision of effective medical and health care services for everyone presents one of the knottiest and most controversial of modern problems. Any successful resolution depends on *statistics,* to provide information about specific needs; *sociology,* for understanding of the mores and life styles of the people to be served; and *economics,* to assure financial feasibility.

Study of various aspects of health care delivery takes place in several settings: public health services at all levels; community health councils; foundations; universities; large trade unions; professional associations; national voluntary health agencies; and large medical complexes. Partial achievement is evident in: establishment of clinics; nonprofit, commercial, and government-sponsored prepaid health insurance plans; and other progressive projects to ensure effective and prompt delivery of health services to all members of the community, irrespective of their economic status.

Need for personnel in medical and health statistics, sociology, and economics will continue through the foreseeable future, since society itself is dynamic and methods of health care delivery must continually adapt to its changing patterns.

SOCIOLOGIST

The science of sociology deals with man as a social animal, seeking to discover how his customs, attitudes, family, neighborhood, ethnic group, trade union, political organization, church or synagogue, or economic and social stratum affect his life. The Medical Sociologist is most concerned with how all these factors affect his health. The knowledge he gathers is invaluable for agencies planning public health programs, hospitals, clinics, health education, and similar projects.

JOB DUTIES

The Sociologist makes his contribution largely through research, which takes him out among the people he is studying, rather than gathering information about them from books. He becomes part of the community he is studying, seeking answers to his questions from the people themselves. He explores, for example, the relationship between national origin or income-level and illness rates, seeking clues in group customs, or in social stress to which the group is exposed. He may try to learn why a certain group of people won't go to a doctor when they should, and won't follow his advice when they do. He may be assigned to evaluate a community's total health needs, and such facilities as exist, and how they can be supplemented or reorganized to give better service.

The Sociologist may develop pilot projects in the community, to study their effectiveness. When he has completed his data-gathering and evaluation, he may recommend courses of action to the hospital, health council, or other group who employed him, or he may report his findings as part of the material for future research.

He may spend part of his time teaching in a university or professional school.

EDUCATION, TRAINING, AND EXPERIENCE

A Sociologist with a master's degree is likely to find his first job in the health field as a staff assistant in a fairly large public health organization or a medical center, or as a member of a university research group working on health problems. As he gains experience, opportunity arises for advancement in these settings, although working ahead toward his Ph.D. in the meantime gives him a great advantage. Few persons lacking the doctorate degree can reach full senior faculty status in a professional or graduate school, or become research director in a major health organization.

JOB RELATIONSHIPS

Varies with the employment situation.

PROFESSIONAL AFFILIATIONS

American Sociological Association
1722 N. Street, N.W.
Washington, D.C. 20036

Sociologist: (DOT) 054.088-038

Anthropologist: (DOT) 055.088-010

MEDICAL ECONOMIST

Medical care in the United States is a gigantic enterprise that cares for tens of millions of patients each year, at a cost of billions of dollars. It is the task of the Medical Economist to find means of delivering the highest quality of health and medical care to the most people at the lowest cost.

JOB DUTIES

The Medical Economist uses research techniques to answer questions apropos of health care planning. Questions may be general, and of nationwide importance; or of a specific, local nature. Typical assignments might be to determine the relative economy of individual doctor-patient practice versus group practice; appropriate level of fringe benefits for medical care in a labor-management contract; or comparative values of differing types of health insurance. He may also study such matters as geographic distribution of doctors and other health personnel.

He may base his study on compilation of statistics and studies already in existence, and garnered from various sources. He may authorize or conduct a poll, or issue questionnaires, to amass original data. Or he may set up pilot and control programs to ascertain facts.

On completion of data-gathering, he analyses and evaluates the facts, draws conclusions, and applies them to practical planning of methods to be followed or recommended.

He usually publishes his work, so that his material becomes available to other researchers.

EDUCATION, TRAINING, AND EXPERIENCE

The Medical Economist should have a baccalaureate degree in economics, with courses in economic theory and history, public and international finance, money and banking, labor, consumer economics, statistics, and accounting. Since few colleges offer undergraduate or graduate courses specifically geared to economics of health, special graduate education is needed. A master's or doctor's degree in such health-oriented areas as public health administration, medical care administration, hospital administration, health statistics, epidemiology, or the sociologic aspects of health is desirable.

JOB RELATIONSHIPS

Varies with employment situation.

PROFESSIONAL AFFILIATIONS

National Center for Health Services Research and Development
5600 Fishers Lane
Parklawn Building
Rockville, Maryland 20852

Economist: (DOT) 050.088-014

9

HEALTH EDUCATION

Health Education is a relatively new profession. Its purpose is to bridge the gap between medical knowledge and techniques and the use people make of them. For example, it does no good for medical science to have a means for curing a type of cancer if the patients who have it do not go to a doctor.

The ultimate goal of health education is action. Therefore, the Health Educator must not only inform people about good health practices; he must persuade them to utilize them.

There are many obstacles that he must overcome. There may be emotional resistance, language barriers, social and economic barriers, psychological blocks, and apathy.

Sometimes the difficulties in taking health action are not on the part of the people in a community, but with the institutions that provide health services. For example, clinic hours may not be such that working people can get there. Clinic personnel may be curt and impersonal in their treatment of patients, or fail to make explanations in terms patients can understand.

Thus, the Health Educator must work with other health personnel in the community, to help them plan and deliver health care that the public can and will use.

With major changes taking place in the delivery of health care at local, regional, and national levels, participation of health educators in planning groups is increasingly in demand.

Major employers of health educators are local, regional, and Federal public health services, and schools. Voluntary health organizations also utilize their services, although they may be called by such titles as Director of Education, or Director of Information. Other employers are hospitals, clinics, industry, agricultural extension services, colleges and universities. In the past twenty-five years, the number of professional health educators has grown from five hundred to two thousand, and opportunities continue to increase.

As a science, health education derives from sociology, psychology, educational psychology, and the behavioral sciences, as well as from the biological and health sciences. Young persons preparing for careers in this field must gain background in all of these disciplines, and skills in every form of communications.

PUBLIC HEALTH EDUCATOR

At the local level, the Public Health Educator has the advantage of personal contact with individuals and groups within the community. At regional and national levels, he must depend to a great extent on use of the mass communications media: Television, radio, films, newspapers, and specially printed materials.

JOB DUTIES

Regardless of the level at which he works, the Health Educator must have a thorough knowledge of the public that he serves and the structure of its organized groups and institution, such as schools, churches, health agencies, welfare organizations, labor unions, and the like. Perhaps the Health Educator will help them to recognize health problems in their communities and stimulate them to action. Such problems might have to do with environmental pollution, chronic disease, over-population, drug abuse, or any of hundreds of ills that plague society. The Health Educator knows that community group action usually results in solutions to problems that will work for that community. He may assist by contacting resources, helping to organize a conference, plan a campaign, or develop a television series about the problem the group is tackling. He may supply educational materials, or help groups to develop their own.

Thus, whether helping a ghetto neighborhood plan its own health center, or helping representatives from state agencies agree on needed regional medical facilities, the Health Educator helps people to help themselves, by bringing needs and resources together to form new partnerships for health.

Frequently, improving health care involves training: inservice training for health workers already in the community; preparation of young people coming into health careers; training of health aides who will help improve communications among the poor; and training of citizen volunteers who are ready to assume community leadership. The Health Educator contributes by consulting on the development of training programs, by suggesting creative methods, and even by training the local personnel who will do the training in the community.

At all levels, the Health Educator must be adept at public speaking, writing, and utilization of all available media.

EDUCATION, TRAINING, AND EXPERIENCE

Because the profession is relatively new, health educators today have come from many backgrounds. Some have strengths in administration or social welfare, or public administration, or community organization. Others were once in nursing, teaching, environmental health, and similar occupations. In any case they reinforced their original college background with courses in the physical and social sciences and education. Some went on to professional study in the field of health education.

Requirements are becoming standardized today, with a master's degree in health education as the requirement for positions of leadership. For the most part, such programs are offered by universities having schools of public health. They include training in fundamental public health areas, such as disease control and environmental health, and in-depth preparation in educational program planning, and in theory and methods analysis of health education problems. Many institutions offering these programs also have financial assistance available for students.

An increasing number of colleges and universities are now offering a bachelor's degree in community health education. These programs include the biological and social sciences, and basic health education skills. They qualify the student for many community jobs, and for entrance into graduate school.

JOB RELATIONSHIPS

Vary with the employment situation.

PROFESSIONAL AFFILIATIONS

Society for Public Health Education, Inc.
655 Sutter Street
San Francisco, California 94102

Public Health Educator: (DOT) 079.118-010

SCHOOL HEALTH EDUCATOR

Modern health education in schools is not what was once called hygiene, nor is it blood-and-bones physiology, nor physical education. From nursery school into college, health education deals with day-by-day living, helping children and young people develop the knowledge, attitudes, and skills they need to live healthfully and safely. School health educators cooperate closely with the physicians and nurses who serve the schools, and they participate in community health activities as representatives of the school health education program.

Depending on the school system and the grades covered, health courses usually include such subjects as family-life education, first aid, safety education, choice and use of health products and services, nutrition, personal hygiene, and community health. Mental health and good human relations are also included.

JOB DUTIES

The School Health Educator is responsible for developing the health education curriculum for each grade of the schools she serves. She may work in a single school, or an entire school system. Whatever the size of her jurisdiction, she exercises leadership in maintaining an adequate, well-balanced program, and in getting all groups in the school and community interested in the health of the school child to work together effectively.

In small schools, the Health Educator may be the only teacher of the subject, and may not devote all of her time to it. Although increasing numbers of school systems are employing full-time health educators, it is wise for a beginner fresh from college to have a second teaching field, such as social studies, science, or physical education. In larger systems, she may act as supervisor, furnishing materials and guidance for classroom teachers.

EDUCATION, TRAINING, AND EXPERIENCE

The School Health Educator must be certified in her state to teach at the level at which she is employed. In some school systems and levels, a bachelor's degree with a background in the biological, behavioral, and social sciences, and health education is acceptable. However, a master's degree in health education is rapidly becoming a minimum requirement. A doctorate in health education often is required for college positions.

Universities having schools of public health often have courses in health education leading to advanced degrees, as do some other colleges and universities. Most of them have scholarship funds available.

JOB RELATIONSHIPS

Vary with the employment situation.

PROFESSIONAL AFFILIATIONS

American Association for Health, Physical Education,
    and Recreation (AAHPER)
1201 Tenth Street N.W.
Washington, D.C. 20036

School Health Educator: (DOT) 079.118-010

NUTRITIONIST

A Nutritionist is an educator who teaches people about good eating habits, and helps people who have special nutritional needs, such as old people, poor people, foreign-born groups, mothers with young babies or children whose conditions require special diets. She often supplies nutrition information for radio and television programs, or newspaper columns.

Nutritionists work mainly in government and voluntary health agencies concerned with community health or the needs of special groups. A Nutritionist may work as consultant on a health team, along with physicians, social workers, public health nurses, dental hygienists, and other professionals, training them to counsel the people they serve.

JOB DUTIES

A Nutritionist may work directly with individuals or groups of people who need her advice and teaching; or she may convey information by means of written articles, brochures, radio or television interviews. She may conduct demonstrations, actually showing food preparation, or employing audiovisual aids.

Nutritionists are in demand for international technical assistance programs, to work with people in underdeveloped countries, where the relationship of food and good health is not yet understood. In these circumstances, she must be innovative, adapting her program to make good use of foodstuffs the people already have, and presenting new diet ideas in a manner that will be acceptable to their culture and customs.

EDUCATION, TRAINING, AND EXPERIENCE

Although the work of the Nutritionist is not exactly like that of the Dietitian, the required preparation for their careers is similar. A bachelor's degree is required, generally in home economics, with emphasis on food and nutrition, and courses in psychology, sociology, and teaching. High school courses in chemistry and other basic sciences are helpful.

A career Nutritionist should find work in a related field, such as hospital dietetics, home economics teaching, or extension work for a few years after college graduation, and then proceed to a master's degree or doctorate in public health nutrition. Advanced degrees and experience are necessary to reach such positions as nutrition consultant or director of nutrition services in public health departments or voluntary health and welfare organizations.

JOB RELATIONSHIPS

Vary with the employment situation.

PROFESSIONAL AFFILIATIONS

American Dietetic Association
620 North Michigan Avenue
Chicago, Illinois 60611

Nutritionist: (DOT) 077.128-022

Research Nutritionist: (DOT) 077.081-010

10

HEALTH INFORMATION AND COMMUNICATION

Health information and communication takes place on several levels. At the most highly professional levels, physicians, research scientists, and others report their clinical and research findings to each other in specialized journals. This kind of professional communication may also be presented on closed circuit television, or in films or in lectures accompanied by audiovisual material.

On the second level, medical and health professionals wish to inform the general public in regard to current developments and good health practices. Voluntary agencies, too, wish to tell the public about their particular interests, to keep people involved in the initiation and support of adequate health facilities in the community. Public health officials want to educate the public, and also to keep avenues open to communicate such newsworthy items as threatening epidemics, and campaigns against venereal and other diseases. Newspapers, magazines, radio, television, and films become the media of choice in these circumstances.

On another level, textbooks and supplementary materials concerned with health information and education must be written.

Each of these facets of health information and communication requires specific writing styles and techniques. At all levels, writers work with illustrators, medical illustrators, and photographers. Description of the work of Medical Illustrator and Photographer will be found in the section on the Clinical Laboratory, since they are most likely to work on technical materials.

In addition to writers, Medical Editors form a specially trained group of professionals employed by publishers of medical books, textbooks, and journals, public health groups, and voluntary organizations. These Editors must have strong backgrounds in medical science and terminology, including knowledge of symbols and abbreviations used in medicine. In addition, they must frequently be able to rewrite professional material with clarity for other scientists to comprehend, or simplify it for the understanding of nonprofessionals.

All of these specialists may be employed on the staffs of publishers, professions, pharmaceutical houses, research centers, voluntary organizations, or public health departments. However, many of them work as free lances, sometimes as generalists, but often as specialists in certain types of writing, or writing for certain media.

SCIENCE WRITER

The Science Writer is an experienced journalist who specializes in scientific subjects, including medicine and health. He may write for newspapers, magazines, radio, television, or for scientific or professional publications.

JOB DUTIES

It is the job of the Science Writer to acquaint his readers with what is happening in the fields of science and medicine: new treatments for cancer or heart disease; improved surgical techniques; or research on mental illness, as examples.

The Science Writer must not only report, he must interpret and explain new and complex technical matters so that they will be understandable to the readers. He must be objective and accurate in presenting facts, because they are critical, and because the scientists, physicians, and health administrators from whom he gets his material will hesitate to talk freely unless they know that he is competent and trustworthy. Also, the confidence of his reading public depends on his care and integrity.

EDUCATION, TRAINING, AND EXPERIENCE

Many Science Writers began their careers as general news reporters, and through personal interest and additional training, fitted themselves to write authoritatively in the fields of science and medicine. Necessary background for good science writing consists of good general education and journalism, plus knowledge of the physical and social sciences. A writer must be reasonably well informed in every branch of science and medicine, since he works with a diversity of specialists.

Minimum requirements for a young writer should be four years of college, and a bachelor's degree, preferably in English or journalism, and concentration on science courses. The beginner must prove his worth as a general writer and journalist before he can begin to specialize in science writing. A real grasp of the subject and the ability to write it interestingly demand training as well as aptitude and experience.

JOB RELATIONSHIPS

Vary with the employment situation.

PROFESSIONAL AFFILIATIONS

Council for the Advancement of Science Writing, Inc.
201 Christie Street
Leonia, New Jersey 07605

Science Writer: (DOT) 139.088-033

HEALTH INFORMATION SPECIALIST

The Health Information Specialist is a science writer who is employed by a health organization as its link with the news media. Information Specialists work in practically every kind of health organization and institution, public and private, from local to national levels. This writer's work is valuable, because the people who support health programs through voluntary contributions or taxes are entitled to know what their money is helping to accomplish.

JOB DUTIES

The work of the Health Information Specialist is creative, in that he not only informs, but transmits information in such a way as to reach and attract as many people as possible, and influence them toward a favorable attitude in regard to his organization, and to use its services.

He uses every communications medium available: leaflets, brochures, newspapers, magazines, exhibits, radio, television, films, and other audiovisual materials.

In a large organization he may have a staff of editorial assistants who may do abstracting, or library research, or prepare first drafts. In a small organization, he may have to do everything himself.

He works closely with the organization's executive staff and other staff members, advising them on the news value of their programs, and interpreting them to the public.

EDUCATION, TRAINING, AND EXPERIENCE

Except for government agencies, which require civil service examinations, qualifications and training requirements differ widely. The Health Information Specialist should plan on taking a four-year college course, and acquiring a bachelor's degree, preferably in journalism, and backed up with courses in biological, medical, and social sciences. General experience on newspapers, or in radio or television stations, or in film production is helpful.

JOB RELATIONSHIPS

Workers supervised: May have Editorial Assistants and clerical staff.
Supervised by: Chief Executive of the employing organization.
Promotion from: No formal line of promotion, but may move up from Editorial Assistant with additional training and experience.
Promotion to: No formal line of promotion.

PROFESSIONAL AFFILIATIONS

Council for the Advancement of Science Writing, Inc.
201 Christie Street
Leonia, New Jersey 07605

Science Writer: (DOT) 139.088-033

TECHNICAL WRITER

The Technical Writer's specialty is writing science material for professionals, the people who are involved in scientific activities. His job is a direct result of scientific progress, which has multiplied the need for communication within scientific fields.

JOB DUTIES

Not all scientists who must report on their work in scientific papers are proficient as writers: others who could do their own writing cannot spare the time from their basic work. The Technical Writer prepares reports, either for administrative purposes or for scientific journals; he prepares instruction manuals for various kinds of laboratory technicians; he prepares equipment specifications, contract proposals, and other business documents that serve as connecting links between the scientist and the persons who will manufacture or use his latest technological product. He may prepare proposals, in search of grants for research projects.

In technical writing, the emphasis is on specific data, spelled out in detail, to provide a clear, concise picture, no matter how complex the subject may be.

A Technical Writer must be thoroughly familiar with his subject, which assumes a substantial background of technical information and intensive, continuing study of the area to be covered. In some cases, Technical Writers assist in preparing charts, diagrams, photographs, and other illustrative material.

EDUCATION, TRAINING, AND EXPERIENCE

There are no hard and fast requirements for this specialty, but few employers would consider an applicant with less than a bachelor's degree in one of the basic sciences plus a minor in English or journalism; or a degree in English or journalism, with a minor in science. Some Technical Writers take advanced degrees in one of the sciences. Beginning writers are often assigned to assist experienced staff members.

JOB RELATIONSHIPS

Workers supervised: Assistant Writers, clerical staff.
Supervised by: Varies with employment situation.

Promotion from: No formal line of promotion, but may be promoted from Assistant Technical Writer.

Promotion to: No formal line of promotion.

PROFESSIONAL AFFILIATIONS

Society of Technical Writers and Publishers, Inc.
1010 Vermont Avenue N.W.
Washington, D.C. 20005

Technical Writer: (DOT) 139.388-014

11

RELATED PROFESSIONS

A number of professions that bear directly on patient care are practiced independently outside of such usual health structures as hospitals, public health services, schools, and voluntary agencies, although some of them also have a place in these milieux. Each of them in some way supplements the practice of medicine, and requires education and training related to that discipline.

MEDICAL ASSISTANT

Wherever a physician is in practice, he is likely to need a general factotum—a highly intelligent, efficient being who can relieve him of all duties except those only he can perform. That person is the Medical Assistant, who combines the roles of secretary, receptionist, administrative aide, clinical aide, and countless other functions. She is the contact between the physician and his patients, his professional associates, and his suppliers of equipment and medications.

Most Medical Assistants work in doctors' offices, although some work in group-practice offices, clinics, or hospitals.

JOB DUTIES

The Medical Assistant manages the physician's office, assists him in giving some examinations and in emergency situations. She answers the telephone and sets appointments, receives patients, and reassures them if they are nervous or ill. She takes patients' medical histories, and arranges hospital admissions.

She greets representatives from various firms that sell medical supplies, and places the physician's order.

She types medical reports and fills out insurance forms.

Her job requires friendliness, a cheerful manner, kindness, adaptability, stamina, good judgment, neatness, and accuracy. She is well aware that her manner and attitude influence the impression patients and others form about the physician and his methods of practice.

Preparation for work as a Medical Assistant should begin in high school, with basic secretarial, typing, English, mathematics, and health science courses. Ideally, after graduation the student should enroll in one of the two-year associate degree programs offered by community and junior colleges, which give a broad foundation in basic medical assistance skills, including a period of practical training in a doctor's office. A graduate of these programs may apply for certification and membership in the American Association of Medical Assistants.

Some one-year courses and other short courses are available in colleges, technical, and vocational schools; and state employment offices have information about on-the-job training programs in their localities.

JOB RELATIONSHIPS

Workers supervised: Possible clerical help.
Supervised by: The Physician.
Promotion from: No formal line of promotion.
Promotion to: No formal line of promotion.

PROFESSIONAL AFFILIATIONS

American Association of Medical Assistants
Suite 1510
One East Wacker Drive
Chicago, Illinois 60601

Medical Assistant: (DOT) 079.368-022

OPTICIAN

When a patient has visited his eye doctor and been fitted for glasses, someone has to fill the doctor's prescription. This is the business of the Dispensing Optician. If the Optician has a great many customers who come to him for glasses, he employs other opticians, known as Dispensers. He may also employ some beginners, known as Apprentice Technicians, whom he trains in the work of lens grinding and fitting. (In states where opticians are licensed, this knowledge is needed to pass the examination. Students who go to accredited opticianry schools get this experience in their courses.)

JOB DUTIES

The Dispensing Optician and his assistants measure each patient's facial contours in order to select the frame and lens shape that will best suit the patient. Then the lenses must be ground in accordance with the prescription, edged to fit the frame, and assembled into the finished glasses. This "benchwork" may be done in the shop.

Now that more than five million Americans wear contact lenses, the scope of the Optician's work has broadened. In fitting them, he also follows the doctor's prescription, but he must make very exacting measurements of the corneas of the patient's eyes. In addition, he must work very skillfully with precision instruments which measure the power and curvature of each lens. Finally, it is the Optician who instructs patients on inserting, removing, and caring for the delicate thin plastic disks.

A trained Optician may open his own shop, work for someone else as a Dispenser, or enter into other phases of optical work. Opportunities for women are excellent.

EDUCATION, TRAINING, AND EXPERIENCE

Standards for the sixteen schools of opticianry in the United States, and for vocational schools offering such courses, are set by the American Board of Opticianry, Buffalo, New York. An applicant for apprenticeship must have a high school education and be at least 17 years old. The term of apprenticeship is three years (6,000 hours) and includes a minimum of 150 hours per year of related instruction. The first six months of the program is probationary.

If an apprentice progresses rapidly he may achieve the level of journeyman within the time of instruction.

Seventeen states require Dispensing Opticians to be licensed; California and Hawaii also license opticianry establishments; and Connecticut and New Jersey require that Optical Technicians be licensed.

JOB RELATIONSHIPS

Workers supervised: The Dispensing Optician supervises Dispensers and Apprentices.
Supervised by: State laws where they exist.
Promotion from: Apprentice and Journeyman to Dispenser.
Promotion to: None.

PROFESSIONAL AFFILIATIONS

Guild of Prescription Opticians of America, Inc.
1250 Connecticut Avenue, N.W.
Washington, D.C. 20036

Optician: (DOT) 713.381-014

Optician, Apprentice: (DOT) 713.381-018

Optician, Contact Lens Dispensing: (DOT) 711.381-018

Optician, Dispensing: (DOT) 713.251-010

OPTOMETRIST

Medical eye care can be given only by an Ophthalmologist, who is basically a physician with special training in defects and diseases of the eyes. However, the Optometrist is educated and trained to examine eyes and prescribe eye glasses or contact lenses as needed, or recommend other optical treatment to improve eyesight. If evidence of eye injury or disease is present, he refers the patient to an Ophthalmologist.

JOB DUTIES

The Optometrist examines and tests eyes, fits lenses, and writes prescriptions. When the lenses have been ground in an optical laboratory, he fits them to frames suitable for the patient's features.

Much of the research and development through which contact lenses evolved were done by Optometrists, and some Optometrists now devote their entire practice to prescribing them, fitting them, and training patients to use them properly.

Optometrists are also playing a leading role in correction of children's vision problems, especially in use of vision training and orthoptics. Many serve as consultants to schools.

Telescopic and microscopic lens systems that aid children and elderly persons who have certain types of failing vision are further developments of optometry.

Many Optometrists are in private practice, although there are many opportunities for them in industries, hospitals, government agencies, and the Armed Forces, and great need for them in research. It is estimated that 20,000 new Optometrists will be needed during this decade.

EDUCATION, TRAINING, AND EXPERIENCE

Students looking toward optometry as a career should begin taking science courses in high school, so that they acquire background in mathematics, physics, chemistry, biology, neurology, physiology, anatomy and psychology before they begin professional training. All colleges of optometry require two years of college before entrance, and today many students complete four years of college first. All colleges in the United States and Canada that are accredited by the American Optometric Association require completion of a four-year course of professional training, leading to the degree of Doctor of Optometry (O.D.). Optometrists must be licensed in the state where they practice.

There are many scholarships available for optometric study, some of them from state associations, some from colleges; and there is financial assistance from the government available under the Health Professions Educational Assistance Act.

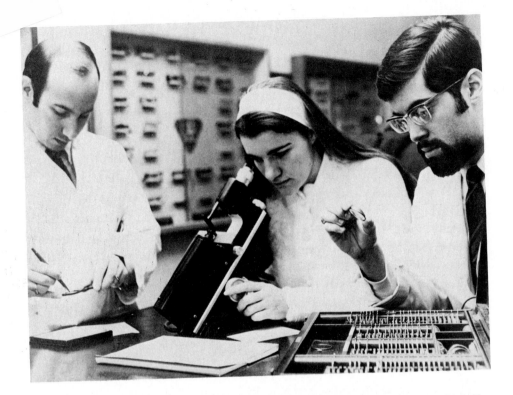

Students of optometry must acquire a practical knowledge of mechanical optics, including characteristics of ophthalmic glass, and skills of lens grinding, adaptation and fitting.
Photo courtesy of the American Optometric Association

JOB RELATIONSHIPS

Except as a young Optometrist may break into the field by working as assistant to an established man, or joining an industry, Optometrists work independently.

PROFESSIONAL AFFILIATIONS

American Optometric Association
7000 Chippewa Street
St. Louis, Missouri 63119

Optometrist: (DOT) 079.108-026

ORTHOPTIST

Many Ophthalmologists employ assistants called Orthoptists to treat patients who have the condition familiarly known as "crossed eyes." Many Orthoptists are women, and they have a highly specialized job in helping children and adults overcome this handicap.

JOB DUTIES

The Orthoptist uses exercises, which teach the patient's eyes to work together as a team and see with properly fused vision. The Ophthalmologist supervises her work. Like any teacher, the Orthoptist must be able to win the cooperation and confidence of her patients, and for this she needs a calm, understanding personality.

EDUCATION, TRAINING, AND EXPERIENCE

A candidate for this profession must be at least 20 years old, and have completed at least two years of college or comparable education before applying to one of the schools giving a 15-month course in orthoptics. (One school requires four years of college before acceptance.)

Alternatively, a candidate may elect to enter a training center for the same period of practical work under supervision of a Certified Orthoptist, combining this with the basic two-month course offered by the American Orthoptic Council.

Although there is no legal requirement for certification, almost all orthoptists are certified.

JOB RELATIONSHIPS

Workers supervised: None.
Supervised by: Ophthalmologist.
Promotion from: No formal line of promotion.
Promotion to: No formal line of promotion.

PROFESSIONAL AFFILIATIONS

American Orthoptic Council
3400 Massachusetts Avenue, N.W.
Washington, D.C. 20007

Orthoptist: (DOT) 079.378-030

OSTEOPATH

Osteopathic physicians are licensed to practice in all of the United States, although about half of the 14,000 now in practice work in Florida, Michigan, Missouri, Ohio, Pennsylvania, Texas, and New Jersey. Most of them are in private practice, and utilize the 310 osteopathic hospitals. They are also eligible for admittance to the medical and surgical staffs of many tax-supported hospitals throughout the country.

JOB DUTIES

Osteopathy, which was developed toward the end of the last century, stresses the importance of body mechanics to health, and emphasizes the use of manipulation to detect and correct faulty structure. In dealing with illness and injury, osteopathic medicine makes major use of manipulative therapy, combining it with the use of drugs, operative surgery, physical therapy, and other methods, depending on the individual diagnosis.

EDUCATION, TRAINING, AND EXPERIENCE

There are seven colleges of osteopathic medicine accredited by the American Osteopathic Association. Their graduates receive the degree of Doctor of Osteopathy (D.O.).

Minimum entrance requirement in all these colleges is three years of college work in an accredited college or university, although almost all applicants today have completed the regular four years of college and earned a bachelor's degree. Some colleges that have a three-year entrance requirement grant a baccaleureate degree on completion of the first year of osteopathic training. In general, osteopathic colleges require chemistry, biology, physics, and English as prerequisites for admission.

Curriculum in osteopathic colleges includes basic science subjects such as anatomy, physiology, pathology, bacteriology, immunology, biochemistry, histology, embryology, pharmacology, and public health. In addition, osteopathic principles, diagnosis, manipulative therapy, and other subjects are taught in the first half of the course. During the second half, clinical subjects are combined with practical training in the osteopathic hospitals with which these colleges are affiliated. After receiving his degree, the Doctor of Osteopathy must serve a 12-month rotating internship in one of these hospitals.

The basic course in osteopathic medicine is designed for general practitioners, but specialization courses are offered in anesthesiology, internal medicine, dermatology, neurology and psychiatry, obstetrics and gynecology, ophthalmology and otorhinolaryngology, pathology, pediatrics, proctology, radiology, rehabilitation medicine, and surgery.

Requirements for licensing differ widely in the various states.

JOB RELATIONSHIPS

The Osteopath in private practice works independently.

PROFESSIONAL AFFILIATIONS

American Osteopathic Association
212 East Ohio Street
Chicago, Illinois 60611

Osteopathic Physician: (DOT) 071.108-010

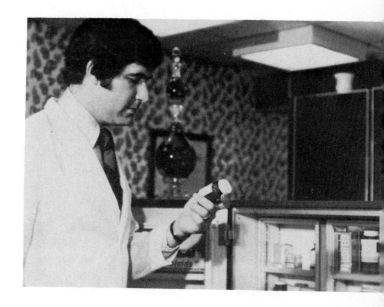

A neighborhood Pharmacist exercises care in double-checking physicians' prescriptions before he fills them, and double-checking his labeling on the container.
Photo courtesy of American Association of Colleges of Pharmacy

PHARMACIST

The neighborhood Pharmacist, unlike his counterpart who works in an institutional setting, is often the first health professional seen by persons seeking help. Consequently, he dispenses advice as well as medications, guiding the people of his community to other professionals competent to treat their specific health problems. In effect, his drugstore becomes a center for health information in the neighborhood.

JOB DUTIES

The primary responsibility of the Pharmacist is to compound and dispense medicine on the order of a physician or other qualified practitioner. To perform his function, he must be thoroughly acquainted with the physical and chemical properties of drugs, and their effects on the human system. He must also know how a drug will react in laboratory tests of blood and human tissues. On occasion he may need to advise physicians on the effects that certain drugs may have in combination with others.

The neighborhood Pharmacist is also a business man, who may have to hire and supervise clerical staff and assistant pharmacists, buy and sell merchandise, both health-related and otherwise.

His ethics must be above question, since he is entrusted with storage and distribution of dangerous and habit-forming drugs, and he must be scrupulous in handling them. He must be meticulous about cleanliness, orderliness, and accuracy in compounding drugs, since his work affects human welfare and life.

EDUCATION, TRAINING, AND EXPERIENCE

To obtain a degree in pharmacy, a student must complete a five- or six-year program of education after graduation from high school. The five-year program leads to the degree of Bachelor of Pharmacy; the six-year program leads to the degree of Doctor of Pharmacy. Some colleges of pharmacy accept students following high school graduation and give the entire course themselves. Others permit or require two years of college. However, there is no exception to the rule that at least three years of professional education in either the five- or six-year course must be acquired at an accredited college of pharmacy. There are 72 such schools in the United States and Puerto Rico.

The prospective Pharmacist should begin his planning in high school, getting as good a background as possible in English, mathematics, history, and government or social studies. Courses in the basic sciences are helpful.

There is great opportunity for members of minority groups in this profession. Colleges of pharmacy consider aptitude as important as high grades in accepting applicants.

JOB RELATIONSHIPS

The neighborhood Pharmacist works independently. He supervises only his own employees.

PROFESSIONAL AFFILIATIONS

American Pharmaceutical Association
2215 Constitution Avenue, N.W.
Washington, D.C. 20037

National Association of Boards of Pharmacy
77 West Washington Street
Chicago, Illinois 60602

American Society for Pharmacology and Experimental Therapeutics
9650 Rockville Pike
Bethesda, Maryland 20014

American Association of Colleges of Pharmacy
850 Sligo Avenue
Silver Spring, Maryland 20910

Pharmacist: (DOT) 074.181-010

PODIATRIST

Since three out of four persons have foot trouble, the Podiatrist, whose profession is foot care, fulfills an important role in the delivery of health services. As medical science has lengthened the life span, resulting in large numbers of elderly persons in the population, the need for his work has increased. Although most Podiatrists

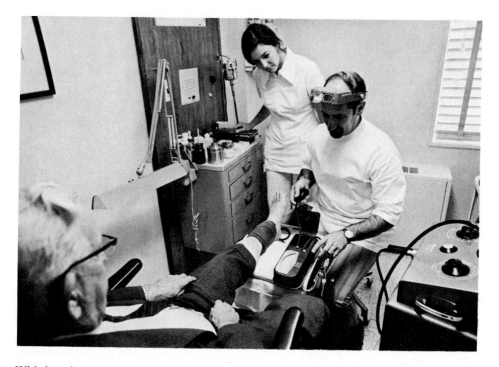

With lengthening life span and a large proportion of older people in the population, the incidence of foot disabilities has increased, and podiatry has become a valuable adjunct to the practice of medicine.

Photo courtesy of the American Podiatry Association

are in private practice, many of them also work in hospitals and nursing homes on a regular basis. Others are on the staffs of hospitals, in government health programs, in the Armed Forces, and on the faculties of colleges of podiatry. A few do research work.

The field is far from overcrowded, and is open to women, although only about six per cent of practicing podiatrists are women at present.

JOB DUTIES

The Podiatrist diagnoses and treats diseases and deformities of the feet, or tries to prevent their occurrence. The problems he encounters range from simple corns to foot difficulties that require special shoes or appliances.

Podiatrists consult and cooperate with other medical personnel, and are alert to symptoms of such diseases as diabetes or arteriosclerosis, which may first become evident in the feet and legs. If a patient with such symptoms is not already under medical care, the Podiatrist will urge him to seek such help. Conversely, physicians may refer patients with diseases that affect the feet to a Podiatrist for auxiliary care.

A knack for mechanical work and deft hands are helpful in the Podiatrist's work, since he uses electrical equipment and small tools, and must be able to make and adjust such devices as casts and braces.

EDUCATION, TRAINING, AND EXPERIENCE

The prospective Podiatrist must graduate from high school and complete at least two years of college work before he can be eligible for entrance into a college of podiatry. There are only five such colleges accredited by the American Podiatry Association in the United States. Students should write to the schools of their choice before starting preliminary college work, so that they can match their preprofessional courses to requirements. Scientific subjects are emphasized in college as well as in the four years of professional study. One- and two-year residencies are also available to students who want further training, or who must meet particular licensing requirements in certain states. State board examination is required for licensing in all states.

JOB RELATIONSHIPS

Except as Podiatrists join the staffs of institutions, they work independently.

PROFESSIONAL AFFILIATIONS

American Podiatry Association
20 Chevy Chase Circle
Washington, D.C. 20034

Podiatrist: (DOT) 079.108-030

PSYCHOLOGIST

Psychology is the science of human behavior, and holds an important place in the health field because it is concerned with mental health. Along with psychiatry, psychiatric nursing, and psychiatric social work, it contributes both to prevention of mental illness and to its diagnosis and treatment, even though it is a nonmedical science.

JOB DUTIES

The Psychologist looks first at the individual and his reactions to his environment in terms of his family, job, and other social circumstances.

If he is a *Clinical Psychologist,* he assists in diagnosis and treatment of patients with mental or emotional problems. He designs and conducts research, either alone or as part of an interdisciplinary team of scientists. He applies his knowledge of human behavior to the care and treatment of handicapped or disturbed persons. He helps persons who are social misfits to learn new and better patterns of behavior. He works directly with patients, and confers with other people who have contact with him either professionally or socially.

A *Counseling Psychologist* applies the same principles to help people "find themselves," so that they can deal with their own problems and take advantage of their fullest potentials through self-understanding. This kind of work strives to prevent mental illness. It is appropriate in industries, colleges, communities agencies, and in the rehabilitation of handicapped persons.

A *School Psychologist* is concerned primarily with psychological factors as they are involved in the learning process and the general well-being of school-age children. He diagnoses the needs of gifted, handicapped, and disturbed children, and plans and carries out corrective programs to help them succeed in their school work and adjust to everyday pressures. He observes the children, sometimes administering and evaluating various tests; studies school records; and confers with children, their families, teachers, physicians, and others who are associated with each child. He may serve as consultant to the school administration and to parent groups.

The *Social Psychologist* is concerned with the behavioral patterns of groups rather than individuals. He studies the way social attitudes develop, and how members of families and neighborhoods react to each other. An example of the way his work affects health might be found in a study of how people get their ideas about traffic accidents, and why they do (or don't) feel a sense of responsibility about highway safety.

Psychology is basically a research profession, and the *Research Psychologist* on the mental health research team contributes to increasing understanding of mental capacity and intelligence, and the effect of emotions on health. From this, improved methods for diagnosing and treating, or preventing, mental illness can be developed.

Psychologists who concentrate on development and administration of tests to measure peoples' mental, emotional, and social characteristics are called *Psychometrists*. The products of their labors are used in all forms of applied psychology.

EDUCATION, TRAINING, AND EXPERIENCE

Anyone planning a career in psychology should look toward obtaining a doctoral degree, and devoting at least one year to internship in a supervised clinical experience, to become a diplomate of the American Board of Examiners in Professional Psychology.

High school years are not too early to get a good start in mathematics, science, and foreign languages. Those planning to obtain a Doctor of Philosophy degree (Ph.D.) need not major in psychology in undergraduate college years, but it is advisable to take some work in that direction.

Financial help is available from government and other sources for students engaged in graduate study. Many graduate students in this field get part-time work as teachers or laboratory assistants that gives them useful experience.

Most psychologists are in salaried employment rather than private practice. They work in industries, institutions, the Armed Forces, public health agencies, and schools. About one-third of them are women. Demand for psychologists is high, and employment outlook stable.

Forty-two states, the District of Columbia, and four Canadian provinces require psychologists to be licensed or certified. Such legal recognition usually calls for a doctoral degree plus one or two years of qualifying experience. In addition, psychologists work under a professional code of ethics.

JOB RELATIONSHIPS

Depend on employment situation.

PROFESSIONAL AFFILIATIONS

American Psychological Association
1200 Seventeenth Street, N.W.
Washington, D.C. 20036

Clinical Psychologist: (DOT) 045.108-022

Counseling Psychologist: (DOT) 045.108-026

Psychometrist: (DOT) 045.088-030

Social Psychologist: (DOT) 045.088-026

School Psychologist: (DOT) 045.108-034

VETERINARIAN

Veterinary medicine has many applications, and many relationships to the practice of medicine in humans and human health care. Animals are subject to many ills, and are able to transmit diseases to humans, either directly, or—as in the case of cattle that have tuberculosis or brucellosis—through the meat and milk we consume. In the research laboratory, the study of disease in animals contributes enormously to the advancement of medical science.

The young Veterinarian can direct his career into any one of several channels. About 60 per cent of all veterinarians are engaged in private practice, caring for pets and farm animals. About 11 per cent are in the public health field, working for the Federal government, state or local agencies, or such international agencies as the United States Foreign Operations Administration, World Health Organization, or the Food and Agriculture Organization of the United Nations. Veterinary medicine is also important in the United States Armed Forces. A few veterinarians with special talents go into teaching in schools of veterinary medicine, public health, or medicine.

Veterinarians are employed in various kinds of research laboratories. In those associated with universities or medical centers, or in private foundations, or those related to the National Institutes of Health, they are not only responsible for the good health of the laboratory animals, but work as part of investigative teams with other scientists. In laboratories of commercial concerns who manufacture biologicals or pharmaceuticals for human or animal use, they may conduct their research independently, within any one of a number of basic science specialties.

JOB DUTIES

Private Practice: Most veterinarians handle all kinds of domestic animals, although the city Veterinarian usually concentrates on household pets, while the rural Veterinarian practices largely with cows, horses, swine, sheep, or poultry. A small number of veterinarians specialize in zoo or circus animals, or animals that are raised for their fur. Wherever they practice, they perform all the medical and surgical services needed by animals, including inoculations against diseases, treatment of illness or injury, deliveries of larger animals such as horses and cows; and they counsel on animal feeding and care. They are also likely to do some work for public health agencies in their communities.

The city Veterinarian usually has a fully equipped hospital for the pets he treats, which makes establishing such a practice very expensive for a beginner. Usually, young Veterinarians work for an older practitioner, as assistant or junior partner, for a number of years before they either take over the business or set up their own practice. In addition to strictly medical and surgical services, the city Veterinarian may offer boarding facilities, grooming and training services, and supervision of breeding of valuable animals.

The rural practitioner must also make a considerable financial outlay before he gets started. He must be able to invest several thousand dollars in drugs, instruments, and transportation equipment. In very large territories, a small private plane, and radio-telephone facilities between plane or car and office may be needed. Veterinarians with very large practices sometimes build animal hospitals or clinics, to which their patients can be brought for medical treatment or surgery.

The rural Veterinarian inoculates farm animals against the diseases to which they are prey. In addition, he has the responsibility for teaching farm families how to protect themselves, by sanitary procedures and proper handling of infected animals, against diseases the animals can transmit to people.

Rural Veterinarians frequently combine private practice with part-time work for Federal, state, or local government. This public service may be concerned with control or eradication of animal diseases, or it may involve the inspection of foods of animal origin, such as meat and poultry.

Public Health: Veterinarians in the United States Public Health Service develop programs for controlling animal diseases that affect public health, help the states establish similar programs, and act as consultants in other Public Health Service activities. Other functions of veterinary medicine in the Public Health Service are collection and evaluation of statistical data on human illnesses caused by animals, study of the effects of air pollution on animals, and basic research on chronic and communicable diseases.

The Agricultural Research Service of the United States Department of Agriculture uses a full-time staff of Veterinarians to inspect meat in packing plants, and to work throughout the country on control and eradication of animal diseases. Other Veterinarians in this department supervise stockyards, inspect poultry, and enforce the quarantine and other rules about importing and exporting animals and animal products. They also do research work, and supervise the licensing of companies that manufacture serums and vaccines for animals; and supervise the production of serums, antitoxins, and other biologicals used to prevent or treat diseases in humans.

The United States Food and Drug Administration also employs Veterinarians. At the county and city level, they often inspect food and dairy products, and assure that they are produced and sold in clean surroundings.

A new responsibility for Veterinarians is participation in radiological health programs in various health administrations. They are playing an important role in military and civil defense programs, by studying how to protect men and animals against atomic, biological, and chemical attacks.

Internationally, Veterinarians provide economic and technical aid in underdeveloped countries, most notably in helping them to improve their flocks and herds to build up food supplies, and in control and eradication of diseases in both animals and people.

The Veterinarian who looks toward a career in public health needs special education in addition to his veterinary medical degree. A year or two of veterinary practice, followed by postgraduate study in an accredited school of public health leading to a master's degree in public health is recommended.

The Armed Forces: Veterinarians in the United States Armed Forces have the responsibility of giving medical care to military animals, such as guard dogs. However, they are often assigned as part of a medical team to work on newly recognized diseases of animals and man. As a member of the medical department, the Veterinarian cooperates with physicians, dentists, nurses, and other health personnel on problems that affect the health of the Armed Forces, in training and in the field, at home and abroad. As food inspectors, Veterinarians were largely responsible for the low incidence of food poisoning and food-borne diseases among troops during World Wars I and II, and during the Korean and Vietnam conflicts. By rejecting substandard food products, and developing more effective ways of producing, preparing, preserving, and serving foods, they made a valuable contribution.

Veterinarians in the Armed Forces, like those in civil defense, are involved in research to protect the public as well as our troops against atomic, biological and chemical attacks or accidents.

Research Laboratories: Within the scope of individual research laboratories, their organization, structure, and purpose, Veterinarians are responsible for laboratory animal care. However, there are also many basic science specialties available to them: anatomy, bacteriology, epidemiology, parasitology, pathology, pharmacology, physiology, and virology.

The specific job duties of Veterinarians in any of these specialties correspond to those described for Chiefs and Technologists in each of these scientific branches.

EDUCATION, TRAINING, AND EXPERIENCE

High school graduation, plus two years at a liberal arts or agricultural college are the minimum prerequisites for entrance to an approved college of veterinary medicine. Four years of college and a bachelor's degree are recommended. Latin, which helps in understanding medical terminology, and courses in organic and inorganic chemistry, biochemistry, zoology, botany, physics, English composition, and speech are recommended undergraduate courses.

In 1971, there were 18 approved veterinary schools in the United States and three in Canada, which offer four-year courses leading to Doctor of Veterinary Medicine (D.V.M.). With the exception of the one at the University of Pennsylvania, all the colleges in the United States are located at state-supported institutions. States that do not have veterinary schools of their own cooperate with schools in other states. Women students are admitted to all of these schools. Prospective students should inquire about entrance requirements from the school of their choice soon after they begin their first year of undergraduate work, since prerequisites vary from school to school, and time must be allowed to accomplish them before applying for admission.

An additional two years of postdoctoral study in an accredited school of public health, leading to a master's degree in public health, are required for most jobs in that field. Additional courses beyond the basic veterinary medical school curriculum may be required for specialization in laboratory research.

After graduation from a college of veterinary medicine, the student must pass the examination given by the Board of Veterinary Medical Examiners in the state in which he wishes to practice, and must be licensed in that state. Licenses granted in one state are not necessarily valid in others.

JOB RELATIONSHIPS

Workers supervised: Depends upon job situation.
Supervised by: Depends upon job situation.
Promotion from: Usually no formal line of promotion.
Promotion to: Usually no formal line of promotion.

PROFESSIONAL AFFILIATIONS

American Veterinary Medical Association
600 South Michigan Avenue
Chicago, Illinois 60605

Veterinarian: (DOT) 073.108-014

Veterinarian, Laboratory Animal Care: (DOT) 073.081-010

Veterinarian, Public Health: (DOT) 073.108-018

Veterinary Anatomist: (DOT) 073.081-014

Veterinary Bacteriologist: (DOT) 073.081-018

Veterinary Epidemiologist: (DOT) 073.081-022

Veterinary Livestock Inspector: (DOT) 073.181-010

Veterinary Meat Inspector: (DOT) 168.284-014

Veterinary Parasitologist: (DOT) 073.081-026

Veterinary Pathologist: (DOT) 073.081-030

Veterinary Pharmacologist: (DOT) 073.081-034

Veterinary Physiologist: (DOT) 073.081-038

Veterinary Virologist: (DOT) 073.081-042

Veterinary Virus-Serum Inspector: (DOT) 073.281-010

12

HEALTH CAREERS IN THE ARMED SERVICES

Medical and health career opportunities in the United States Armed Services fall into two categories: (1) Training programs, in which the professional education of the enlisted man or woman is subsidized, with the promise of a specified length of service on active duty on completion of the course; and (2) Direct appointments of qualified persons, still with an active duty obligation for persons who have not had previous military service.

The Army, Navy, and Air Force all have programs in both categories. Full information may be obtained from the following sources:

Army: The Surgeon General
                Attention: DASG—PTP
            Washington, D.C. 20314

Navy: Chief, Bureau of Medicine and Surgery
            Navy Department
            Washington, D.C. 20390

Air Force: Air Force Military Personnel Center
                Attention: SGS
            Randolph Air Force Base, TX 78148

All opportunities are open equally to men and women.

All services have minimum and maximum ages at which they will accept applications. However, in the student training programs these are well suited to young adults in college and postgraduate years. In the appointments programs, applicants' qualifications must meet the requirements of the rank commensurate with their age.

Student Programs

Professional careers for which the Army, Navy, and Air Force offer scholarships and/or training include:

- Medicine
- Osteopathy
- Dentistry
- Veterinary Medicine
- Psychology
- Occupational Therapy

- Nursing
- Sanitary Engineering
- Social Work
- Optometry
- Dietetics
- Physical Therapy

Military rank is conferred on each student, with reserve status while he or she is attending school, or active status if the student is serving an intership in a military institution or installation.

Direct Appointments

Appointments are available for personnel in the following professions:

- Medicine
- Osteopathy
- Dentistry
- Veterinary Medicine
- Occupational Therapy
- Pharmacy
- Biochemistry
- Bacteriology
- Health Physics
- Podiatry
- Parasitology
- Audiology
- Public Health Nutrition
- Hospital Administration

- Nursing
- Sanitary Engineering
- Optometry
- Dietetics
- Physical Therapy
- Virology
- Social Work
- Entomology
- Clinical Psychology
- Aerospace Physiology
- Bioenvironmental Engineering
- Speech Therapy
- Public Health Administration
- Health Care Administration

Commissions granted in the various Reserves and National Guards do not entail active duty except in a war or national emergency.

In many careers, such as Nursing, there is opportunity for advancement within the services through further education.

APPENDIX A

INFORMATION GUIDE

The following listing of health professions organizations, compiled by the National Health Council, Inc., constitutes an authentic and unified source of career information.

LIST OF CAREER FIELDS

Basic Sciences and Engineering

American Institute of Physics
American Physiological Society
American Society of Biological
  Chemists, Inc.
American Society of Microbiology
Society of Nuclear Medicine
U.S. Atomic Energy Commission—
  Division of Technical Information

Clinical Laboratory and Related Technical Services

Biomedical Engineer
Biomedical Equipment Technician
  Biomedical Engineering and
    Instrumentation—Branch, NIH
  Biomedical Engineering Society
  Engineers Joint Council
Blood Bank Technologist
  American Association of Blood Banks
  American National Red Cross
  National Hemophilia Foundation
Cytotechnologist
  American Cancer Society
  American Society of Clinical Pathologists
  American Society of Medical
    Technologists
  American Medical Technologists
Electrocardiograph (EKG or ECG)
Technician
  American Hospital Association

Electroencephalograph (EEG) Technician
  American Society of Electroencephalo-
    graphic Technologists
Histologic Technician
  American Society of Clinical Pathologists
  American Society of Medical
    Technologists
  American Medical Technologists
Laboratory Assistant
Medical Technologist and Technician
  American Medical Technologists
  American Society of Clinical Pathologists
  American Society of Medical
    Technologists
  National Committee for Careers in
    the Medical Laboratory
Nuclear Medical Technologist and
Technician
  American Society of Clinical Pathologists
  American Society of Medical
    Technologists
  American Society of Radiologic
    Technologists
  Society of Nuclear Medical
    Technologists
Radiologic (X-Ray) Technologist
and Technician
Radiation Therapy Technologist
  American Society of Radiologic
    Technologists

Additional Resources
Association of Schools of Allied
Health Professions
American Medical Association
U.S. Atomic Energy Commission

Dental Services

Dentist
American Association of Dental Schools
American Dental Association
Dental Assistant
American Dental Assistants' Association
Dental Hygienist
American Dental Hygienists' Association
Dental Lab Technician
National Association of Certified
Dental Labs
Additional Resources
Veterans Administration

Dietetics and Nutrition

Dietetian
Dietary Assistant
Dietary Aide
American Dietetic Association
Nutritionists
American Home Economics Association
Additional Resources
Food and Drug Administration
Institute of Food Technologists

Environmental Health

Air Pollution
Industrial Hygienist
American Industrial Hygiene Association
Sanitarians
International Association of Milk, Food
and Environmental Sanitarians, Inc.
National Environmental Health Association
Safety Engineer
American Society of Safety Engineers
Systems Safety Analyst
National Safety Council
Additional Resources
American Public Health Association
National Tuberculosis and Respiratory
Disease Foundation
Planned Parenthood—World Population

Health and Medical Research

American Diabetes Association
American Heart Association
American Lung Association
Arthritis Foundation
National Association for Mental Health
National Cystic Fibrosis Research
Foundation

National Easter Seal Society for Crippled
Children and Adults
National Hemophilia Foundation
National Kidney Foundation
National Multiple Sclerosis
National Society for the Prevention
of Blindness
United Cerebral Palsy

Home Care

Home Health Aide
Homemaker
National Council for Homemaker—
Home Health Aide
Additional Resources
National Council on the Aging
Hospital Administration, Business
and Clerical Specialties
Accountant
American Association of Hospital
Accountants
Hospital Financial Management
Association
Administrator
American College of Hospital
Administrators
American Hospital Association
American Nursing Home Association
Association of University Programs
in Hospital Administration
Business Office Manager
Controller
Hospital Financial Management
Association
National Executive Housekeepers
Association, Inc.
Medical Assistant
Medical Secretary
American Association of Medical
Assistants
American Medical Technologists

Information and Communications
American Journal of Art Therapy
Association of Medical Illustrators
Biological Photographic Association, Inc.
Blue Cross Association
Council for the Advancement of
Science Writing
National Association for Music
Therapy, Inc.
Society for Public Health Education
Society of Technical Communications

Library

Medical Science Librarian
American Library Association
Medical Library Association
Medical Record Administrator

Medical Records
Medical Records Technicians
American Medical Record Association

Medicine

Family Physician
American Academy of Family Physicians
Association of American Medical Colleges
American Medical Association
American Medical Women's Association
National Medical Association
Osteopathic Physician
American Osteopathic Association
Pathologist
Inter Society Committee on Pathology
Information
Pediatrician
American Academy of Pediatrics
Physiatrist (Physical Medicine)
American Academy of Physical
Medicine and Rehabilitation
Podiatrist
American Podiatry Association
Veterinarian
American Veterinary Medical Association

Mental Health

Psychiatric Aide
National Association for Mental Health
Psychiatrist
American Psychiatric Association
Psychologist
American Psychological Association

Nursing Services

Nurses Aide
Orderly
Ward Clerk
American Hospital Association
Nurse Anesthetists
American Association of Nurse
Anesthetists
Industrial Nurses
American Association of Industrial Nurses
Nurse Midwives
American College of Nurse Midwives
Maternity Center Association
Practical Nurse
National Association for Practical
Nurse Education
National Federation of Licensed
Practical Nurses
Registered Nurse
American Nurses' Association
Nursing Educational Programs
ANA—NLN Committee on Nursing
Careers

Pharmacy

Pharmacy Clerk
American Association of Colleges
of Pharmacy
Registered Pharmacist
American Pharmaceutical Association
Additional Resources
American Society for Pharmacology and
Experimental Therapeutics, Inc.

Physician's Assistant

Physician's Assistant
American Association of
Physician's Assistant
American Medical Association

Public Health

Public Health Services
American Association for Health, Physical
Education, and Recreation
Educators
Society for Public Health Education
Additional Resources
American Public Health Association

Rehabilitation

Music Therapist
National Association for Music
Therapy, Inc.
Occupational Therapy Assistant
Occupational Therapist
American Occupational Therapy
Association
Orthotists and Prosthetics
American Orthotic and Prosthetic
Association
Physical Therapy Aide
Physical Therapy Assistant
Physical Therapist
American Physical Therapy Association
Recreational Therapist
National Association of Recreational
Therapists, Inc.
National Recreation and Parks Association
Additional Resources
American Association for Rehabilitation
Therapy, Inc.
American Corrective Therapy
Association, Inc.
American Rehabilitation Counseling
Association
Association of Medical Rehabilitation
Directors and Coordinators
Goodwill Industries of America, Inc.
National Association for Retarded
Children

National Easter Seal Society for Crippled
Children and Adults
National Rehabilitation Counseling
Association
Registry of Medical Rehabilitation
Therapists and Specialists
United Cerebral Palsy Association
Veterans Administration

Respiratory Therapist

American Association for Respiratory
Therapy
American Medical Association

Social Services

Psychiatric Social Worker
Social Work Aide
Social Work Assistant
American Social Health Association
National Association of Social Workers
National Commission for Social
Work Careers

Additional Resources
American National Red Cross

Speech and Hearing

Audiologist
Speech Pathologist
Teachers of the Deaf
American Speech and Hearing Association
National Association of Hearing
and Speech Agencies

Vision Care

Ophthalmologists
American Association of Ophthalmology
Optician
Guild of Prescription Opticians
Optometrist
Optometrist Assistant Technician
American Optometric Association
Orthoptist
American Orthoptic Council
Additional Resources
National Society for the Prevention
of Blindness

REFERRAL LIST OF SOURCE AGENCIES

**American Academy of
Family Physicians**
Volker Boulevard at
Brookside
Kansas City, Missouri
64112

**American Academy of
Pediatrics**
1801 Hinman Avenue
Evanston, Illinois 60204

**American Academy of
Physical Medicine and
Rehabilitation**
30 North Michigan Avenue
Chicago, Illinois 60602

**American Academy of
Physicians' Associates**
Duke University Medical
Center, Box 2914 CHS
Durham, N.C. 27706

**American Association for
Health, Physical Education,
and Recreation**
1201 Sixteenth St., N.W.
Washington, D.C. 20036

**American Association for
Respiratory Therapy**
7411 Hines Place
Dallas, Texas 75235

**American Association of
Blood Banks**
Suite 1322,
30 North Michigan
Chicago, Illinois 60602

**American Association of
Dental Schools**
211 East Chicago Avenue
Chicago, Illinois 60611

**American Association of
Hospital Accountants**
840 North Lake Shore Dr.
Chicago, Illinois 60601

**American Association of
Industrial Nurses, Inc.**
79 Madison Avenue
New York, New York
10016

**American Association of
Medical Assistants**
One East Wacker Drive
Chicago, Illinois 6061

**American Association of
Nurse Anesthetists**
111 East Wacker Drive
Suite 929
Chicago, Illinois 60601

**American Association of
Ophthalmology**
1100 17th Street, N.W.
Washington, D.C. 20036

American Cancer Society
219 East 42nd Street
New York, New York
10017

**American College of
Hospital Administrators**
840 North Lake Shore Dr.
Chicago, Illinois 60611

**American College of
Nurse-Midwives**
50 East 92nd Street
New York, New York
10028

**American Congress of
Rehabilitation Medicine**
30 North Michigan Avenue
Chicago, Illinois 60201

**American Corrective
Therapy Association**
Public Relations Officer
1781 Begen Avenue
Moutain View, Calif. 94040

**American Dental Assistants
Association**
211 East Chicago Avenue
Chicago, Illinois 60611

American Dental Association
211 East Chicago Avenue
Chicago, Illinois 60611

American Dental Hygienists Association
211 East Chicago Avenue
Chicago, Illinois 60611

American Diabetes Association
18 East 48th Street
New York, New York 10017

American Dietetic Association
620 North Michigan Avenue
Chicago, Illinois 60611

American Heart Association
44 East 23rd Street
New York, New York 10010

American Home Economic Association
2010 Massachusetts Ave. N.W.
Washington, D.C. 20036

American Hospital Association
840 North Lake Shore Dr.
Chicago, Illinois 60611

American Industrial Hygiene Association
25711 Southfield Road
Southfield, Michigan 48075

American Institute of Physics
335 East 45th Street
New York, New York 10017

American Journal of Art Therapy
Box 4918
Washington, D.C. 20008

American Library Association
50 East Huron Street
Chicago, Illinois 60611

American Lung Association
1740 Broadway
New York, New York 10019

American Medical Association
535 North Dearborn Street
Chicago, Illinois 60610

American Medical Record Association
Suite 1850,
875 North Michigan Avenue
Chicago, Illinois 60611

American Medical Technologists
710 Higgins Road
Park Ridge, Illinois 60068

American Medical Women's Association, Inc.
1740 Broadway
New York, New York 10019

American National Red Cross
17th and D Streets, N.W.
Washington, D.C. 20006

American Nurses' Association
10 Columbus Circle
New York, New York 10019

ANA-NLN Committee on Nursing Careers
10 Columbus Circle
New York, New York 10019

American Nursing Home Association
1025 Connecticut Avenue N.W.
Washington, D.C. 20036

American Occupational Therapy Association
251 Park Avenue South
New York, New York 10010

American Optometric Association
7000 Chippewa Street
St. Louis, Missouri 63119

American Orthoptic Council
3400 Massachusetts Ave.
Washington, D.C. 20007

American Orthotic and Prosthetic Association
1440 N Street, N.W.
Washington, D.C. 20005

American Osteopathic Association
212 East Ohio Street
Chicago, Illinois 60611

American Association of Colleges of Pharmacy
850 Sligo Avenue
Silver Spring, Md. 20910

American Pharmaceutical Association
2215 Constitution Ave., N.W.
Washington, D.C. 20037

American Physical Therapy Association
1156-15th Street, N.W.
Washington, D.C. 20005

American Physiological Society
9650 Rockville Pike
Bethesda, Maryland 20014

American Podiatry Association
20 Chevy Chase Circle, N.W.
Washington, D.C. 20015

American Psychiatric Association
1700-18th Street, N.W.
Washington, D.C. 20009

American Psychological Association
1200-17th Street, N.W.
Washington, D.C. 20036

American Public Health Association
1015-18th Street, N.W.
Washington, D.C. 20036

American Rehabilitation Counseling Association
1605 New Hampshire Ave.
Washington, D.C. 20036

American Speech and Hearing Association
9030 Old Georgetown Road
Washington, D.C. 20014

American Social Health Association
1740 Broadway
New York, New York 10019

American Society for Pharmacology and Experimental Therapeutics, Inc.
9650 Rockville Pike
Bethesda, Maryland 20014

American Society of Electroencephalographic Technologists
University of Iowa
Division of EEG &
Neurophysiology
500 Newton Road
Iowa City, Iowa 52240

American Society of Biological Chemists
9650 Rockville Pike
Bethesda, Maryland 20014

American Society of Clinical Pathologists
2100 West Harrison Street
Chicago, Illinois 60612

American Society of Medical Technologists
Suite 1600,
Hermann Professional Bldg.
Houston, Texas 77025

American Society of Microbiology
1913 Eye Street, N.W.
Washington, D.C. 20006

American Society of Radiologic Technologists
645 North Michigan Ave.
Suite 620
Chicago, Illinois 60611

American Society of Safety Engineers
850 Busse Highway
Park Ridge, Illinois 60068

American Veterinary Medical Association
600 South Michigan Ave.
Chicago, Illinois 60605

Arthritis Foundation
1212 Ave. of the Americas
New York, New York
10036

Association of American Medical Colleges
One Dupont Circle, N.W.
Washington, D.C. 20036

Association of Medical Illustrators
Medical College of Georgia
Augusta, Georgia 30902

Association of Medical Rehabilitation Directors and Coordinators
Franklin Delano Roosevelt
V.A. Hospital
Montrose, New York 10548

Association of Schools of Allied Health Professions
One Dupont Circle,
Suite 300,
Washington, D.C. 20036

Association of University Programs in Hospital Administration
One Dupont Circle,
Suite 420,
Washington, D.C. 20036

Biological Photographic Association
P.O. Box 12866
Philadelphia, Pa. 19108

Biomedical Engineering and Instrumentation
Division of Research
Services, National
Institutes of Health
9000 Wisconsin Avenue
Bethesda, Maryland 20014

Biomedical Engineering Society
P.O. Box 1600
Evanston, Illinois 60204

Blue Cross Association
840 North Lake Shore Dr.
Chicago, Illinois 60611

Council for the Advancement of Science Writing, Inc.
201 Christie Street
Leonia, New Jersey 07605

Engineers Joint Council
345 East 47th Street
New York, New York
10017

Goodwill Industries of America, Inc.
9200 Wisconsin Avenue
Washington, D.C. 20014

Guild of Prescription Opticians of America, Inc.
1250 Connecticut Avenue
N.W.
Washington, D.C. 20036

Hospital Financial Management Association
840 North Lake Shore Dr.
Chicago, Illinois 60611

Institute of Food Technologists
221 North La Salle Street
Suite 2120,
Chicago, Illinois 60601

International Association of Milk, Food and Environmental Sanitarians, Inc.
P.O. Box 437
Shelbyville, Indiana 46176

Intersociety Committee on Pathology Information
9650 Rockville Pike
Bethesda, Maryland 20014

Maternity Center Association
48 East 92nd Street
New York, New York
10028

Medical Library Association, Inc.
919 North Michigan
Avenue, Suite 2023,
Chicago, Illinois 60611

National Association for Mental Health
1800 North Kent Street
Rosslyn, Virginia 22209

National Association for Music Therapy, Inc.
P.O. Box 610
Lawrence, Kansas 66044

National Association for Practical Nurse Education and Services
1465 Broadway
New York, New York
10036

National Association for Retarded Children
2709 Avenue E East
Arlington, Texas 76011

National Association of
Certified Dental
Laboratories
3801 Mount Vernon
Avenue
Alexandria, Virginia 22305

National Association of
Hearing and Speech
Agencies
919-18th Street, N.W.
Washington, D.C. 20006

National Association of
Social Workers
Two Park Avenue
New York, New York
10016

National Committee for
Careers in the Medical
Laboratory
9650 Rockville Pike
Bethesda, Maryland 20014

National Commission for
Social Work Careers
Two Park Avenue
New York, New York
10016

National Council for
Homemaker-Home Health
Aide Services, Inc.
1740 Broadway
New York, New York
10019

National Council on the
Aging
1828 L Street, N.W.
Washington, D.C. 20036

National Cystic Fibrosis
Research Foundation
3379 Peachtree Road
Atlanta, Georgia 30326

National East Seal
Society for Crippled
Children and Adults
2023 West Ogen Avenue
Chicago, Illinois 60612

National Environmental
Health Association
1600 Pennsylvania Avenue
Denver, Colorado 80203

National Executive
Housekeepers Association,
Inc.
Business and Professional
Building
Gallipolis, Ohio 45631

National Federation of
Licensed Practical Nurses,
Inc.
250 West 57th Street
New York, New York
10019

National Hemophilia
Foundation
25 West 39th Street
New York, New York
10018

National Kidney
Foundation
116 East 27th Street
New York, New York
10016

National Medical
Association
1717 Massachusetts Ave.
N.W. #602
Washington, D.C. 20036

National Multiple
Sclerosis Society
257 Park Avenue South
New York, New York
10010

National Recreation and
Park Association
1700 Pennsylvania Avenue
N.W.
Washington, D.C. 20006

National Rehabilitation
Counseling Association
1522 K Street, N.W.
Washington, D.C. 20005

National Safety Council
425 North Michigan
Avenue
Chicago, Illinois 60611

National Society for the
Prevention of Blindness
Inc.
79 Madison Avenue
New York, New York
10016

Planned Parenthood-
World Population
810 Seventh Avenue
New York, New York
10019

Registry of Medical
Rehabilitation Therapists
& Specialists
4975 Judy Lynn
Memphis, Tennessee 38118

Registry of Medical
Technologists
P.O. Box 4872
Chicago, Illinois 60680

Society for Public Health
Education
655 Sutter Street
San Francisco, Calif. 94102

Society of Nuclear
Medicine
211 East 43rd Street
New York, New York
10017

Society of Nuclear
Medical Technologists
1201 Waukegan Road
Glenview, Illinois 60025

Society of Technical
Writing & Publishers
1010 Vermont Ave., N.W.
Washington, D.C. 20005

United Cerebral Palsy
Association
66 East 34th Street
New York, New York
10016

ADDITIONAL RESOURCES

U.S. Army
The Surgeon General
AT.: DASG-PTP
Washington, D.C. 20314

**U.S. Atomic Energy
Commission**
Division of Technical
Information Extensions
P.O. Box 62
Oak Ridge, Tenn. 37830

U.S. Navy
Chief, Bureau of Medicine
and Surgery
Navy Department
Washington, D.C. 20390

U.S. Air Force
Air Force Military
Personnel Center
AT.: SGS

**Food and Drug
Administration**
Parklawn Personnel Office
Parklawn Building
5600 Fishers Lane
Rockville, Maryland 20852

MEDIHC Program
National Institutes of
Health
Manpower Education
9000 Rockville Pike
Bethesda, Maryland 20014

**National Institutes of
Health Bureau of Health
Manpower Education
Information Office**
9000 Rockville Pike
Bethesda, Maryland 20014

Public Inquiries
Health Services and Mental
Health Administration

Public Health Service
Room 5-B-29
5600 Fishers Lane
Rockville, Maryland 20852

Public Health Service
Office of Public Inquiries
Bethesda, Maryland 20034

U.S. Employment Service
Department of Labor
Washington, D.C. 20210

U.S. Office of Education
Division of Vocational and
Technical Education,
Health Occupations
Washington, D.C. 20202

**Veterans Administration
(054)**
810 Vermont Ave., N.W.
Washington, D.C. 20420

APPENDIX B: STATE
AND LOCAL HEALTH CAREERS PROGRAMS

Alabama

Director
Health Careers Council of Alabama
901 South 18 Street
Birmingham, Alabama 35205

Alaska

Executive Director
Alaska State Hospital Association
1135 West 8th Street, Suite 3
Anchorage, Alaska 99501

Arizona

Assistant Executive Director
Arizona Hospital Association
635 West Indian School Road
Phoenix, Arizona 85013

Arkansas

Director
Health Careers Program
Arkansas Hospital Association
P.O. Box 2181
Little Rock, Arkansas 72203

California

Executive Director
Health Manpower Council of
  California
One Camino Sobrante
Orinda, California 94563

Project Director
Health Careers Program
National Medical Association Foundation
1635 East 103 Street
Los Angeles, California 90002

Director
Health Professions Council of
  San Francisco
1487 Fourth Avenue
San Francisco, California 94122

Assistant Executive Director
Hospital Council of Southern California
4777 Sunset Boulevard
Los Angeles, California 90027

Canada

Hospital Careers Consultant
Ontario Hospital Association
24 Ferrand Drive
Don Mills, 402, Ontario

Coordinator of Information Services
Manitoba Hospital Association
377 Colony Street
Winnipeg, 2, Manitoba

Director
Education Service
L'Association Des Hospitaux de la
  Province de Quebec
505 oest, boul Dorchester 1202
Montreal, 128, Quebec

Director
Alberta Hospital Association
2108 A Street, N.W.
Calgary, 61, Alberta

Colorado

Associate Director
Colorado Hospital Association
3150 East Third Avenue
Denver, Colorado 80206

Executive Director
Colorado Health Careers Council, Inc.
1809 East 18 Avenue
Denver, Colorado 80218

Connecticut

Executive Vice President
Connecticut Hospital Association
P.O. Box 1966
New Haven, Connecticut 06509

Delaware

Director of Health Manpower
Association of Delaware Hospitals, Inc.
1401 Pennsylvania Avenue
Wilmington, Delaware 19806

District of Columbia

Project Director
Health Careers Program
National Medical Association
    Foundation
1013 12th Street, N.W.
Washington, D.C. 20005

Assistant Executive Director
Hospital Council of the National
    Capital Area
1812 K Street, N.W.
Washington, D.C. 20006

Florida

Coordinator
Hospital-Health Careers
South Florida Hospital Association
Two Coral Way
Miami, Florida 33131

Public Relations Director
Florida Hospital Association
P.O. Box 6905
Orlando, Florida 32803

Executive Director
Florida Health Manpower Council
One Davis Boulevard
Davis Island
Tampa, Florida 33606

Georgia

Director
Georgia State Scholarship Commission
100 Mitchell Street, S.W.
Atlanta, Georgia 30303

Executive Secretary
Health Careers Council of Georgia, Inc.
P.O. Box 151
St. Joseph's Infirmary
Atlanta, Georgia 30303

Hawaii

Executive Director
Hospital Association of Hawaii
200 North Vineyard Boulevard,
    Suite 507
Honolulu, Hawaii 96817

Idaho

Executive Director
Idaho Hospital Association
P.O. Box 7482
Boise, Idaho 83707

Illinois

Executive Director
Health Careers Council of Illinois
410 North Michigan Avenue
Chicago, Illinois 60611

Indiana

Executive Director
Indiana Health Careers, Inc.
2905 North Meridian
Indianapolis, Indiana 46208

Iowa

Director
Health Manpower and Public Affairs
Iowa Hospital Association
1906 Ingersoll Avenue
Des Moines, Iowa 50309

Kansas

Director of Education
Kansas Hospital Association
P.O. Box 417
Topeka, Kansas 66601

Kentucky

Program Coordinator
Health Careers in Kentucky
1415 Saint Anthony Place
Louisville, Kentucky 40204

Louisiana

Director
Health Careers Development Program
Louisiana Hospital Association
P.O. Box 53352
New Orleans, Louisiana 70150

Maine

Executive Director
Health Council of Maine
133 State Street
Augusta, Maine 04330

Maryland

Executive Director
Maryland Hospital Education and
  Research Foundation
1301 York Road
Lutherville, Maryland 21093

Massachusetts

Executive Director
Massachusetts Health Careers Council
c/o Massachusetts Heart Association
  Inc.
85 Devonshire Street
Boston, Massachusetts 02109

Manager, Personnel Services
Massachusetts Hospital Association
5 New England Executive Park
Burlington, Massachusetts 01803

Michigan

Associate Director
Michigan Hospital Association
2213 East Grand River Avenue
Lansing, Michigan 48912

Executive Vice President
Michigan Health Council
P.O. Box 1010
East Lansing, Michigan 48823

Coordinator
Health Careers Council of
  Calhoun County
252 Beckwith Drive
Battle Creek, Michigan 49015

Director
Health Manpower Council of
  Southeast Michigan
United Community Services of
  Metropolitan Detroit
51 West Warren Avenue
Detroit, Michigan 48201

Minnesota

Director
Manpower, Training and Education
Twin City Hospital Association
2329 University Avenue, S.E.
Minneapolis, Minnesota 55414

Project Director
Minnesota Health Careers Council
2333 University Avenue, S.E.
Minneapolis, Minnesota 55414

Mississippi

Planning Assistant
Health Manpower Recruitment Program
Mississippi Hospital Association
4880 McWillie Circle
Jackson, Mississippi 39206

Missouri

Project Director
Missouri Health Careers Program
P.O. Box 1044
Jefferson City, Missouri 65101

Director
Missouri Health Careers Program
c/o Washington University Medical
  School and Associated Hospitals
660 South Euclid Avenue
St. Louis, Missouri 63110

Montana

Executive Director
Montana Hospital Association
P.O. Box 543
Helena, Montana 50601

Nebraska

Chairman, Health Careers
Nebraska Inter-Agency Health
 Planning
c/o Nebraska State Medical Association
1902 First National Bank Building
Lincoln, Nebraska 68508

Nevada

Director
Health Careers Program
Nevada Hospital Association
3660 Baker Lane
Reno, Nevada 89502

New Hampshire

Executive Director
New Hampshire Health Careers
 Council
61 South Spring Street
Concord, New Hampshire 03301

New Jersey

Executive Director
New Jersey Health Careers
 Service, Inc.
375 West State Street
Trenton, New Jersey 08618

Director
Education and Recruitment
New Jersey Hospital Association
1101 State Road
Princeton, New Jersey 08540

New Mexico

Executive Director
New Mexico Hospital Association
3010 Monte Vista Boulevard, N.E.
Albuquerque, New Mexico 87106

New York

Director
Office of Special Health Manpower
 Program
New York State Health Department
84 Holland Avenue
Albany, New York 12208

Staff Associate
Hospital Association of New York
 State
15 Computer Drive
Albany, New York 12205

Senior Recruitment Representative
Rochester Regional Office
New York State Department of Health
119 Main East
Rochester, New York 14604

Personnel Associate
Western New York Hospital
 Association
2005 Sheridan Drive
Buffalo, New York 14223

Staff Associate
Health Manpower Services
United Hospital Fund of New York
3 East 54th Street
New York, New York 10022

North Carolina

Health Careers Coordinator
Regional Health Council of
 Eastern Appalachia
210 Green Street
Morgantown, North Carolina 28655

Assistant Director
Health Careers Program
North Carolina Hospital Association
P.O. Box 10937
Raleigh, North Carolina 27605

Coordinator
Health Careers for Piedmont Carolina
1323 Kingscross Drive
Charlotte, North Carolina 28211

North Dakota

President
North Dakota Council on Health
 Careers
North Dakota School of Pharmacy
Fargo, North Dakota 58102

Ohio

Director
Health Careers of Ohio
P.O. Box 5574
Columbus, Ohio 43221

Executive Director
Health Careers Association of
    Greater Cincinnati
2400 Reading Road
Cincinnati, Ohio 45202

Director of Health Manpower
Mid-Ohio Health Planning Federation
P.O. Box 2239
Columbus, Ohio 43216

Director
Health Manpower
Health Planning Association of
    Northwest Ohio
225 Allen
Maumee, Ohio 43537

Health Careers Coordinator
The Greater Cleveland Hospital
    Association
1001 Huron Road
Cleveland, Ohio 44115

Coordinator
Tri-County Health Careers Committee
P.O. Box 689
Canton, Ohio 44701

Oklahoma

Executive Director
Oklahoma Council for Health Careers
N.E. 15th Street
Oklahoma City, Oklahoma 73104

Pennsylvania

Executive Director
Pennsylvania Health Council, Inc.
933 Kranzel Drive
Camp Hill, Pennsylvania 17011

Director
Health Careers Program
United Health Services
225 South 15th Street
Philadelphia, Pennsylvania 19102

Director
Health Manpower Program
Hospital Council of Western
    Pennsylvania
Chatham Center
Pittsburgh, Pennsylvania 15219

Assistant Director
Hospital Association of Pennsylvania
P.O. Box 608
Camp Hill, Pennsylvania 17011

Puerto Rico

Director
Puerto Rico Hospital Association
Doctors Medical Center
800 Hippodrome Avenue
Santurce, Puerto Rico 00909

Rhode Island

Assistant Executive Director
Hospital Association of Rhode Island
121 Dyer Street
Providence, Rhode Island 02903

South Carolina

Chairman
South Carolina Health Manpower
    Council
P.O. Box 75
Columbia, South Carolina 29204

Health Careers Consultant
South Carolina Appalachian
    Region Health Policy and
    Planning Council
P.O. Box 6708, Station B
Greenville, South Carolina 29606

South Dakota

Coordinator
Health Manpower Development
    Program
State Department of Health
Office Building No. 2
Pierre, South Dakota 57501

Chairman
Health Careers Committee
South Dakota Hospital Association
222 East Capitol
Pierre, South Dakota 57501

Tennessee

Director
Tennessee Health Careers Programs
210 Reidhurst Avenue
Nashville, Tennessee 37203

Texas

Director
Texas Health Careers Program
Texas Hospital Association
P.O. Box 4553
Austin, Texas 78765

Utah

Utah State Medical Association
42 South Fifth East
Salt Lake City, Utah 84102

Executive Director
Utah State Hospital Association
455 East Fourth Street #10
Salt Lake City, Utah 84111

Vermont

Executive Director
Health Careers Council of Vermont
5 Maple Street
Randolph, Vermont 05060

Virginia

Director
Virginia Health Careers
Virginia Council on Health and
    Medical Careers
1100 East Franklin Street
Richmond, Virginia 23219

Washington

Program Specialist
Coordinating Council for Health
    Occupational Education
P.O. Box 248
Olympia, Washington 98504

Administrator
Health Manpower Project
Smith Tower
Seattle, Washington 98104

West Virginia

Assistant Director
West Virginia Hospital Association
1219 Virginia Street, East
Charleston, West Virginia 25301

Wisconsin

Health Manpower Coordinator
Hospital Council of Greater
    Milwaukee Area
9800 West Bluemound Road
Milwaukee, Wisconsin 53226

Coordinator
Wisconsin Careers Program
P.O. Box 4387
Madison, Wisconsin 52711

Wyoming

Executive Director
Wyoming Hospital Association
P.O. Box 2594
Cheyenne, Wyoming 82201

APPENDIX C: RECOMMENDED
FILMS ON HEALTH CAREERS

The following list of 16 mm. color films, and filmstrips depicting careers in health care was compiled by the American Hospital Association. Other films and film-strips on specific careers may be available for purchase or loan from the professional organization representing each career.

When requesting loan of a film, indicate first and second choices of dates for screening it.

Careers in the Allied Health Services: This 28-min., 16 mm. color film provides an overview of jobs in hospitals and other health care institutions that require less than a baccalaureate degree. Careers covered include licensed practical nurse, dental hygienist, nursing assistant, histologic technician, cytotechnologist, and op-tician. Available for rental ($3 the first day and $1.50 each additional day) from the University of South Carolina, College of General Studies, Audio-Visual Di-vision, Columbia, South Carolina 29208. Please list catalog number 520C and title.

Code Blue: This 27-min., 16 mm. color film presents black professionals on the job to encourage minority group viewers to consider careers in the health field. One professional voices some of the arguments made by minority youth when con-sidering a health career: it takes too long, it costs too much, and it's too hard. He then answers each point. Dramatic impact is provided by using scenes of an actual birth throughout the film. Available for purchase for $110.50 from the National Audiovisual Center, Washington, D.C. 20409, or on loan from Modern Talking Pictures Service, Inc., 2323 New Hyde Park Rd., New Hyde Park, New York 11040.

The Fixing Business: This 14-min., 16 mm. color film of the Association of University Programs in Hospital Administration describes the career of a hospital administra-tor and demonstrates how he can be an agent for change and new direction in the health care system. Available for purchase for $150 from AUPHA/Screen-scope Inc., One Dupont Circle, Suite 420, Washington, D.C. 20036. Also avail-able for rental from AUPHA for $5 per day.

For Today and Tomorrow: This 22-min., 16 mm. color film explains the training and functions of a physical therapist by following the teenage victim of a surfing accident through hospitalization, rehabilitation, and subsequent enrollment in an educational program. For information on distribution, write to Royce P. Noland, Executive Director, American Physical Therapy Association, California Chapter, 658 Ocean Street, Santa Cruz, California 95060.

Health Careers I, II, III, IV: Four 13 min. color filmstrips with narration on records, describe a wide variety of health careers and the requirements for entering them. Available for previewing in record or tape kits, from Lawren Productions, Inc., 4133 Wooster Avenue, San Mateo, California 94403. Cost: record kit—$10.00, tape kit—$11.50.

Horizons Unlimited: This 28-min., 16 mm. color film presents a variety of careers in the hospital, explaining the educational backgrounds, professional skills, and aspirations of each. The American Medical Association film stresses that there are many health occupations other than physician and nurse. Available on loan from Modern Talking Pictures, Inc., Prudential Plaza, Chicago, Illinois, or from the American Hospital Association.

In a Medical Laboratory: This 28-min., 16 mm. color movie shows the parts played by laboratory personnel in the diagnosis and treatment of three patients. Available through state and local pathologists and medical technologist societies, through local chapters of the American Cancer Society, and through medical schools. For a list of distributors, write to the National Committee for Careers in Medical Technology, 9650 Rockville Pike, Bethesda, Maryland 20014.

Is a Career in the Health Services for You?: This 14-min., 16 mm. color film emphasizes the service nature of health occupations, the broad variety of jobs available in health care settings, and the excitement generated in the health field by continuing technologic and medical advances. A quiz at the end of the film helps viewers determine whether they might be suited for a health career. Available for purchase for $190 from AIMS, P.O. Box 1010, Hollywood, California 90028. Also available for preview from either AIMS or Counselor Films, Inc., 1422 Chestnut Street, Philadelphia, Pennsylvania 19102.

Jobs in the Health Field: This 15-min., 16 mm. color film describes some of the jobs available in the health field and the qualifications required. Available free from local U.S. Employment Service Office, U.S. Department of Labor.

A Matter of Opportunity: This 22-min., 16 mm. black and white film, produced by the American Medical Association, uses black medical students to present the difficulties facing the black man in a medical career. Available from Modern Talking Pictures, Inc., 160 Grand Avenue, Chicago, Illinois 60610.

The O.D.'s—Vision Care Specialists: This 15-min., 16 mm. color film focuses on optometry as a career. Optometrists and optometric students describe the profession and its many fascinating facets. Scenes show a preschool vision examination, learning disability testing and therapy, a laser examination, and fitting of contact lenses. Available for purchase for $98.50 from Audience Planners, Inc., 200 S. LaSalle Street, Chicago, Illinois 60604, or on loan from Modern Talking Pictures Services, Inc., 2020 Prudential Plaza, Chicago, Illinois 60601.

On the Side of Life: This 8-min., 16 mm. color film aims at motivating high school students toward nursing as a career. Nurses are shown working in a hospital, for the Peace Corps, in the armed services, and for the Visiting Nurses Association. Available for purchase for $55.00 from Stage 3516, 124 East 36th Street, New York, New York. Also available on loan from Johnson & Johnson, 501 George Street, New Brunswick, New Jersey 03903.

The People Shop: This 18-min., 16 mm. sound color film is directed primarily to children in the third through seventh grades. The film shows children in typical hospital situations such as having a tonsillectomy and getting a broken bone set. Not only does the film expose the student to the people who work in the hospital, it explains many of the services offered by a community hospital. Available for purchase for $220 or for rental at $22 per day from Aspect IV Educational Films 21 Charles Street, Westport, Connecticut 06880.

Seven for Suzie: This 13½-min., 16 mm. color film shows how seven members of the rehabilitation team—physical therapist, occupational therapist, social workers, speech pathologist, psychologist, recreation specialist, and special education teacher—work together and separately to help the handicapped child work, play, improve her speech, and prepare for regular school life. Printed material describing the rehabilitation professions and listing sources of further information is available to supplement the film. Prints may be borrowed from state Easter Seal societies or purchased, at $50.00 each, from Careers in Rehabilitation, National Easter Seal Society, 2023 West Ogden Avenue, Chicago, Illinois 60612.

Summer of Decision: This 29-min., 16 mm. black and white film, produced in 1959 for the Council of Social Work Education, presents an overview of social work as a career. Available free from Association Films, Inc., 561 Hillgrove, LaGrange, Illinois 60525.

Target: Occupational Therapy: This 15-min., 16 mm. movie depicts the challenges of occupational therapy and rewarding experiences. Available from American Occupational Therapy Association, 6000 Executive Boulevard, Rockville, Maryland. For loan or purchase. Cost: $40.00 for black and white, $70.00 for color.

What About Tomorrow?: This 18-min., 16 mm. color film is a motivational film to encourage black children to choose dentistry as a career. The film introduces a central character, Bobby, who becomes interested in the dental profession. Dr. Stevens fosters this interest by employing Bobby in a summer job. While working in the dentist's office, Bobby learns what auxiliary dental workers do as well as the functions of a dentist. Available on loan from Modern Talking Pictures, Inc., 2020 Prudential Building, Chicago, Illinois 60611.

Yesterday, a Student . . . Tomorrow, a Nurse: This 10-min., 16 mm. color film takes the documentary approach and features students in classroom and clinical situations. It is designed for use by recruiters from hospital schools or nursing, and others concerned with attracting young men and women to nursing as a career. Available from the American Hospital Association for $100. Also available for rental at $6.00 a day.

Index

INDEX